MANAGING ORGANISATIONAL CHANGE

Allan Ramdhony & Christoph Thiele

MANAGING ORGANISATIONAL CHANGE

Sage

1 Oliver's Yard
55 City Road
London EC1Y 1SP

2455 Teller Road
Thousand Oaks
California 91320

Unit No 323-333, Third Floor, F-Block
International Trade Tower, Nehru Place,
New Delhi 110 019

8 Marina View Suite 43-053
Asia Square Tower 1
Singapore 018960

Library of Congress Control Number: 2023941035

British Library Cataloguing in Publication data

A catalogue record for this book is available from the British Library

Editor: Amy Minshull
Assistant editor: Charlotte Hegley
Production editor: Martin Fox
Copyeditor: Christine Bitten
Proofreader: Sarah Cooke
Indexer: Adam Pozner
Marketing manager: Lucia Sweet
Cover design: Francis Kenney
Typeset by: C&M Digitals (P) Ltd, Chennai, India

ISBN 978-1-4462-9830-5
ISBN 978-1-4462-9831-2 (pbk)

CONTENTS

List of Figures   xi
List of Tables   xiii
List of Case Studies   xv
Online Resources   xvii
Acknowledgements   xix

1 Introduction   1

PART I   A SYSTEMIC APPROACH TO CHANGE   13

2 The Nature of Change and Role of Change Management   15

3 Strategic Change   49

4 Theories and Models of Change Management   81

PART II   A DIALOGIC APPROACH TO CHANGE   113

5 Reactions to Change   115

6 Culture Change   145

7 Leading Change   175

8 Communicating Change   213

PART III   A PROCESSUAL APPROACH TO CHANGE   243

9 Implementing Change   245

10 Evaluating Change   279

11 Sustaining Change   305

12 Conclusions   337

Glossary   347
Index   359

DETAILED CONTENTS

List of Figures	xi
List of Tables	xiii
List of Case Studies	xv
Online Resources	xvii
Acknowledgements	xix

1 Introduction — **1**

1.1 Conceptual framework — 1
1.2 Aim and objectives — 3
1.3 Book structure — 4
1.4 Pedagogical approach — 7
1.5 How to use this book — 8
1.6 Overarching learning outcomes — 10
1.7 References — 10

PART I   A SYSTEMIC APPROACH TO CHANGE — **13**

2 The Nature of Change and Role of Change Management — 15

Learning outcomes — 15
2.1 Introduction — 15
2.2 Philosophical underpinnings — 16
2.3 Typology of organisational change — 22
2.4 The theory of punctuated equilibrium — 27
2.5 Causes of organisational change — 29
2.6 The role of change management — 32
2.7 Exploring the links between OD, PM and CM — 34
2.8 Conceptual nugget: Adopting a systemic approach to change management — 38
2.9 Key learning points — 41
2.10 Independent learning — 46
2.11 References — 46

3 Strategic Change — 49

Learning outcomes — 49
3.1 Introduction — 49
3.2 Meaning of strategic change — 50
3.3 Change agency: Determinism v. Voluntarism — 52
3.4 Approaches to strategic change — 55
3.5 Diagnostic tools to facilitate strategic change — 65

3.6 Conceptual nugget: Leading strategic change in a VUCA business world   71
3.7 Key learning points   74
3.8 Independent learning   78
3.9 References   79

4   Theories and Models of Change Management   81

Learning outcomes   81
4.1 Introduction   81
4.2 Key change theories   82
4.3 Characteristics of a good change model   88
4.4 Critical review of popular organisational change models   90
4.5 Conceptual nugget: The superior value of systemic models   106
4.6 Key learning points   108
4.7 Independent learning   111
4.8 References   111

PART II   A DIALOGIC APPROACH TO CHANGE   113

5   Reactions to Change   115

Learning outcomes   115
5.1 Introduction   115
5.2 The psycho-social factors underlying human reactions to change   116
5.3 Types of reactions to change   118
5.4 The coping cycle   121
5.5 Resistance to change   127
5.6 Conceptual nugget: Managing resistance to change as dialogic practice   135
5.7 Key learning points   137
5.8 Independent learning   142
5.9 References   143

6   Culture Change   145

Learning outcomes   145
6.1 Introduction   145
6.2 The complex and multidimensional concept of culture   146
6.3 Layers of organisational culture   150
6.4 The cultural web   153
6.5 Organisational subcultures   156
6.6 Strategies for managing cultural change   160
6.7 Managing cultural diversity in an international context   164
6.8 Conceptual nugget: A dialogic model for managing culture change   167
6.9 Key learning points   170
6.10 Independent learning   173
6.11 References   173

7   Leading Change   175

Learning outcomes   175
7.1 Introduction   175

7.2 The meaning of leadership   176
7.3 Leadership through the ages: Implications for organisational change leadership   177
7.4 Leaders v. managers   182
7.5 Key leadership theories   184
7.6 Contemporary approaches to organisational change leadership   196
7.7 Conceptual nugget: Dialogic leadership   203
7.8 Key learning points   206
7.9 Independent learning   210
7.10 References   210

8 Communicating Change   213

Learning outcomes   213
8.1 Introduction   213
8.2 Human communication and organisational change   214
8.3 Shannon and Weaver's model of communication   217
8.4 Why do organisations fare badly in communicating change?   219
8.5 Clampitt et al.'s typology of communication strategies   222
8.6 Choosing the right medium for communicating change   226
8.7 Organisational silence   229
8.8 Conceptual nugget: A dialogic model for communicating change   230
8.9 Key learning points   235
8.10 Independent learning   240
8.11 References   240

PART III   A PROCESSUAL APPROACH TO CHANGE   243

9 Implementing Change   245

Learning outcomes   245
9.1 Introduction   245
9.2 Approaches to change implementation   246
9.3 Methods of change implementation   248
9.4 Combining Lean with Six Sigma: LSS   267
9.5 Conceptual Nugget: A filtering device for selecting change
        implementation methods   270
9.6 Key learning points   272
9.7 Independent learning   276
9.8 References   277

10 Evaluating Change   279

Learning outcomes   279
10.1 Introduction   279
10.2 Evaluation in the context of organisational change   280
10.3 Operationalising a process model of change evaluation   282
10.4 The Balanced Scorecard   286
10.5 Change evaluation in SMEs   292
10.6 Conceptual nugget: A critical approach to change evaluation   295
10.7 Key learning points   298

10.8 Independent learning 303
10.9 References 303

11 Sustaining Change 305

Learning outcomes 305
11.1 Introduction 305
11.2 On change sustainability and sustaining change 306
11.3 The impact of the public discourse of sustainability on business organisations 308
11.4 Embedding sustainability in the value chain 311
11.5 Strategies for sustaining change 315
11.6 Conceptual nugget: A seven-step practical framework for sustaining change 324
11.7 Key learning points 329
11.8 Independent learning 334
11.9 References 334

12 Conclusions 337

12.1 Introduction 337
12.2 Achievement of aim and objectives 337
12.3 Summary review of conceptual nuggets 339
12.4 Concluding remarks 346

Glossary 347
Index 359

LIST OF FIGURES

1.1	Conceptual framework underpinning textbook	2
1.2	Book structure	4
1.3	Key features of textbook	9
2.1	Prevailing organisational change orthodoxy	19
2.2	Organisational change as a case of punctuated equilibrium	27
2.3	Links between CM, OD and PM	34
2.4	A systemic approach to change management	38
2.5	A case of punctuated equilibrium at Hosco	44
3.1	Key features of strategic change	50
3.2	Mintzberg's pattern of strategy formation and development	60
3.3	Key components of KUKA's change strategy	77
4.1	Lewin's three-step model of change	90
4.2	Kirkpatrick's (2001) linear model of organisational change	92
4.3	Weisbord's (1976) six-box model of organisational change	97
4.4	Kotter's (1980) integrative model of organisational dynamics	101
4.5	The Burke-Litwin (1992) causal model of organisational performance and change	103
4.6	Key features of systemic models	107
4.7	Application of the Burke-Litwin model to Sheraton Edinburgh	109
5.1	Highlighting the dynamic nature of Kirkpatrick's basic types of reactions to change	119
5.2	A basic version of the coping cycle	121
5.3	Mapping out stages of the coping cycle against key change-related variables	125
5.4	Application of the coping cycle to monitor performance	126
5.5	A systemic mapping of organisational resistance to change	134
5.6	Managing resistance to change as dialogic practice	136
5.7	Henkel's New Leadership Commitments (NLC)	139
5.8	Spectrum of employee reactions to Henkel's NLC	140
6.1	A dialogic model for managing culture change	168
7.1	Hersey and Blanchard's model of situational leadership	191
7.2	Contemporary approaches to change leadership	196

7.3	Key elements and transformative effects of dialogic leadership	203
7.4	Leading change through conversational practice	208
8.1	Shannon and Weaver's model of communication	217
8.2	Causes and consequences of poor organisational communication	220
8.3	Clampitt et al.'s (2000) typology of communication strategies	223
8.4	Media richness and level of interactivity of organisational communication media	227
8.5	The negative relational dynamics and impact of organisational silence	230
8.6	A dialogic framework for change communication	232
8.7	COVID-19-induced digitalisation of AutoCo's communication strategy	238
9.1	Applying BPR to the key processes of the value chain	249
9.2	Process map for procuring a component part for a production department	256
9.3	Core principles of Lean management	258
9.4	Application of VSM	262
9.5	Six Sigma performance and quality standards	263
9.6	Core principles of Six Sigma	264
9.7	The Six Sigma DMAIC process	265
9.8	LSS: Combining Lean and Six Sigma	268
9.9	Filtering device for selecting change implementation methods	271
9.10	The building blocks of the TPS as an integrated socio-technical system	273
10.1	A process model of change evaluation	280
10.2	Key dimensions of the Balanced Scorecard	287
10.3	A critical approach to change evaluation	296
10.4	Tata Motors' expansion of the BSC	300
10.5	Map of TMG's strategic objectives against its triple bottom lines	301
11.1	Sustainability as a multidimensional concept	309
11.2	Embedding sustainability in the value chain	311
11.3	Mapping out the multidimensional approach to sustainability change at BuildCo	331
11.4	Stock and flow diagram representing dimensions of BuildCo's sustainability strategy	332
11.5	Outputs of simulation exercise for sustainable change at BuildCo	333
12.1	Tree infographic: Key conceptual nuggets	339

LIST OF TABLES

2.1	Dichotomous conceptions of organisational change	22
2.2	Key features of dichotomous types of organisational change	24
2.3	Mapping out the key roles and responsibilities of change agents, OD practitioners and project managers	38
2.4	Major overhaul of Hosco's deep structures	45
3.1	Identifying key features of strategic change	52
3.2	The primary focus and key features of improvised, ambidextrous and quantum approaches to strategic change	65
3.3	PESTLE: Key macro-level forces impacting strategic change in a global business context	65
3.4	Key factors of a SWOT analysis	68
3.5	Key components of a strategic change canvas	70
3.6	Operationalising VUCA into an analytical framework: Implications for strategic change	72
4.1	Matching actions with relevant theory	87
4.2	Main strengths and limitations of Lewin's change model	92
4.3	Applying Weisbord's change model as a consultancy tool	100
4.4	Comparative analysis of change models	106
5.1	Monitoring reactions to change	121
5.2	Typology of resistance to organisational change	128
6.1	Matching distinguishing cultural features with relevant metaphors	149
6.2	Overview of Schein's layers of organisational culture	150
6.3	Key dimensions of the cultural web	158
6.4	Turning the cultural web into an effective change tool	158
6.5	Strategies for managing culture change	160
6.6	A summary overview of Hofstede's model of national cultures	164
6.7	Using Hofstede's model of national cultures as a change tool to manage cross-cultural teams	166
6.8	Practical application of dialogic model	170
7.1	The key differences between change leaders and managers	182
7.2	Key eras of leadership theory	184
7.3	Change leaders as born and made	186
7.4	Prominent continuums of leadership styles	188

8.1	Key features of communication tools used by large IT-driven companies	229
9.1	Comparative analysis of Lean, Six Sigma and LSS	270
10.1	An operational framework for a processual approach to change evaluation	283
10.2	Evaluation system for household furniture company	286
10.3	Example of financial performance metric	288
10.4	Example of customer satisfaction metric	288
10.5	Example of business processes metric	289
10.6	Example of learning and growth metric	289
10.7	Application of the BSC across sectors	290
11.1	Strategies for sustaining change	316
11.2	Comparative analysis of change strategies for sustaining change	323
11.3	Seven-step practical framework for sustaining change	324
11.4	Assessment of TSL's approach to sustaining change	328

LIST OF CASE STUDIES

2.1	The Alibaba Group: Navigating challenges and driving creative change	25
2.2	Hewlett-Packard: A prime example of upward causation	31
2.3	Hosco: Compelling evidence for punctuated equilibrium and systemic change	43
3.1	NHS England: Battling COVID-19 and becoming stronger	54
3.2	British Airways: A planned approach to strategic change	56
3.3	Biogen: A swift strategic response to emergent challenges	58
3.4	KUKA: Shaping the future of robotics in a VUCA business world	75
4.1	Indonesia's Krakatau Steel: From industry laggard to leader	93
4.2	Unicorn: Deploying a profit-focused change strategy	99
4.3	Sheraton Edinburgh: Applying the Burke-Litwin model to mitigate the impact of COVID-19	108
5.1	Bitter union-led strike action at Heathrow Airport	127
5.2	The Volkswagen scandal	129
5.3	Managing reactions to leadership and culture change at Henkel	138
6.1	Mumbai Dabbawala: Culture as a lever for high-performance standards	152
6.2	Aetna: Targeted culture change for a major turnaround	162
6.3	Dutch bank ING: Clearing a cultural path for agile transformation	171
7.1	Eric Schmidt: Combining leadership styles to drive innovation at Google	190
7.2	The rise and fall of a world-class woman leader	201
7.3	Jeff Skoll: An exemplar of 21st century leadership	207
8.1	Nike: Showing agility in tackling a communication crisis	222
8.2	Atlassian: Driving change through a suite of collaborative software products	225
8.3	AutoCo: COVID-19 as a catalyst for digital communication strategy	236
9.1	T-Mobile: Re-engineering from the perspective of the customer	254
9.2	Bosch Connected Industry: Taking Six Sigma to a new level through digital technology	266
9.3	The Toyota Production System: An exemplar of Lean implementation	273
10.1	Amazon QuickSight: Scaling business intelligence for SMEs	293
10.2	Evaluating change in a micro business	294
10.3	TATA Motors Group: Expanding the Balanced Scorecard in pursuit of sustainable value creation	299

11.1   IKEA: A trendsetter in sustainability change   314
11.2   GSK Consumer Healthcare: Exploring the possibility of a Community
       of Practice in sustaining innovative change   320
11.3   Sustaining change: Tata Steel's Shikhar25 programme   327
11.4   Simulation modelling as a driver of sustainability change at BuildCo   330

ONLINE RESOURCES

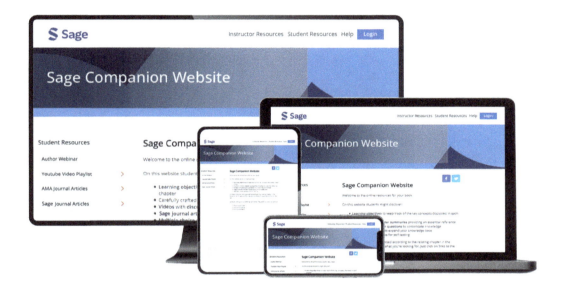

This textbook is accompanied by online resources to aid teaching and support learning. To access these resources, visit: https://study.sagepub.com/ramdhony.

For Lecturers

- A **Teaching Guide** providing practical guidance and support and additional materials for each chapter.
- **PowerPoint Decks** that can be downloaded and adapted to suit individual teaching needs.
- A **Testbank** that provides multiple-choice questions that can be used in class, for exams and in a virtual learning environment.

ACKNOWLEDGEMENTS

Allan would like to thank all those who have had an input into this book: students, colleagues and external reviewers whose feedback has been invaluable.

Many thanks to Dr Tina Bass for her contribution in the early development stage of Chapter 3. Sincere thanks also to Dr Indra Dusoye and Dr Timur Erim for having each contributed an end-of-chapter case study.

Allan would also like to thank Dr Christoph Thiele as co-author who, despite joining the project late, has brought a much needed practitioner perspective to it and shown his unwavering support whilst juggling work and family commitments.

Special thanks to all the editors at Sage – Ruth Stitt, Charlotte Bush, Sunita Patel, Lyndsay Oliver, Kirsty Smy, Nina Smith and Amy Minshull – for their constant support, timely feedback and encouragement in bringing this project to completion.

Finally, a big thank you to my wife Bianca, for her tremendous help with research, referencing and proof-reading – I could not have done it without you.

Christoph would like to thank Dr Allan Ramdhony, as lead author, academic mentor and friend. As your former doctoral student, I felt privileged to have joined the project to demonstrate the practical value of the theories laid out in this book. I am looking forward to working together with you in the future.

I would like to express my sincere gratitude to Bianca Ramdhony for her effective and kind approach to managing the smooth delivery of bite-sized work packages in this project. You have helped me tremendously.

Thanks to the Sage team for their professional support and advice.

Last, but not least, I want to thank my wife, Esther, our four children – Bastian, Liam, Sophie, and Niklas – for their patience and understanding.

1

INTRODUCTION

Welcome to this textbook on managing organisational change. It is an undisputed fact that the ability to effectively manage change is a unique competence that separates successful organisations from those that struggle to stay afloat and stay ahead of the competition. Yet, achieving change success remains a tall order and is considered one of the most challenging endeavours across modern-day organisations (Nag et al., 2007). Although the ubiquitous and grim statistic pointing to the 70 % failure rate of change initiatives has been debunked as lacking in reliable empirical evidence, context-insensitive and at best a perceptual estimate (e.g. see Ashkenas, 2013; Beer and Nohria, 2000; Hughes, 2011), it does point to the long-standing uncertainty, perception of high risk and angst surrounding organisational change.

While change failure is often ill-defined, the fact remains that a significant number of organisations are not achieving their change goals and losing out on their investments in change initiatives. The reasons underlying change failure are manifold but tend to revolve around recurrent key factors such as: the absence of a clear change strategy, weak leadership, poor communication, rigid cultural value systems, inability to respond to emergent environmental changes, stakeholder resistance to change, and a lack of emphasis on creativity and innovation (e.g. see Dawson and Andriopoulos, 2017; Lofquist, 2011; Miller Cole, 2019).

However, this does not mean that all change initiatives are doomed to failure or that organisations are 'genetically predestined' to either succeed or fail, irrespective of the good will and efforts of change agents – which would leave organisational change management (OCM) redundant, exhausted and conceptually closed as a distinctive field of research and practice. In contrast, we endorse the more optimistic view that, despite the fact that OCM is not an exact science, it can still provide the answers to the challenges and dilemmas facing change agents in an increasingly dynamic and unpredictable business world. However, for this to happen, OCM has to evolve in sync with the world around it and remain accommodating of ongoing research, consultancy work and a diversity of pedagogical approaches through which it can renew its legitimacy and (re)-engage change stakeholders.

1.1 Conceptual framework

Figure 1.1 presents the conceptual framework that underpins our alternative perspective on OCM. It consists of three conceptual pillars which are explained below.

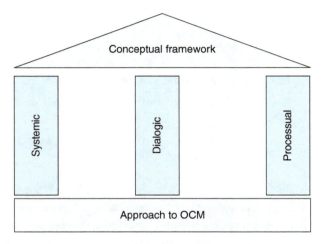

Figure 1.1 Conceptual framework underpinning textbook

A systemic approach to OCM

A systemic approach to OCM views the changing organisation as a *complex, adaptive ecosystem* which is in a dynamic relationship with the forces of change at play within its external environment. Attention is also given to the inner workings of the organisation and to how its different parts or sub-systems interact to create value that may be of benefit to both organisational stakeholders and the wider community over which it has an influence. Importantly, a systemic approach to change is amenable to different forms of causal modelling which can allow for an in-depth understanding of the complex web of causal relationships underlying an organisation's change situation and of their emergent properties that can have a significant bearing on change outcomes (Allan, 1997; Nadler and Tushman, 1980).

Moreover, a systemic approach to change sees the organisation as a living organism in a symbiotic and mutually beneficial relationship with its external environment – placing an emphasis on the organisation's responsibility to demonstrate good stewardship of its external environment if it is to survive and grow in the longer term (Kast and Rosenzweig, 1972).

A dialogic approach to OCM

A dialogic approach to OCM carries the ideal of change initiatives brought under the binding principle of free dialogue – warranting the suspension of unequal power relations between change stakeholders and a continuous and cooperative process of interpretation and negotiation through which they can achieve shared understanding around the change initiatives and coordinate their action towards mutually beneficial goals (Bakhtin, 1981; Habermas, 1987).

As such, a dialogic approach to OCM is *non-episodic*, where it plays out as a continuous conversational process, *plurivocal* in that it is accommodating of a multiplicity of independent voices and perspectives, and *co-constructive* as it allows for the co-creation of meaning around change initiatives and a collaborative approach to their design and implementation as key determinants of change success (Francis et al., 2013; Ramdhony and D'Annunzio-Green, 2018).

A processual approach to OCM

A processual approach to OCM underlines the fact that organisational change is not a one-off event or occurrence but an on-going, continuous and never-ending process of formation and development without any clear end point or final destination. It has been argued that even discrete change initiatives with set timelines have to be seen as 'nodes' in the continuous process of change an organisation has to undergo throughout its life cycle – where the impact of such discrete change initiatives has to be accounted for when charting the change trajectories of organisations over the longer term (Martic, 2019).

A processual approach to OCM also elicits thinking about the temporal dimension of organisational change, drawing attention to how it is shaped by past experiences of success and failure, current challenges and opportunities and the vision of a desired future state which exert an influence over strategic choices and particular courses of action (Pettigrew, 1985). Lastly, another feature of a processual approach to OCM which is of particular relevance here, is the focus on the distinct yet interlocking stages of the change management process, which include the following: the development of a change plan with clear strategic goals and objectives, its effective implementation through the deployment of necessary resources, and the application of meaningful evaluative criteria and performance indicators to assess its outcomes as a basis for taking corrective measures or sustaining change efforts.

These three conceptual pillars underpin the structure of this textbook (which is discussed in the next section) and importantly, inform the development of a set of conceptual nuggets (presented at the end of each substantial chapter) which arise from each of the key topics covered in this textbook and which represent its unique contribution to OCM.

1.2 Aim and objectives

It is in this spirit that we present this new textbook on OCM. Our overriding aim is to provide an *alternative perspective* on OCM that can advance student understanding of this discrete field of research and practice. Our key objectives are as follows:

- To capture the essence of OCM.
- To provide an alternative perspective of OCM as a distinctive field of research and practice.
- To address the emerging trends and contemporary issues in OCM.
- To inform the practice of OCM.
- To meet the learning needs of students on both undergraduate and postgraduate business and management programmes.

1.3 Book structure

The structure of the book rests upon the three conceptual pillars (refer to Figure 1.1) which account for its three main parts and provide the parameters for the development of the key topics covered in the subsequent chapters – as shown in Figure 1.2 below.

Apart from the introductory chapter which sets the scene for what follows and a concluding chapter which brings the textbook to a close with a distillation of the key issues and concerns arising from it, the body of this textbook consists of three main interlocking parts.

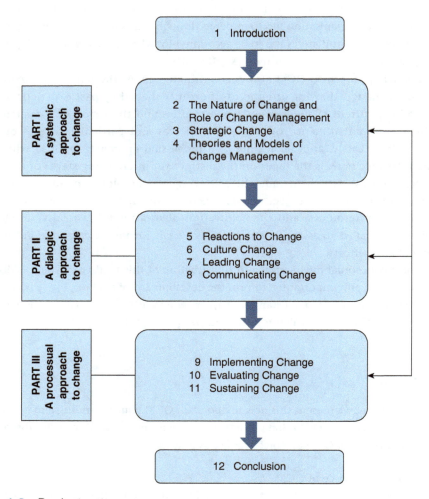

Figure 1.2 Book structure

Part I – A systemic approach to change

The first part of the book is grounded in systems thinking and consists of a first block of three chapters which primarily deal with the 'hard dimension' of OCM. Chapter 2, *The Nature of*

Change and Role of Change Management, begins with a discussion of the nature of organisational change, focusing on the philosophical commitments, basic assumptions, key typologies and causes underlying it. It then considers the role of OCM before exploring its links with Organisational Development (OD) and Project Management (PM) as distinct areas of organisational functioning. The conceptual nugget for this chapter advocates a systemic approach to change management and provides a discussion of its key features and benefits.

Chapter 3, *Strategic Change*, unpacks the key features of strategic change before explaining the meaning of the notion of human agency in the context of strategic change with reference to the key philosophical concepts informing it. The chapter then presents a critical review of different approaches to strategic change. It proceeds to consider a set of diagnostic tools that can be used to facilitate strategic change, showing how these can be applied in practice. The final section of the chapter presents our conceptual nugget which considers the implications of the VUCA (*Volatile, Uncertain, Complex and Ambiguous*) business world for strategic change.

Chapter 4, *Theories and Models of Change Management*, contains a critical examination of a selection of change theories and models and considers their implications for effective change management. The chapter begins with a discussion of the key theories that have informed the development of some of the most widely known change models. It then identifies a set of criteria that can allow for a robust assessment of the value of change models before providing a critical review of a number of popular models with particular attention to their key strengths and limitations. The conceptual nugget for this chapter underlines the 'superior value' of systemic change models and distils their key features in light of the preceding discussion.

Part II – A dialogic approach to change

The second part of the textbook is mainly concerned with the 'softer dimension' of OCM and consists of a block of four chapters focusing on its psychological and socio-cultural dimensions. Chapter 5, *Reactions to Change*, provides a discussion of the psycho-social factors influencing human reactions to change before considering a couple of models of human reactions to change to show how these can be used as sensitising tools to effectively manage employee reactions throughout the change process. The chapter then turns attention to the notion of resistance to change to discuss its various types, underlying causes and the meanings that can be attached to it as a social systemic and discursive phenomenon. The conceptual nugget for this chapter entails the development of a model for managing resistance to change as 'dialogic practice'.

Chapter 6, *Culture Change*, begins with the consideration of a set of alternative definitions and metaphors of culture change, leading to a distillation of its key features as a complex and multidimensional concept. It then provides a critical review of well-established models of culture change and shows how they can be used as practical tools to diagnose and frame organisational culture change. Some consideration is given to the underlying causes of organisational subcultures and to their impact on culture change.

The chapter moves on to consider a range of change strategies and tools for managing organisational culture change. Our conceptual nugget for this chapter puts forward a dialogic model for managing culture change and elicits thinking about ways to effectively translate it into practice.

Chapter 7, *Leading Change*, draws attention to the multidimensional, dynamic and emergent nature of change leadership before providing a brief historical overview of political leadership to establish its links to organisational change leadership. The chapter then revisits one of the most recurrent themes in the change literature regarding the differences between change leaders and change managers, developing an argument as to their distinctive yet complementary roles in the pursuit of change success. The chapter proceeds to critically examine in chronological order (from early 1940s to date) some of the most prominent leadership theories to draw out their relevance to organisational change leadership and consider their practical implications. The conceptual nugget for this chapter develops a model of dialogic leadership and explains how it can serve as a lever for contemporary approaches to leadership.

Chapter 8, *Communicating Change*, completes the second part of the textbook and focuses on effective communication as one of the key determinants of change success. The chapter begins by distilling the key features of human communication in light of its historical development and considering their implications for organisational change. It then critically examines a seminal model of communication, drawing attention to its limitations which call for a more sophisticated approach to change communication. It proceeds to explain the key causes and consequences of poor communication after which it considers a typology of change strategies that can be used as a diagnostic tool to assess the effectiveness of change communication. It then carries out an assessment of a range of communication media that change leaders can employ to communicate more effectively before giving some consideration to the notion of organisational silence which can have adverse effects on the change process and outcomes. The conceptual nugget for this chapter proposes a dialogic model of change communication that can allow for a balanced approach to collective sense making and the achievement of shared understanding around change initiatives.

Part III – A processual approach to change

This final part of the textbook places an emphasis on the importance of treating organisational change as a process and integrates both its hard and soft dimensions. Chapter 9, *Implementing Change*, begins by drawing the distinction between directed and facilitated approaches to change implementation, leading to an argument in favour of a reconciliation of both approaches to effectively address the needs and interests of both organisation and employees. The chapter then provides a critical evaluation of three popular change implementation methods: Business Process Reengineering, Lean and Six Sigma and shows how they can be applied in practice. The chapter proceeds to consider how the combination of Lean and Six Sigma (referred to as Lean Six Sigma) can have synergistic effects and enable a greater balance between organisational and employee needs. The conceptual nugget for this chapter involves the development of a filtering device that can prove valuable in selecting appropriate change implementation methods.

Chapter 10, *Evaluating Change*, begins by explaining the meaning and purpose of evaluation in the context of organisational change whilst underlining the importance of a processual approach to change evaluation. It then develops a processual model to explain the key stages and features of a processual approach to change evaluation and shows how such a model can be operationalised and translated into practice. The chapter proceeds to critically examine one of the most widely used evaluation tools, the Balanced Scorecard, to discuss its key dimensions and benefits whilst drawing attention to the criticisms that have been leveled against it. The chapter then considers the different evaluative tools SMEs can employ to monitor and improve their business processes and performance. The conceptual nugget for this chapter advocates a critical approach to change evaluation and outlines a set of principles to this effect.

Chapter 11, *Sustaining Change*, begins by drawing the distinction between change sustainability and sustaining change and considering the impact of the wider public discourse of sustainability on organisational change. The chapter then shows how sustainability can be embedded into an organisation's value chain with due attention to the principles underpinning such an exercise. The chapter moves on to consider a range of strategies that can be deployed to sustain organisational change, outlining in the process their key features, methodologies and implications for sustaining change. Our final conceptual nugget presents a seven-step framework that provides concrete guidance on how to successfully sustain organisational change.

1.4 Pedagogical approach

This textbook is primarily targeted at top-tier undergraduate and postgraduate students across business schools who are studying organisational change management as either a core or an optional module. It does not presuppose prior knowledge of OCM and is structured in such a way as to enable students to gradually develop their knowledge of the subject matter as they progress through the chapters and engage with the key topics covered therein.

From a pedagogical perspective, the textbook blends theoretical explanation with empirical evidence and practical insights to enable a grounded yet imaginative approach to OCM – where it not only preserves a unity between theory and practice but at times 'runs ahead of practice' to challenge the reader to re-imagine OCM and think about creative ways of doing organisational change and transforming practice in the face of change failures and challenges arising from an increasingly complex and unpredictable business environment (Collier, 1994). The aforementioned conceptual nuggets at the end of each chapter are designed to do just that.

The textbook combines a range of teaching and learning materials to support both lecturers and students.

Lecturers can access a range of online resources to aid teaching including:

- PowerPoint slides for each of the key topics covered in this textbook.
- A teaching guide giving pointers on how to approach each topic and carry out the exercises included in each chapter.
- A set of multiple-choice questions covering all key topics to test student learning and progress.
- Links to online audio-visual materials and free-access journal articles that can serve to illuminate the key concepts and issues discussed under each key topic.
- Access to a selection of case studies from the publisher's database that are of particular relevance to the topics covered in this textbook.

Students can use the following materials to support their learning:

- Reflective exercises to deepen understanding of the key issues relating to OCM.
- Practical exercises to experiment with a wide range of change tools and techniques.
- A rich library of case studies spanning all substantial chapters which provide valuable insights into the practical reality of modern-day organisations in relation to the key topics addressed in this textbook.
- Links to free-access journal articles and book chapters that can serve to illuminate some of the key concepts and issues discussed.
- Links to online learning resources such as video-clips and podcasts to benefit from alternative perspectives from academics, consultants and practitioners on key change issues and concerns.

As digital learners, we endorse an approach to learning rooted in *connectivism* which views smart learning as socially distributed and happening through both physical and virtual networks (Shrivastava, 2018). We therefore encourage students to draw on the above pedagogical features and use them as a solid platform to expand their knowledge of OCM both through face-to-face and online interaction with lecturers, fellow students and colleagues.

In terms of timeframe, we want to draw attention to the fact that we have adopted a modular approach to both the structure and content of the textbook and it is our view that it can be realistically covered over a single semester and mapped against current OCM modules taught across universities in the UK and elsewhere. Finally, the textbook also aims to strike a chord with change managers and other practitioners who will hopefully find its contents particularly useful in enabling them to experiment with a wide range of change tools and techniques to frame effective change strategies and ideally transform practice to drive change initiatives towards their successful completion.

1.5 How to use this book

This textbook contains a set of key features that will help you navigate through its contents, enrich your learning experience and achieve its intended learning outcomes – as highlighted in Figure 1.3.

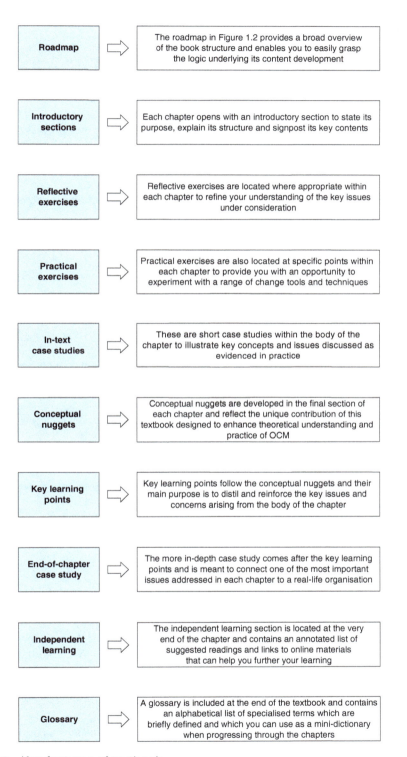

Figure 1.3 Key features of textbook

1.6 Overarching learning outcomes

Upon completion of this textbook, you will be able to:

- Gain an in-depth understanding of the complex nature of organisational change and of the critical role of OCM across modern-day organisations.
- Explain the meaning and implications of a systemic, dialogic and processual approach to organisational change.
- Critically examine the key concepts, theories, models and principles underpinning OCM as a distinctive field of research and practice.
- Apply a range of practical tools and techniques to effectively implement, evaluate and sustain organisational change.
- Deploy innovative strategies to enhance OCM practices in your current or future organisation.

REFLECTIVE EXERCISE

Think about a recent change that your organisation or an organisation with which you are familiar has gone through and answer the following questions:

1   Would you consider the change a success or a failure?
2   What could be the main reasons underlying such success or failure?

As you embark on your learning journey with us, we take this opportunity to wish you all the best with your studies and endeavours as a change agent.

1.7 References

Allan G. (1997) 'A holistic model for change management', in F.A. Stowell, R.L. Ison, R. Armson, J. Holloway, S. Jackson and S. McRobb (eds), *Systems for Sustainability*. Boston, MA: Springer, pp. 703–707.

Ashkenas, R. (2013) 'Change management needs to change', *Harvard Business Review*. [Online] Available at: https://hbr.org/2013/04/change-management-needs-to-cha.html (accessed 31 May 2022).

Bakhtin, M.M. (1981) *The Dialogic Imagination: Four Essays*. Austin: University of Texas Press.

Beer, M. and Nohria, N. (2000) 'Cracking the code of change', *Harvard Business Review*, *78* (May– June), 133–141.

Collier, A. (1994) *Critical Realism: An Introduction to Roy Bhaskar's Philosophy*. London: Verso.

Dawson, P. and Andriopoulos, C. (2017) *Managing Change, Creativity and Innovation*, 3rd edn. London: Sage Publications Ltd.

Francis, H.M., Ramdhony, A., Reddington, M. and Staines, H. (2013) 'Opening spaces for conversational practice: A conduit for effective engagement strategies and productive working arrangements', *International Journal of Human Resource Management*, *24*(14), 2713–2740.

Habermas, J. (1987) *The Theory of Communicative Action: Reason and the Rationalization of Society*, Vol. *1*. Cambridge: Polity Press.

Hughes, C. (2011) *Changes and Challenges in 20 Years of Research into the Development of Executive Functions*. [Online] Available at: https://onlinelibrary.wiley.com/doi/full/10.1002/icd.736 (accessed 5 May 2022).

Kast, F. and Rosenzweig, J. (1972) 'General systems theory: Applications for organization and management', *The Academy of Management Journal*, *15*(4), 447–465. Available at: www.jstor.org/stable/255141 (accessed 2 June 2022).

Lofquist, E.A. (2011) 'Doomed to fail: A case study of change implementation collapse in the Norwegian Civil Aviation Industry', *Journal of Change Management*, *11*(2), 223–243.

Martic, K. (2019) *Digital Transformation (DX): Best Practices for Driving Change*. [Online] Available at: https://blog.smarp.com/digital-transformation-dx-best-practices-for-driving-change (accessed 10 April 2022).

Miller Cole, B. (2019) *Innovate Or Die: How a Lack Of Innovation Can Cause Business Failure*. [Online] Available at: www.forbes.com/sites/biancamillercole/2019/01/10/innovate-or-die-how-a-lack-of-innovation-can-cause-business-failure/#597313fb2fcb (accessed 3 June 2022).

Nadler, D.A and Tushman, M.L. (1980) 'A model for diagnosing organizational behavior', *Organizational Dynamics*, *9*(2), 35–51. Available at https://doi.org/10.1016/0090-2616(80)90039-X (accessed 3 June 2022).

Nag, R., Corley, K.G. and Gioia, D.A. (2007) 'The intersection of organizational identity, knowledge, and practice: Attempting strategic change via knowledge grafting', *Academy of Management Journal*, *50*(4), 821–847.

Pettigrew, A. (1985) 'Contextualist research and the study of organizational change processes', in E. Lawler (ed.), *Doing Research that is Useful for Theory and Practice*. San Francisco: Jossey Bass, pp. 53–72. Available at https://ifipwg82.org/sites/ifipwg82.org/files/Pettigrew.pdf (accessed 15 May 2022).

Ramdhony, A. and D'Annunzio-Green, N. (2018) 'A dialogic reframing of talent management as a lever for hospitableness', *Worldwide Hospitality and Tourism Themes*, *10*(1), 14–27.

Shrivastava, A. (2018) 'Using connectivism theory and technology for knowledge creation in cross-cultural communication', *Research in Learning Technology*, *26*. [Online] Available at: https://journal.alt.ac.uk/index.php/rlt/article/view/2061/pdf (accessed 15 May 2022).

PART I
A SYSTEMIC APPROACH TO CHANGE

2

THE NATURE OF CHANGE AND ROLE OF CHANGE MANAGEMENT

Learning Outcomes

After completing this chapter, you should be able to:

- Understand the philosophical underpinnings of change and consider their implications for organisational change.
- Describe the main types of organisational change and apply them as a diagnostic tool to real-life organisations.
- Explain the theory of punctuated equilibrium and its application to the process of organisational change.
- Gain an insight into the complex web of causal relationships underlying organisational change and appreciate the value of causal modelling in driving change success.
- Outline the defining features of change management and discuss its links with OD and PM as distinct areas of organisational functioning.
- Discuss the key features, benefits and limitations of a systemic approach to change management.

2.1 Introduction

The purpose of this chapter is to develop a sound understanding of the nature of organisational change and the role of change management in leveraging the resources of an organisation and effectively achieving its strategic goals and objectives. The chapter begins by outlining the key philosophical underpinnings of change to draw attention to the role of philosophy in shaping our understanding of the nature of change and to consider its implications for organisational change. In the same breath, some of the most common assumptions about organisational change are critically examined, leading to a working definition of organisational change.

The chapter then unpacks the key meanings of a set of dichotomous types of organisational change which have been used to describe the nature of organisational change and provide an example of how they can be used as a diagnostic tool. The chapter proceeds to briefly explain the theory of punctuated equilibrium and show how it has been applied to the process of organisational change and enabled a more sophisticated understanding of the phenomenon. The chapter then provides a discussion on the causes underlying organisational change, drawing attention to the value of causal modelling in driving change success.

The next section brings the focus on the role of change management to outline its key defining features before exploring its links with Organisational Development and Project Management as distinct areas of organisational functioning. The final section presents our conceptual nugget for this chapter which advocates a systemic approach to change management and provides a discussion of its features and benefits which, in our view, far outweigh its limitations. The chapter concludes with a summary of key learning points arising from the preceding discussion and an end-of-chapter case study which provides some compelling evidence for punctuated equilibrium and systemic change in a Scottish healthcare organisation.

2.2 Philosophical underpinnings

The role of philosophy in organisational change management

Philosophy can be viewed by some as mentally taxing and of limited relevance to organisational change management. It is however, in our view, a key determinant of how change agents make sense of reality and develop a shared mental model of who they are and what they want to achieve in this reality. Thus, like any sentient entity, organisations undergoing change inevitably have to reckon with the same kind of existential questions:

- How do we see the world around us?
- What do we stand for?
- What is it that we want to do?
- How do we do it?
- How do we survive and grow while doing it?

While these bottom line questions are critical in the development of a sound change strategy and business model, they have a *philosophical import*. So, when doing change, organisations have to open up spaces for 'defining philosophical moments' in order to make sense of their operating context, articulate their core values, vision and mission, outline their strategic objectives and commit the necessary resources to achieve such objectives in order to ensure their survival, continuity and growth in the longer term. Thus, the way organisations do change is a reflection of their philosophical commitments and, importantly, of their basic assumptions – whether conscious or tacit – of the very nature of change, which is discussed in the following section.

The nature of change

Views on the nature of change in Western philosophy can be traced back to Ancient Greek philosophers, more particularly Parmenides and Heraclitus, who had opposing worldviews. Parmenides, who lived between c.515–445 BCE, contended that for the world to exist, it must be permanent and unchanging. So, for Parmenides, *nothing in the very nature of the world really changes*, and *change itself is just an illusion*, a product of deceitful appearances and flawed human perception. On the other hand, Heraclitus, who was a contemporary of Parmenides, entertained a view of the world as dynamic and ever-changing. For Parmenides, the actual illusion is the impression that the world is fixed and permanent when in fact, everything around us is in a perpetual state of flux (Mannion, 2007). *Nothing ever stands still* and *change is the only constant.*

Implications for organisational change

When applied to organisational change, Parmenides's worldview is but a short step away from an image of the organisation as static and locked in a *status quo* in which there is no room for any real change – perpetuating a deterministic view of change agents as impotent actors having to operate in a fundamentally unchanging business environment which remains beyond human influence. In contrast, Heraclitus' worldview throws up images of the organisation as fluid and dynamic and in constant interaction with its ever-changing operating context – ascribing greater freedom and power to change agents to both respond to and have a shaping influence over the forces at play within it (Harvey, 1996).

However, the pertinent question remains: *What, in an organisational context, can and cannot be changed?* Answers to such a question are always subject to contention. Notwithstanding this fact, we are of the view that some defining features of an organisation are less susceptible to change than its other, more malleable components. For example, the core social values (such as social justice, human rights, well-being of communities, etc.) that define a social enterprise are unlikely to change without destroying its *raison-d'être* and institutional integrity – even in the case of a major change in its strategy, structures and processes. The same argument may apply to healthcare organisations and governmental agencies that exist for a specific purpose and whose missions and strategic objectives are relatively enduring even in the face of major shifts in the wider external environment.

From a different vantage point, some might argue that *organisations cannot not change*, given the increasingly volatile and hypercompetitive business environment in which they have to operate. But then again, we would have to cycle back to our previous argument to underline the fact that, even if business organisations have to be always open to change in order to remain competitive, there are certain aspects of their business models that cannot remain in a perpetual state of flux if they have to make good on their strategic choices or stay true to their core values and mission. All in all, what can and cannot be changed is a matter of degree and very much dependent upon the specific context, purpose and strategic imperatives of the changing organisation.

On external and internal flows

The image of the organisation having to contend with external and internal flows has often been used to explain the complex nature of organisational change and the challenges involved in managing it. External flows refer to the numerous processes, relations, disruptions and other shock waves in the wider operating context of the organisation. External processes and relations can take the form of money transfers, inbound and outbound transportation of raw materials and finished products, and working relationships with external stakeholders such as business partners, consultancy firms, suppliers and customers. Disruptions and shock waves are the daunting challenges and events over which any single organisation has very little or no control. These can include things such as political turmoil, economic recessions, a sudden intensification of competitive rivalry, shifts in consumer preferences, technological innovations, natural disasters and other systemic disturbances that can adversely (and suddenly) impact performance, productivity and business continuity – the recent COVID-19 pandemic being a case in point.

On the other hand internal flows refer to the dynamic processes, activities and relations that occur within the boundaries of the organisation. They can include things such as production processes, communication patterns, employee relationships, processes of learning and knowledge transfer, technological applications and other ongoing value-adding activities underpinning an organisation's product offerings. Internal flows are 'bounded' – i.e. they are contained within organisational boundaries which arguably, make them easier to monitor and control – which is what all organisations endeavour to do to optimise performance, productivity and profit. However, one has to remember that internal flows are in constant tension with external flows and subject to their disruptive effects – which can make them equally difficult to manage.

The image of external and internal flows draws attention to the complex, multidimensional and dynamic nature of organisational functioning. Even more importantly, it casts light on the challenges associated with managing change within an organisational setting and the creative role that change agents are called to play in meeting those challenges.

Common assumptions about organisational change

In this sub-section, we further explore the nature of organisational change by critically examining some of the most common assumptions underlying it as encapsulated in the catchphrases highlighted in Figure 2.1.

Figure 2.1 Prevailing organisational change orthodoxy

Assumption 1: Change is the only constant

The assumption that *change is the only constant* arises from a recognition of the increasingly chaotic and unpredictable business context in which modern-day organisations have to operate and the need for change agents to relentlessly battle the forces of change as the only means to survive and stay ahead of the competition. However, one might argue that organisations cannot always manage change at the 'edge of chaos' and cope with never-ending disruptions, which in any case is not tenable. In most cases, enough time has to be allowed for the absorption of the shock and disturbances caused by change; and even more importantly, for the stabilisation of new ways of working over a desired time period which is vital to the successful achievement of the change goals and objectives. This is a point that we will discuss in more depth in later chapters.

Assumption 2: Change or die

Another common assumption about organisational change is captured in the rather intimidating imperative, *change or die*. Its legitimacy is perhaps best explained by the growing list of organisations that failed to effectively respond to major shifts in their external environment and, as a result, had to fold their businesses. One organisation that is often cited as a case example to justify this assumption is Blockbuster Entertainment Inc., a provider of video games and home movies rental service.

Blockbuster initially experienced worldwide success as it offered a convenient way for its customers to enjoy their favourite games and movies in the comfort of their homes. However, despite the emergence of rivals such as Netflix and Amazon, whose business models were based on online video streaming, Blockbuster did not promptly engage with Internet technologies based on the wrong assumption that its customers would still prefer the in-store shopping experience to a faceless video-on-demand online service – which eventually led to its demise (Miller Cole, 2019). Blockbuster's ill-fated story seems to lend some credence to the view that organisations have to either *change or die*.

However, upon closer examination of the sequence of events that led to Blockbuster's fatal end, it becomes clear that the company's failure cannot be solely attributed to its refusal to change. The fact is that Blockbuster made a serious attempt to jump on the online streaming bandwagon through a series of acquisitions and business partnerships to create a video-on-demand online service that could compete with rival offerings. It is therefore not a refusal to change that caused Blockbuster's demise. The company *did change but still died*. The fact is that there were multiple interrelated causes underlying Blockbuster's termination: a lack of industry foresight and innovative flair, poor timing of change interventions, wavering partnerships, and a loss of touch with its customer base (Reisinger, 2009). Perhaps the better lesson to be learned here is that *change is no guarantee of success*; and the demise or success of an organisation is not so much dependent on its readiness to change as on the *process of how it goes about doing change*.

Assumption 3: The pace of change is ever-increasing

The claim that *the pace of organisational change is ever-increasing* is defensible. It is undeniable that since the Industrial Age which revolutionised the way of doing business, there has been a convergence of technologies and scientific disciplines that have had a 'quickening effect' on the pace of organisational change (Spiegel-Rösing and de Solla Price, 1977). For instance, the convergence of information and communication technologies (ICTs) has led to the flourishing of e-commerce and allowed for rapid forays into previously untapped markets on a global scale. Amazon was among the first companies in the 1990s to successfully exploit ICTs and has transformed itself over the years into a global conglomerate that will undoubtedly be a central figure in the history books on e-commerce.

The ongoing development of ICTs has brought about the *Industrial Internet of Things* which involves the integration of industrial machinery and equipment, production processes and logistics with relevant software applications and network connectivity to enable companies to leverage their supply chain on a global scale (Greengard, 2015). Undoubtedly, this new development in ICTs will further accelerate the pace of technological change and commercial activity across industries. Other high-profile converging technologies and disciplines that are already having a quickening effect on the pace of organisational change across industries include: robotics (the interface between mechanical engineering and computer science), nanotechnology (the merging of physics and chemistry), artificial intelligence (AI) (the leveraging of computers and smart machines to carry out tasks that mimic, and even outperform, human intelligence) and space technology (the intersection between astronomy, space engineering and communications).

However, a caveat is in order here. While it would be fair to say that the pace of change is, generally speaking, increasing, it is important to recognise the fact that there are significant variations across sectors and industries. McGahan's (2004) insightful research into how industries change shows that the type, intensity and pace of change are dependent on the extent to which core assets and core activities are under threat. Industries with relatively stable core assets and activities (such as the commercial airlines and long-haul trucking) tend to change progressively and incrementally while those whose core assets and activities run the risk of becoming quickly obsolete (e.g. travel agencies and makers of landline handsets) usually need to change relatively faster and undergo radical change – which, however, as aptly remarked by McGahan, does not need to happen overnight.

Assumption 4: Change is the primary driver of business success

Although in essence true, the claim that *change is the primary driver of business success* has also to be qualified. As previously mentioned, it is not change itself that is a determinant of business success but the ability to manage it effectively. Organisational change is not an end in itself but a lever for optimising organisational functioning in view of the forces at play within the operating context of the organisation and its strategic choices and desired outcomes. Therefore an unqualified claim of change as the primary driver of business success falls short of the complex web of contextual variables and set of skills that are needed to ensure and sustain change success. While the common assumptions about organisational change discussed above contain some partial truths, they can also limit the possibility of a richer and more nuanced understanding of the phenomenon and of the challenges arising from it.

REFLECTIVE EXERCISE

1 Why is philosophy relevant to organisational change management?
2 What are your own philosophical views on the nature of organisational change?
3 What, in an organisational context, can and cannot be changed?
4 What do you think of the common assumptions about organisational change discussed in the preceding sub-section?

What then is organisational change?

In light of the above discussion, one has to recognise the sheer complexity and multidimensional and dynamic nature of organisational change which defies any single, definite definition. There are, however, many valuable definitions of organisational change in both academic and trade literature that, if not all encompassing, offer some illuminating insights into its key features and purpose. The common denominator of all these definitions is a representation of organisational change as a *deliberate move* towards some *desired state* in an attempt to ensure the *survival and growth* of the organisation.

We reinforce the key meanings attached to organisational change highlighted above but also take stock of what has been discussed so far in the following definition:

A process whereby an organisation deliberately adapts its strategy and ways of working in response to forces of change in its external environment in order to achieve competitive advantage and ensure its survival, continuity and growth in the longer term.

2.3 Typology of organisational change

Dichotomous conceptions of organisational change

Even a cursory review of both academic and trade literature would indicate a tendency towards a dichotomous mode of thinking in explaining the different types of organisational change – where the phenomenon is treated as a series of binary opposites and split into two mutually exclusive categories. Table 2.1 contains a list of some of the most common binary opposites used to describe organisational change.

Table 2.1   Dichotomous conceptions of organisational change

Dichotomous conceptions of organisational change	
Operational	Strategic
Localised	Organisation-wide
Continuous	Discontinuous
Evolutionary	Revolutionary
Incremental	Transformational

Operational v. strategic change

Operational change usually refers to the changes that are made to work structures, processes and activities in order to improve their effectiveness and efficiency – e.g. redefining roles and responsibilities, opening up new communication channels and establishing new production control systems. Strategic change is pitched at a higher level and usually involves long-range planning and a significant change to the overarching goals and business model of an organisation in response to certain threats and opportunities in order to achieve competitive advantage. For example, to remain competitive a manufacturing company might need to expand its business to new markets or develop new products that match those offered by its rivals in terms of both quality and price.

Localised v. organisation-wide

The main difference between these two types of change is one of *scope*. Localised change refers to a type of change contained within a particular department or functional area or at a particular level of the organisation – e.g. the digitalisation of HR processes or a reshuffling of roles and responsibilities at managerial level. Organisation-wide change encompasses the whole organisation and has a greater impact on the way the organisation conducts its business and on the working lives of organisational members – e.g. a major restructuring exercise entailing the closure of several business units and redundancy of low-level employees.

Continuous v. discontinuous change

Continuous change can involve a form of planned change which is broken down in smaller stages over a period of time. It can also refer to an approach to change as a never-ending journey to enable the organisation to respond in a moderate and timely manner and on an on-going basis to emerging challenges and opportunities in the external environment without an exclusive focus on long-term performance. On the other hand, discontinuous change involves a sharp and sudden break from current ways of working that occurs over a relatively short period of time and can have a dramatic effect on organisational performance. For example, discontinuous change can result from an urgent need to develop a new business model (such as an abrupt shift from brick-and-mortar to e-commerce) to keep up with technological innovations and outperform rivals.

Evolutionary v. revolutionary change

The distinction between these two types of organisational change hinges on the *pace* of the change. Like biological evolution across species which happens over successive generations, evolutionary organisational change takes place incrementally or in small steps to ensure the organisation's survival and growth over time. Evolutionary change can be seen in the slow, gradual modification, reconfiguration and development of organisational structures, processes and activities as the organisation adapts to the changes in its external environment. Revolutionary organisational change entails a rapid and radical break from old and current ways of doing things. It often calls for a change in leadership, cultural values, structures, business models and strategies. Moreover, revolutionary change is often unplanned, emergent and can also take the form of remedial action to ensure the survival of an organisation and guide it towards a more sustainable future.

Incremental v. transformational change

Incremental organisational change is typically low-intensity, localised and entails a gradual process of step-by-step adjustments or modifications. For example, a company may make a series of small adjustments to its after-sales service in response to customer feedback to improve it on a continuous basis. In most cases, the optimisation of production processes and product quality is achieved incrementally through minor corrective measures and tentative improvements based on regular monitoring and evaluation exercises. Moreover, there is the view that incremental change can be cumulative in effect – where timely and small-scale changes can enable the organisation to respond promptly to its external environment, foregoing the need for large-scale, unanticipated and often chaotic change.

In sharp contrast, transformational change is typically high-intensity, organisation-wide, radical and, in most cases, irreversible – where the organisation does something completely different from what it was doing before and can morph into something completely different from its original state. Transformational change can entail a major shift in an organisation's strategic orientation alongside significant changes to its structural arrangements, product portfolio, production processes and cultural value system. For example, transformational change may be required in the case of a merger where the companies involved have to integrate their core cultural values, develop innovative products and services and expand into international markets.

Finally, we just want to underline the fact that: (i) the dichotomies used to describe different types of change in some cases carry overlapping meanings and (ii) the types of change they describe are not mutually exclusive and can complement each other – for example, an organisation which, for whatever reason, has undergone transformational change can sustain the change through incremental adjustments and improvements.

PRACTICAL EXERCISE

Carry out the following exercise to familiarise yourself with the key meanings attached to the **dichotomous conceptions** of organisational change.

Once again, go through the section on *Typology of organisational change* and use Table 2.2 below to map out in the right-hand column the key features of each of the dichotomous types of organisational change listed in the column on the left.

Table 2.2 Key features of dichotomous types of organisational change

Dichotomous types of organisational change	Key features
Operational v. strategic change	Operational: Strategic:
Localised v. organisation-wide	Localised: Organisation-wide:
Continuous v. discontinuous change	Continuous: Discontinuous:
Evolutionary v. revolutionary change	Evolutionary: Revolutionary:
Incremental v. transformational change	Incremental: Transformational:

Can you identify the similarities and differences in meaning across the dichotomous types of organisational change covered in this section?

Van de Ven and Poole's modes of change

Van de Ven and Poole (1995) developed an alternative typology of change which is worth mentioning as it provides some valuable additional insights into the nature of organisational change. While the theoretical foundations underpinning their typology is beyond the scope of this book, we will only briefly consider here the distinction it draws between two main modes of change: a prescribed mode of change v. a constructive mode of change.

A prescribed mode of change

A prescribed mode of change 'channels the development of entities in a pre-specified direction, typically of maintaining and incrementally adapting their forms in a stable, predictable way' (Van de Ven and Poole, 1995, p. 522). With regard to organisational change, a prescribed mode of change is planned and charts a clear path for organisational development and the achievement of pre-determined goals and objectives. It is also referred to as first-order change as it involves a form of incremental, gradual, evolutionary change that is derived from past and current practices and progresses in a fairly stable and predictable manner. Like an incremental approach to change, a prescribed mode of change has a cumulative effect and can add up over time to a large-scale change, in terms of both impact and quality.

A prescribed mode of change entails a low level of uncertainty. Since it is rooted in past practices and unravels in a continuous and predictable manner, organisational members can anticipate to some extent its progress path and outcomes. Moreover, because a prescribed mode of change follows a continuous developmental path and allows for organic growth, it enables the organisation to build on its own capabilities and resources and importantly, retain its identity throughout the change process.

A constructive mode of change

By contrast, a constructive mode of change 'generates unprecedented, novel forms that, in retrospect, often are discontinuous and unpredictable departures from the past' (Van de Ven and Poole, 1995, p. 522). With regard to organisational change, a constructive mode of change is emergent as goals and objectives arise from the change process, leading to completely new working practices and unpredictable outcomes. It is also referred to as second-order change in that it entails a form of radical, discontinuous, revolutionary change that forces a break from the past and progresses in an unstable and unexpected manner – which can cause a high level of uncertainty among organisational members and a constant need to make sense of things and track its progress.

Importantly, a constructive mode of change warrants, on the part of change agents, a greater sense of purpose and an ability to resolve the conflicts and contradictions arising from the change process as they endeavour to break away from past practices and generate effective solutions to drive innovative change.

CASE STUDY 2.1

The Alibaba Group: Navigating challenges and driving creative change

Applying Van de Ven and Poole's typology of modes of change as a diagnostic tool

Introduction

Founded by Jack Ma in 1999, the Alibaba Group is a China-based multinational technology company that operates as one of the world's leading e-commerce companies. The

(Continued)

Alibaba Group has grown into a massive business hosting online marketplaces which provide access to consumer goods, payment services, cloud computing and digital entertainment. With a firm commitment to technological innovation, Alibaba has been instrumental in shaping China's digital economy. Recently, the company expanded its operations beyond China, tapping into Southeast Asian and other global markets.

Challenges on all fronts

Over the past few years, however, the Alibaba Group has been facing challenges on all fronts. Back in April 2021, Alibaba was fined a record-breaking $2.75 billion by China's antitrust regulator for abusing its dominant market position to coerce traders into conducting business exclusively through its online platform, to the detriment of competitive rivals, consumers and the wider Chinese economy. Such a heavy fine represented around 4% of the company's 2019 domestic revenues – signalling a hardening of China's position against what it considers as bullying tactics on the part of mega corporations.

Since then, the Alibaba Group has been under intense scrutiny which has shaken the trust of its customer base. The COVID-19 lockdown only served to complicate matters further, causing supply chain disruptions and a significant decrease in business activity and revenues. In addition, the company was experiencing difficulties abroad – where, for example, it could no longer facilitate access of US businesses to the Chinese market while facing stiff competition from well-established rivals such as Amazon and eBay.

Splitting giant Alibaba into six baby Babas

In March 2023, in response to the punitive action of China's antitrust regulator, Alibaba publicly announced its plan to undertake a major restructuring exercise designed to split the giant organisation into six distinct business units or what has been referred to as 'baby Babas'. Each business unit will have its own board of directors and CEO. As the controlling shareholder, the Alibaba board will continue to have control over the boards of these new companies. While five out of the six units will have the ability to raise capital and seek stock market listing, *Taobao Tmall Commerce Group*, by far the biggest revenue contributor will remain fully owned by the parent company.

According to top management, this restructuring exercise will enable the Alibaba Group to address the ever-increasing size of the company in one fell swoop. The massive size of the company was the major cause of slow decision-making, weak accountability and a real 'drag on performance'. It is hoped that the new structural configuration will enable the independent business units to 'become more agile' and be able to 'respond faster' to market changes by giving them a greater focus and the freedom to 'chart their own paths', and demonstrate a greater entrepreneurial spirit – with a positive knock-on effect on shareholder value.

Conclusions

The major change initiative facing the Alibaba Group is seen by key stakeholders as a smart strategic response by top management and a creative way of navigating the challenges arising from its operating context – as it serves the dual purpose of enabling the company to effectively address current challenges while setting it on track towards a promising future. However, for investors, this future remains uncertain. There is still the fear of constant scrutiny by the government and it is a well-known fact that the profitability of new business ventures is something that is highly unpredictable and very difficult to measure through failsafe metrics.

Sources: Horwitz (2023); Lee (2023); Nga (2023).

Activity

Apply Van de Ven and Poole's typology of modes of change to the Alibaba Group's impending change initiative.

1   How would you describe the main mode of change that is underway across the Alibaba Group? Why?
2   What are the potential benefits and pitfalls of Alibaba's proposed change initiative?

2.4 The theory of punctuated equilibrium

The theory of punctuated equilibrium was developed by paleontologists Stephen Jay Gould and Niles Eldredge and was first introduced to the world in 1972. Punctuated equilibrium is a revision of Darwin's gradualist theory which views the evolution of the species as a relatively steady and gradual process. As such, it posits that the process of evolution entails long periods of relative stability interspersed with shorter bursts of disruptive and rapid change during which significant evolution occurs (Bernstein, 1988). While the theory of punctuated equilibrium is still hotly debated in scientific circles and the subject of ongoing research, we shall content ourselves here to apply it, at the most basic level, to the process of organisational change – as illustrated in Figure 2.2.

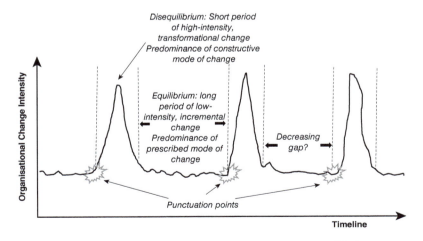

Figure 2.2   Organisational change as a case of punctuated equilibrium

Figure 2.2 illustrates the application of a basic understanding of punctuated equilibrium to the process of organisational change. In this case, organisational change is seen as consisting of *relatively longer periods of low-intensity, incremental change punctuated by shorter, compact periods of high-intensity transformational change* that can either be triggered by major disturbances in the external environment or be the result of a deliberate strategic choice (highlighted by the punctuation points in Figure 2.2).

Link to Van de Ven and Poole's modes of change

The theory of punctuated equilibrium can be nicely linked to Van de Ven and Poole's (1995) modes of change explained in the preceding sub-section. When the organisation is going through relatively longer periods of low-intensity, incremental change, it is in a *predominantly prescribed mode of change* that progresses in a fairly stable and predictable manner. However, when the organisation experiences short bursts or compact periods of high-intensity transformational change, it operates in a *predominantly constructive mode of change* characterised by a discontinuous and radical break from past practices.

Decreasing gap between transformational spikes

Hayes (2021) makes the compelling remark that the gap between high-intensity, transformational spikes is *decreasing* – which would explain in part why there is a noticeable increase in the pace of change across industries, the IT industry being a case in point. Gersick's (1991) research tends to validate this phenomenon whilst drawing attention to how periods of high-intensity, disruptive change warrant the alteration of the organisation's *deep structures*.

Changing the organisation's deep structures

Tushman and Romanelli (1985) refer to the organisation's deep structures as the key domains of organisational activity including: (i) strategic goals and objectives, (ii) core cultural values and ethical principles, (ii) structural arrangements and work patterns, (iv) the mode of governance and power distribution and (v) processes designed to optimise organisational performance and create value and competitive advantage. These domains of activity are interdependent and determined by the organisation's fundamental choices over time in response to environmental challenges and opportunities. As such, deep structures tend to be well-entrenched and persistent – until they are 'knocked off their bases' in times of high-intensity, transformational change and replaced by new strategies, cultures, structures, power distributions and processes which then 'take hold' during periods of relative stability and become established as the organisation's deep structures.

The value of the theory of punctuated equilibrium lies in the way it foregrounds the alternate patterns of stability and change and the relative balance that is needed between the two to bring about sustainable change. Moreover, the theory has been substantiated by ample empirical evidence across disciplines and industries (Gersick, 1991). The end-of-chapter case study provides additional empirical evidence in support of punctuated equilibrium.

1   What is the meaning of *punctuated equilibrium* in the context of organisational change?
2   How is the theory of punctuated equilibrium linked to Van de Ven and Poole's *modes of change*?
3   What does the term *deep structures* refer to? When are deep structures subject to change?

2.5 Causes of organisational change

Organisational change is underpinned by a complex web of causal relationships that have a significant impact on its design, implementation and outcomes. In this section, we consider both the external and internal causes impacting organisational change while drawing attention to the importance of thick causal explanations and causal modelling in driving change success and the possibility of upward causation with reference to a real-life organisation.

External causes

There is a multiplicity of external causes at different levels of analysis that can impact organisational change. At the macro level, a good example would be political measures relating to international trade that can either open up or limit the possibility for international ventures and foreign direct investment – leading to either a slowing down or an acceleration of the pace of business globalisation and a cascading effect on an organisation's international market development strategy. This brings to mind the on-going trade war between the US and China, which has brought about a raft of protectionist trade tariffs in response to what is perceived by the US as China's 'longstanding malpractices' – e.g. the cyber-enabled theft of intellectual property and the pressured transfer of US technologies to Chinese companies (US Trade Representative Office, 2018). Such protectionist measures have had an adverse impact on corporate foreign direct investment and have forced some organisations such as Samsung and General Motors to curb their international activities and close down plants in China (Manabe, 2019).

At industry level, a good example of an external causal factor which can have a significant impact on organisational change is the on-going competitive rivalry driven by innovative technological applications – where companies have to continuously leverage their technological architecture to remain competitive. For instance, Nike, the leading provider of athletic shoes and clothing, managed to stay ahead of the competition during the COVID-19 pandemic by deploying an online library of resources (including the Nike Training Club App, Digital Fitness Challenges and livestream workouts on YouTube) where customers could interact and play with global athletes from their living rooms or backyards. In so doing, Nike was able to extend its e-commerce strategy into 'social commerce' and found a way to reverse the social distancing brought about by COVID-19 and boost their direct online sales while outperforming their competitors (Beaverton, 2020).

Internal causes

Internal causes that have the most significant impact on change initiatives are those arising at the strategic level – e.g. the development of a new business model to enable a major business turnaround, a restructuring exercise to cut costs and enhance the performance or the deployment of a new communication model designed to frame culture change and muster employee commitment. For example, among the many internal causes driving the major restructuring exercise at Tesla (the well-known manufacturer of electric cars, solar-powered batteries and spaceships), those that were cited as of pressing importance by CEO Elon Musk included: the need for a flatter organisational structure to improve communication between teams, the need to streamline processes to speed up the production of a new car model and the need for the company to become more sustainably profitable (Sage, 2019).

The need for thick causal explanations of organisational change

Organisational change cannot be reduced to one single occurrence or a flat, linear sequence of events that would allow for only a weak understanding of the causes driving change. This is perhaps why change agents sometimes fail to see the connection between key causal relationships at play within a particular change context and tend to remain impervious to the 'causal blind spots' that can prevent the successful completion of change projects. There is a growing recognition of the need for *thick causal explanations* of organisational change – which can enable a more robust understanding of the complex web of reinforcing and countervailing causal mechanisms underlying change and how they can lead to change success or failure (Fleetwood and Hesketh, 2011).

For example, however visionary and sound a new business strategy can be, it is unlikely to succeed if change agents fail to identify and effectively address countervailing causal powers such as employee resistance or technological misapplication that can have a highly adverse impact on change outcomes. This is nothing new, but approaching such issues from a *causal perspective* and integrating them into smart causal models can make a significant difference and enable change agents to develop meaning-rich and context-sensitive insights into the forces driving or constraining change projects – thus, increasing the likelihood of change success.

The value of causal modelling

As hinted above, causal modelling can prove to be a valuable diagnostic exercise through which change agents can generate thick causal explanations of organisational change and increase the likelihood of change success. A smart causal model can enable change agents to:

- Map out the significant causes underlying their change initiatives.
- Gain a sound understanding of the nature of the relationships between such causes.
- Identify causal chains that can enable or constrain the achievement of desired change outcomes.
- Track emergent causal influences throughout the change process.
- Plot evidence-based courses of action to achieve both planned and emergent strategic goals and objectives.

Upward causation

Finally, we need to say a few words on the possibility of upward causation in the context of organisational change. So far, the discussion has focused mainly on downward causation – especially in the case of external causal variables which are usually portrayed as operating in a higher sphere of events and 'hitting' the organisation from above. However, it is important to consider the fact that an *organisation can have a causal impact on its wider operating context*, where, for example, a company's strategic choices and innovative product offerings can change the competitive dynamics across its industry – which can be construed as a case of *upward causation*. The following case study provides another compelling example of upward causation.

---CASE STUDY 2.2---

Hewlett-Packard: A prime example of upward causation

Introduction

In their thought-provoking and well-revered book, *Competing for the Future*, Hamel and Prahalad (1996) provide evidential support for the possibility of upward causation in the context of organisational change. Hamel and Prahalad's main argument is that sustainable success is not for those organisations that conform to traditional ways of thinking and that are only reactive to external change drivers. The future belongs to organisations that challenge the status quo, are adept at out-of-the-box thinking and able to regenerate their strategy and shape the forces at play within their industry. Hamel and Prahalad cite IT company Hewlett-Packard as a business organisation that has done just that.

Changing the rule of the game

Since its humble beginnings in 1938 in a car garage, Hewlett-Packard has repeatedly transformed itself and creatively re-developed its product portfolio to not only gain competitive advantage but also change the rule of the game across its industry. In 1939,

(Continued)

Hewlett-Packard targeted a niche market with its first audio oscillator for testing sound equipment which was famously used by Walt Disney. After the Second World War, the company consistently made a series of smart strategic moves and developed new imaginative products targeting much larger markets worldwide including: the cesium beam instrument to synchronise the globe's atomic clocks in 1964, the very first desk calculator in 1968 and its highly successful HP LaserJet printer in the early 80s.

Shaping customer demand

Between 2000 and 2010, Hewlett-Packard opened research labs in India, China, Russia, Japan and Israel and acquired Compaq and Palm Inc. This allowed the company, in collaboration with Microsoft, to become a prime producer of personal computers, personal digital assistants and smartphones. More recently in 2015, Hewlett-Packard made another decisive strategic move by splitting into two discrete companies – with one focusing on the production of personal computers and the other on products and services for businesses (see also Hall, 2020).

It is through a sustained process of strategic re-positioning, judicious acquisitions and strategic alliances (coupled with its renowned 'high-motivation-high-performance' approach to people management) that Hewlett-Packard has managed to develop an impressive range of innovative electronic engineering and computing products that have over time shaped demand and appealed to different generations of customers.

Conclusions

For Hamel and Prahalad, Hewlett-Packard is an exemplary case of industry foresight and strategic regeneration made possible by technological innovation and an exceptional ability to tap into customer needs and expectations. This has allowed the organisation to repeatedly re-invent itself whilst exerting a powerful shaping influence over its external environment by spearheading imaginative ways of doing business and setting new standards of product quality and customer satisfaction.

Questions

1   Why is Hewlett-Packard a good example of *upward causation*?
2   How did Hewlett-Packard manage to maintain a shaping influence over its external environment over the years?

2.6 The role of change management

Now that we have examined the nature of organisational change in some detail, it is appropriate at this point to consider ways to effectively manage it. In doing so, we outline the defining features of Change Management (CM) and explore its links with the distinct disciplines of Organisational Development (OD) and Project Management (PM), which is a key theme in the change literature.

Defining change management

There are as many definitions of CM as there are textbooks on the subject matter. This is understandable given the sheer complexity of this vital organisational activity and the alternative vantage points from which it can be described. Moreover, some would argue that any single definition of CM would fail to do justice to its multidimensional nature and the multiplicity of meanings that can be attached to it.

While having their own limitations, most definitions of CM have a common denominator: an intent to *move* the organisation from its *current* state to a *desired* state. It is worth underlining the fact that this movement from one state to another tends to be primarily *instrumental* in orientation – i.e. the process of managing change is typically locked in a means-end relationship and driven by an overriding purpose which is to optimise its resources to achieve the strategic interests of an organisation as a complex system, further the interests of (dominant) organisational stakeholders and ensure business continuity and growth in the longer term.

In light of the above, we put forward an instrumental yet non-exhaustive definition of CM as:

A multidimensional process that aims to leverage the resources of an organisation as a complex system to effectively achieve its strategic goals and objectives and ensure its continuity and growth in the longer term.

Key features of CM

In deconstructing the above definition, we identify the key perspectives informing CM as follows:

- A *strategic* perspective – to gain and maintain competitive advantage geared toward business continuity and long-term growth.
- A *resource-based* perspective – to optimise the financial, material, technological and human resources of the organisation in order to achieve its strategic goals and objectives.
- A *process* perspective – to enable a systematic and continuous approach to the planning, implementation, coordination and evaluation of change projects in order to ensure their successful completion.
- A *systems* perspective – to develop a sound understanding of how key functional domains and activities of an organisation interact to ensure its optimal functioning.

Thus, to be effective, CM warrants a multi-perspectival approach and a complex set of unique skills and competences that can generate competitive advantage and sustainable business success.

2.7 Exploring the links between OD, PM and CM

In this section we discuss the links between OD, PM and CM as distinct yet overlapping and mutually reinforcing areas of organisational functioning. The basic Venn diagram in Figure 2.3 highlights the primary focus of each discipline and their shared focus which lies at the intersection of their practical boundaries. It also provides a structure for the following discussion.

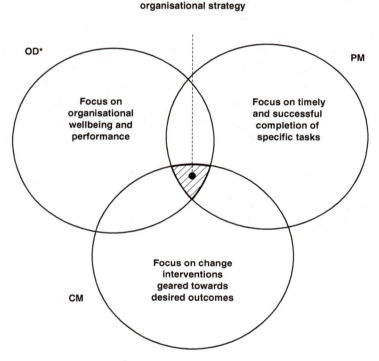

* Moving clockwise, starting point for following discussion

Figure 2.3   Links between CM, OD and PM

Organisational Development – OD

The primary focus of OD is on the optimisation of organisational well-being and performance. To this effect, OD adopts a holistic and planned approach to maximise and sustain organisational effectiveness and performance whilst building capability to effectively cater to the physical, psychological and social well-being of employees at all levels of the organisation (Creasey et al., 2015). Some of the most salient principles and interventions of OD include:

- Maintaining a robust alignment between OD activities and the organisation's strategic and performance objectives.
- Deploying strategic interventions to enhance business planning and organisational capability to diagnose challenges and opportunities and choosing optimal strategic solutions to drive the organisation forward.

- Developing positive core cultural values and organisational behaviours through HR interventions focused on enabling leadership, teamwork, positive group dynamics and relational networks.
- Promoting collaborative learning at all organisational levels via learning and development interventions such as training, coaching, mentoring, team working and action learning.
- Maximising the value of the organisation's resources via techno-structural interventions such as Business Process Reengineering, Lean and Six Sigma.
- Employing sound evaluative measures to gauge the impact of employee engagement, learning and well-being on organisational performance.
- Sustaining an organisation-wide commitment to change and continuous improvement (CIPD, 2022).

Project Management – PM

The primary focus of PM is on the timely and successful completion of specific tasks. By definition, PM involves the application of particular processes, knowledge, skills and resources to achieve specific outcomes according to set standards and within a set timescale and budget (McDowell, n.d.). Unlike OD, PM is not an on-going process or 'business-as-usual'. As highlighted in the definition, PM draws on a specific set of skills and resources for a specific period of time to achieve specific outcomes. Moreover, PM usually takes place within a matrix structure, where employees from different functional areas and with different skills, expertise and experiences come together under the leadership of the project manager. After the completion of the project, they usually disband to resume their usual work activities or join another project.

It is important to note that a particular project can run in parallel with main business activities or in tandem with other projects, under the leadership of different project managers. Alternatively, a project manager can be in charge of several projects with different deadlines and outcomes. The PM process can be broken down into clearly identifiable stages that take the project 'from start to finish'. These stages account for the project life cycle and include:

- *Initiation*: defining the purpose and business value of the project – which can be of particular importance in selling it to other organisational stakeholders.
- *Planning*: paying particular attention to resource commitments, required skills and expertise, key deliverables and timescales of the project – to provide the much-needed parameters for the successful implementation of the project.
- *Execution*: putting the project into action and deploying the necessary resources to ensure its successful implementation.
- *Monitoring and control*: Keeping tabs on the progress of the project against appropriate evaluative measures while addressing emerging problems and taking corrective action to ensure the project outcomes are delivered on time and within budget.
- *Closure*: Confirming the completion of the project and communicating its results to key stakeholders as per the intended outcomes and expected quality standards (Donato, 2022).

It has to be said that the stages of the project life cycle can overlap (e.g. monitoring and control can span the whole project life). However, the primary function of the project life cycle is to enable project managers to have a handle on the flow of activities and the timings of the project's key deliverables, leading to its successful completion.

Change Management – CM

Since the defining features of CM have already been described above, we will focus here on how it compares with OD and PM along the dimensions of scope of application, focus of efforts and level of engagement (Creasey et al., 2015).

In terms of *scope of application*, CM is viewed as involving focused interventions geared towards specific outcomes, which can last for only a short time or span multiple years. In contrast, OD entails a holistic and on-going process that encompasses the whole organisation and is driven by a commitment to continuous improvement in organisational well-being and performance. PM is focused on very specific tasks or activities and involves only a selection of organisational members who work as a team over a relatively short period of time to deliver more narrowly focused outcomes.

In terms of *focus of effort*, CM is often seen as focused on individual performance while OD is concerned with optimising organisational functioning and performance as a whole. For PM, the focus of effort is on the performance of the project team. In terms of *level of engagement*, CM is structured around ways to engage individual employees and enhance their performance in line with the strategic objectives of the organisation. On the other hand, OD is concerned with high-order engagement interventions designed to continuously improve organisational functioning and performance. As for PM, the level of engagement is restricted to project team members and their contributions to the successful completion of the project.

The intersection of OD, PM and CM

At the intersection of CM, OD and PM lies a shared focus on the effective achievement of the organisation's strategic objectives. While, as explained above, the activities that can be subsumed under each of these domains of organisational functioning bear certain differences, such activities are underpinned by the same core cultural values and can be mutually reinforcing and converge towards a shared purpose and the realisation of commonly desired outcomes.

Moreover, the effectiveness of all three domains rests upon the same key principles:

1 The need for a collaborative approach to problem solving and the generation of innovative solutions.
2 The need for positive cultural values and enabling behaviours and group dynamics to optimise learning and performance.
3 The need for effective communication and participation to sustain commitment and effort.
4 The need for robust evaluative measures to track progress.
5 The need to maintain an alignment between performance outcomes and strategic objectives.
6 The need to optimise organisational effectiveness.

Typically, in a change situation, OD would focus on what needs to be improved at a higher level of organisational functioning and play a leading role in addressing issues such as the reformulation of the mission and strategy of the organisation, the delineation of new core cultural values and leadership behaviours, new people management principles, process redesign and formation of new teams or functional groups. CM would provide more explicit guidance at a more 'granular level' where more detailed information is needed regarding things such as specific job roles, key performance indicators for individual employees and teams, and required change in attitudes and behaviours. PM could involve the set-up of project teams or task forces that would combine resources and talents scattered across the organisation to focus on problem solving and the development of innovative solutions that could then be 'fed into' the change process (Creasey et al., 2015).

Thus, while there are clear conceptual differences between CM, OD and PM, they can bring unique yet complementary, mutually reinforcing contributions to change success; and changing organisations can greatly benefit from an increasing convergence of these discrete areas of organisational functioning.

PRACTICAL EXERCISE

Merging CM, OD and PM activities in a merger situation

Read the following scenario before carrying out the activity and addressing the questions that follow.

You are the newly appointed CEO of a medium-sized company which has recently merged with a rival company of similar size based in another country. It is hoped that this strategic move will enable the merged company to expand its market internationally and develop a range of new products that will contribute to a significant growth in revenues and profits. Together with the other senior members of the Board, you are in the process of developing a strategic change plan that will help the merged company to achieve its new strategic objectives.

You have been advised by one of the senior HR managers that the talent pool of the newly merged company includes well experienced change agents, OD practitioners and project managers and that they could all bring valuable contributions to the implementation of the change plan. You have decided to follow the advice of the senior HR manager and invited all the employees with experience in OD, PM and CM to sit on the next change management committee to plot a course of action to ensure the successful implementation of the new strategic change plan.

The new change initiative calls for major changes in the following areas: strategy, leadership, cultural values, people management, technology application and process management. There is also a clear recognition among the change leadership team that the success of the new change initiative will depend to a large measure upon the commitment, creativity and performance of all employees.

Activity

In preparing for the next change management committee, you want to be clear in your mind about how you will make the best use of the talents and experiences of the change agents, OD practitioners and project managers in implementing the new strategic plan. You have called in the senior HR manager who advised you about this. With his help, you want to map out the different roles and responsibilities you want to assign to each category of employees listed in Table 2.3. You can refer back to the discussion in this section to help you with this exercise.

(Continued)

Table 2.3 Mapping out the key roles and responsibilities of change agents, OD practitioners and project managers

Category of employees	Key roles and responsibilities
Change agents	
OD practitioners	
Project managers	

Questions

1   What was the value of conducting this exercise?
2   What key contributions could each category of employees identified in Table 2.3 bring to the change initiative?
3   What can you do as CEO to support such contributions?

2.8 Conceptual nugget: Adopting a systemic approach to change management

In line with one of the conceptual pillars underpinning this textbook, we advocate, in this final section, a systemic approach to change management. Figure 2.4 foregrounds the key elements of such an approach that will be critically examined in the following discussion.

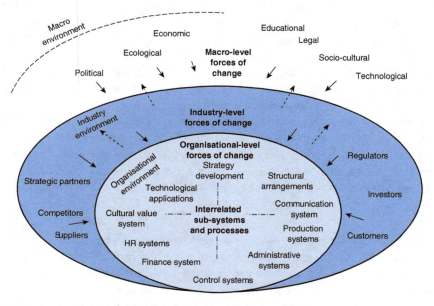

Figure 2.4 A systemic approach to change management

The organisation as a complex ecosystem

Figure 2.4 portrays the organisation as a complex ecosystem. The term ecosystem is a concept that is rapidly gaining traction across the change management landscape. An ecosystem refers to a community of living organisms and to the physical environment with which they have a dynamic relationship (*Encyclopaedia Britannica*, 2023). Importantly, the focus is on the way these living organisms are interconnected and interact with each other and their environment to survive and grow.

When transposed to the business context, the concept of an ecosystem locates the *organisation as a living organism* within its external environment with which it has a *dynamic relationship* – where the organisation and its external environment impact each other and are engaged in some form of symbiotic relationship through which both can survive, endure and prosper. In Figure 2.4, *the macro and industry environments* and the forces of change at play within them account for the organisation's external environment.

The notion of an ecosystem also elicits thinking about the inner workings of a living organism that serve to keep it alive and in harmony with its environment. In a business context, the *internal environment* refers to the way the different parts or sub-systems of an organisation are purposefully configured and interact *to create collective value* that may be of benefit to both internal stakeholders (e.g. managers, employees and owners) and external stakeholders (e.g. customers, shareholders, suppliers, business partners, the wider community, etc.). In Figure 2.4, the inner circle represents the organisation's internal environment and provides examples of the *key interrelated and interacting sub-systems and processes that underlie the forces of change* at play within it.

In light of the above, the first important point we want to make is twofold. A systemic approach to change management can: (i) allow for a *multi-levelled and complex understanding* of the key environmental forces impacting an organisation undergoing change, and (ii) enable *informed decision-making* as to how its interrelated sub-systems and processes can be reconfigured to generate greater collective value to the benefit of all key stakeholders.

A web of causal relationships

A systemic approach to change management can enable change agents to map out a complex web of causal relationships that underlie their change situation. Figure 2.4 foregrounds the three main levels of causal analysis that provide the parameters for this exercise: the macro, industry and organisational environments. The major causal factors in the macro environment that can have a significant impact on both the industry and organisational levels (as shown by the downward arrows in Figure 2.4) can be of a political, ecological, economic, legal, educational, socio-cultural or technological nature – which can be identified via common diagnostic tools such as PESTLE and SWOT analyses.

The key causal entities in the industry environment that have an immediate effect on the competitive positioning of the organisation include competitors, suppliers, strategic partners, regulators, investors, customers, etc. – all of which can be mapped out via tools such as Porter's

5-Forces model (which is highly valuable in gauging the causes underlying the competitive intensity of an industry) and the industry life-cycle model (which enables an insight into the causes impacting the stage of development of an industry and the strength of competitive rivalry within it).

To gain an understanding of the significant causal forces in the organisational environment, change agents can have recourse to tools such as the value chain analysis (which can be used to trace the causal links between the value creating activities of the organisation) or simulation modelling to assess the causal impact of various alternative business processes and practices. Moreover, various types of bespoke causal maps or canvases can be used to explore the causal relationships between the sub-systems (as shown in the inner circle in Figure 2.4) that account for organisational functioning and the creation of value.

Importantly, Figure 2.4 also draws attention to the possibility of *upward causation* in the context of organisational change (indicated by the upward dotted arrows) – where an organisation can have a causal impact across its industry and sometimes even the macro environment through the development of innovative product offerings and the creation of new customer demands – an outstanding example being mobile Internet devices that have changed the competitive dynamics at industry level and caused a shift in customer preferences, lifestyle and demand at a global level.

The second important point we want to make with regard to a systemic approach to change management is that it *is amenable to different forms of causal modelling* that can enable an *in-depth analysis* of the complex web of causal relationships that underlie the change process and of their emergent properties that can have a significant bearing on the change outcomes.

Beyond dichotomous thinking

A systemic approach to change management goes beyond a rigid dichotomous, either–or mode of thinking. It is accommodating of the view that organisational change does not have to be *either* incremental *or* transformational. It has already been shown in a previous section of this chapter how incremental and transformational change can follow each other in a repeated pattern (see section on The theory of punctuated equilibrium). A systemic perspective can add to an understanding of the relationship between incremental and transformational change to show how both can happen simultaneously.

For example, an automotive company interested in setting up a new branch in another country to sell one of its most successful luxury car models to niche markets in that particular country. Such a strategic move might necessitate only minor incremental changes to the production sub-systems of the company to accommodate the needs and preferences of the new target markets and to comply with the law. However, the strategic move might warrant a transformation of its cultural value system to demonstrate greater sensitivity in dealing with new customers and colleagues from a different cultural background.

The final important key point we want to make here is that a systemic approach to change can serve to *deepen our understanding of the relationship between incremental and transformational change* and underline the fact that *both types of change can happen simultaneously*.

Limitations

A systemic approach to change management also has certain limitations. First, systems theory and modelling has often been criticised for being overly complex and esoteric which makes it unappealing to busy practitioners who do not have the time or the inclination to engage with it. Second, a systemic approach to change management can also be resource intensive and expensive which makes it difficult to get top-management buy-in and access to sufficient funding, especially when more straightforward and less costly ways of doing change are readily available. Third, most organisations do not possess the necessary competences and technical expertise to effectively engage in systemic change. Finally, there is still a lack of evidence of success in this area which means that a lot of organisations would be unwilling to invest in and experiment with systemic change management.

However, we are of the view that the benefits of systemic change far outweigh its limitations. The lack of evidence of successful systemic change can lead to a form of circular reasoning – where the lack of evidence results in an unwillingness of organisations to engage in systemic change which is the reason why there is a lack of evidence of successful systemic change – and so on and so forth. To break out of this unproductive cycle, there is a need to make the concept of systemic change more accessible to practitioners, raise awareness about its potential benefits, stimulate investments in training and development and encourage wider experimentation in this area – which would produce more compelling evidence on not only the practical value of a systemic approach to change management but also on the challenges arising from it.

REFLECTIVE EXERCISE

1   What are the key benefits of a systemic approach to change management?
2   What are its key limitations?
3   What can be done to promote a systemic approach to change management?

2.9 Key learning points

The following key learning points have been covered in this chapter:

1   The *philosophical commitments* of change leaders and their assumptions about the nature of change have a significant influence on their approach to organisational change. While views about organisational change may differ, *what can and cannot be changed* is very much dependent upon the specific context, purpose and strategic imperatives of the changing organisation. This textbook defined organisational change as a *process* whereby an organisation *deliberately adapts its strategy* and *ways of working* in response to forces of change in its external environment in order to *achieve competitive advantage* and ensure its *survival, continuity and growth* in the longer term.

2   Some of the most common dichotomies used to identify and describe different types of organisational change addressed in this chapter include *operational v. strategic, localised v. organisation-wide, continuous v. discontinuous*, and *evolutionary v. revolutionary* change. Van de Ven and Poole's alternative typology of *prescribed v. constructive modes of change* can also be used as a valuable diagnostic tool to describe organisational change.

3   When applied to the process of organisational change, the theory of punctuated equilibrium portrays it as consisting of *relatively longer periods of low-intensity, incremental change* (when the organisation is in a predominantly prescribed mode of change) punctuated by *shorter, compact periods of high-intensity transformational change* (when an organisation is in a predominantly constructive mode of change). Periods of high-intensity, disruptive change warrant the alteration of the organisation's *deep structures*, which refers to the organisation's strategy, culture, power distribution and processes.

4   Organisational change is underpinned by a complex web of causal relationships that can have a significant impact on its design, implementation and outcomes. This web of causal relationships consists of *external causal factors* operating at macro and industry levels and *internal causal factors* at play within the boundaries of the organisation. *Thick causal explanations* of organisational change can enable agents to develop a meaning-rich and context-sensitive understanding of the causal forces driving or constraining change projects – thus, increasing the likelihood of change success. Moreover, *upward causation* occurs when an organisation exerts a causal impact on its wider operating context, where, for example, a company's strategic choices and innovative product offerings can change the competitive dynamics across its industry.

5   This textbook defined change management as a *multidimensional process* that aims to *leverage the resources* of an organisation as a complex system to *effectively achieve its strategic goals and objectives* and *ensure its continuity and growth* in the longer term. While change management, organisational development and project management are distinct areas of organisational functioning, they have a *shared purpose* which is the effective achievement of the organisation's strategic objectives. As such, they can bring *unique* yet *complementary, mutually reinforcing contributions* to change success and changing organisations can greatly benefit from an increasing *convergence* of these discrete areas of organisational functioning.

6   A systemic approach to change management views the organisation as a *complex ecosystem* and locates it *as a living organism* within its external environment with which it has a dynamic and symbiotic relationship. It also elicits thinking about the internal environment of the organisation and how its interrelated sub-systems and processes are purposefully configured and interact to create collective value that may be of benefit to all key stakeholders. The main benefits of a systemic approach include the following: (i) a *multi-levelled and complex understanding* of the key environmental forces impacting an organisation, (ii) *informed decision-making* as to how its interrelated sub-systems and processes can be reconfigured to generate greater value, (iii) an *in-depth analysis* of the complex web of causal relationships that underlie the change process and (iv) a *deeper*

understanding of the relationship between incremental and transformational change. The limitations of a systemic approach to change include: the complex and esoteric nature of systems theory and modelling, the lack of top-management buy-in and access to sufficient funding, the lack of competence and technical expertise, and the lack of evidence of success in this particular area.

—END-OF-CHAPTER CASE STUDY 2.3—

Hosco: Compelling evidence for punctuated equilibrium and systemic change

Introduction

Hosco is one of the largest Health Boards in Scotland with a workforce of around 29,000 staff. It provides a comprehensive range of healthcare services to a diverse population of over 850,000 within Scotland. Since Hosco's establishment in 2001, there has been a feeling among staff that uncertainty and change had been the only constant, as evidenced by the following comment by a Head of Department:

- With the new government nothing is certain anymore … we all know they've got their eyes on the NHS … all this talk about debt and how we need to tighten budgets … we've been told that the organisation needs to be 'fit for purpose' and the Single System Working is now fundamentally important.

The Single System Working entailed a whole system redesign aimed at modernising service delivery in view of the political commitments of a newly elected government and Hosco's aspiration to become one of the world's top 24 healthcare systems.

Key drivers of change

The key drivers of change that caused Hosco to embark on a whole system redesign included *inter alia*: (i) the new strategic objectives of the Scottish Government Health Directorate to reduce health inequalities, adopt an inclusive stakeholder approach to service redesign and locate patients at the core of healthcare provision; (ii) a period of economic downturn leading to financial pressures and the imposition of cost-reduction measures and saving targets calling for a major shift in the organisation's skill mix and service configuration; (iii) a felt responsibility at board level for the organisation to take a leading role in deploying technology-based projects and processes, notably for e-recruitment, e-learning, patient management system and biomedical research; and (iv) changes in patient demographics with an increase in elderly and migrant populations and a shift in balance of care warranting a move from hospital-based to community-based healthcare.

(Continued)

A case of punctuated equilibrium

The type of change that Hosco has gone through since the turn of the century provides some convincing evidence for a case of punctuated equilibrium which is illustrated in Figure 2.5 below.

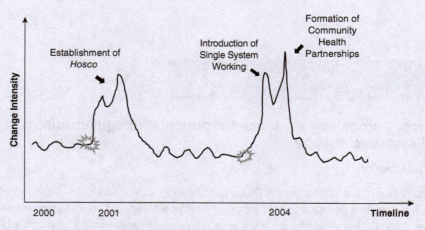

Figure 2.5 A case of punctuated equilibrium at Hosco

At the turn of the century, Hosco was still part of a wider national healthcare service which had so far been relatively stable for the past two decades. In view of the key macro-level change drivers mentioned above, the organisation was thrust into transformational mode. The first wave of high-intensity, transformational change occurred in 2001. It involved a major restructuring exercise leading to the establishment of Hosco as an umbrella organisation responsible for all healthcare services in Scotland and brought the then self-governing health trusts under its aegis as a unified health board.

After a relatively stable period of adaptation to the new centralised way of working, the second wave of transformational change occurred in 2004 with another major restructuring exercise involving back to back the introduction of the Single System Working and the formation of Community Health Partnerships, leading to the set-up of Hosco's three main divisions: University Hospitals Division, Primary Care Services and Community Health Partnerships. This second spike of transformational change was a marked attempt to remove further barriers impeding system improvement and to bring, in line with the Scottish Government's directive, the National Health Service closer to the community.

A systemic approach to change

The two compact periods of transformational change that Hosco went through can be viewed as a major strategic move which enabled the organisation to re-position itself within its operating context and, through service modernisation, ensure its effectiveness in the longer term. This called for an uncoupling and a major overhaul of the organisation's key sub-systems and processes forming its deep structures as highlighted in Table 2.4 – which was a conscious and deliberate approach to change from a systemic perspective.

Table 2.4 Major overhaul of Hosco's deep structures

Strategy	Culture	Structure	Power Distribution	Process
Re-alignment with the Scottish Government's national health strategic objectives towards a healthier Scotland. Development of Key Performance Indicators to measure achievement of new strategic objectives and ensure system improvement.	Establishment of *The Hosco Way* – a new motto to embed a new cultural value system based on an ethos of person-centredness, partnership and integrity as key determinants of continuous service improvement.	Major restructuring exercise to support Single System Working and enable an integrated approach to service delivery. Formation of Community Health Partnerships to move service delivery points closer to community.	Centralised board of governance responsible for strategic planning, resource allocation and organisational performance. Devolved decision-making powers at divisional level to ensure effectiveness and efficiency of service at point of delivery.	Technology-enabled process improvement based on LEAN principles and targeting research and development, HR practices and patient experience to reduce waste, and maximize efficiency and added value.
Hosco's **Deep Structures**				

Conclusions

A number of key issues can be distilled from this case study: first, it provides some compelling empirical evidence for punctuated equilibrium where the organisation went through a relatively stable and longer period of adaptation and experimentation between the two spikes or punctuations of high-intensity, transformational change in 2001 and 2004. One could argue that the analytical lens used to make sense of the empirical data was already informed by the theory of punctuated equilibrium and thus pre-determined the research findings. However, the two short bursts of transformational change separated by a longer period of relative stability at Hosco were clearly discernible, irrespective of the theoretical lens used in this particular study. Second, the case study draws attention to how Hosco had to make discrete yet mutually reinforcing changes within each of its key sub-systems and processes forming its deep structures to enable a holistic and smooth transition to its new Single System Working – suggesting a systemic approach to change management. Finally, the case study has cast light on the dynamic tension between the external and internal drivers of change and importantly, has shown how these drivers can coalesce to form a complex causal web that underlies organisational change.

Questions

1 Look back at the key drivers of change that led Hosco to embark on a whole system re-design. Which of those factors do you think may have had the most influence on the organisation's change programme?

(Continued)

2   To what extent does the change initiative at Hosco support the theory of punctuated equilibrium?
3   Consider the changes Hosco made to its deep structures in its strategic move towards service modernisation. In what way does this account for a systemic approach to change?

2.10 Independent learning

You can access the following sources to deepen your knowledge of some of the key theories, concepts and issues covered in this chapter.

Myers, P., Hulks, S. and Wiggins, L. (2012) *Organisational Change: Perspectives on Theory and Practice*. Oxford: Oxford University Press, Chapter 2, pp. 17–32. Contains an informative review of the external trends and internal causes driving organisational change.

Systems Theory of Organization: www.youtube.com/watch?v=1L1c-EKOY-w. An excellent 10-minute introduction to systems theory and the key concepts associated with it – which will consolidate your understanding of how it applies to organisations and how it fits into our overall approach to change management.

2.11 References

Beaverton, O. (2020) *Nike, Inc. Reports Fiscal 2020 Fourth Quarter and Full Year Results*. [Online] Available at: https://news.nike.com/news/nike-inc-reports-fiscal-2020-fourth-quarter-and-full-year-results (accessed 1 March 2023).

Bernstein, P.L. (1988) 'The theory of punctuated equilibrium', *The Journal of Portfolio Management*, 15(3), 12–17.

CIPD (2022) *Organisation Development*. [Online] Available at: www.cipd.org/uk/knowledge/factsheets/organisational-development-factsheet/#what (accessed 2 May 2023).

Creasey, T., Jamieson, D.W., Rothwell, W.J. and Severini, G. (2015) 'Exploring the relationship between Organization Development and Change Management', in W.J. Rothwell, J. Stavros and R.L. Sullivan (eds), *Practicing Organization Development: Leading Transformation and Change*, 4th edn. New Jersey: John Wiley & Sons, Inc., pp. 330–337.

Donato, H. (2022) *5 Phases of Project Management Life Cycle You Need to Know*. [Online] Available at: https://project-management.com/project-management-phases/ (accessed 30 April 2023).

Encyclopaedia Britannica (2023) *Ecosystem*. [Online] Available at: www.britannica.com/science/ecosystem (accessed 2 February 2023).

Fleetwood, S. and Hesketh, A. (2011) *Explaining the Performance of Human Resource Management*. Cambridge: Cambridge University Press.

Gersick, C. J. G. (1991) 'Revolutionary change theories: A multilevel exploration of the punctuated equilibrium paradigm', *Academy of Management Review*, 16(1), 10–36.

Greengard, S. (2015) *The Internet of Things*. USA: MIT Press.

Hall, M. (2020) *The Editors of Encyclopaedia Britannica: Hewlett Packard Company*. [Online] Available at: www.britannica.com/topic/Hewlett-Packard-Company (accessed 8 July 2022).

Hamel, G. and Prahalad, C. K. (1996) *Competing for the Future*. Boston, MA: Harvard Business School Press.

Harvey, D. (1996) *Justice, Nature and the Geography of Difference*. UK: Blackwell Publishing Ltd.

Hayes, J. (2021) *The Theory and Practice of Change Management*, 6th edn. London: Red Globe Press.

Horwitz, J. (2023) *China's Alibaba to Break up Empire into Six Units as Jack Ma Returns Home*. [Online] Available at: www.reuters.com/markets/deals/alibaba-splits-into-six-units-that-may-pursue-individual-ipos-bloomberg-news-2023-03-28/ (accessed 1 May 2023).

Lee, J. (2023) *Alibaba Tells Investors Its Overhaul Will Make The Business More 'Agile' With Market Changes*. [Online] Available at: www.cnbc.com/2023/03/30/alibaba-executives-conference-call.html (accessed 1 May 2023).

Manabe, K. (2019) *Trade War Hammers Foreign Investment in China and Southeast Asia*. [Online] Available at: https://asia.nikkei.com/Spotlight/Datawatch/Trade-war-hammers-foreign-investment-in-China-and-Southeast-Asia (accessed 14 February 2023).

Mannion, J. (2007) *Essential Philosophy: Everything You Need to Understand the World's Greatest Thinkers*. Cincinnati: F+W Publications.

McDowell, Z. (n.d.) *What is Project Management?* [Online] Available at: www.planview.com/resources/guide/what-is-project-management/ (accessed 30 April 2023).

McGahan, A. (2004) 'How industries change', *Harvard Business Review*. [Online] Available at: https://hbr.org/2004/10/how-industries-change (accessed 12 December 2022).

Miller Cole, B. (2019) *Innovate or Die: How a Lack of Innovation Can Cause Business Failure*. [Online] Available at: www.forbes.com/sites/biancamillercole/2019/01/10/innovate-or-die-how-a-lack-of-innovation-can-cause-business-failure/#597313fb2fcb (accessed 11 November 2022).

Myers, P., Hulks, S. and Wiggins, L. (2012) *Organisational Change: Perspectives on Theory and Practice*. Oxford: Oxford University Press.

Nga, L. (2023) *Alibaba's Decision to Break Out Its Empire Could Be Game Changing*. [Online] Available at: https://www.nasdaq.com/publishers/the-motley-fool (accessed 1 May 2023).

Reisinger, D. (2009) *Blockbuster Streaming: Too Late*. [Online] Available at: https://www.cnet.com/news/blockbuster-streaming-too-late/ (accessed 12 December 2022).

Sage, A. (2019) *Employees Sour on Tesla amid Cost-cutting, Layoffs*. [Online] Available at: www.reuters.com/article/us-tesla-workers-idUSKCN1TB1AJ (accessed 2 December 2022).

Spiegel-Rösing, I. and de Solla Price, D. (eds) (1977) *Science, Technology and Society: A Cross-Disciplinary Perspective*. London: Sage Publications.

Tushman, M. L. and Romanelli, E. (1985) 'Organizational evolution: A metamorphosis model of convergence and reorientation', *Research in Organizational Behavior*, 7, 171–222.

US Trade Representative Office (2018) *Findings of the Investigation into China's Acts, Policies and Practices Related to Technology Transfer, Intellectual Property, and Innovation under Section 301 of the Trade Act of 1974*. [Online] Available at: https://ustr.gov/sites/default/files/Section%20301%20FINAL.PDF (accessed 5 December 2022).

Van de Ven, A. H. and Poole, M. S. (1995) 'Explaining development and change in organizations', *Academy of Management Review*, 20(3), 510–540. [Online] Available at: https://www.jstor.org/stable/258786 (accessed 1 May 2023).

3

STRATEGIC CHANGE

Learning Outcomes

After completing this chapter, you should be able to:

- Define strategic change and discuss its key features.
- Explain the meaning of human agency in the context of strategic change and discuss the key philosophical concepts underlying it.
- Consider a range of alternative approaches to managing strategic change.
- Apply a set of well-known diagnostic tools to facilitate strategic change.
- Gain an understanding of how the concept of the VUCA business world can be used as an environmental scanning tool and consider its implications for strategic change.

3.1 Introduction

The purpose of this chapter is to help you develop a sound understanding of strategic change and apply a set of practical frameworks and diagnostic tools to effectively manage it. The chapter begins by defining strategic change before unpacking its key features. Next, the chapter explains the meaning of human agency in the context of strategic change and provides a discussion of key philosophical concepts underlying it. The chapter proceeds to present a review of a range of approaches to strategic change (from the traditional to the more experimental), craft approaches that reflect contemporary issues and concerns. The chapter moves on to consider a set of well-known diagnostic tools that can be used to facilitate strategic change and show how these can be applied in practice. The final section of the chapter presents our conceptual nugget which considers the implications of the VUCA (*Volatile, Uncertain, Complex and Ambiguous*) business world for strategic change. The chapter concludes with a summary of the key learning points arising from the preceding discussion and an end-of-chapter case study, focusing on a German high-tech company's approach to strategic change in a VUCA business environment.

3.2 Meaning of strategic change

Strategic change is a complex notion that carries multiple meanings informed by various theoretical perspectives and practical experience. In this opening section, we first provide a definition of strategic change and proceed to consider its key meanings in the following discussion.

Definition of strategic change

We define strategic change as:

> The modification or major overhaul of an organisation's strategy and the deployment of the necessary resources to enable it to effectively respond and sometimes shape the dynamic forces at play within its operating context in an attempt to achieve competitive advantage and ensure its long-term survival and growth.

In unpacking the above definition, we want to draw attention to the key features highlighted in Figure 3.1, which are explained in the following discussion.

Type of change

Strategic change can involve different types of change – from a modification or refinement to a major overhaul or radical transformation of the current strategy. (Refer to the section *Typology of organisational change* in Chapter 2).

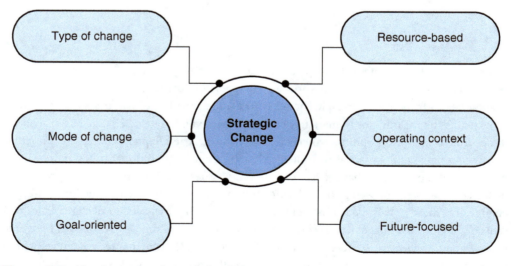

Figure 3.1   Key features of strategic change

Resource-based

Strategic change is dependent upon a range of necessary resources which have to be optimally configured to enable its successful implementation. Such resources include a wide array of different things such as human capital, intellectual capital, raw materials, financial assets, machinery and equipment, digital architectures, communication structures, etc.

Mode of change

The mode of strategic change can be a reaction in response to the dynamic forces at play within the external environment or a proactive attempt to exert a shaping influence on it – more on this in the following section.

Operating context

Strategic change does not happen in a vacuum but takes stock of the context in which it is going to play out. This warrants a thorough analysis of key contextual factors having a significant bearing on the strategic change process such as: the external drivers of change, the internal capabilities of the organisation, the intensity of industry rivalry, and the needs and demands of target markets.

Goal-oriented

An effective change strategy contains a clear intent and a set of goals and objectives that are spelt out in SMART terms – the primary aim of which is to leverage the activities of the organisation's value chain in order to generate sustainable competitive advantage.

Future-focused

While strategic change can be deployed to achieve short and middle term goals, it is, by definition, future-focused to ensure the survival, continuity and, ideally, growth of the organisation in the longer term. To this end, strategic change involves not only *insight* (a deep understanding of the current situation) but also *foresight* (an ability to anticipate the future outcomes of the organisation's strategic choices).

PRACTICAL EXERCISE

To help you consolidate your understanding of the preceding discussion, match the descriptions in the left column in Table 3.1 to the key features of strategic change highlighted in Figure 3.1.

(Continued)

Table 3.1 Identifying key features of strategic change

Strategic change	
Description	**Key feature**
Involves an in-depth analysis of the factors which can have a significant bearing on the strategic change process.	
Aims to leverage the activities of the organisation's value chain in order to generate sustainable competitive advantage.	
Focus on long-range planning to ensure the survival, continuity and ideally growth of the organisation in the longer term.	
Dependent on human capital, intellectual capital, raw materials, financial assets, machinery and equipment, digital architectures, communication structures, etc.	
Can involve modification or major overhaul of the current strategy.	
Can be a reaction in response to the dynamic forces at play within the external environment or a proactive attempt to exert a shaping influence on it.	

3.3 Change agency: Determinism v. voluntarism

Change agency

Before considering the notion of change agency, it is useful to first explain the meaning of *human agency* which is the focus of attention here. Human agency refers to an *intentional* action designed to *produce* a particular outcome. In being *intentional*, human agency entails a state of mind characterised by an intent, a sense of purpose, a desire, an imagination, and a belief in one's capacity to do something. In aiming to *produce* a particular outcome, human agency is an embodied form of causal power that is instrumental, means-end oriented and aims to achieve certain goals or results (e.g. see Hartwig, 2007).

When the above meanings attached to human agency are applied to strategic change, one can speak of change agency as: (i) change agents' *intentional action* driven by an intent, a vision and a certain level of confidence in their ability to positively affect or change for the better the current strategy of their organisation, and (ii) a form of *causal power embodied in change agents* that aims to generate certain desired strategic outcomes.

On determinism and voluntarism

The philosophical concepts of determinism and voluntarism are at the core of an understanding of human agency. In this sub-section we look at the key meanings of each of these concepts and consider their implications for strategic change.

Determinism

Determinism posits that when people make certain decisions or follow particular courses of action, they are only reacting to (mainly external) forces which 'impact them' and over which they have little or no control – i.e. their decisions and actions are 'determined' by such forces. In its most extreme form, determinism precludes the possibility of free will and severely constrains intentional human action and causal powers.

With regard to strategic change, determinism locks change agents in a rather passive and reactive mode of thought and behaviour and constrains their ability for intentional strategic action – where change agents can but react to the forces of change in their operating context and the overriding purpose of strategic change is to adapt and respond to such forces in order to either minimise their potentially adverse effects or capitalise on the opportunities that they present.

It can be argued that a determinist approach to strategic change could induce greater sensitivity to the uncontrollable events in the external environment – allowing for timely responses that can keep the organisation in tune with the major drivers of change whilst following the safest, least-risky strategic routes to ensure business survival and growth. However, determinism (especially its more extreme versions) tends to lock change agents in a world of uncontrollable events which cast them in a restrictive strategic role with limited causal power and little confidence in their ability to have any major influence on the process of strategic change.

Voluntarism

On the other hand, voluntarism posits that people are free and unrestrained in their ability to make their own decisions and follow chosen courses of action. Voluntarism, in its most extreme form, sees human beings as having complete freedom and autonomy in making choices about their lives and 'making things happen'. Thus, voluntarism ascribes to human beings a greater agentive role and causal power in shaping the world around them.

With regard to strategic change, voluntarism portrays change agents as having a degree of control over their environment and being able to exercise free will in making informed strategic choices and following deliberate courses of action. Moreover, while ascribing a much more proactive role to change agents in the process of strategic change, voluntarism opens up the possibility for them to exercise greater causal powers and take a leading role in 'shaping' the forces of change at play within their change situation in pursuit of innovative change, competitive advantage and industry leadership – where change leaders such as Jeff Bezos of Amazon and Elon Musk of Tesla and SpaceX come to mind.

However, it can be argued that pushing the voluntarist envelope too far can lead to over-confidence and overly risky courses of action resulting in strategic change failure. In any case, even sound and well-crafted strategies are not a guarantee of success, especially in highly volatile and unpredictable external environments where the element of chance can weigh heavily on change outcomes.

A tempered understanding of strategic change agency

We are in favour of a more tempered, moderate understanding of human agency in the context of strategic change. We take the view that change agents are neither totally free nor totally bound when conducting strategic change. To paraphrase Marx, change agents can make their own strategic choices but generally not under conditions of their own making. Change agents have to grapple with the indeterminate forces at play within their operating context which are beyond their immediate control – which, however, does not preclude change agents from exercising a degree of freedom and free will in crafting innovative strategies to creatively respond to these indeterminate environmental forces or even exert a shaping influence upon them.

A good example would be the socio-political shaping of new technologies (such as the Internet of things, cloud computing, nanotechnology) over which any single organisation has little or no control but which can have disruptive effects on their industry. In this case, change agents might have no other choice but to respond to such technological disruptions if they want their organisations to remain competitive. However, in so doing, change agents can be highly proactive and display their creative powers in grappling with these disruptive technologies and deploying innovative change strategies to stay ahead of the competition and even shape the competitive dynamics across their industry.

Thus, a more moderate approach to the issue of human agency aims to: (i) demonstrate how the *process of strategic change consists of both determinist and voluntarist elements* which are very difficult to disentangle in practice, and (ii) bring to attention how change agents have to both deal with the *givens* (or pre-existing conditions over which they have little control) and *exercise their free will and causal powers* in the deployment of innovative change strategies. The mini case study below provides you with an opportunity to refine your understanding of this issue.

CASE STUDY 3.1

NHS England: Battling COVID-19 and becoming stronger

The COVID-19 outbreak forced the National Health Service in England to implement a rapid and radical change strategy. Over an exceptionally short period, work patterns were reconfigured, staff upskilled, leadership roles broadened at point of need and digital technology leveraged to enable remote working and boost up online services. The aim of this frantic strategic activity was to maintain service continuity and swiftly respond to the medical emergencies and work pressures brought about by the global pandemic.

The way the organisation responded to the pandemic demonstrated remarkable resilience, astute strategic capabilities and an innovative mindset. However, management is already thinking. The focus is now very much on what can be learned from the experience of battling COVID-19 and how this can make the organisation stronger. Although a full audit of the organisation's response to the pandemic is not feasible yet, management have started to take stock of what went well, what needs to be stopped and what needs to be done differently. The knowledge gathered from this exercise will inform strategic change which aims to build NHS England's responsiveness and resilience in the event of similar crises in the future and uphold the organisation's commitment to the continuous improvement of the healthcare system across the country.

Source: Rastrick (2020)

Questions

1   Can you identify the determinist and voluntarist elements in NHS England's approach to strategic change in response to COVID-19?
2   What are your views on the role of human agency in the context of strategic change?

3.4 Approaches to strategic change

This section contains a review of a range of approaches to strategic change – beginning with the 'traditional' approaches that are well-established in the literature before considering some of the more experimental approaches that reflect contemporary issues and concerns.

Planned v. emergent strategic change

Coram and Burnes (2001) point out that approaches to strategic change in the literature tend to fall into two broad camps: those that follow the *planned approach* and those leaning towards the *emergent approach*.

Planned approach to strategic change

The planned approach represents a *holistic, rational* and *proactive* way of dealing with strategic change with a focus on long term effectiveness and performance. On adopting a *holistic approach*, planned strategic change involves setting the whole organisation on a new strategic course and providing direction for changes to all of its key sub-systems and processes that may be required to enable the organisation to achieve its strategic goals and objectives – e.g.

renewing the cultural value system, reconfiguring current structures, enhancing communication systems, tightening control systems, optimising production processes, building new project teams, deploying new technologies, developing new performance management and reward systems, etc.

CASE STUDY 3.2

British Airways: A planned approach to strategic change

In 2008, British Airways, the biggest airline in the UK, was going through a financial crisis. On top of a worldwide economic recession, the company registered a pre-tax loss of £401m while having to grapple with increased competitive pressures from low cost airlines. Management felt that they had to take decisive action and come up with a sound business strategy to turn around the fortunes of the company. They developed a centralised, comprehensive strategic plan with formal controls led from the top and which included the following key features:

- Downsizing and voluntary redundancy to create a leaner organisational structure and lower operating costs.
- A reduction in flight prices to compete with low-cost airlines.
- Significant pay cuts for pilots.
- Optimising performance of cabin crews.
- Emergency training for staff to improve customer service.
- The modernisation of current fleet of aeroplanes.
- Increased corporate responsibility for environmental performance and business partnerships.

The major focus on the reduction of employment costs met with resistance from the Union and led to staff walkouts and strike action – a situation which was aggravated by the eruption of a volcano in Iceland which caused the cancellation of thousands of flights in Northern Europe and other security alerts. Despite these setbacks, BA managed to turn the situation around after two years, reporting a £158m profit for the six months to September 2010.

Source: Djurovic (2011)

Questions

1   Why does BA's change initiative represent a planned approach to strategic change?
2   Why do you think the strategic plan met with resistance from the Union?
3   Would you rate the strategic change at BA as a success?

Planned change is *rational* in that it entails a systematic process of diagnosis, forecasting, formulation, implementation and evaluation. As such, it aims to identify the environmental challenges and opportunities arising from the organisation's change situation, estimate resource requirements and performance targets and predict future outcomes. Finally, planned change is *proactive* in that it is underpinned by a voluntarist outlook – which, as previously explained, views change agents as having a degree of control over their environment and being able to exercise free will in making informed strategic choices and following deliberate courses of action.

Criticisms

While the planned approach can be seen as a sign of the commitment, competence and creativity of change agents in driving the organisation forward, it is also the subject of some criticisms. First, planned change is usually contained within the higher realm of top management and more often than not imposed on those operating at the lower levels of the organisation. The fact that planned change is usually led from the top makes it easier for managers to slip into a rigid, autocratic mode of orchestrating change which frustrates the possibility for a more empowering and collaborative approach.

Second, there is an in-built lack of flexibility in 'planning ahead' as managers cannot account for all the variables at play within an increasingly dynamic and unpredictable environment before the actual implementation of the strategic change plan – and 'sticking to the plan', however rational and smart it may be, can leave the organisation stuck in its ways, impervious to emerging external influences and liable to strategic drift.

Finally, planned change is based on the rather naive assumption that consensus and commitment can be readily achieved around change projects even when it is forced upon others – obscuring in the process the political and the 'messy' nature of organisational change and the fact that a good strategic plan is no guarantee of success unless it is effectively implemented through all its key stakeholders. This is in part why the change initiative at BA was met with resistance from the union; and an assessment of its change strategy cannot solely be based on performance and financial outcomes but has to factor in its impact on all organisational stakeholders.

Emergent approach to strategic change

The emergent strategic change approach is based on the view that planned strategic change is not applicable to all change situations, where rigid adherence to pre-determined plans can rapidly isolate the organisation and desensitise it from its external environment. In contrast to planned strategic change, an emergent approach to strategic change is *adaptive, ad hoc* and *reactive*. In being *adaptive*, emergent strategic change enables timely changes to the original change plan to enable the organisation to adjust its course of action to suit the dynamic conditions in its external environment. Emergent strategic change is also ad hoc in that it 'accounts for the unplanned'. The initial strategic plan changes as the organisation addresses the challenges and opportunities arising from its external environment; and it is not before the completion of the implementation phase that the change strategy is 'fully formed'.

Finally, an emergent approach to strategic change is *reactive* because it is underpinned by a determinist outlook – where the most important responsibility of change agents is to effectively respond to the forces of change in their operating context to either minimise their potentially adverse effects or capitalise on the opportunities that they present.

—CASE STUDY 3.3—

Biogen: A swift strategic response to emergent challenges

The US pharmaceutical and life sciences company Biogen is an example of a company that had to rapidly alter its strategy to effectively cope with external events beyond its control. In 2017, Biogen had to grapple with a disastrous situation at one of its production facilities after the Caribbean was hit by a hurricane that killed 1,000 people and caused billions of dollars of damage.

Biogen reacted swiftly to the situation by modifying its strategy to ensure business continuity and to keep the company on track towards the effective achievement of its strategic goals and objectives. Top management first ordered a risk assessment exercise to identify the problems caused by the hurricane that posed an immediate threat to Biogen's value chain and competitive base. Next, the company set up an emergency communication network to facilitate employee participation and the adoption of a concerted approach to strategic renewal designed to leverage the company's value chain. Lastly, scenario planning was used to predict potential outcomes and plot the most viable course of action to expedite change implementation and the desired outcomes.

The revamped strategy entailed, among other things, the set-up of alternative procurement arrangements, the relocation of the production line and extensive collaboration with industry partners. Through the timely modification of its strategic plan, Biogen was able to limit the damages caused by the hurricane and swiftly resume its operations – unlike other companies which had to shut down their operations for months in the aftermath of the hurricane.

Source: Resilinc Corporation (2018)

Questions

1   What were the key features of the strategic change at Biogen?
2   Why do you think that Biogen was able to adjust its strategy in such a short time?

Criticisms

The emergent approach to strategic change can be viewed through a more critical lens. First, there is the argument that emergent strategic change tends to downplay the importance of strategic vision and foresight and the need for a sound business plan without which an organisation could hardly survive in increasingly competitive markets. However, it has to be said that an emergent approach to change does not preclude proper planning; nor does it downplay the importance of strategic vision and foresight. In fact, an emergent approach to change strategy has more to do with the ability of change leaders to draw on their strategic flair and modify their initial strategy in timely fashion to ensure business continuity and sustain competitive advantage – as evidenced in the Biogen case study.

Second, emergent strategic change could be interpreted as a sign of incompetence – where change leaders are mostly clueless and only able to 'muddle through' a continuous process of testing and experimentation in response to unpredictable environmental changes. Third, an emergent strategic approach can also be viewed as a drain on resources and employee commitment as too much effort is focused on the continuous reformulation of the change strategy while blurring the focus on its actual implementation. Finally, the need to achieve shared understanding and consensus around the change strategy each time it is revised in view of emergent environmental changes can be quite taxing and time-consuming whilst preventing any real progress in the face of shifting goals and objectives.

Logical incrementalism: Navigating a middle course between planned and emergent change

Quinn (1980) developed the concept of logical incrementalism to explain how change agents can navigate a middle course between planned and emergent change. Logical incrementalism integrates elements of both planned and emergent approaches to strategic change – where change agents can not only formulate a sound and clear strategic plan prior to its implementation but are also given the freedom and flexibility to modify and revise such a plan in response to unanticipated environmental changes throughout the change process. Thus, logical incrementalism integrates the provision of both a clear strategic direction and the possibility of timely adaptation throughout the change implementation process – a process referred to by Burnes (1996) as 'choice management' or *planning for the unplanned*.

Empirical evidence

Quinn (1993) found evidence for logical incrementalism in the research that he conducted at Xerox, IBM and General Motors. He noticed that managers driving change were themselves able to clearly spell out their strategies only after many of the key elements of these strategies had already been implemented. This suggests that the strategies that were actually implemented were a combination of direction and adaptation, planning and unplanned reactions to external events.

Another more recent example of 'logical incrementalism in practice' is that of John Lewis Partnership, the UK's largest employee-owned business and parent company of John Lewis stores and Waitrose supermarkets. The organisation has a flexible approach to strategic change – where a strategic plan is designed by top management but left open to enable the organisation to continuously adapt to 'situations as they arise' and enhance customer value and experience, which is a key determinant of the company's business success (O'Regan and Ghobadian, 2012).

Mintzberg: Towards a deeper understanding of strategic change

While Mintzberg's work is more focused on strategy *per se*, his conceptualisation of strategy as a pattern of formation and development does provide some additional insights into the process of strategic change which are worth mentioning here. Figure 3.2 illustrates Mintzberg's pattern of strategy formation and development.

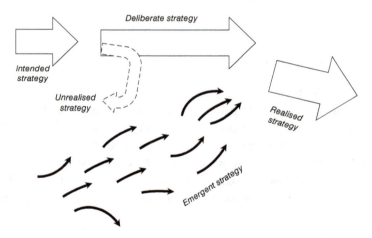

Figure 3.2   Mintzberg's pattern of strategy formation and development

Source: Mintzberg, H. (1978) 'Patterns in strategy formation', *Management Science*, 24(9), 934–948. https://www.researchgate.net/publication/227444830_Patterns_in_Strategy_Formation. Reproduced with permission.

Mintzberg's longitudinal research in the area points to the fact that one would hardly find instances of either purely planned or purely emergent strategies in actual practice. As shown in Figure 3.2, most strategic approaches tend to involve a combination of planned and emergent strategies. In the figure, the *intended strategy* represents a planned approach to strategy and involves the development of a plan of action to achieve certain predetermined goals and objectives. The *deliberate strategy* represents the components of the strategic plan that are actually implemented or translated into practice. The *unrealised strategy* includes those parts of the intended strategy that prove to be impractical or counterproductive and that are discarded at some point along the implementation process.

The *emergent strategy* is not part of the initially planned, intended strategy but comes about as a response to unforeseen challenges and opportunities in the external environment. The emergent strategy is then combined with the deliberate strategy to produce the *realised strategy* – a blend of both intended and unintended strategic outcomes, which bring to mind Mintzberg and Waters' (1985) famous remark that strategy walks on two feet, one deliberate, the other emergent.

A deeper understanding of strategic change

Mintzberg's research contribution has enabled a deeper understanding of strategic change along the following lines:

- It has blurred the dividing lines between planned and emergent strategies and shown how in the real world they can intertwine to form a pattern of strategic decision-making and action and produce a mix of both intended and unintended outcomes.
- It underlines the importance of both having a solid plan and a clear direction for strategic change and building the adaptive capacity of an organisation to promptly respond to emerging threats and opportunities arising from its external environment.
- It is a powerful reminder that no change strategy is written in stone but is always subject to revision, correction, expansion or whatever it takes to ensure the survival and growth of the organisation.
- Finally, Minztberg's conceptualisation of strategy finds some echo in Quinn's notion of logical incrementalism (discussed above) and, in our view, provides a conceptual foothold for the consideration of more recent approaches to strategic change, which are briefly discussed in the following section.

Strategic improvisation

There is a growing recognition of the need for a more agile, improvised and 'craft approach' to strategic change in an increasingly dynamic, diverse and unpredictable global business context. Strategic improvisation speaks to the ability of change leaders to reconfigure the resources of their organisation to effectively address the (mostly unanticipated) opportunities and threats arising from their business environment (Alsaqal et al., 2021; Mintzberg, 1987). One of the defining features of strategic improvisation is that it endorses a decentralised, collaborative and empowering approach to strategic change – where change leaders set out and clearly communicate the broad strategic goals of the organisation and then empower teams and individuals at all organisational levels to creatively contribute to the successful achievement of such strategic goals throughout the change implementation process, taking into consideration the unpredictable forces of change that can have a significant impact on the organisation.

In light of the above, the key objectives of strategic improvisation include:

- A primary focus on building the adaptive capacity of the organisation so that it can swiftly address emerging challenges and opportunities arising from its operating context.

- A commitment to continuous organisational development, performance improvement and the collaborative creation of competitive value.
- An emphasis on the need to constantly leverage the resources of the organisation in pursuit of innovative business solutions and sustainable competitive advantage.

Finally, strategic improvisation warrants the application of certain principles, notably the need for:

- Strategic flexibility: To enable the organisation to promptly reconfigure its resources and adapt its strategy in response to significant environmental changes.
- Strategic vigilance: To emphasise the importance of remaining sensitive to major trends and events that can significantly impact the organisation's strategic agenda.
- Innovation: To swiftly apply new technologies and optimise processes and practices to create innovative products, customer value and competitive advantage.
- Entrepreneurial orientation: To proactively drive strategic change by seizing business opportunities, taking calculated risks and demonstrating ingenuity and determination in spearheading new business ventures.

The late Steve Jobs could be seen as an exemplar of a business leader who was adept at strategic improvisation. When Jobs returned to Apple as interim CEO in 1996, the company was in dire straits, strapped for cash and facing stiff competition from its main rival Microsoft. Instead of fighting Microsoft head on, Jobs devised a clever strategy through which he secured a US$150 million investment from Microsoft in return for non-voting shares together with the assurance that Microsoft would support its Office software on the Mac platform for the next five years.

Jobs also managed to streamline Apple's product line, reduce operating expenses and open new high-street stores to sell Apple's products directly to customers. In 1998, Jobs introduced the iMac which, by the end of that year, became the highest-selling PC in the US. A few years later, he led Apple's early foray into online music with the iPod and mobile phone business with the iPhone. Job's strategic moves turned Apple into one of the most successful IT companies in the world whilst proving himself a master craftsman in strategic improvisation (Gallagher, 2023).

Ambidextrous strategic change

An ambidextrous approach to strategic change places an emphasis on the ability of change leaders to *concurrently* deploy different strategies across different business contexts or deploy different strategies *in succession* within a single or several business contexts. There are four key types of ambidextrous strategic change, depending on the two key dimensions of diversity (the number of different contexts in which an organisation has to operate) and dynamism (the degree of stability and pace of change in those different business contexts). These account for the 'portfolio' of ambidextrous strategic change, including:

Separation: A strategic approach which is appropriate for organisations having to operate in diverse but relatively stable environments. Separation is managed from the top and involves splitting up different business units that need different strategic styles which can be deployed concurrently – e.g. separating a mature business unit that requires a strategic approach designed to maximise efficiency from a start-up business that warrants an innovative and flexible change strategy.

Switching: A strategic approach which is appropriate for companies operating in dynamic but less diverse environments. Here, change leaders have to change their strategies in succession and in tandem with the changes in their business environment – by *switching* between different strategic styles. Amazon is often cited as an example of a company that was able to switch from an exploration strategic phase to an exploitation strategic phase as it first had to explore the possibilities of the Internet for retailing before moving on to exploit the Internet and use it as a platform for retailing at a global level.

Self-organising: A strategic approach which is appropriate for companies operating in both diverse and dynamic business environments. In this case, leading strategic change from the top becomes impractical. Therefore, it is more effective to split business units and leave it to teams and individuals to *self-organise* and decide for themselves which strategic approach is best for each unit according to the strategic imperatives and competitive dynamics faced by each discrete unit.

Ecosystem approach: A strategic approach which is appropriate for companies operating in highly diverse and dynamic business environments – where managing a large number of different strategic styles becomes internally untenable. In this case, it makes sense for change leaders to adopt an ecosystem approach and have recourse to external parties with specific expertise and experience to manage strategic change across different business units requiring different strategic styles. Apple is seen as a company which has used the ecosystem approach with considerable success – where it mobilises an ecosystem of external business partners to deploy the different strategic styles that are needed across its different business ventures (see Reeves et al., 2013).

Finally, we just want to remark that it is understandable why an ambidextrous approach to strategic change is gaining traction across the business world – as more and more companies are 'going global' and are having to compete in different business environments with different competitive dynamics that cut across different countries and regions.

Quantum strategic change

While we do not have the space here to consider in any detail the implications of quantum technology for change management, we will simply mention the fact that quantum strategic change rests upon the ability of business organisations to harness technological innovations brought about by quantum technology (more precisely, the second quantum revolution) as a catalyst for entrepreneurship, new business models and product development, and the generation of competitive advantage.

The first quantum revolution (which happened nearly a century ago) brought about transistors, semiconductors and lasers that led to significant advances in computing, non-invasive imaging technology, optical fibre communication, navigation technology and other commonly-used devices such as digital cameras, Blu-ray, LEDs and barcode scanners. The second quantum revolution (which began in the 1960s) has been mostly driven by the convergence of physics and information science and given rise to what is referred to as quantum information science (QIS) (Boladian et al., 2023).

One of the greatest promises of QIS is the next-generation quantum computers that can process big data, solve complex problems and that over time will be capable of learning and making predictions. While quantum computing is still in an experimental stage, its application to society and industry is wide-ranging and expected to enable major advancement across key sectors such as healthcare, finance, education, the military and of course, business.

The application of quantum technology (and in particular quantum computing) to business is manifold. It can impact all value-added activities from financial investments, inventory budgeting, through production processes and logistics to marketing, sales and advertising. For example, quantum technology can enable the consolidation of cybersecurity, stronger predictions in financial trading, the development of breakthrough products, big data marketing, and the optimisation of storage and transportation of goods.

At a more strategic level, quantum technology can enable predictive simulation modelling and scenario planning to develop more informed business plans and plot the most effective courses of action. Big industry players such as Google, Airbus and BMW are already experimenting with quantum computing. Another high-profile example is IBM Quantum Systems – which provides access to quantum computing to more than 125 organisations, including educational institutions, research labs, start-ups, and Fortune 500 companies (Cision PR Newswire, 2017).

Quantum strategic change locates quantum technology at the core of strategic change and places an emphasis on the role of change leaders in harnessing its power to develop innovative products and services that can generate value and competitive advantage whilst taking a long-term approach in addressing the current and future needs of all key stakeholders and society at large. As such, quantum strategic change requires from change leaders a 'quantum mindset' that entails industry foresight, an entrepreneurial stance and active experimentation with quantum technologies in the pursuit of sustainable change success – which could be viewed as its key principles (Cuenca-Gomez, 2021).

REFLECTIVE EXERCISE

To familiarise yourself with the concepts of strategic improvisation, ambidextrous strategic change and quantum strategic change, read once again the preceding sections on these three approaches to strategic change. Use Table 3.2 to map out the primary focus and key features of each of those approaches.

Table 3.2 The primary focus and key features of improvised, ambidextrous and quantum approaches to strategic change

Approach to strategic change	Primary focus	Key features
Strategic improvisation		
Ambidextrous strategic change		
Quantum strategic change		

- What are the key differences between each of these approaches to strategic change?
- Do you think they can be used in concert as a multidimensional theoretical lens to frame strategic change? If yes, how?

3.5 Diagnostic tools to facilitate strategic change

This section covers three of the most popular diagnostic tools that change leaders can employ to facilitate strategic change: the PESTLE analysis, the SWOT analysis and the business canvas.

PESTLE analysis

The mnemonic PESTLE stands for Political, Economic, Socio-cultural, Technological, Legal and Environmental. As a diagnostic tool, the PESTLE analysis is quite straightforward and enables a quick yet thorough scanning of the external environment and a sound understanding of the opportunities and threats arising from it – which is vital to a well-informed, evidence-based approach to strategic decision-making and action. Table 3.3 outlines some of the most salient factors under each of the dimensions of the PESTLE framework, which are of increasing concern to modern-day organisations operating in a global business context.

Table 3.3 PESTLE: Key macro-level forces impacting strategic change in a global business context

Political	– Impact of geopolitical tensions on international trade – Extent of government intervention in business – Implications of political in/stability, government policies and actions on (foreign) business investments, (global) supply chains, market growth and business continuity across countries and larger geographical areas
Economic	– Emergence of new economic blocs such as BRIC (Brazil, Russia, India, China) and MINT (Mexico, Indonesia, Nigeria and Turkey) – Production costs associated with the internalisation of production processes, labour, marketing and distribution channels – Key indices such as economic growth, exchange and interest rates, inflation rates, unemployment levels, consumer pricing, income disparity and purchasing power

(Continued)

Table 3.3 (Continued)

Socio-cultural	– Change in demographics – Level of education – Shifts in customer lifestyles, preferences and buying patterns – Health consciousness and vaccination rates – Cultural diversity and emergence of global culture – Changing attitudes towards gender equality, racial inclusion and social equity – New flexible-work patterns and career pathways – Move towards collaborative partnerships and strategic alliances
Technological	– Development in GRIN (Genetics, Robotics, IT, Nanotechnology) and quantum computing – Rapid pace of digitisation of administrative work, automation of production processes and service delivery – Exponential growth of Internet-based work, social commerce, live streaming and global commercial activity – R&D activity driven by disruptive technological innovation
Legal	A raft of laws regulating international and local business including: – Foreign direct investments, licensing, franchising, exports/imports – Mergers and acquisitions – Finance – Taxation – Health and Safety – Fair labour and worker compensation – E-commerce, online marketing and advertising – Data protection and privacy – Cybersecurity – Intellectual property and copyright – Consumer protection
Environmental	– Challenge of climate change – Increased pressure from environmental interest groups for greater consistency in the move towards eco-friendly modes of energy consumption, production, transportation and waste management systems – Growing body of innovative research into the use of renewable energies and sustainable development – Greater social awareness of the importance of reducing environmental pollution in all its forms and protecting the earth's natural resources

As Table 3.3 is largely self-explanatory, we simply want to draw attention to the following key issues:

i   Against the backdrop of the rapid globalisation of business activity, change strategists have to increasingly grapple with political and economic drivers of change that cut across local, national, regional and global contexts.

ii   At the socio-cultural level, there is a trend towards flexible work patterns, a more humanistic approach to the employment relationship, collaborative partnerships and strategic alliances as key determinants of business continuity and long-term success. There is also a sense of urgency around building organisational capacity to manage cultural diversity with the growing internationalisation of business activity and the emergence of a global culture.

iii   Technological development is happening fast in many scientific fields and its application to industry and to social and domestic life is forcing business organisations to change the way they operate, integrate machines and human labour, and engage with customers. The key determinant of successful technological application for a business organisation is its ability to press technology in the service of its strategic goals and objectives and create innovative products and services which are of unique value to its target customers.

iv   In a global business context, change strategists have to comply with a wide range of laws at local, national and international levels which makes jumping through legal hoops to maintain the legitimacy of businesses increasingly complex and challenging.

v   Finally, the wider public discourse around climate change and increasing pressure from environmental activists have placed the onus on organisations to develop ecologically sound business models and take responsibility for minimising pollution and protecting the earth's natural resources. Environmental concerns and sustainable development are now an integral part of strategic change.

SWOT analysis

The PESTLE analysis is usually used in conjunction with the SWOT analysis. The acronym SWOT stands for *Strengths, Weaknesses, Opportunities* and *Threats*. As a diagnostic tool, the SWOT analysis consists of two main dimensions:

i   The first dimension, which includes *Strengths* and *Weaknesses*, is inward-looking and allows for a resource-based approach to strategic change. To this end, it focuses on the factors and resources that are internal to the organisation – especially things over which change leaders have some degree of control and that can be (re)-configured to provide the optimal support for strategic change and help the organisation achieve and maintain competitive advantage.

ii   The second dimension is outward-looking and focuses on the key threats and opportunities arising from the external environment. If left unattended, immediate threats could endanger the organisation and sap its competitive advantage. On the other hand, opportunities that can have a positive impact on desired strategic outcomes need to be promptly seized.

Table 3.4 provides an example of a commonly used template for carrying out a SWOT analysis. It highlights some of the key factors that change leaders need to consider when planning for strategic change.

Table 3.4 Key factors of a SWOT analysis

Strengths	Weaknesses
– High-quality standard of services and product offerings – Scarce material resources such as invested capital, infrastructure (such as well-situated buildings, communication and transport systems, global supply chains), proprietary technologies, etc. and intangible assets (such as strong brand, goodwill and intellectual property) that separate the organisation from its competitors – Unique and difficult to imitate core competences, specialist skills and technological expertise that account for significant competitive advantage – Innovative R&D into improving current services/ products and developing new ones	– Waste and inefficiencies in the production system – Inability to meet current customer demands – Inability to improve cost effectiveness and match the pricing models of market rivals – Inability to compete in certain markets due to limited resources and product portfolio – Lack of skilled labour or technical expertise – Deficiencies in market intelligence and specialist knowledge – Inconsistencies in delivery and after-sales service – Lack of investment in R&D
Opportunities	**Threats**
– Underserved markets or increase in demand for the company's product line – Trend towards deregulation opening up possibility for market development – Government support or subsidies in promoting the sales of eco-friendly products – Relaxation of laws pertaining to international trade or foreign investments – Technological developments that can potentially be integrated into current production system – Industry shift towards collaborative partnerships and strategic alliances	– Economic stagnation or recession – Emergence of new competitors – New products and value propositions by immediate competitors – Shortage or rising costs of raw materials – Shrinking demand for current product offerings – Technology risks such as cyber attacks, electronic data breaches, online platform vulnerabilities, etc. – Adverse consequences of new taxation policies – Negative press reviews or media coverage

Whilst the list included in Table 3.4 is certainly not exhaustive, it does give a broad idea of some key factors within both the internal and external environments that change agents may have to contend with when planning for strategic change. These environmental factors need to be outlined in more specific terms when applied to the particular context of the organisation. However, some of the more important points that have to be kept in mind with regard to the purpose and benefits of the SWOT analysis include the following:

- It provides a solid framework for a quick yet sound assessment of the competitive position of the organisation before embarking on a new strategic course.
- It allows for a quick assessment of the VRIN (Valuable, Rare, Inimitable and Non-substitutable) resources at the disposal of an organisation and that are of 'strategic value'.
- It allows change leaders to take stock of what the organisation is currently doing well whilst identifying its shortcomings and areas that need to be improved in view of the new strategic plan.
- It can be used to refine the PESTLE analysis and single out the key trends and variables in the external environment that pose a potential risk to the organisation and those that offer unique opportunities that need to be seized to optimise the chances of strategic change success.
- Finally, the SWOT analysis provides the parameters for the collection of the necessary data to enable an evidence-based approach to strategic change.

Conducting PESTLE and SWOT analyses

Using Table 3.3 and Table 3.4 as templates, carry out a separate PESTLE and SWOT analysis for one of the following three well-known multinational companies listed below.

1   Samsung   2   PepsiCo   3   Nike

Do an online search to find the information that you will need to complete this exercise.

Strategic change canvas

The strategic change canvas is a powerful visual and flexible tool for designing and making a compelling case for a new strategic plan. The primary purpose of the strategic change canvas is to enable change leaders to map out and gain a panoramic understanding of the new change strategy. Table 3.5 provides an example of the key components that can be included in a strategic change canvas – although these can vary depending upon the specific context and requirements of the strategic change. Moreover, as a visual tool, the strategic change canvas can include not only text (which should be kept to a minimum) but also all sorts of diagrams, clipart and pictures to facilitate communication and shared understanding.

Table 3.5 Key components of a strategic change canvas

Scope	Purpose	Vision	Implementation	Impact
What do we want to achieve?	*Why* do we need to do this? *Why* are these goals and objectives worth pursuing?	*What* do we stand for?	*How* are we going to do this? *What* methods will we use?	*Who* will benefit from the change?
	Timing *When* do we have to deliver its key outputs?		**Key roles and responsibilities** *Who* will lead the change? *Who* will do what?	
Resources *What* will it take?	**Context** *Where* will we have to concentrate our efforts? *Where* will we find the best opportunities and greatest challenges?		**Success Criteria** *How* will we know if the change strategy has been successful?	

Importantly, a strategic change canvas brings together the 'bottom-line questions' that change leaders need to effectively address to increase the likelihood of change success. As highlighted in Table 3.5, these bottom-line questions turn on the *what*, the *why*, the *when*, the *how* and the *who* of strategic change – which provide a holistic framework for the groundwork that needs to be carried out prior to the implementation of the change strategy. When properly addressed, these bottom-line questions can enable change leaders to:

- Delimit the scope of the new strategic change
- Clarify its purpose, goals and objective
- Articulate the vision driving the change strategy
- Agree on implementation milestones and set clear deadlines for key deliverables and intended outcomes
- Specify the resource requirements
- Identify (emerging) challenges and opportunities
- Choose appropriate methods to implement the change strategy
- Assign key roles and responsibilities to drive the change process
- Assess the impact of the change strategy on key stakeholders
- Select evaluative measures to monitor change progress and determine its level of success

Finally, it is important to underline the fact that a strategic business canvas does not only bring together the key components that account for strategic change success but also it can serve to bring together people who can effectively contribute to its design and implementation. As such, a strategic change canvas can be used as a powerful communication tool to enable collaboration, transparency, trust and co-creation of meaning around new change strategies. The following exercise provides you with an opportunity to get a feel of how to build a strategic change canvas.

Building a strategic change canvas

Think of yourself as the owner and manager of a mid-sized hotel with 80 beds somewhere in Europe. Thanks to government subsidies your hotel barely survived two disastrous years of the pandemic, during which you not only used up all your savings but also lost half of your staff. Now, as demand is picking up, you find yourself unable to operate at full capacity because you do not have enough staff to maintain the high service standards for which your hotel is renowned. Worse still, the cost of energy and other supplies is on the rise which means that your current revenues just about cover your expenses.

You realise that your business is in serious trouble and that you need to put in place a new strategy fairly quickly if it is to stay afloat. You have enlisted the help of a friend who is a business consultant and you have a meeting with her in two weeks' time. In the meantime, she has sent you a blank strategic change canvas that she usually uses with her other clients (see Table 3.5 above). She has asked you to go through the questions in each of its boxes and to start jotting down your tentative answers to these questions across the canvas. She said you could 'blow out' the canvas on a flip chart so that you have enough space for including text, images, charts or whatever other visual forms you think are appropriate to express your ideas and views about the new strategy that you want to implement. You will then have the opportunity, together with other senior staff members, to review and refine the canvas at the meeting with your business consultant friend, which will form the basis for the development of the new change strategy for your hotel.

For now, your task is to start mapping your ideas across Table 3.5. To help you with this exercise, you can go online to find examples of completed strategic change canvasses.

3.6 Conceptual nugget: Leading strategic change in a VUCA business world

For the conceptual nugget of this chapter, we consider the challenges of leading strategic change in a VUCA business world. The acronym VUCA stands for *Volatile, Uncertain, Complex* and *Ambiguous*. It was first used by the military in the US following the September 11 terrorist attack on the World Trade Centre in New York City to describe the emergence of a radically different world marked by violence, insecurity and anxiety on a global scale. Today, the term VUCA has been 'co-opted' and applied to the business world – and pertinently so, given the external challenges and threats that business organisations have to grapple with in the form of turbulent international politics, relentless wars, worldwide socio-economic inequality and crises, climate change-related disasters, disruptive technologies that can shake up whole industries and health issues of global proportions (Bennett and Lemoine, 2014).

But what is of particular relevance here is how the notion of a VUCA business world can be turned into an analytical framework (and effectively complement the PESTLE and SWOT analyses) to help frame strategic change in an increasingly unstable and unpredictable global business context. Table 3.6 below provides an indication of how the concept of the VUCA business world can be broken down and 'operationalised' into an *environmental scanning tool* that can be used to frame strategic change.

Table 3.6 Operationalising VUCA into an analytical framework: Implications for strategic change

Leading strategic change in a VUCA business world			
Dimension	**Description**	**Examples**	**Approach to strategic change**
Volatility	Refers to the speed, magnitude and erratic nature of change – leaving the business environment in a state of flux and instability, bringing about unexpected threats and challenges	– Sharp fluctuations in pricing of commodities following natural disasters or in times of war – Abrupt employee turnover across particular sectors in the wake of global health crises – Sudden trend towards corporate mergers and acquisitions of start-ups	– Commit resource buffers and build capacity for greater agility and adaptability in response to unforeseeable challenges – Conduct on-going risk assessments and match change investments – Develop vision that can turn threats into opportunities and secure the organisation's future
Uncertainty	Describes a business environment where there is no discernible trend or pattern of events – resulting in many unknowns and limiting full understanding of the current situation or making it hard to predict the future	– Inability to predict the impact of a new product launch on customer preferences and buying behaviours – Insufficient information to anticipate employee response to the introduction of new terms and conditions of service – Application of new technology with which industry players and customers are not familiar	– Develop a risk management plan to lessen uncertainty and enable a better understanding of the organisation's future prospects – Enhance business intelligence by extending the range of data mining and analytical tools to enable data-driven strategic decisions – Invest in training on how to manage through uncertainty, foster innovation and seize opportunities in dynamic markets
Complexity	Describes the change situation as an elaborate system of interconnected parts and relationships – making it too chaotic and overwhelming to manage	– Conducting business in many countries with different trade regulations, stakeholder expectations and cultural values – A company that manufactures a wide range of products targeted at different markets across a global distribution network – A large and decentralised company with increasing levels of functional specialisation and silo working – limiting cross-functional communication and opportunities for collaboration and innovation	– Build capacity to manage complexity to drive the organisation forward in increasingly chaotic and competitive environments – Set up enabling structures and build trusting relationships to facilitate communication and collaboration as a precondition for effective problem-solving and innovative change

Leading strategic change in a VUCA business world

Dimension	Description	Examples	Approach to strategic change
Ambiguity	When the causal relationships underpinning the change situation are unclear and available data are open to multiple interpretations – making it very difficult to make informed strategic choices	– Working towards unclear goals, deadlines and stakeholder expectations on a project designed to reduce current production costs – Confusion surrounding the impact of a merger on a company's current work practices, employee relations and cultural values – Lack of understanding as to how to provide customer support for a new technology product which is outside employees' current capabilities	– Set up task force to investigate causal relationships impacting intended strategic outcomes – Facilitate communication and collaboration to integrate alternative perspectives in strategy development – Support organisational learning, knowledge transfer, experimentation and innovation to seize competitive opportunities in ambiguous change situations

The descriptions of the VUCA business world in Table 3.6 are not set in stone and there may be slight differences in the way other authors have explained the term. Moreover, the examples given here are just an indication of the many problems and challenges that change agents might have to contend with in a VUCA business world; and there are many more examples that change agents will be able to identify when the VUCA lens is applied to the actual context of the organisation.

However, the more important point that needs to be extracted from Table 3.6 is this: the VUCA analytical framework is not a scaremongering device but a *solutions concept* and a *strategic tool*. While the VUCA analytical framework tends to paint a rather bleak picture of an unstable, chaotic and utterly unpredictable business world to which most organisations are bound to fall victim, it can (as shown in the right-hand column of Table 3.6) be employed as a powerful strategic tool to both mitigate threats and plot courses of action to effectively seize opportunities arising from an organisation's external environment (Schoemaker et al., 2018).

Implications of the VUCA business world for strategic change

It is important at this point to focus attention on the key implications of the VUCA business world for strategic change – as outlined below.

A reinforcement of strategic change as a mix of planned and emergent change

The notion of the VUCA business world serves to reinforce Quinn's and Mintzberg's conceptualisations of strategy as a mix of planned and emergent change borne out of the dynamic interaction between an organisation and its external environment – where a growing awareness of the ever-increasing complexity and unpredictable nature of the business world further blurs the line between strategy formulation and strategy implementation and provides greater legitimacy to an understanding of strategic change as an agile, adaptive and emergent process in response to environmental changes over which change agents have hardly any control (Mintzberg, 1987; Mintzberg and Waters, 1985).

Business acumen rooted in systems practice

The VUCA business world warrants the development of a type of business acumen rooted in systems practice, where change agents have to develop their ability to manage their organisations as complex adaptive systems – calling for the development of an in-depth understanding of the complex web of causal relationships that underpins organisational functioning and the change situation as a whole. Importantly, change leaders have to be able to promptly identify and react to the causal dynamics that might have the greatest impact on the organisation's strategic orientation and capacity to generate competitive advantage (Reeves et al., 2016).

A democratic brand of leadership

Operating in the VUCA business environment requires a departure from traditional, top-down approaches to change leadership. Making sense of and navigating the VUCA business world is beyond the ability and the parochial interests of a sole individual or small group of people operating in an ivory tower detached from other change stakeholders and the practicalities of the change situation (Kelly, 2019). The VUCA business world warrants a brand of democratic leadership that can let go of the need to command and control. It enjoins change leaders to empower all key stakeholders so that they can make a valuable contribution in helping the organisation grapple with increasingly complex and overwhelming business contexts.

This involves creating a unity of purpose, setting up support structures for stakeholder involvement, effective communication and collaboration and a distribution of leadership responsibilities – as a means of developing shared understanding, trusting relationships and organisation-wide commitment to strategic change. In short, the VUCA business world calls for a type of leader who can not only lead others but also release the leadership potential of others in the pursuit of competitive advantage and strategic success (Ibarra and Scoular, 2019).

An experimental approach to learning

In a VUCA business world, there is rarely any certainty as to whether a chosen strategy will actually work and whether the risks are worth the investment. It is often said that uncertainty is the catalyst of learning. However, learning in the VUCA business world cannot be constrained by past experiences. What is required here is an experimental approach to learning where employees and other actively involved change stakeholders are encouraged to try out new ideas, test different working methods and find innovative solutions that can be of 'strategic value' and 'yield' competitive advantage (Luca and Bazerman, 2021). As such, experimental learning is characterised by a high tolerance for mistakes, a focus on creativity and innovation, and a virtuous cycle of learning and unlearning, practical application and evaluation that can drive the organisation forward in an increasingly uncertain and unpredictable business environment.

REFLECTIVE EXERCISE

1   Explain in your own words the meaning of a VUCA business environment.
2   What are the implications of a VUCA business environment for strategic change?

3.7 Key learning points

The following key learning points arising from this chapter include:

1   Strategic change involves the *modification or major overhaul* of an organisation's strategy and the deployment of the *necessary resources* to enable it to effectively *respond and sometimes shape* the dynamic forces at play within its *operating context* in an attempt to *achieve competitive*

advantage and ensure its *long-term* survival and growth. In unpacking the key features of strategic change, one has to pay attention to the *type* of change involved, the *resource requirements*, the *mode* of change, the *operating context* in which it is going to play out, its *goals and objectives* and its focus on business survival, continuity and growth in the *longer term*.

2　Change agency refers to: (i) change agents' *intentional action* driven by an intent, a vision and a certain level of confidence in their ability to positively affect or change for the better the current strategy of their organisation, and (ii) a form of *causal power* embodied in change agents that aims to generate certain desired strategic outcomes. The two main philosophical views underpinning human agency in the context of strategic change include: (i) *determinism* in which external forces of change are seen as beyond the control and free will of change agents who can but react to such forces, and (ii) *voluntarism* which endorses a view of change agents as having a degree of control over their environment and being able to exercise free will in making informed strategic choices and following deliberate courses of action. This textbook upholds the more moderate view that *the process of strategic change consists of both determinist and voluntarist elements* and brings to attention how change agents have to both deal with pre-existing conditions over which they have little control and exercise their free will and causal powers in the deployment of innovative change strategies.

3　The main approaches to strategic change identified in this textbook include: (i) the *planned approach* which entails a holistic, rational and proactive way of dealing with strategic change; (ii) the *emergent approach* which is adaptive, ad hoc and reactive; (iii) Quinn's *logical incrementalism* and Mintzberg's *pattern of strategy formation and development* which in their own ways integrate elements of both planned and emergent approaches to strategic change; (iv) *strategic improvisation* which places an emphasis on an agile, improvised and 'craft approach' to strategic change; (v) *ambidextrous strategic change* which consists of a portfolio of different types of approaches to strategic change depending on the two key dimensions of diversity and dynamism; and (vi) *quantum strategic change* which locates quantum technology at the core of strategic change and places an emphasis on the role of change leaders in harnessing its power to create value and competitive advantage.

4　This chapter considered three popular diagnostic tools that change leaders can employ to facilitate strategic change: (i) The *PESTLE analysis* which allows for a sound understanding of the opportunities and threats arising from an organisation's external environment; (ii) the *SWOT analysis* which focuses on both the internal resources of the organisation and the key threats and opportunities arising from the external environment; and (iii) the *strategic change canvas* that is a powerful visual and communication tool that brings together the key components that account for strategic change success and that can enable collaboration, transparency, trust and co-creation of meaning around new change strategies.

5　The concept of the VUCA (*Volatile, Uncertain, Complex and Ambiguous*) business world can be broken down and 'operationalised' into an *environmental scanning tool* that can be used to effectively frame strategic change. Its key implications for strategic change include: (i) a reinforcement of *strategic change as a mix of planned and emergent change*; (ii) the need for a type of *business acumen rooted in systems practice* and the ability to manage organisations as complex adaptive systems; (iii) a *democratic brand of leadership* that can release the leadership potential of others in the pursuit of competitive advantage and strategic success; and (iv) *an experimental approach to learning* characterised by a high tolerance for mistakes, a focus on creativity and innovation, and a virtuous cycle of learning and unlearning, practical application and evaluation that can drive the organisation forward in an increasingly uncertain and unpredictable business environment.

—END-OF-CHAPTER CASE STUDY 3.4—

KUKA: Shaping the future of robotics in a VUCA business world

Introduction

KUKA, a leading firm in industrial automation, was founded in 1898. Headquartered in Augsburg, Germany, KUKA offers robotics-enabled solutions to international customers in a variety of sectors such as automotive, electronics, metal and plastic, consumer goods, e-commerce/retail, and healthcare. In 2021, the company employed around 14,000 people and generated a revenue of 3.3 billion USD. According to KUKA's Mission 2030 statement, the firm 'will support manufacturing companies of any size to meet tomorrow's requirements by providing intuitive and intelligent automation solutions'. KUKA also seeks to extend industrial intelligence to every corner of the world by creating a global network of experts in robotics and facilitating access to flexible automation solutions.

Unprecedented challenges in a VUCA business environment

However, KUKA is facing unprecedented challenges arising from an increasingly VUCA (*Volatile, Uncertain, Complex and Uncertain*) business environment. As both KUKA and most of its customers operate within the manufacturing industry, they all have to face more or less the same problems: unforeseen shortages of shipping containers, unstable prices, and the erratic supply of input materials such as steel, plastics and semiconductors, all of which have resulted in severe disruptions in its supply chain. KUKA has up to now struggled to deal with the new level of *volatility* and *uncertainty*. In addition, staying ahead of the competition is a constant challenge in the fast-paced and increasingly competitive high-tech industry and strategic success is far from being a given. This is why KUKA has to keep investing heavily in experimental research and development – the outcomes of which are, more often than not, unknown, without any guarantee of success or return.

In terms of *complexity*, KUKA faces challenges at different levels. At the technological level, the effective integration of robots and software requires high engineering and programming capabilities. At a social level, embedding new technology into diverse business communities with different cultural and educational backgrounds and legal requirements remains a tall order. At the economic level, key concerns such as recessions, inflation, unemployment and uneven distribution of wealth across target markets makes it very difficult to predict sales performance and identify growth opportunities.

Moreover, one of KUKA's strategic endeavours to take high-end robotics and automation to new industries and mass markets remains fraught with ambiguity. Access to reliable data in this area is very limited. Variables such as level of engagement with robotics and automation, level of technical expertise, nature of human–robot integration and their causal relationships with customer demand and sales performance remain elusive – which makes informed strategic decision-making, business forecasting and the identification of leverage points and success factors extremely difficult.

Three strategic pillars

In response to those daunting challenges, KUKA has embarked on a new strategic journey which rests upon three pillars: *technological leadership*, *diversified growth* and *operational efficiency*. Figure 3.3 foregrounds the key change drivers arising from KUKA's VUCA business environment, the three foundational pillars of the company's change strategy and its intended outcomes.

Technological leadership

Technological leadership refers to KUKA's ambition to identify, develop and implement new technologies that can help the company achieve its new strategic goals. To stay ahead of the competition KUKA will need to develop a better understanding of the technological megatrends impacting its operating context which will underpin the development of adaptable products and solutions. For example, KUKA is currently experimenting with cobots (collaborative robots), industrial robots that can safely operate in tandem with human beings in a shared workspace and optimise human–machine integration. Also, in its drive for technological leadership, KUKA fosters a culture of innovation and collaboration both within and outside of its organisational boundaries – where, for example, it runs 25 KUKA colleges around the world, offering e-learning courses whilst providing access to expert knowledge in robotics. With its 'Tech-meets-Talent' initiative, KUKA also aims to get

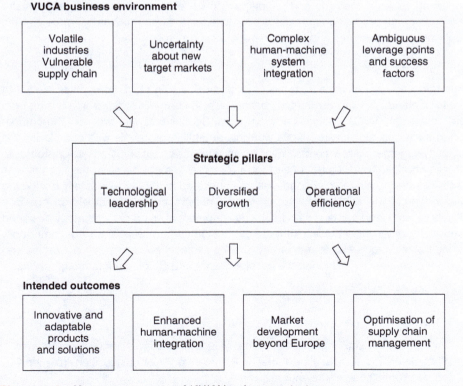

Figure 3.3 Key components of KUKA's change strategy

(Continued)

young people interested in MINT (mathematics, information technology, natural sciences, and technology) subjects and engaged in exploring the possibilities of robotics.

Diversified growth

Through diversified growth, KUKA aims to spread its business across different sectors and geographic regions in order to reduce the risk of losses due to increased volatility across its current target markets. KUKA has traditionally partnered with the automotive industry across Europe and will continue to be a useful asset in spearheading automation, digitalisation and electrification processes within that particular market. However, the firm is putting out feelers to other sectors such as healthcare and is widening its market reach to include, for example, emerging Asian markets.

Operational efficiency

The primary aim of automation and industrial robotics is the maximisation of efficiency, productivity and profit – which is why operational efficiency is an integral part of KUKA's DNA and one of the pillars of its change strategy. A good example which demonstrates KUKA's commitment to operational efficiency is its iiQKA robot-operating system, an easy-to-use starter package for beginners developed in close collaboration with customers and partners. iiQKA combines powerful software and an intuitive and graphical user interface to help companies automate and monitor their production systems at the push of a button. Another example is KUKA's AIVI (a control system based on Artificial Intelligence connecting vehicles, machine and people) which will enable customers to have greater control over their production processes to enable faster throughput times, more efficient supply chain management and higher productivity and profitability.

Conclusions

A number of key issues arise from this case study. First, high-tech companies like KUKA have to contend with unprecedented challenges and competitive pressures arising from their increasingly VUCA business environments. Second, staying ahead of the competition in such business environments warrants an ability to grapple with complexity and ambiguity together with a commitment to an innovative, solutions-based approach to strategic change. Third, there is need for a robust alignment between the key streams of activities driving strategic change – as demonstrated by the three mutually reinforcing pillars underpinning KUKA's change strategy. Finally, successful strategic change in a VUCA business world perhaps calls for the development of an outreach strategy designed to move the organisation closer to its target customers and enable it to become more attuned to their needs – as evidenced by KUKA's efforts in engaging with customers and the wider community in exploring the possibilities for and shaping the future of robotics.

Sources: KUKA (2020, 2021, 2022)

Questions

1   What are the key challenges that KUKA has to face in its external business environment?
2   What makes the company's external environment a VUCA business environment? Refer to Table 3.6 to frame your answer.
3   What are the three pillars of KUKA's change strategy? How can these three pillars enable KUKA to stay ahead of the competition and prosper in the longer term?

3.8 Independent learning

If you want to consolidate your understanding of strategic change, you can access the following materials online:

Martin, R.L. (2022) *A Plan Is Not a Strategy*: www.youtube.com/watch?v=iuYlGRnC7J8. Prof Roger Martin draws the distinction between planning and strategy. He provides a definition of strategy and explains the steps for developing a good strategy while emphasising the need for the organisation to leave its comfort zone.

Systems Innovations (2016) *VUCA Environments*: www.youtube.com/watch?v=rLOLdTjdnsY. This short video explains the origin of the term VUCA. It draws the distinction between the traditional approach to strategy in a non VUCA world and how to develop strategies in an increasingly complex world.

Managing Transformations in a VUCA World: https://soundcloud.com/inpractice_loaydirar/ managing-transformations-in-a-vuca-world. This podcast highlights the need for organisations to adapt and thrive amidst rapid change and consider adopting the VUCA model, which would help them navigate the volatile, uncertain, complex and ambiguous nature of the current environment.

Mintzberg, H. and Waters, J. A. (1985) 'Of strategies, deliberate and emergent', *Strategic Management Journal*: www.jstor.org/stable/2486186. This seminal article by Mintzberg and Waters will enable you to further develop your understanding of their notion of strategy as a pattern of decision-making and activity and it also provides a good starting point for the research exercise that you have to do for this particular topic.

3.9 References

Alsaqal, A. H., Ahmed, H. A. and Alsaadoun, S. K. H. (2021) 'Strategic improvisation and its impact on organizational development for business organizations', *Journal of Management Information and Decision Sciences*, 24(6). [Online] Available at: www.abacademies.org/articles/ strategic-improvisation-and-its-impact-on-organizational-development-for-business-organizations.pdf (accessed 2 February 2023).

Bennett, N. and Lemoine, G. J. (2014) 'What a difference a word makes: Understanding threats to performance in a VUCA world', *Business Horizons*, 57(3), 311–317. [Online] Available at: https://doi.org/10.1016/j.bushor.2014.01.001 (accessed 1 October 2022).

Boladian, R., Daccache, C., Matar, S. and Sabol, M. (2023) *The Rise of National Quantum Strategies*. [Online] Available at: www.kearney.com/industry/aerospace-defense/article/-/ insights/the-rise-of-national-quantum-strategies (accessed 10 May 2023).

Burnes, B. (1996) 'No such thing as a "one best way" to manage organisational change', *Management Decision*, 34(10), 11–18.

Cision PR Newswire (2017) *IBM Announces Collaboration with Leading Fortune 500 Companies, Academic Institutions and National Research Labs to Accelerate Quantum Computing.* [Online] Available at: www.prnewswire.com/news-releases/ibm-announces-collaboration-with-leading-fortune-500-companies-academic-institutions-and-national-research-labs-to-accelerate-quantum-computing-300571228.html (accessed 11 May 2023).

Coram, R. and Burnes, B. (2001) 'Managing organisational change in the public sector – Lessons from the privatisation of the Property Service Agency', *International Journal of Public Sector Management*, 14(2), 94–110. [Online] Available at: https://doi. org/10.1108/09513550110387381 (accessed 6 October 2022).

Cuenca-Gomez, E. (2021) *Becoming a Quantum Company: A Change Management Approach for Quantum Technologies and the Quantum Mindset.* [Online] Available at: https://quantumstrategyinstitute. com/2021/11/11/becoming-a-quantum-company/ (accessed 10 May 2023).

Djurovic, B. A. (2011) *Transformational Change or Not?: The Case of British Airways (2008–2010).* [Online] Available at: https://papers.ssrn.com/sol3/papers.cfm?abstract_id=1947296 (accessed 20 October 2023).

Gallagher, W. (2023) *How Steve Jobs saved Apple with the iMac 25 years ago.* [Online] Available at: https://appleinsider.com/articles/23/05/06/how-steve-jobs-saved-apple-with-the-imac-25-years-ago (accessed 10 May 2023).

Hartwig, M. (ed.) (2007) *Dictionary of Critical Realism.* London: Routledge.

Ibarra, H. and Scoular, A. (2019) 'The leader as coach', *Harvard Business Review*, November–December, 1–17.

Kelly, R. (2019) 'Future-proofing organisations for leadership 4.0', in R. Kelly, *Constructing Leadership 4.0: Swarm Leadership and the Fourth Industrial Revolution.* Cham, Switzerland: Palgrave Macmillan. [Online] Available at: https://doi.org/10.1007/978-3-319-98062-1_7 (accessed 5 December 2022).

KUKA (2020) *White Paper: Future Production Fast Forward.* [Online] Available at: https://www.kuka.com (accessed 8 November 2022).

KUKA (2021) *KUKA Sustainability Report.* [Online] Available at: https://www.kuka.com/-/media/kuka-corporate/documents/ir/reports-and-presentations/sustainability-reports/kuka-sustainability-report-2021.pdf?rev=72d1663802ef4cbca307ba3dcef2c9f3 (accessed 8 November 2022).

KUKA (2022) *KUKA Annual Report 2021.* [Online] Available at: www.kuka.com/-/media/kuka-corporate/documents/ir/reports-and-presentations/en/annual-report/annual-report_2021.pdf?rev=-1&hash=99AC1CD91DDA07C76759E84735EA2F7A (accessed 10 December 2022).

Luca, M. and Bazerman, M. H. (2021) *The Power of Experiments: Decision Making in a Data-Driven World.* Cambridge, MA: MIT Press.

Mintzberg, H. (1978) 'Patterns in strategy formation', *Management Science*, 24(9), 934–948.

Mintzberg, H. (1987) 'Crafting strategy', *Harvard Business Review*, July/August. [Online] Available at: https://hbr.org/1987/07/crafting-strategy (accessed 15 September 2022).

Mintzberg, H. (2009) *Tracking Strategies: Toward a General Theory of Strategy Formation.* New York: Oxford University Press.

Mintzberg, H. and Waters, J. A. (1985) 'Of strategies, deliberate and emergent', *Strategic Management Journal*, 6(3), 257–272.

O'Regan, N. and Ghobadian, A. (2012) 'John Lewis Partnership lessons in logical incrementalism and organic growth: A case study and interview with the Chairman, Mr Charlie Mayfield', *Journal of Strategy and Management*, 5(1), 103–112. [Online] Available at: https://doi.org/10.1108/17554251211200473 (accessed 18 October 2022).

Quinn, J. B. (1980) *Strategies for Change: Logical Incrementalism.* Homewood: Richard D. Irwin, Inc.

Quinn, J. B. (1993) 'Managing strategic change', in C. Mabey and B. Mayon-White (eds), *Managing Change.* London: Paul Chapman/Open University, pp. 65–84.

Rastrick, S. (2020) *Capturing the Impact of New Ways of Working for Allied Health Professionals Arising from the COVID-19 Response.* [Online] Available at: www.england.nhs.uk/blog/capturing-the-impact-of-new-ways-of-working-for-allied-health-professionals-arising-from-the-covid-19-response/ (accessed 15 October 2020).

Reeves, M., Haanaes, K., Hollingsworth, J. and Scognamiglio, F. (2013) *Ambidexterity: The Art of Thriving in Complex Environments.* [Online] Available at: www.bcg.com/publications/2013/strategy-growth-ambidexterity-art-thriving-complex-environments (accessed 2 February 2023).

Reeves, M., Levin, S. and Ueda, D. (2016) 'The biology of corporate survival', *Harvard Business Review*, January–February, 1–17.

Resilinc (2018) *Biogen & Resilinc Case Study: Proactive Risk Mitigation in Hurricane Season.* [Online] Available at: www.resilinc.com/learning-center/white-papers-reports/proactive-risk-mitigation-in-hurricane-season/ (accessed 25 October 2022).

Schoemaker, P. J. H., Heaton, S. and Teece, D. J. (2018) 'Innovation, dynamic capabilities, and leadership', *California Management Review*, 61(1), 15–42. [Online] Available at: https://doi.org/10.1177/0008125618790246 (accessed 30 September 2022).

4

THEORIES AND MODELS OF CHANGE MANAGEMENT

Learning Outcomes

After completing this chapter, you should be able to:

- Understand a range of change theories that underpin the study of change management and that have served as a basis for the development of popular change models.
- Discuss the key characteristics of a good change model.
- Critically examine different types of organisational change models with reference to their key elements, processes and intended outputs.
- Apply a selection of change models to the practical context of real-life organisations and case examples reflecting the business realities of modern-day organisations.

4.1 Introduction

This chapter will enable you to develop a critical understanding of a set of well-known change theories and models and provide you with the opportunity to apply them to the practical context of real-life organisations. The chapter begins with a discussion of a selection of theories that have informed the development of some of the most widely known change models, outlining their key features and implications for effective change management. The chapter then considers what constitutes a good change model to provide a solid foundation for assessing the value of the change models discussed in the following section. The chapter proceeds to critically review a number of popular organisational change models to describe their key elements, underline their value in framing change and draw attention to their limitations or the criticisms that have been levelled against them. This particular section also contains practical exercises and case studies that provide you with an opportunity to apply some of the models discussed to both real-life case examples and fictitious cases that reflect the business realities of modern-day organisations. The conceptual nugget for the chapter is presented in a final key section to underline the 'superior value' of systemic change models and distil their key features in light of the preceding discussion. The chapter concludes with an outline of the key learning points before presenting the end-of-chapter case study which entails a practical application of a popular systemic change model to an organisation operating within the hospitality industry.

4.2 Key change theories

While there is a plethora of theories that underpin change management and modelling, we consider below some of the most salient ones that have informed the development of some of the most widely known change models, which are presented in the final section of this chapter.

Field theory

Field theory is of central importance in the study of organisational change and one can easily appreciate how it has served as a basis for the development of so many change models, some of which are discussed in the last section of this chapter. Field theory is derived from Lewin's interest in Gestalt psychology (a school of thought that focuses on how the human brain perceives and makes sense of things as a complete whole and not as isolated components) and group behaviour (Burnes, 2020). Field theory entails the following key features:

- A holistic approach warranting attention to the change situation as a whole and which is conveyed by the notion of field. Thus, effective change management should begin with an organisation-wide scoping of the change requirements and an identification of the group of interdependent variables that can generate particular change outcomes.
- A thorough force-field analysis of the change situation – which is usually presented in topological maps to show the strength and direction of the forces driving change and those constraining it at different points in time.
- An examination of how organisational stakeholders interact with the changing environment and of how their perceptions, experiences and feelings impact their attitudes and patterns of behaviour towards the proposed change.

Systems theory

There is some overlap between field theory and systems theory. Both theories warrant a holistic approach to change where change agents are encouraged to consider the change situation as a whole. Both theories also locate the organisation within its wider environment and pay attention to how the organisation interacts with it. However, systems theory places an even greater emphasis on how the organisation evolves as a dynamic and organic entity within its wider environment. Systems theory also pays particular attention to the interaction between the many parts or sub-systems of the organisation – where the basic idea is that *the whole is greater than the sum of its parts*, which means that the combined effects of the organisation's sub-systems is far greater than the sum of the separate effect of each individual sub-system.

In a change situation, the organisation as a 'whole system' is made up of a number of sub-systems – which can include political, cultural, structural, social, technological, developmental, motivational and other functional sub-systems. Importantly, such sub-systems are causally interconnected and their combined effects lead to the generation of change outcomes which are specific to the 'organisation in context' (Mele et al., 2010). Systems theory has served as a strong basis for the development of some of the more recent and robust 'systemic' change models – which are accommodating of multiple dimensions, perspectives and interests and can be distinguished from the more straightforward one-dimensional, linear and step-by-step change models which tend to reflect the unitary interests of top management. Examples of both types of change models are discussed in the final section of this chapter.

Process theory

Process theory can take on different meanings across different fields of study. In the context of organisational change, process theory primarily refers to the three-stage activity (Input – Process – Output) which has provided an infrastructure for the development of many organisational change models. The *Input* stage entails the raw materials and other resources (labour, information, capital, entrepreneurship, etc.) that are fed into the next *Process* stage where they are transformed, leading to the *Output* stage: the production of valuable goods and services that meet customer expectations and quality standards whilst addressing the interests of wider stakeholder groups (Niederman, 2021).

More generally, process theory promotes a view of organisational change as a *continuous process*, paying particular attention to how the organisation dynamically interacts with and evolves within its external environment – which, as will be shown later on, is also foregrounded in many change models.

Communication theory

Effective communication is widely recognised as a key determinant of change success – which explains why communication theory is one of the building blocks of change modelling. Communication theory informs a set of key principles and precepts relating to:

i   the clarity, tonality and directionality of the change message

ii   the quality and effectiveness of the medium or channel used to convey the change message

iii   the creation of the opportunity for stakeholder feedback and open dialogue as a means of reaching consensus around the change plan, the terms and conditions of the change implementation and the coordination of action towards the achievement of change goals and objectives

iv   the impact of effective communication on employee commitment, motivation and performance as a necessary condition for sustainable change (see Chapter 8 for a more detailed discussion of communication in the context of change).

Importantly, communication theory also alerts change agents to the plurality of stakeholder interests – especially across large organisations – and to the opposing forces that can hinder change progress. In such cases, effective communication is of the essence (Harikkala-Laihinen, 2022). There is a significant critical stream of literature on communication theory that enjoins change agents to open up democratic spaces for open dialogue and enabling conversations between key organisational stakeholders throughout the change process to: (i) allow for the prompt resolution of conflict, (ii) constructively address potential sources of resistance and (iii) facilitate on-going negotiation and consensus around the terms and conditions of change implementation vital to sustainable change success.

Motivation theory

The theory of human motivation is also of central importance in change management and a core element in the development of change models. Change experts and practitioners are increasingly sensitive to the impact of employee motivation on change success and greater attention is being paid to how it can be effectively managed. Motivation theory has now reached a stage of development where it can provide change agents with rich insights into both the content (*the what*) and the process (*the how*) of human motivation. In terms of content, there is a wide array of models identifying different types and sources of human motivation (e.g. extrinsic, intrinsic, autonomous motivation, working conditions, relational networks and other supporting mechanisms) that speak to the satisfaction of the physiological, psychological, social and developmental needs of human beings (D'Annunzio-Green and Ramdhony, 2019; Ryan and Deci, 2000).

In terms of process, there is now a greater understanding of stakeholder dispositions, perceptions and attitudes about the change situation – and even more importantly, of regulatory behaviours of employees in making sense of the implications of change and aligning their own values, needs and interests with those of the changing organisation. Change agents now have at their disposal a comprehensive motivational toolbox which can be used to create the working conditions and set up the supporting mechanisms to optimise employee motivation, commitment and performance levels in pursuit of the desired change outcomes.

Leadership theory

There is an ever-growing stream of specialist literature on leadership that can be drawn upon to inform organisational change. Leadership theories most relevant to organisational change relate to the desirable traits of effective change leaders, the different leadership styles that befit different change situations, the nature of the exchange relationships between the leader and their followers, and the emergent role and responsibilities that are thrust upon modern-day leaders (Northouse, 2013). (These theories are treated in more depth in Chapter 7.)

The distinction between leaders and managers is a recurrent theme in the change literature. Change managers are appointed by the organisation and their roles and responsibilities involve maintaining the status quo and attending to current organisational functioning through proper planning, resource allocation, staffing and ensuring that the change goals and objectives are efficiently achieved. By contrast, the status of change leaders is legitimated through the dynamic exchange relationship between the leader and their followers.

The roles and responsibilities of change leaders are mainly concerned with:

i   creating a vision for change
ii   providing a clear direction towards the achievement of change goals and objectives
iii effectively communicating with stakeholders and building the necessary coalitions to smooth the process of change implementation
iv   motivating and building the capability of employees to muster their commitment to change
v   aligning their needs and interests with those of the organisation as a way of optimising their performance levels in view of the intended change outcomes. Generally speaking, these are the basic theoretical assumptions about leadership that underlie the development of most change models.

Culture theory

Culture theory seeks to understand the nature of the relationship between organisational members (such as senior executives, middle and line managers, and employees) within the context of their everyday activities as they cope with the challenges arising from both the internal and external environment. In this regard, culture theory pays particular attention to the cultural value system of the organisation – i.e. the taken-for-granted assumptions, beliefs and values held by organisational members which are shaped over time by a process of learning and adaptation and which tend to be validated by experiences of past success and failures (Schein, 1992). Because it is rooted in past experiences and actions spanning over a relatively long period, the cultural value system is usually well entrenched and inevitably has a strong influence on the perceptions, behaviours and relationships of organisational members and importantly, on their attitudes towards change. Since cultural values are often unconsciously held, they can be difficult to shift in spite of the need to do so in cases of radical, transformational change.

For culture change to happen, the literature emphasises the need for strong leadership and empowered agency that can effectively unpick and reframe the current cultural value system and take concrete action to institutionalise new cultural values that align with the organisation's change goals and objectives. The ability to effectively manage the cultural dimension of organisational change can have a significant bearing on its intended outcomes – which is why culture theory is another building block of change modelling.

Contingency theory

Contingency theory is closely associated with the work of Fred Fiedler in the early 1960s. In the context of organisational change, it speaks to the ability of change agents to be sensitive to the dynamic nature of the change situation and base their strategic decisions and chosen courses of action on a sound analysis of the shifting forces at play within it. A contingency approach to organisational change places an emphasis on the following:

- The need for different styles of change leadership depending on different change situations.
- The need to consider the multiple factors that can impact on change initiatives across different situations – e.g. type of change, characteristics of key organisational stakeholders, power structures, the organisation's core cultural values, etc.
- The need to be flexible throughout the change process and effectively respond to emerging variables and issues that can have a significant impact on the intended change outcomes.
- It might sometimes be necessary to 'change the intended change outcomes' themselves in case of a drastic change in strategic orientation.
- In light of the above, contingency theory places an emphasis on the need to move away from a deterministic and highly prescriptive approach to change to one that is more adaptive, open-ended and emergent.

However, the contingency theory has been criticised for the lack of compelling research and valid measures to substantiate its claims – especially those related to the ability of the leader to change and adapt their style to different situations (Northouse, 2013). Sometimes, the situation might need to be changed to match the dominant style of a new change leader – which, in some cases, is exactly what needs to be done for the survival and continuity of the organisation. Contingency theory has also been taken to task because of its one-sided focus on the leader in the leader–exchange relationship – where the leader is the one adapting their style and *doing things to people* as opposed *to doing things with them* and being responsive to employees and seeking their collaboration and commitment in the pursuit of desirable change outcomes (Sivaruban, 2021). Finally, if pushed too far, contingency theory can lock change agents in a reactive, fire-fighting role where all they can do is respond to the shaping power of the external environment – thus, closing off the possibility for change agents and initiatives to exert a shaping influence on their external environment through the development of new business models and innovative products.

PRACTICAL EXERCISE

The following exercise will help you consolidate your understanding of the key issues and concerns arising from each of the change theories discussed above.

- Match the actions described in Table 4.1 with the appropriate theory.

Table 4.1   Matching actions with relevant theory

Action	Theory
Scope the change situation as a whole to identify the interdependent variables that can generate particular change outcomes.	
Set up supporting mechanisms to optimise employee motivation, commitment and performance levels.	
Provide the opportunity for feedback and open dialogue to reach consensus and coordinate action.	
Provide a clear direction towards the achievement of change goals and objectives.	
Carry out a force-field analysis of the change situation to show the strength and direction of the forces driving and constraining change.	
Reframe the current organisational value system and take concrete action to institutionalise new values that align with the change goals and objectives of the organisation.	
Place an emphasis on the need to move away from a prescriptive approach to change to one that is more adaptive and emergent.	
Develop an understanding of the organisation evolving as a dynamic and organic entity within its wider environment.	
Align the needs and interests of employees with those of the organisation as a way of optimising performance levels.	
Examine how employees' perceptions, experiences and feelings impact their attitudes and patterns of behaviour towards the proposed change.	
Promptly resolve conflict and address potential sources of resistance.	
Stress the need for different styles of change leadership depending on different change situations.	
Map out the political, cultural, structural, social, technological, developmental and motivational dimensions of the proposed change programme.	

4.3 Characteristics of a good change model

While views may differ about what constitutes a good change model, it has to be said that there is no such thing as a perfect model. As mental representations of how something works in the real world, all change models are products of human perception and interpretation – and are, as a result, subjective, selective, tentative and biased. As such, all change models are carriers of only 'partial truths' about the real world (which is itself dynamic and in a constant state of flux) and subject to refinement, revision and correction. British statistician George E.P Box famously said that *all models are wrong, but some are useful* (Box, 1979).

   While the controversy raised by Box's statement is beyond the scope of this book, it does provide a starting point for a tempered view of the value of change models. As partial representations of reality and products of the human mind (and its flawed assumptions), all models (including change models) are never 'totally true' and to some extent always wrong. However, models can be useful if the 'partial truth' they carry is upheld in reality and can be used to achieve desired goals and objectives – which would then qualify them as 'good models'.

What makes a good change model?

A good model is as simple as possible

As noted above, no single model can ever represent a complete picture of reality or lay claim to the whole truth. However, even if imperfect and incomplete, a good change model should be as simple as possible. If a change model is overly complex and bogged down in details to the point of confusion, this would defeat its primary purpose – which is to help change agents make sense of a particular organisational process or activity 'in context' and choose an appropriate course of action to improve it. This brings to mind the so-called Bonini's paradox (named after a Stanford business professor) where the more complex and accurate a model is, the less clear and useful it becomes (Bonini, 1963; Dutton and Starbuck, 1971). Therefore, a simple change model is one that is clear, easy to understand, and enables change agents to swiftly get to grips with a change situation and confidently develop an action plan to effectively address it.

A good model represents reality as accurately as possible

However, simplicity does not necessarily mean an unavoidable compromise on accuracy. A simple model can still score high on accuracy. This can be achieved by being economical and paying attention only to the core elements or key variables at play within a change situation. This can allow for a narrow-focused and highly precise analysis of individual elements, the nature of their relationships with each other and of their combined effects on the change outcomes. Accuracy also allows change agents to place a value on the significance of change variables and, importantly, to reliably identify variables which change agents can influence (and thus effectively manage) and those that are beyond their control (and only react to or cope with).

A good model allows for causal explanations

A sound change model is sophisticated enough to allow for causal explanations. It does not stop at identifying the main stages or core elements of a change situation but enables change agents to explore and examine the cause-and-effect relationships between the key variables within it. In change models, causal relations are usually mapped out by different types of arrows showing the directionality and sometimes the weight of impact (denoted by the thickness of the arrow and other mathematical signs) of the causal relationships between key change variables. As such, causal models have a high *explanatory power* in that they allow for a grounded examination and explanation of the complex web of causal relationships that underlie the change process and the specific change outcomes it generates.

A good model enables a systemic understanding of change

A good model is multidimensional and enables the development of a systemic understanding of change – where change issues are not addressed in isolation but are critically examined within the web of causal factors and relationships underlying the change situation. This allows for a holistic, multidimensional approach to change which locates the diagnosis of change problems and the generation of effective solutions to address them within the 'wider scheme of things' and in light of their potential impact on the organisation as a whole. Systemic models stand in stark contrast to linear, sequential models which only identify the core elements, stages and sequence of activities of a change process without any emphasis on their underlying causal relations.

A good model is a springboard for action

A good model, however sophisticated, is not meant to be just a mental exercise with no hope of having any impact in the real world. While good models should be informed by sound theory and rigorous empirical research, they should also serve as a springboard for action geared toward practical outcomes – or, as Lewin would have it, they should effectively bridge the gap between theory and practice (Hughes, 1981). Therefore, a sure sign of a good model is its practical orientation. Whilst change models should be theoretically grounded and based on solid evidence, they should also open up the possibility for concrete, follow-up action to improve practice.

REFLECTIVE EXERCISE

1   Why is there no such thing as a perfect change model?
2   What is the main difference between systemic and linear models?
3   Refer back to the key characteristics of a good change model. Do you think a single model can integrate all these characteristics?

4.4 Critical review of popular organisational change models

Lewin's 3-step model of change

Lewin's three-step approach to change remains one of the most quoted models across both academic and trade literatures and has served as the foundation for change modelling since its first inception in the late 1940s. To paraphrase Hendry (1996), one has merely to scratch the surface of most change models – even the more recent ones – to find the change principles and precepts that underpin Lewin's sequential, three-step model of change. The first conceptualisation of Lewin's three-step approach to change can be found in a *Human Relations* article he published in 1947 in which he describes successful change as a process involving the following three aspects: unfreezing of current level, moving to a new level and freezing organisational life on the new level (Lewin, 1947).

While there has been some contention regarding whether the actual three-step model of change (which took shape after his death) can be attributed to Lewin, it is based on a wide range of issues and concerns which arise from his lifelong research in field theory and organisational development (Burnes, 2020). Figure 4.1 is one of many representations of Lewin's three-step model of change. Its simplicity (for which it has often been criticised) in fact hides an in-depth and complex understanding of organisational change management which is briefly discussed next.

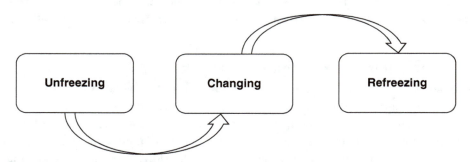

Figure 4.1 Lewin's three-step model of change

Source: Adapted from Lewin, K. (1947) 'Frontiers in Group Dynamics', *Human Relations*, 1(1), 5–41.

Unfreezing

The first step of Lewin's model involves a process of *unfreezing*. It involves an attempt at 'destabilising the status quo' – i.e. upsetting the balance between the forces driving and restraining change which tends to keep the organisation in a state of equilibrium and locks it in a 'frozen' state. In practical terms, this means increasing the strength of the forces for change while decreasing that of the forces against change. Strengthening the forces for change needs strong leadership that can create a sense of urgency and a readiness for change among organisational stakeholders. To this effect, change leaders need to develop a clear change plan that is informed by a sound diagnosis of the change situation and an understanding of the challenges and opportunities arising from it. Change leaders also need to effectively communicate with stakeholders to convince them of the necessity and potential benefits of the proposed change and build a common vision of the future and a coalition to transform it into reality.

To decrease the forces against change, there is a need to identify and promptly address sources of resistance and conflict that can have a negative impact on the change implementation and outcomes. A collaborative approach to change can allow for greater stakeholder inclusion and participation which is critical in reducing the alienating feelings of fear, isolation, helplessness and loss that people can experience in the face of the unknown and that can destroy their trust in change leaders and nip their commitment in the bud even before the change implementation (Hussain et al., 2018).

Changing

The next step in Lewin's model, *changing*, has to do with the implementation of the change initiative. It is a transitional phase that allows the organisation to move towards new ways of working – which, especially in the case of transformational change, call for new mindsets, new attitudes and behaviours, and new skills and competences. To facilitate this transition, change leaders must put in place the appropriate support mechanisms such as training, coaching and mentoring focused on culture change, and competency building and participative forums to involve, empower and motivate employees, and apply evaluation measures to closely monitor change progress.

Refreezing

This last stage of *refreezing* is to emphasise the need to 'make change stick' and to ensure that the organisation does not regress to its previous state and revert back to the old ways of working. There is therefore a need at this stage to consolidate new processes, reinforce new behaviours, embed new cultural values and solidify new working relationships to uphold the desired levels of performance and productivity. Crucial activities at this stage include on-going learning and development opportunities at both individual and collective levels, appropriate reward systems to positively reinforce desirable behaviours, management support to effectively address emerging challenges and maintain employee motivation and commitment and the celebration of success at key milestones of the change process to sustain the momentum of change.

Criticisms levelled at Lewin's change model

Lewin's model has been criticised for being simplistic and prescriptive whilst remaining insensitive to the context of change and the wide array of variables within it (Burnes, 2004). However, the beauty of Lewin's model is that its simplicity hides the complexity and the richness of the principles, theoretical issues and fieldwork that informed its development. As such, it is a well-grounded and logical model that leaves change agents a lot of freedom to deconstruct and apply it to context – which also explains why it has served as a basis for the development of other, more recent change models and is testimony to Lewin's lasting contribution to organisational change management.

Another recurrent criticism which has been directed at Lewin's model relates to its last refreezing stage. The main issue of contention here is the fact that refreezing the organisation locks it once again into a new status quo whilst reducing the possibility for further change – which does not make much sense given the *increasingly* dynamic, emergent and unpredictable global business context. This boils down to a question of interpretation. The term refreezing does not necessarily pose a problem if it refers to the 're-stabilisation' of the organisation to give enough time for the new ways of working to 'take hold' and generate the intended outcomes – in which case refreezing does not have to be permanent or close off the possibility for further change. This issue is discussed at greater length in Chapter 11 on sustaining change.

REFLECTIVE EXERCISE

To consolidate your understanding of Lewin's three-step model, use Table 4.2 to jot down your thoughts about what you would consider to be its main strengths and limitations in light of the above discussion.

Table 4.2 Main strengths and limitations of Lewin's change model

Lewin's three step model of change	
Strengths	Limitations

Kirkpatrick's linear model of organisational change

Figure 4.2 below presents the key stages of Kirkpatrick's linear model of organisational change which is critically examined in the discussion that follows.

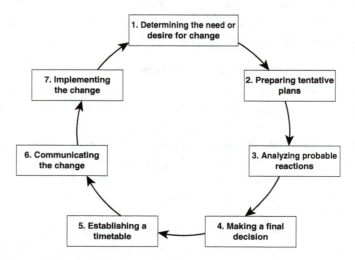

Figure 4.2 Kirkpatrick's (2001) linear model of organisational change

Source: Kirkpatrick, D. L., (2001) *Managing Change Effectively: Approaches, Methods, and Case Examples*. Taylor and Francis. Reproduced with permission.

Kirkpatrick's (2001) model of change is a linear model of organisational change – i.e. it portrays organisational change as a step-by-step process where one stage follows the other in a neat sequence. As such, it is very simple and easy to understand, which perhaps explains its popularity with practitioners. But the most outstanding quality of Kirkpatrick's model is that it is very economical and contains only the core elements of organisational change which are logically sequenced and provide broad yet clear parameters for a planned approach to change – where change is pre-determined, developed into a well-timed plan of action and then effectively communicated and implemented, leading to another change cycle.

Kirkpatrick's model is also underpinned by a voluntarist outlook (refer to Chapter 3) – where change agents are portrayed as in control of the change situation and able to take the necessary steps to respond to (if not pre-empt) the challenges facing the organisation. Hence, Kirkpatrick places change managers in the driving seat, knowledgeable and capable of making informed decisions at each critical stage of the change process to ensure progress and success – a view of change as driven from the top which sits well with managers.

On the downside, Kirkpatrick's model can be criticised for being economical to a fault. It is so broad that it does not give much attention in terms of both the context and content of change. There is little scope for the consideration of the variables at play within each of the key stages of the model, let alone for a sound understanding of their cause-and-effect relationships that can have a significant impact on the change implementation and outcomes. Moreover, while the model is oriented towards action and practical outcomes, it comes across as prescriptive in that it promotes a view that there is one best way to conduct organisational change, irrespective of context. Finally, it tends to obscure the political dimension of change (which relates to sources of resistance and the dynamics of negotiation and conflict) and labours under the unitarist impression that organisational change is unproblematically driven from the top and flows smoothly from a common purpose and a single (unitary) interest shared by all employees.

The case study below provides you with the opportunity to apply the Kirkpatrick model to a real-life organisation and use it as a tool to assess the change initiative it describes.

CASE STUDY 4.1

Indonesia's Krakatau Steel: From industry laggard to leader

Applying the Kirkpatrick model to a real-life organisation

Introduction

Krakatau Steel (KS) is Indonesia's biggest steel maker and public enterprise that operates a complex value chain to manufacture a wide range of steel-based products such as hot iron coils and plates used in ship building and for the construction of oil and gas pipes, heavy duty vehicles and certain home appliances. KS has 6,000 employees and plays a substantial role in the development of Indonesia's economy. Until recently, KS had to face major challenges in the form of increasing global competition, digitisation trends and a steep

(Continued)

fall in product demand, mainly from developed economies. For almost a decade, KS had to grapple with increasing financial losses and debts amounting to 2.5 billion USD. It was only in 2020 that KS recorded its first profit following significant measures to transform the ailing company from industry laggard to leader.

IT-enabled change

In 2019, while KS was still on the brink of bankruptcy, senior management set up an ambitious turnaround plan that included the following key features: restructuring financial relationships with lenders, improving partnerships with subsidiaries and associations, organisation-wide cost-reduction and optimisation of efficiency, culture change and capability-building to ensure business continuity and growth in the longer term. Newly digitalised processes enabled KS to effectively monitor the effects of change measures. A 'digital tower' was set up to integrate various data sources from sales, operations and finance, allowing change leaders to make informed and timely decisions. In addition, KS had to hire employees with IT skills and train new leaders in order to ease the adoption of a 'digital culture'.

Prioritising transparent communication

Having to work within strict parameters and tough deadlines (everything had to be in place within 12 months), KS leaders considered transparent communication a top priority to make sure employees clearly understood what was expected from them, what they had to do and when. In view of the possibility of negative reactions to the new strategy, change leaders endeavoured to act as good role models and spared no effort to maintain an open channel of communication with employees who, as a result, felt engaged and empowered to fully participate in the change process.

Moving forward

As KS strives to maintain its position as an industry leader, senior managers see the need to keep moving forward and sustaining the momentum of change as the top priority. The focus is now on creating value through cost reduction, increasing operational efficiency and the implementation of a cash-flow optimisation system as well as control measures to reduce energy consumption and utility costs across the company's main plants. Importantly, senior management have expressed their unwavering commitment to strengthening the company's relationships with its customers across all segments through continuous investments.

Sources: Krakatau Steel (2021); Razdan (2021)

Activity

Apply Kirkpatrick's linear model of organisational change to the above case study. In doing so, map out the activities and processes associated with the change initiative at Krakatau Steel against each of the key stages of the model.

How well did change leaders perform in light of the recommendations provided by Kirkpatrick at each stage of the model?

Kotter's eight-step checklist of leading change

Kotter's eight-step checklist for successfully designing, implementing, evaluating and sustaining organisational change is one of the most popular change tools taught across business schools and is considered by many as seminal (Kotter, 1996). These eight steps are:

- Establishing a sense of urgency.
- Forming a powerful coalition.
- Developing a vision and strategy.
- Communicating the vision.
- Empowering others to act on the vision.
- Planning for short-term gains.
- Consolidating improvements and producing more change.
- Establishing a change culture as the norm.

Kotter's eight-step checklist is clear and simple yet based on solid empirical evidence and practically oriented. We will not describe these steps in any detail here but want to draw attention to some of the key issues arising from the checklist:

- It underscores the need for change leaders to have a smart vision and the ability to communicate it clearly to stakeholders.
- There is a clear recognition of the political dimension of organisational change and of the need to build a 'powerful coalition' to muster stakeholder commitment and sustain the momentum of change.
- The checklist has a democratic orientation that validates the need for a people-oriented and relational approach to leading change in which employee empowerment plays a key role.
- It emphasises the importance of planning for and celebrating short-term wins as a means of motivating stakeholders and tracking progress toward the ultimate change goals.
- There is a call for institutionalising a culture of change as a critical success factor across business contexts which are becoming increasingly dynamic, competitive and unpredictable.

Criticisms

Although Kotter's eight-step checklist for leading change is clear, easy to apply and of some practical value, it tends, like Kirkpatrick's model, to obscure the complexity of organisational change and pays scant attention to the complex web of causal relationships underlying it. Moreover, Kotter's checklist portrays leadership as a one-off event and does not place enough emphasis on the processual nature of organisational change – the success of which seems to solely depend on the ability of change leaders to neatly follow each of the eight steps.

Kotter's checklist is also top-down and positions change leadership as something that the leader does *to* others which is in itself disempowering and underplays the importance of strong, fully engaged leadership as a key determinant of change success. Finally, Kotter's checklist gives the impression that building powerful coalitions is a straightforward process, and downplays the political tensions and sources of conflict and resistance that can adversely impact the change process and progress towards its intended outcomes.

However, Kotter's checklist has been revamped to take account of emerging challenges within a rapidly changing business context and is still of significant practical value (Kotter, 2012) – as shown in the following exercise.

---PRACTICAL EXERCISE---

Applying Kotter's eight-step checklist for leading change

Suppose you are the newly appointed CEO of a relatively large manufacturing company of 5,000 employees. The company has failed to deliver a profit for the past three years. All salaries have been frozen and staff morale is at an all-time low. The former CEO was not very popular with employees. He was perceived as operating in an ivory tower and nobody really understood what he was trying to do to improve the financial situation of the company. Managers say that they have 'jumped through the hoops' to strike a good working relationship with him but to no avail.

With your arrival, people seem to have a glimmer of hope that things will change for the better and that you will be able to reverse the misfortunes of the company and steer it in the right direction. However, this is a tall order. The current business climate is very competitive, markets seem to be shrinking and industry rivals are all having a tough time staying afloat.

Activity

Using Kotter's eight-step checklist, how are you going to lead the company through the much-awaited change?

Weisbord's six-box model of organisational change

Weisbord's model consists of six boxes accounting for the core elements of organisational change and two-directional arrows that represent the exchange relationship between the organisation and its external environment, as shown in Figure 4.3 below.

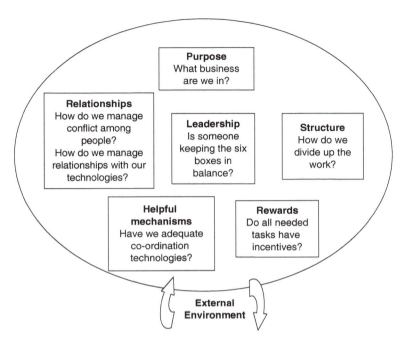

Figure 4.3 Weisbord's (1976) six-box model of organisational change

Source: Weisbord, M. R. (1976) 'Organizational diagnosis: Six places to look for trouble with or without a theory', *Group and Organization Studies*, 1(4), 430–447. Article with figure also on Sage website https://journals.sagepub.com/doi/pdf/10.1177/105960117600100405. Reproduced with permission.

Weisbord's (1976) six-box model adopts a non-linear, systemic approach to organisational change. As such, it represents the organisation as an open, living system in a symbiotic relationship with its external environment – which is emphasised by the two-directional arrows at the bottom of Figure 4.3. A symbiotic relationship in this case means that like a living organism, the organisation cannot exist in a vacuum but exists and evolves together with its external environment which is itself dynamic and in a constant state of flux. It is therefore important for the organisation to remain in *alignment* with its external environment if it is to survive and grow within it – which is the central premise on which Weisbord's model is based.

The model also warrants a robust *alignment* between the six boxes that account for the core elements of the organisation's internal environment. Therefore, activities within each of the six boxes have to be interconnected and mutually reinforcing and beneficial.

- First, an organisation needs to have a clear change strategy and business model which leaves no doubt as to its overriding purpose and mission (What business are we in?).
- Second, the organisation has to be (re)-structured in such a way as to enable the effective implementation of the chosen change strategy. To this effect, organisational activities have to be judiciously divided and coordinated across functional areas (How do we divide up the work?).

- Third, change agents need to put in place an effective reward system that will build and sustain stakeholder commitment and motivation which is a necessary condition for change success. Activities which can have a significant influence on the change outcomes have to be prioritised and attached to rewards which are of particular value to stakeholders (Do all needed tasks have incentives?).
- Fourth, the technologies employed to implement the change strategy have to be compatible and harnessed to the change outcomes – i.e. they have to work well together and effectively support functional activities vital to the achievement of the strategic goals and objectives (Have we adequate co-ordination technologies?).
- Fifth, Weisbord's model invites attention to the relational context and socio-technical aspect of change. As such, it alerts change agents to the need to address in a timely fashion the potential sources of resistance and conflict that can negatively impact change outcomes. It also brings to attention the need to ensure a seamless and empowering interface between technology and people which critically impacts the quality of decision-making, chosen courses of action and performance levels throughout the change process (How do we manage conflict among people? How do we manage relationships with our technologies?).
- Finally, the Weisbord model gives central importance to the type of enabling leadership that is needed to drive change and maintain a much-needed balance between the functional activities that fall under the five other core elements (Is someone keeping the six boxes in balance?).

The key strengths of the Weisbord model include: (i) it uses simple language (a non-technical business speak) and asks clear, practical bottom-line questions that are easy to understand and resonate with practitioners; (ii) it integrates the strategic, structural, technological, relational and motivational dimensions of change to allow for a holistic, organisation-wide understanding of the resource implications for effective change implementation; and (iii) it elicits thinking about the type of enabling leadership roles and responsibilities vital to a balanced approach to change and long-term success.

However, although the Weisbord model is multidimensional, it is not a causal model. No particular attention is given to the key variables at play within each of the six boxes which are foregrounded in the model; and neither does it trigger any specific thought about their possible cause-and-effect relationships. The responsibility for causally unpacking the six boxes and establishing their causal links is entirely left to change agents who might find it too daunting a task. For this very reason, it might be argued that the Weisbord model barely qualifies as such. It might be viewed by some as a mind map or loose conceptual framework at best designed for the development of an initial systemic understanding of the change situation and its resource implications.

Unicorn: Deploying a profit-focused change strategy

Using Weisbord's change model as a consultancy tool

Founded in 2019, Unicorn is a Latin American technology start-up company that provides an online delivery service. With its innovative application of Internet technologies and a primary focus on customer service, Unicorn is revolutionising the way people shop and receive their purchases that is accommodating of their busy lifestyles. Despite its rapid growth and substantial external funding over the past few years, the company is still struggling to run profitably as it operates in markets with razor-thin margins and investors are threatening to withdraw their financial support.

The CEO is convinced that the only way out of this difficult situation is to embark the company on a profit-focused change strategy. They have asked one of the senior managers to write a report to give an update on the current status of the company which will inform the development of the new strategy. The key issues arising from the report are as follows:

– Unicorn is facing intense competition from established and emerging industry players. As much as the firm benefited from the surge in demand during the COVID-19 pandemic it is now confronted with the impact of high interest rates and inflation – which has adversely impacted on the purchasing power of current customers, resulting in a drop in demand for the company's services.

– The senior management team remain committed to the well-being of the organisation and to the advancement of e-commerce across Latin America, which is an integral part of its initial strategic agenda.

– The company was recently restructured to better serve different target markets with the set-up of regional divisions reporting to the senior management team located in the company headquarters.

– Unicorn has an efficient logistics system in place which has received generally good feedback from customers but there is still room for improvement when compared to immediate competitors.

– The company is facing public scrutiny regarding how it treats its drivers who are mostly 'freelancers' and are not entitled to the benefits of permanent staff – which is the main cause of a high turnover rate among drivers.

– There is a lack of clarity regarding who should take a leading role in addressing the current challenges facing the company.

(Continued)

Activity

Imagine you are a hired consultant having to advise the CEO on how to develop and implement their new change strategy. In order to do so, you have decided to use Weisbord's model as a diagnostic tool to help you develop an initial understanding of Unicorn's unique change situation and the challenges arising from it.

In light of the information distilled from the senior manager's report to the CEO, address the questions in each of the component boxes of the Weisbord's model and consider the nature of the external environment in which Unicorn operates (refer to Figure 4.3 above). Use Table 4.3 to outline your answers which will frame the discussion when you have your meeting with the CEO.

Table 4.3 Applying Weisbord's change model as a consultancy tool

External environment What are the key external factors impacting the company?	
Purpose What business are we in?	
Structure How do we divide up the work?	
Rewards Do all needed tasks have incentives?	
Helpful mechanisms Have we adequate coordination technologies?	
Relationships How do we manage conflict among people? How do we manage relationships with our technologies?	
Leadership Is someone keeping the six boxes in balance?	

Kotter's integrative model of organisational dynamics

Figure 4.4 presents Kotter's (1980) integrative model of organisational dynamics which is another systemic model that views the organisation as an open system and focuses on the dynamic relationships between its interconnected parts (or sub-systems) and their impact on key organisational processes.

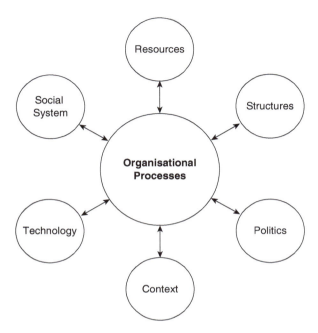

Figure 4.4 Kotter's (1980) integrative model of organisational dynamics

Source: Adapted from Kotter, J. P. (1980) 'An integrative model of organizational dynamics', in E. E. Lawler, D. A. Nadler and C. Cammann (eds), *Organizational Assessment: Perspectives on the Measurement of Organizational Behavior and the Quality of Work Life*. New York: Wiley, p. 282.

The centerpiece of Kotter's model is the key production processes of the organisation that have to do with the transformation of resource inputs (e.g. raw materials, energy, equipment, technologies, transportation, information, etc.) into desirable outputs (products, delivery, services, etc.). The model also highlights the sub-systems that have a direct input into the production process and significantly impact it – and which, starting from the top end of the model and moving clockwise, include:

Resources: such as buildings, machinery, employees, inventories and cash flows.

Structures: formal hierarchical configurations, division of functional activities, informal networks, collaborative partnerships, etc.

Politics: power relations, spheres of decision-making, coalitions and opposition groups, and sources of conflict and resistance to change.

Context: the immediate internal environment in which the production process and other related activities take place and the external environment which includes variables such as the political and economic climate, relevant legal frameworks, industry forces, social expectations and so on.

Technology: the technological applications upon which the organisation's core product and service are dependent.

Social system: the organisation's cultural value system, the nature of the employment relationship, and relational networks both within and external to the organisation.

Like all other systemic models, Kotter's model is multidimensional and non-linear. It emphasises the interconnectedness of the sub-systems described above and their combined causal effects on the organisation's production process – where such effects can be either positive or negative. Moreover, the organisational processes at the centre of the model can also 'act back on' the sub-systems and exert a causal influence over them – which is indicated by the double-sided arrows in the model. Importantly, this points to the dynamic nature of the complex web of causal relationships that underpin the organisation's production process and that can change over time – underlining, at the same time, the need to manage change on an on-going basis to maintain optimal levels of performance and productivity throughout the change process.

However, given the complexity of the causal relationships accounted for in Kotter's model, managing them effectively and maintaining a balance between the sub-systems identified therein remain a real challenge – especially where corrective measures in one sub-system can have a constraining effect on another sub-system – e.g. the adoption of a new technology to address a deficiency in the production process can serve the interests of dominant groups but lead to redundancy and a deterioration of the employment relationship. Hence, corrective action to enable system adaptation can have ramifications that are largely beyond the control of change agents – and which are difficult to predict however sophisticated and detailed the application of the model to its practical context. Moreover, it might be argued that the model does not place enough emphasis on the type of enabling leadership that is needed to manage organisations as complex systems and maintain a healthy balance between its sub-systems.

The Burke-Litwin causal model of organisational performance and change

Figure 4.5 presents the Burke-Litwin (1992) model of organisational performance and change which is one of the most comprehensive systemic models that has struck a chord with academics and practitioners alike. From an academic perspective, the model is informed by sound theory, empirical and extensive consultancy work that satisfy the important criteria of rigour and validity. From a practitioner perspective, the model is detailed and explicit but not to the point of being overwhelming and, as such, provides thorough yet clear parameters for an informed approach to change implementation. Its key features are considered in the following discussion.

As shown in Figure 4.5, the original Burke-Litwin model has been slightly modified (with the addition of a few labels in italics) to facilitate understanding of its key features discussed below.

Adopting a systems approach to organisational change

The Burke-Litwin model comprises 12 interrelated factors. As an open systems model, it locates the organisation within its wider context with which it has an exchange relationship – with *inputs* from the external environment (represented by the box at the top of the model) and *outputs* in terms of individual and organisational performance (represented by the box at the bottom of the model) which in turn 'act back on' the external environment (as highlighted by the feedback loops between the two boxes). The remaining 10 boxes represent the internal factors (or sub-systems) that have a causal influence on the process of converting inputs into outputs.

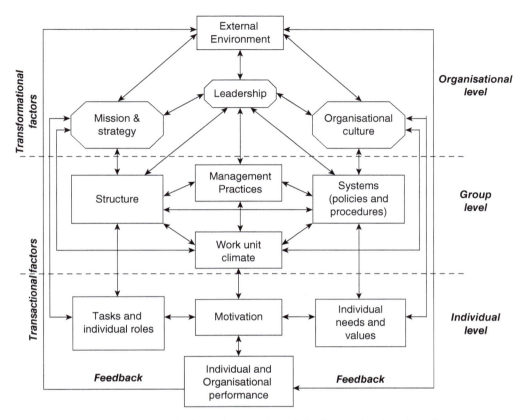

Figure 4.5 The Burke-Litwin (1992) causal model of organisational performance and change

Source: Adapted from Burke, W. W. and Litwin, G. H. (1992) 'A causal model of organizational performance and change', *Journal of Management*, 18(3), 523–545. https://carleton.ca/leader/knowledge-hub/wp-content/uploads/A-Causal-Model-of-Organizational-Performance-and-Change.pdf

Taking causality in the weighted direction

Unlike many change models (e.g. Weisbord's model considered above), the Burke-Litwin model goes beyond mere description to develop a rich 'causal complex' that underlies the transformation of change inputs into desirable outputs. This rich causal complex is formed by the 10 boxes representing the internal causal factors in Figure 4.5. As shown in the figure, these internal factors are linked by bi-directional arrows to show how they exert a mutual influence on each other. In this respect, the Burke-Litwin model addresses both the *what* and the *how* of causality – where, based on sound theory and reliable empirical evidence, it prioritises a set of the key causal factors impacting organisational change (*the what*) and maps out their casual links which underpin the achievement of the change goals and objectives (*the how*).

The Burke-Litwin model goes a step further in that, following the authors themselves, it takes causality in a 'weighted direction' (Burke and Litwin, 1992, p. 540) – it ascribes a greater weight to the causal factors at the top end of the model in comparison to those at the lower end. Thus, the external environment, mission and strategy, leadership and organisational culture are viewed as major factors which can have greater causal weight and greater influence on the performance outputs of the organisation.

Distinguishing between transformational and transactional factors

The factors at the upper end of the model are seen as 'transformational factors' because they underpin transformational change – which is needed when for example, disruptions or emerging challenges and opportunities in the external environment (e.g. new government regulations, increased competitive rivalry, technological breakthroughs or shifting customer demands) warrant a major change to the organisation's mission, strategy and culture, and call for completely new values and behaviours.

The remaining boxes below the transformational factors in the model have more to do with change of a transactional nature. They contain factors which are referred to by Burke and Litwin (1992) as *transactional variables* and which are associated with incremental change. These include: the current structural arrangements (hierarchies, functional divisions, working relationships), management practices (routine activities relating to supervision and motivation of subordinates), systems (policies and procedures, management information systems, HRM systems, etc.) and work unit climate (experiences, feelings and expectations of employees within local work units or functional areas) – all of which have a direct impact on individual employees' tasks and roles, motivation, and needs and values (Burke and Litwin, 1992). Thus, minor alterations or fine-tuning of such transactional variables are enough for small, gradual and continuous improvements without the necessity of any significant change to transformational factors such as the organisation's overall strategy and culture or prevailing leadership style.

Accounting for different types of learning

The distinction that is drawn in the Burke-Litwin model between transactional and transformational change variables also allows it to account for different types of learning. Transactional variables relate more to a type of learning which organisational learning theorists Argyris and Schön (1978) refer to as *single-loop learning*. This type of learning is focused on continuous improvement, where learners modify their behaviours and take action to solve problems or correct mistakes without addressing their root causes or making any significant change to existing practices. Thus, transactional variables in the Burke-Litwin model are mostly concerned with a type of learning that aims to improve existing practices and *doing things right* within the current mode of thinking (see also Hayes, 2021).

By contrast, changing the transformational variables in the Burke-Litwin model calls for another type of learning which is identified by Argyris and Schön (1978) as *double-loop learning*. This type of learning involves challenging and modifying prevailing beliefs and assumptions in order to identify and understand the causes underlying observed problems and concerns and take action that can radically change existing practices. Thus, transformational variables in the Burke-Litwin model are mostly concerned with a type of learning that enables change agents to *do different things* and establish new ways of thinking and doing things.

Allowing for a 'level-of-analysis' approach to change

As indicated by the dividing lines and the labels on the right-hand side of Figure 4.5, the Burke-Litwin model allows for three main levels of analysis, starting from the top: the organisational level, the group level and the individual level. At the organisational level, the Burke-Litwin model allows for an organisation-wide diagnosis of change requirements and importantly, the determination of whether the proposed change needs to be transformational or transactional. Analysis at group level is focused on the changes that have to be made across work units, functional areas and teams to align this level of organisational functioning to the new change strategy. At the individual level, the focus of the analysis is on the behaviours, knowledge and skills required of employees to perform well in their tasks and individual roles, their motivational and developmental needs, and on their personal values and interests – all of which have to be in sync with the cultural value system and strategic objectives of the change initiative.

The Burke-Litwin model is unquestionably a much stronger model than the others considered in this chapter – in that it is rooted in sound theory and solid evidence and has a high explanatory power which allows for an in-depth understanding of the causal relationships underlying the change process. However, the complex causal web that it allows change agents to create, can quickly become overly complicated, creating a barrier to swift action which is often a key determinant of change success. Moreover, Burke and Litwin (1992) lay claim to the predictive capability of their model. But there is a big difference between enabling an understanding of the causal relationships that underpin a change process and allowing for a forecast of their outcomes, whether in the immediate or distant future – even more so in the global business context which is fluid, fast-paced and increasingly unpredictable.

Finally, it is important to underline the fact that the range of change models covered in this chapter is by no means exhaustive. There are many other models with their own merits and limitations that change agents can find useful and more applicable to their particular change situations. The main criteria behind their selection include: (i) the extent to which they are representative of the main types of models prevalent in the change literature (whether linear or systemic, causal or descriptive, prescriptive or analytic, etc.) and (ii) the extent to which they are theoretically grounded, evidence-based and committed to practical outcomes.

PRACTICAL EXERCISE

Comparative analysis of change models

This exercise will allow you to consolidate your understanding of the change models covered in this chapter. Having read this section of the chapter and taken relevant notes, complete Table 4.4, noting down only keywords or key points in each cell. Once you have completed your analysis, discuss your main findings with your fellow students.

(Continued)

Table 4.4 Comparative analysis of change models

Change model	Type	Key elements	Strengths	Limitations
Lewin				
Kirkpatrick				
Weisbord				
Kotter				
Burke-Litwin				

There are many other change models that, for the sake of brevity, were not included in the critical review carried out here. Go online and find out more about other popular change models which resonate with practitioners, for example:

McKinsey 7S model
Nadler and Tushman congruence model
ADKAR model of change
Boston Consulting Group Change Delta model

Questions

1 How would you describe the type of each of the models you have researched?
2 How do they compare with the models covered in this chapter?

4.5 Conceptual nugget: The superior value of systemic models

In line with one of the conceptual pillars underpinning this textbook, we reiterate and reinforce the 'superior value' of systemic change models and distil their key features in simple terms as our 'take away message' for this chapter – as highlighted in Figure 4.6.

Holistic

Systemic models are *holistic* in that they allow change leaders to look at the change situation as a whole and develop a rich understanding of the different parts of which this whole is made up.

Importantly, systemic models show how these different parts are interconnected and how their combined effects can potentially generate outcomes that are far greater than the sum of the separate effect of each individual part.

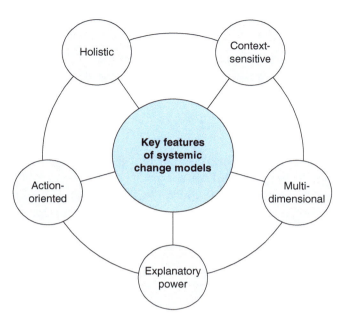

Figure 4.6 Key features of systemic models

Context-sensitive

Systemic models are context-sensitive in that they not only cast a light on the 'inner working' of the different components that account for the internal context of the organisation but also locate the organisation within the external context with which it interacts and can have a mutually shaping exchange relationship.

Multidimensional

Like Kotter's integrative model of organisational dynamics, systems models can accommodate multiple dimensions, perspectives and interests that distinguish them from one-dimensional, linear models. As such, they bring under a single conceptual framework the multiple dimensions – political, cultural, structural, social, technological, developmental, motivational, etc. – that can have a significant impact on the change outcomes.

Explanatory power

Systemic models have a high explanatory power. As exemplified by the Burke-Litwin model, they can be used to map out the dynamic relationships between the interconnected parts of a changing organisation and allow for a robust understanding of the complex web of causal relationships underlying the change process and its intended outcomes.

Action-oriented

Systemic models are action-oriented as they are meaning-rich and can be used to frame informed courses of action geared towards the achievement of change objectives – as will be demonstrated in the end-of-chapter case study.

4.7　Key learning points

1　A plethora of theories have informed organisational change management and modelling. Some of the most widely recognised theories that have been covered in this chapter include *field, system, process, communication, motivation, leadership, culture and contingency* theories which provide the building blocks for the development of change models and carry valuable principles and precepts for the effective design and execution of change initiatives.

2　A good change model allows for *an accurate representation of the change situation*, a *sound analysis of key change variables* at play within the change situation, a *holistic approach* to change design and implementation, and the provision of a solid platform for action geared towards practical outcomes.

3　*Linear* models of change tend to portray organisational change as a *neat, step-by-step or sequential* process which can be useful for planned, management-led change. Examples include the *Kirkpatrick's model of organisational change* and *Kotter's eight-step checklist for leading change*. On the other hand, systemic change models enable a holistic, multidimensional and context-sensitive approach to organisational change that accounts for its complexity and specificity. They have a high explanatory power, allowing for a robust analysis of the dynamic causal relationships that can have a significant impact on the change process and its intended outcomes.

4　Our conceptual nugget for this chapter has drawn attention to the *superior value of systemic models* in enabling a more informed and robust approach to organisational change. Systemic models are holistic, context-sensitive, multidimensional, action-oriented and have a high explanatory power. Examples include *Weisbord's six-box model of organisational change, Kotter's integrative model of organisational dynamics*, and *Burke-Litwin's causal model of organisational performance and change*.

—END-OF-CHAPTER CASE STUDY 4.3—

Sheraton Edinburgh: Applying the Burke-Litwin model to mitigate the impact of COVID-19

Author: Dr Indravidoushi Chandraprema Dusoye

Introduction

The hospitality industry has been hit hard by the COVID-19 pandemic and it is only now that the World Tourism Organisation (WTO) has recorded the first signs of a gradual recovery. In the UK, the government has confirmed the slow recovery of the hospitality industry but has issued a warning regarding the need to proactively find ways to mitigate the persistent effects of the pandemic and bring the whole industry back on track. Sheraton Edinburgh is a 5-star luxury spa hotel that has left no stone unturned to implement a fast recovery strategy to meet the challenges trailing in the wake of COVID-19, increase its resilience and ensure business continuity and sustainable growth in the longer term.

Bringing the Burke-Litwin model into play

To implement the recovery strategy, senior management decided to bring the Burke-Litwin model of organisational change into play as it was felt that, as an open system and causal model, it could enable a holistic and context-sensitive understanding of the hotel's post COVID-19 change situation and an identification of the key causal factors and variables that could rebuild and drive Sheraton Edinburgh forward. The main purpose of this exercise was not to dwell on the negative effects of the pandemic but to put a positive spin on the current

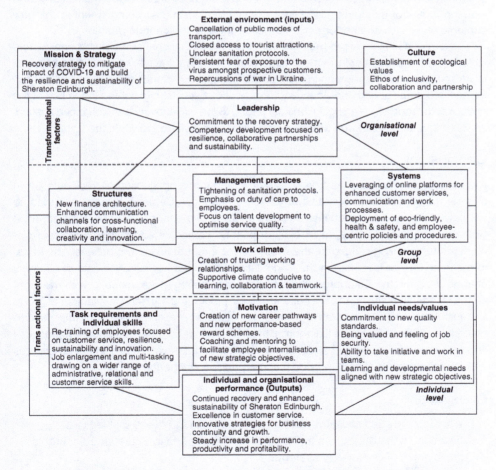

Figure 4.7 Application of the Burke-Litwin model to Sheraton Edinburgh

(Continued)

situation to foreground the key interdependent, mutually reinforcing causal factors and the coordinated courses of action that could effectively translate the intended recovery strategy into practice. Figure 4.7 provides a cursory overview of the key issues and concerns arising from the application of the Burke-Litwin model to Sheraton Edinburgh's change situation.

At the *organisational level* (located at the top end of the figure), it was important to achieve a strict alignment between the transformational factors as key determinants of the strategic change initiative. The new mission and strategy to mitigate the impact of COVID-19 and build the resilience and sustainability of the hotel warranted a committed, competent and empowering type of leadership and the establishment of cultural values marked by an ethos of inclusivity, collaboration and partnership.

At the *group level*, there was need for new structural arrangements, a recalibration of management practices, the development of new IT systems, policies and procedures, and the creation of a supportive work climate to enable a concerted approach to the practical implementation of the recovery strategy. At the *individual level*, the focus was on a re-definition of task requirements and individual skills, addressing the motivational and learning needs of employees, and finding ways to sustain their commitment to the new strategic objectives and performance levels throughout the change process.

The aim of all the changes made to both the transformational and transactional factors included in the Burke-Litwin model was to transform the negative inputs arising from the COVID-19 situation (highlighted in the inputs box at the top of the model) into positive performance outputs at both individual and organisational levels (highlighted in the box at the bottom of the model) – leading, in the near future, to the full recovery and enhanced sustainability of Sheraton Edinburgh whilst ensuring its continuity and growth in the longer term.

Conclusions

A number of key issues arise from Sheraton Edinburgh's application of the Burke-Litwin change model. First, the Burke-Litwin change model can be used as a powerful tool to not only allow for a comprehensive causal analysis of a change situation but also, as in Sheraton Edinburgh's case, to map out a positive course of action to effectively implement strategic change. Second, there is need for a robust alignment between the transformational factors identified in the Burke-Litwin model as key determinants of strategic change. At Sheraton Edinburgh, the new recovery strategy was matched with the 'right type' of leadership style and core cultural values. Finally, the transactional factors at group and individual levels should also be mutually reinforcing and derived from the transformational factors. At Sheraton Edinburgh, the new work structures, management practices and systems were all geared towards the learning and motivational needs of employees and the optimisation of both individual and organisational performance.

Questions

1   What were the key causal variables associated with COVID-19 that led to a downturn in the UK tourism and hospitality industry and to Sheraton Edinburgh's deployment of its recovery strategy?

2 Why was it important for change leaders to first sort out and align the transformational factors before making changes to the transactional factors identified in the Burke-Litwin model?

3 What evaluative measures could be employed to assess the intended performance outputs at both individual and organisational levels? (Refer to the box at the bottom end of model).

4.8 Independent learning

To consolidate your learning of the key dimensions and factors of the change models covered in this chapter, watch the following clips on YouTube. These will help you appreciate both their theoretical foundations and practical value.

Lewin's 3-Stage Model of Change: Unfreezing, Changing & Refreezing: www.youtube.com/watch?v=kerDFvln7hU&t=222s
Weisbord's Six Box Model: www.youtube.com/watch?v=X1QAFHzABgQ
What is John Kotter's 8-Step Change Process?: www.youtube.com/watch?v=e1VDmj1bFFY
Change Model: Burke-Litwin: www.youtube.com/watch?v=c92YT92uFvs

4.9 References

Argyris, C. and Schön, D. A. (1978) *Organizational Learning: A Theory of Action Perspective*. Reading, MA: Addison-Wesley.

Bonini, C. P. (1963) *Simulation of Information and Decision Systems in the Firm*, Englewood Cliffs, NJ: Prentice-Hall.

Box, G. E. P. (1979) 'Robustness in the strategy of scientific model building', in R. L. Launer and G. N. Wilkinson (eds), *Robustness in Statistics*. New York: Academic Press, pp. 201–236.

Burke, W. W. and Litwin, G. H. (1992) 'A causal model of organizational performance and change', *Journal of Management*, 18(3). [Online] Available at: https://carleton.ca/leader/knowledge-hub/wp-content/uploads/A-Causal-Model-of-Organizational-Performance-and-Change.pdf (accessed 1 November 2022).

Burnes, B. (2004) 'Kurt Lewin and the planned approach to change: A re-appraisal', *Journal of Management Studies*, 41(6), 977–1002.

Burnes, B. (2020) 'The origins of Lewin's Three-Step Model of Change', *The Journal of Applied Behavioral Science*, 56(1), 32–59. [Online] Available at: https://doi.org/10.1177/0021886319892685 (accessed 7 November 2022).

D'Annunzio-Green, N. and Ramdhony, A. (2019) 'It's not what you do; it's the way you do it: An exploratory study of talent management as an inherently motivational process in the hospitality sector', *International Journal of Contemporary Hospitality Management*, 31 (10), 3992-4020.

Dutton, J. M. and Starbuck, W. H. (1971) *Computer Simulation of Human Behavior*. New York: Wiley.

Harikkala-Laihinen, R. (2022) 'Managing positive change: Emotions and communication following acquisitions', *Journal of Change Management*, 22(4), 373–400.

Hayes, J. (2021) *The Theory and Practice of Change Management*, 6th edn. London: Red Globe Press.

Hendry, C. (1996) 'Understanding and creating whole organisational change through learning theory', *Human Relations*, 48(5), 621–641.

Hughes, J. M. (1981) 'Theory v. practice: Bridging the gap', *Education + Training*, 23(7), 198–202.

Hussain, S. T., Lei, S., Akram, T., Haider, M. J., Hussain, S. H. and Ali, M. (2018) 'Kurt Lewin's change model: A critical review of the role of leadership and employee involvement in organizational change', *Journal of Innovation & Knowledge*, 3(3), 123–127.

Kirkpatrick, D. L. (2001) *Managing Change Effectively: Approaches, Methods and Case Examples*. Boston: Butterworth-Heinemann.

Kotter, J. P. (1980) 'An integrative model of organizational dynamics', in E. E. Lawler, D. A. Nadler and C. Cammann (eds), *Organizational Assessment: Perspectives on the Measurement of Organizational Behavior and the Quality of Work Life*. New York: Wiley, p. 282.

Kotter, J. P. (1996) *Leading Change*. Boston, MA: Harvard Business Review Press.

Kotter, J. P. (2012) *Leading Change*, 2nd edn. Boston, MA: Harvard Business Review Press.

Krakatau Steel (2021) *Explore to Empower: Company Profile*. [Online] Available at: www.krakatausteel.com/pdf/Laporan%20Tahunan%202021.pdf (accessed 8 March 2023).

Lewin, K. (1947) 'Frontiers in group dynamics: Concept, method and reality in social science; equilibrium and social change', *Human Relations*, 1(1), 5–41.

Mele, C., Pels, J. and Polese, F. (2010) 'A brief review of Systems Theories and their managerial applications', *Service Science*, 2(1–2), 126–135.

Niederman, F. (2021) 'Process theory: Background, opportunity, and challenges', *Foundations and Trends in Information Systems*, 5(1–2), 1–230.

Northouse, P. G. (2013) *Leadership: Theory and Practice*, 6th edn. Thousand Oaks, CA: Sage Publications.

Razdan, R. (2021) *Breathing New Life into a Struggling Giant: An Interview with Krakatau Steel's Silmy Karim*. [Online] Available at: www.mckinsey.com/industries/metals-and-mining/our-insights/
breathing-new-life-into-a-struggling-giant-an-interview-with-krakatau-steels-silmy-karim (accessed 9 March 2023).

Ryan, R. M. and Deci, E. L. (2000) 'Intrinsic and extrinsic motivations: Classic definitions and new directions', *Contemporary Educational Psychology*, 25(1), 54–67.

Schein, E. H. (1992) *Organizational Culture and Leadership*, 2nd edn. San Francisco, CA: JosseyBass.

Sivaruban, S. (2021) 'A critical perspective of leadership theories', *Business Ethics and Leadership*, 5(1), 57–65. [Online] Available at: https://armgpublishing.com/wp-content/uploads/2021/04/Sivanathan_Sivaruban_BEL_1__2021.pdf (accessed 28 February 2023).

Weisbord, M. R. (1976) 'Organizational diagnosis: Six places to look for trouble with or without a theory', *Group and Organization Studies*, 1(4), 430–447.

PART II

A DIALOGIC APPROACH TO CHANGE

5

REACTIONS TO CHANGE

Learning Outcomes

After completing this chapter, you should be able to:

- Gain an insight into the psycho-social factors underlying human reactions to change and appreciate the challenges involved in managing them.
- Consider the main types of human reactions to organisational change.
- Apply models of human reactions to change as sensitising tools to effectively manage employee reactions throughout the change process.
- Explain the meaning of resistance to change and consider its various types and underlying causes.
- Develop an understanding of the role of language and social interaction in shaping resistive conversations and behaviours.
- Discuss the conditions for effectively managing resistance to change as 'dialogic practice'.

5.1 Introduction

The aim of this chapter is to enable you to gain some valuable insights into the key factors underlying human reactions to change and to provide you with the opportunity to apply a range of change tools to effectively manage them. The chapter begins with a discussion of the psycho-social factors influencing human reactions to change, drawing attention to their dynamic nature and the difficulty involved in managing them. The chapter moves on to consider a couple of models of human reactions to change and show how these can be used as sensitising tools to effectively manage employee reactions throughout the change process. It then explains the meaning of resistance to change which is a particular concern of change managers before considering its various types and underlying causes. The chapter devotes some space to consider the notion of resistance to change as a social systemic phenomenon, focusing on the role of language and social interaction in shaping negative background conversations, and resistive attitudes and behaviours. In the final section of the chapter, we present our conceptual nugget which entails the development of a model and an argument in favour of managing resistance to change as 'dialogic practice'. The chapter concludes with an outline of the key learning points before presenting the end-of-chapter case study which focuses on employee reactions to leadership and culture change in a German-based multinational chemical and consumer goods company.

5.2 The psycho-social factors underlying human reactions to change

It is an undisputed fact that different people react differently to change. Is it because of the difference in people? Or is it because of the difference in the social circumstances in which change happens?

Psychological factors

The difference in people is often explained with reference to their individual psychological dispositions. Some people seem to have a 'natural tendency' for change and are generally seen as 'change-ready'. They tend to embrace things that are new and different because they are either easily bored or simply do not like the feeling of being locked into the routine of having to do the same things over and over again. This is why they are constantly on the lookout for new experiences and challenges from which they derive an on-going sense of purpose and intrinsic reward. By contrast, some people are naturally resistant to change and come across as 'change-averse'. They tend to shun away from everything that challenges them to step out of their comfort zone and break away from the routine of their personal and working life. They find it hard to experiment with new things or deal with new situations that they perceive as posing a threat to their physical, mental or emotional well-being (Straatmann et al., 2016).

Social factors

However, the difference in the social circumstances in which change happens should not be underestimated. Since human beings do not evolve in a social vacuum, the immediate socio-cultural environment in which they live and work can have a significant influence on their reactions to change (Burnes, 2014). We can think of a multitude of causal factors such as cultural values, parenting style, peer-pressure, prevailing moral principles and social norms that can serve to either foster or deter a person's disposition towards change. For example, a person 'indoctrinated' by their parents or close relatives in the traditional way of running a family business might not be too amenable to change despite all the indicators in the external environment pointing to the need for an urgent overhaul of their business model. On the other hand, an individual 'educated' in the importance of embracing change as a means of business survival, economic growth and improvement in the standard of living would be much more entrepreneurial and amenable to change, even to that of a more radical or transformational type.

Therefore, the type of immediate socio-cultural environment can be a key determinant of the extent to which people are *change-averse* or *change-ready*. Environments which nurture change aversion are typified by conservative beliefs and values which endorse a view of change as something to be avoided or of last resort. They tend to perpetuate a mode of compliance to the current ways of thinking and doing things. They are characterised by a lack of resources, structures and relationships that can open up opportunities for change.

In marked contrast, environments that are conducive to change readiness are typified by progressive beliefs and values which promote a view of change as something to be embraced. They tend to promote a mode of non-conformity to current ways of thinking and doing things. They are characterised by the availability of enabling resources, structures and relationships that can effectively frame talk and action geared towards sustainable change (Endrejat et al., 2020).

A combination of psychological dispositions and socio-cultural factors

In considering the psychological and social factors underlying human reactions to change, we are inevitably drawn into the longstanding *nature v. nurture* debate which very often creates more questions than answers. Perhaps more realistically, we need to navigate a middle ground to recognise the fact that the way people react to change is dependent on *both their natural psychological disposition and the nurturing socio-cultural factors* to which they are exposed over the course of their personal and working life. However, these two variables are intertwined and difficult to disentangle in reality. This makes it quite hard to determine the weight of their respective influence or the extent to which they are mutually reinforcing or counteracting. It is still fairly safe to state that, given the intricate combinations of psycho-social factors that underlie human behaviour, *different people in different circumstances can react differently to change*.

The dynamic nature of human reactions to change

However, while different people differ in the way they react to different change situations, their reactions to change are not fixed or frozen in time (Vakola, 2016). All too often, typologies of human reactions to change are pigeon-holed into fixed categories such as positive, negative or neutral. In this book, we entertain a view of human reactions as dynamic and subject to change as is the world around them. People's reactions can and do change over time together with the situation in which change unravels. For example, an initially negative reaction to change can either reaffirm itself or mutate into a more positive one – depending on the way the change initiative is managed over time. A shift towards more positive reactions to change could, for instance, be the result of a re-adjustment of the communication strategy to dispel any misunderstanding over the motives driving change and to clarify its potential benefits. But the important point we are trying to make here is this: *there would be no sense in managing human reactions to change if such reactions were fixed*.

The challenges of managing reactions to change

Managing reactions to change is easier said than done. There is no recipe for this vital dimension of change management. It is not surprising that organisations continue to struggle to translate into practice the recommendations of change experts and consultants that emphasise the need to 'get that part of organisational change right'. One would think that by now organisations would have learnt from their past failures and should be adept at managing the reactions of their key stakeholders. But, as mentioned above, the fact remains that human reactions to change are influenced by a complex web of psycho-social factors that can vary significantly across individuals, groups and functional areas – leading to unpredictable outcomes that often lie beyond the reach and control of change agents (Wang and Kebede, 2020).

This does not mean that organisations can waive the need for an informed approach to managing reactions to change without which the chances for change success would be alarmingly slim. Change agents can employ a range of tools and techniques to:

- Identify various types of reactions to change
- Help people cope with change
- Manage resistance to change

These key issues and concerns form the basis of the discussion in the following key sections of this chapter.

---REFLECTIVE EXERCISE---

Once again, skim through the above section and answer the following questions:

1 What are the key factors influencing human reactions to change?
2 Why are human reactions difficult to manage?

5.3 Types of reactions to change

Kirkpatrick's typology of reactions to change

Kirkpatrick (2001) has developed one of the most popular frameworks for identifying reactions to change. He conducted his research at the then *Sears Roebuck*, once the largest retailer in the world that is now in dire straits as a result of increased competition following a series of poor strategic choices compounded by the financial impact of the Coronavirus pandemic (McDowell and Hartmans, 2022). Kirkpatrick's (2001) research is seminal in that it is an early foray into the psycho-social factors impacting people's reactions within the context of organisational change and sets the scene for later developments in the area. He was particularly interested in understanding how employees would react to the sudden change when *Sears Roebuck*, at the peak of its success, decided to relocate all their staff from their out-of-town site to their new quarters in central Chicago, which was at the time the tallest building in the world.

Kirkpatrick provides some valuable insights into the psyche of the individual who tends to resort to a form of calculating rationality when faced with the prospect of inevitable change, harking back to the 'bottom line' question: *what's in it for me?* Kirkpatrick soon found out that individual reactions to change were dependent on the extent to which employees felt they had something to gain or lose from it.

Some employees were enthusiastic about the move to a more central and prestigious building because they felt they would gain from the change in terms of improved working conditions, higher status and even such things as lunchtime shopping. Those employees who were unhappy about the change felt that they were about to lose out on things that were of importance to them, even if such things could have been of particular importance to management: privacy and personal contact with colleagues, travelling costs, a sense of job security and work identity. Still, there was another clearly identifiable group of employees who had mixed feelings about the impending change. For example, they favoured improved working conditions and the prospect of lunchtime shopping but were not so happy about the extra travelling costs for commuting to the city centre or the lack of privacy resulting from the move to more formal and more scrutinised ways of working.

Three basic types of reactions to change

Kirkpatrick distilled his research findings into his now famous typology of three basic reactions to change:

- *Positive Reactions* – when people believe they can gain something from the change.
- *Negative Reactions* – when people believe they can lose something from the change.
- *Mixed Reactions* – when people have mixed feelings or are neutral about the change because they believe that the gains and losses balance out.

The dynamic nature of Kirkpatrick's typology of human reactions to change

We build on Kirkpatrick's typology to reinforce our previous point regarding the dynamic nature of human reactions to change and to explain how people's reactions to change can (and usually do) evolve over time as illustrated in Figure 5.1 below.

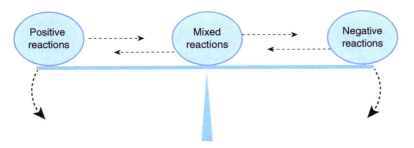

Figure 5.1 Highlighting the dynamic nature of Kirkpatrick's basic types of reactions to change

An initially positive reaction to change (perhaps because of the potential benefits that were effectively 'sold' to employees) can shift towards the opposite pole with a growing perception that 'management talk' about such benefits was just designed to thwart early employee resistance and fast track the change implementation. Conversely, an initially negative reaction to change (perhaps resulting from a misunderstanding of the proposed change) can gravitate towards the positive side following clarification of the change project and its intended benefits. Mixed feelings could tip the balance towards either side of the scale depending on a number of variables which can be hard to manage – e.g. increasing employee mistrust in management leading to mostly negative reactions to the change project or a growing realisation of its value tending towards more positive reactions and a greater employee endorsement of the change goals and objectives.

Using Kirkpatrick's model as a sensitising tool

Importantly, Kirkpatrick's typology can be used as a valuable 'sensitising tool' for managing human reactions to change in an organisational setting in that it:

- allows for a quick and early identification of the 'waves of employee reactions' to change which can have significant impact on the momentum and future course of change projects;
- draws attention to the need to manage reactions to change as an on-going process, given their dynamic and evolving nature;
- can provide a sense of direction and trigger thinking about ways to tip the balance towards more positive reactions throughout the change process;
- can be used to gauge the reactions of employees and other key stakeholders at different levels of analysis: individual, group, or organisational.

The following practical exercise will give you a feel for how you can use Kirkpatrick's typology of reactions to change as a crude but valuable sensitising device at group level.

PRACTICAL EXERCISE

Monitoring reactions to change

Think about a change initiative you have been involved in or witnessed in an organisation with which you are familiar and answer the following questions:

1   What were the initial reactions to the change initiative?
2   How did these reactions evolve over time?

Use Table 5.1 to map out the reactions you have experienced or identified across job categories, using the + sign for positive reactions, the – sign for negative reactions and the letter m for mixed feelings. You can also account for the intensity of those reactions over time by increasing or decreasing the number of signs used as shown in the table.

Table 5.1 Monitoring reactions to change

Job Category	Short-Term	Mid-Term	Long-Term
A	--	---	---
B	--	m	+
C	m	m	++

5.4 The coping cycle

Probing individual responses to change

Another sensitising tool that change agents can use for a deep probing of reactions to change is the coping cycle. It originates from the work of Swiss psychiatrist, Elizabeth Kübler-Ross who found that terminally ill persons or those facing bereavement went through a discernible pattern of psychological responses. Although the coping cycle has been modified and elaborated by many other authors (Carnall, 2003; Scott and Jaffe, 2006), we choose to present it in its simplest form to offer a clear baseline for explaining its key stages – as shown in Figure 5.2.

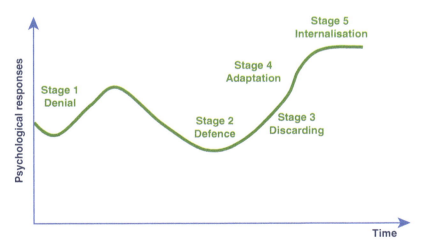

Figure 5.2 A basic version of the coping cycle

As can be seen in Figure 5.2, the coping cycle is a stage model that charts the psychological responses which an individual typically displays when going through a series of transitions in the context of change. The psychological responses or state of mind highlighted at each stage of the cycle can be considered as strong, deep-seated feelings or emotions flowing from a person's mood or state of mind as they cope with the change process. Each stage is briefly described below with the focus on organisational change for the sake of brevity and clarity.

Stage 1: Denial

Denial is a barely visible yet strong emotional response where a person consciously ignores or 'turns a blind eye' to what is happening in their immediate external environment and pretends that it is of little or no consequence to them. In an organisational setting, this can mean carrying on with things as usual and *refusing to come to terms* with the inevitability and implications of impending change. The possible reasons for denial include an initial state of shock leaving the person stunned and unable to pick up the courage to consider ways to cope with the change which might have been experienced as too 'sudden'. It can also result from a natural fear of the unknown – where, for example, a person is overwhelmed by the uncertainties thrown up by the change and finds it hard to think rationally about the meaning of such change – especially in terms of the new behaviours and commitments that will be required of them and the impact on their personal and work life. There is no set time frame for denial or any other stage of the coping cycle. A person might quickly move from one stage to another or become 'stuck' in a particular stage for an indefinite length of time. If left unattended, denial will generally pave the way for the next stage which is defence.

Stage 2: Defence

Defence involves a mechanism which aims to protect or shield oneself from something that is perceived as unfair, reprehensible or even potentially harmful – and thus morally if not legally unacceptable. Defence can manifest itself in many ways of which indifference, anger and depression are the most common.

Indifference is a willful attempt to ignore or feign a lack of interest in the change or the people leading the change – which can close off all channels of communication and delay constructive dialogue around the meaning and real intent of the change initiative.

Anger is a much stronger emotional response with varying levels of visibility. A change situation can result in repressed anger with a low level of visibility. For example, staff at the bottom of the organisational hierarchy with little or no say in the change programme might feel that they are disrespected and shown utter contempt by managers driving the change from the top. Still, they might have no other choice than to suppress their resentment and frustration and keep on doing their job for fear of losing it.

However, anger can be much more visible and expressed in more explicit ways depending on its level of intensity and the perceived gravity of its causes. For example, an action by change agents could be judged by most employees as particularly callous, morally reprehensible, in clear violation of their psychological contract (a set of subjective, unwritten expectations between an employee and their employer) and deserving of condemnation. This might in turn lead to intense feelings of indignation and fury expressed in the form of verbal altercations, strike action and, in some cases, even violent confrontation.

As a form of defence, people can slip into *depression* as a means of closing off or withdrawing themselves from a situation which they find impossible to grapple with in their current state of mind. Depression can involve an unsettling mix of negative feelings such as sadness, anxiety, loneliness, dejection, a sense of loss and disinterest in the new reality brought about by the change. Some people might never recover from this and would be left with no other option than to remove themselves from the change situation. However, as suggested by some experts, depression can also open up a mental space for 'looking inwards' and for deep reflection on how to let go of the past, reorganise one's own life and adjust to the new change situation – which overlaps the next stage in the coping cycle discussed below.

Stage 3: Discarding

As people recognise the inevitability of change, they may move on to the next stage: *discarding*, which involves a tension between the past, the present and the future. This is where they begin to reflect upon how they need to let go of the past, how to accept the new organisational reality, and how they can look forward to the future, however uncertain it might be.

Letting go of the past is mostly about deciding which routines or ways of working will have to be abandoned. For example, a relocation of the workplace might entail abandoning one's initial work–life pattern to accommodate new commuting times.

Accepting the present may mean figuring out what must be done to fit into a new role warranted by the change initiative. This usually entails some form of bargaining to come to an agreement over *what's in it for me* and *for the organisation* – and can include the following: the clarification of new roles and responsibilities, negotiation relating to new pay scales and access to necessary resources, and reaching consensus on realistic target dates for completion of key deliverables and the achievement of change objectives.

Finally, *looking forward to the future* carries a positive slant – where employees begin to think about ways to further adapt to the new organisational reality and consider possibilities for learning and opening up career pathways.

Stage 4: Adaptation

Adaptation can be seen as the process of *enacting one's change resolutions* and plans to achieve a better fit with the new organisational reality. It involves a period of learning new things, testing and trial and error whereby employees can grow into their new roles. This is a time when employees need to gain access to adequate resources, build trusting relationships to facilitate their learning, and raise their levels of confidence and self-efficacy to enhance their performance in the discharge of their new responsibilities. Facilitation of the adaptation process can include formal and on-the-job training, coaching and mentoring, teamwork and communities of practice geared towards the effective achievement of change objectives.

Stage 5: Internalisation

This final stage in the coping cycle is internalisation. This involves *a process of regulation* through which individuals integrate the new objectives and values of the changing organisation and bring these into alignment with their own values and interests. As they make greater sense of the meaning of the change and of their role in it, they become more intrinsically motivated to further their learning and development and to experiment with new ways of working – which are seen as the 'new normal' and as inherently valuable and satisfying. With continuous support and encouragement, the process of internalisation can have a positive impact on employees' identification with the change programme, commitment to the organisation, and willingness to contribute to change success.

Practical application of the coping cycle: A few caveats

While the coping cycle can be a valuable tool for identifying and empathising with people's feelings and personal challenges as they go through the process of change, it has its limitations and some caveats are in order regarding its practical application. These are briefly addressed below.

It is not a definitive model

The coping cycle does not always follow a neat sequence and the naming of its key stages are not fixed in stone. Many other authors have identified additional stages and used different labels for a more nuanced understanding of the emotions that people go through when experiencing change. In any case, emotional responses can overlap the boundaries of each stage of the coping cycle – where, for instance, a person in denial can also be simultaneously experiencing a lot of anger.

Individuals do not always progress along the cycle in a linear fashion

Not all individuals have to progress through the coping cycle in a step-by-step manner as mapped out in the model. Some individuals can get 'stuck' at one particular stage. For example, a person can dwell in the 'defence stage' for so long that they are not able to cope with their negative feelings leading to their exit of the change situation. Others can regress to previous stages – as in the case of an individual at the discarding stage who slips back into the denial or defence stage due to unforeseen issues in their personal life such as serious illness or the loss of a loved one. By contrast, a person can leap forward in the cycle to the adaptation or internalisation stages because they are themselves leading the change or have a lot to gain from it. In short, each individual moves along the coping cycle at their own pace and the direction of that movement is not pre-determined.

Change agents also have to go through the coping cycle

Change agents also have to grapple with their own emotions when leading change and tackling the challenges associated with it. The responsibility to be introspective and positively cope with their own thoughts and feelings is compounded by the need to facilitate the progress of others as they journey along the coping cycle. This is no small feat. For, as representatives of the organisation, they often have to take on a 'buffering role' – especially during the initial stages of the coping cycle – to 'absorb' the negative feelings of employees and lessen their impact on the momentum of change. Such a heavy responsibility can be emotionally draining and counter-productive and calls into question the feasibility of applying the coping cycle, particularly in big organisations where change managers are responsible for a large number of direct reports.

The coping cycle is not readily generalisable

The coping cycle is used to identify and probe responses to change at an individual level. Such responses are therefore subjective and unique to the individual. Moreover, each person can move along the coping cycle at their own pace and in their own particular way. Therefore, it is practically impossible to generalise the findings of the coping cycle to the wider organisation or even to the functional groups within it. However, we believe that, through comparative analysis of individual responses, the coping cycle can allow for a broad-brush understanding of the general mood and patterns of psychological responses at key milestones of the change process.

The coping cycle is not a tried-and-tested tool

Finally, the coping cycle is not a tried-and-tested and refined managerial tool. However, the coping cycle can be used to investigate the mutual relationships between individual psychological responses at each of its stages and identify other variables which can impact change success and which are of particular interest to change agents. These variables can include motivation, commitment, job engagement, performance, etc. and can be explored either

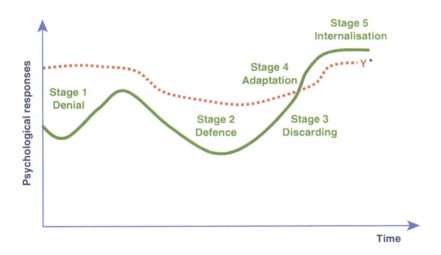

* Y can stand for any change-related variable of interest such as motivation, commitment, performance, etc.

Figure 5.3 Mapping out stages of the coping cycle against key change-related variables

qualitatively or operationalised to enable quantitative snapshot surveys. Figure 5.3 is an illustration of how individual psychological responses might be plotted against other important change-related variables over a set timeframe.

Applying the coping cycle to monitor performance

The following exercise demonstrates how you can apply the coping cycle to manage one of the variables that is represented by the **Y** curve in Figure 5.3. First, read the mini scenario below.

Your organisation has embarked on a major change programme that involves the automation of its production process. This means that a significant number of employees will have to be made redundant while those remaining will have to undergo special training to be able to work on the new production system.

1 As a change manager, how can you use the coping cycle to appraise the performance of employees as they engage with the new production system?

To help you answer this question, we have highlighted along the coping cycle the key issues you will need to consider – as shown in Figure 5.4.

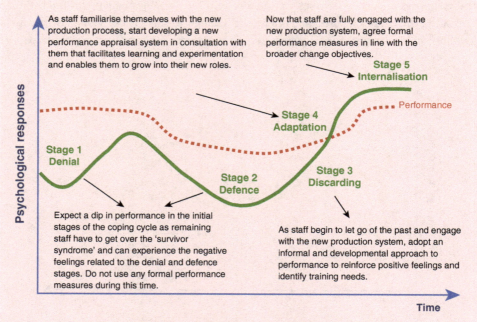

As staff familiarise themselves with the new production process, start developing a new performance appraisal system in consultation with them that facilitates learning and experimentation and enables them to grow into their new roles.

Now that staff are fully engaged with the new production system, agree formal performance measures in line with the broader change objectives.

Stage 5 Internalisation

Performance

Stage 4 Adaptation

Stage 1 Denial

Stage 2 Defence

Stage 3 Discarding

Psychological responses

Expect a dip in performance in the initial stages of the coping cycle as remaining staff have to get over the 'survivor syndrome' and can experience the negative feelings related to the denial and defence stages. Do not use any formal performance measures during this time.

As staff begin to let go of the past and engage with the new production system, adopt an informal and developmental approach to performance to reinforce positive feelings and identify training needs.

Time

Figure 5.4 Application of the coping cycle to monitor performance

5.5 Resistance to change

Meaning of resistance to change

Resistance is usually seen as a negative type of reaction to change and is of particular concern to change agents. However, one of the main points we will develop in this section is that *resistance is not necessarily a bad thing or something to be eliminated or overcome at all costs*. Drawing on the Cambridge dictionary, we use a baseline definition of resistance here as a refusal to accept the terms of a change initiative or an opposing force that acts to either slow down or even stop the flow of change – with the implication that it can have adverse effects on the implementation and intended outcomes of change projects. From this angle, it is understandable why resistance is so much dreaded by change leaders and why 'resistors' are often dismissed as senseless detractors or irresponsible agents that pose a threat to the survival, well-being and sustainability of the organisation (Amarantou et al., 2018).

Such a one-sided and negative view of resistance to change provides the legitimacy for a hard-nosed approach to managing it and for an indiscriminate clampdown on all its forms without much consideration to the underlying causes. Whether outright hostility to all forms of resistance is an expression of an autocratic and repressive approach to change management or symptomatic of the insecurities and fear of change managers it is, more often than not, counter-productive and self-defeating. As pertinently remarked by Knights and Vurdubakis (1994), resistance and counter-resistance are both acts of power which seem to be locked in a mutually reinforcing yet vicious cycle. The more hostile and aggressive change managers are to resistance the more resistance they are likely to generate on the part of the resistors – leading, as is often the case, to open confrontation. The mini-case study below is a prime example of how resistance can be exacerbated and lead to overt public hostility when change measures are perceived as being 'forced from the top' and driven by the dominant interests of change managers.

─CASE STUDY 5.1─

Bitter union-led strike action at Heathrow Airport

The workers union, Unite, at Heathrow Airport Ltd (HAL) undertook a series of strike actions in the wake of the increasingly bitter dispute relating to the organisation's unilateral decision to *fire and rehire* its workforce. The fire and rehire measure saw HAL letting go and re-employing its entire 4,000-strong workforce on considerably inferior contracts with up to 25% permanent pay cuts. According to the Union, this measure was vastly detrimental to employees – some of whom were forced to move house, downsize their properties or give up their cars or were even literally pushed into poverty.

The Union feels that workers have been badly repaid for their commitment to the organisation – especially throughout the COVID-19 pandemic where employees kept on

(Continued)

working despite the increasing health risks to themselves and their families. For the Union, senior management is guilty of using the pandemic as a justification for implementing 'long-held plans' to seal a 'once-for-all' permanent cut in workers' pay – which, from their perspective, is *all about greed and not need* and has left the Union with no other alternative than to take drastic measures in defence of workers' interests.

Source: Unite (2021)

Questions

1 What were the key causes leading to strike actions by the workers union at HAL?
2 Are there actions that senior management could have taken to avoid the strike actions?

Typology of resistance to change

There are many types of resistance to organisational change which have been addressed from different perspectives and levels of analysis. For the sake of brevity, Table 5.2 provides a cursory overview of the typology of resistance that has been identified in the literature.

Table 5.2 Typology of resistance to organisational change

Type of resistance	Description
Overt resistance	When employees express their opposition to the proposed change by either voicing their opinion in the open or through observable attitudes and behaviours.
Covert resistance	When employees discreetly resist change. This is perhaps the most widespread and unaccounted for type of resistance. Can include behaviours such as spreading rumours, making deliberate errors, just going through the motions and resorting to 'go-slow' tactics.
Passive resistance	This type of resistance is less visible and mostly occurs at the individual level. It entails behaviours such as withdrawal, lack of involvement in team work and mental pulling out from the work environment.
Active resistance	This type of resistance is more visible and usually more confrontational. While it can happen at the individual level in the form of sabotage or aggressive behaviours, it mostly happens at group level following a total breakdown in communication and entails collective action such as open revolt and strikes.
Adaptive resistance	This is a less often-mentioned and more subtle form of passive resistance where employees do not fully embrace the change but only do 'just enough' to avoid any repercussions whilst staying on the sidelines and waiting for things to happen – a form of negative adaptation.

REFLECTIVE EXERCISE

Once again, go through the descriptions of the different types of resistance included in Table 5.2.

1   Which type of resistance do you think is the most common across modern-day organisations?
2   Which one would be the most harmful to change initiatives?

Positive value of resistance to change

As argued by Paton and McCalman (2015), not all resistance to change is necessarily negative and detrimental to the interests of the organisation or the wider stakeholder group. Sometimes resistance can prove beneficial to change projects because it is founded on rational and legitimate concerns and triggered from a particular perspective which can be vital to change success but which might have escaped the attention of change leaders. For instance, a change in the production line designed to cut costs might be appealing to change managers but might raise the rightful concerns of assembly workers if the change actually compromises their job security or customer safety. In this case, resistance of the assembly workers to the proposed change could be a positive response were it to lead to actions aimed at achieving a greater balance between employee and organisational needs or minimising risks to customers.

Thus, if positive contributions from 'resistant groups' can be factored into the change agenda based upon their potential to add value to the strategic agenda, they can enable an optimal use of situated knowledge and capabilities across the organisation, timely corrective measures and consistency of practices in the best interests of all stakeholders. What is then needed is for change managers to develop a nuanced understanding of resistance to change as a complex organisational phenomenon that does not always need to be overcome but always effectively managed.

CASE STUDY 5.2

The Volkswagen scandal

Volkswagen (VW), the car giant, was a few years back involved in what has been dubbed the 'diesel dupe'. The Environment Protection Agency (EPA) found that VW had fitted its diesel cars with a 'defeat device' – a software that could detect and 'falsify' the results of tests to measure carbon emission levels. This particular software allowed VW to make bold claims regarding the low emissions of its diesel cars in its global marketing campaign – when in fact, this was far from the truth as these vehicles emitted pollutants up to 40 times above the levels allowed by law.

(Continued)

When this scandal broke out, it quickly spread out to countries such as the UK, Italy, France, South Africa, Canada and of course Germany, which opened a separate investigation into the matter. Graduate students from West Virginia University shot into the limelight when they helped expose VW emission fraud. Customers and other external stakeholders wondered how such a blatant fraud could have been committed without the knowledge of employees and technicians who had been involved in the development of the 'defeat device' for falsifying carbon emission in diesel cars. The fact is that even if some employees had known what was happening, nobody would have dared raise the alarm for the company was at the time known for its culture of fear and punishment, and top management would have clamped down on any employees or groups of employees who would have drawn this issue to their attention, and dismissed them as 'rogue resistant groups' trying to destabilise the company and tarnish its reputation as one of the most successful car manufacturers in the world.

The unfortunate outcome of the 'diesel dupe' scandal was that the company faced an immediate decline in its share price, had to recall millions of cars and pay more than US$32 billion in fines, penalties, financial settlements and buyback costs.

Sources: Hotten (2015); Jung and Park (2017); Jacobs and Kalbers (2019)

Questions

1   Why would employees at VW have been dismissed as 'rogue resistants' had they brought the issue of the 'defeat device' to the attention of top management?
2   How could a more informed approach to managing 'perceived resistance' have led to different outcomes in this particular case?

Causes of resistance to change

You will surely have gathered from the Volkswagen case study that the ability to effectively manage resistance to change rests firmly on an understanding of its underlying causes – which vary according to context. However, it is useful to consider some of the most common causes of resistance to change identified in extant literature.

Conflicting interests

In most organisations, decision-making powers and the formulation of change strategies are contained within the upper spheres of management. As a result, the change agenda mostly reflects the interests of top management and other dominant stakeholder groups with scant attention paid to the interests of employees and subordinates operating at the lower end of the organisational hierarchy.

In Marxist terms, this type of conflict is inherent in the capital–labour relationship upon which modern-day organisations still rest – where we have on the one hand dominant groups in the service of capital whose primary interests lie in its maximisation and the pursuit of performance, productivity and profit; and on the other hand, subordinate groups whose primary interests are to secure a 'fair deal' when selling their labour to organisations, protect their contractual rights and safeguard their jobs. Change agents cannot turn a blind eye to this ongoing source of resistance in the employment relationship which can be exacerbated within the context of change – particularly when the balance tips far too much in favour of dominant groups driving the change.

Fear of the unknown

For Paton and McCalman (2015), resistance to change is something that can never be completely suppressed because one of its key sources is fear of the unknown, which seems to be an integral part of the human psyche. People are naturally apprehensive of the uncertainties of change. The prospect of a loss of stability and control over their own lives can leave people immobilised and unwilling to go with the flow of change. As a 'natural' source of resistance, fear of the unknown can have debilitating effects on change projects and is not something to be ignored or downplayed by change agents.

Misunderstanding

As a common source of resistance, misunderstanding results from a failure to comprehend the real meaning of change and its implications for key stakeholder groups. Misunderstanding is usually attributed to poor communication by change agents and a failure to clarify the purpose of change and provide a sound justification for it. However, we also need to look at the other side of the fence: misunderstanding can also be caused by stakeholders' incorrect interpretation of the evidential basis used by change agents to justify the proposed change. This is why change agents need to ensure that stakeholders correctly interpret the change message – which lends some credence to the saying that change success is more dependent on the shared meaning woven around change rather than the change itself.

Lack of trust

A lack of trust in stakeholders can be linked to a feeling of doubt regarding the ability of change agents to bring the change project to fruition. It can also have to do with the uncertainty regarding the real motives or intentions of change agents, which might not always be in the best interests of all stakeholders. It is often the case that the level of mistrust is related to past behaviours – and the level of mistrust can be particularly high if change agents have in the past repeatedly shown a lack of integrity or deliberately failed to deliver on their promises when implementing change projects.

Perceived violation of the psychological contract

The psychological contract is an implicit and unwritten set of mutual expectations or obligations between an employee and their employer which evolves over the term of the employment relationship (Griep and Cooper, 2019). The psychological contract will tend to remain positive during change as long as these mutual expectations and obligations are met to the satisfaction of both parties. A simple 'breach' of the psychological contract (which is relatively short term with minor effects and seen as beyond the control of the employer) might not have too much of an adverse impact on the change process if promptly addressed and rectified. However, the perception of a violation of the psychological contract (which is relatively long term with major effects and seen as well within the control of the employer) will usually be considered a failure of the organisation to keep their side of the bargain and deliver on their promises.

Culture shock

Organisational members can experience strong feelings of disorientation, stress, anxiety and even depression when suddenly subjected to disruptive change that challenges their long-established ways of life and working habits. For example, the compound effect of job relocation, new roles and responsibilities and the need to commit more time to learning new things can prove too overwhelming for some employees who cannot go beyond the boundaries of their current work–life patterns.

The range of causes of resistance considered above is by no means exhaustive; neither do they always operate in isolation. In real change situations, they can overlap and reinforce each other to form a complex causal web that underlies resistance to change and that can be quite challenging to manage.

Resistance as a social systemic phenomenon

In their compelling paper, Ford et al. (2002) argue in favour of the need for an approach to resistance to change as a social systemic phenomenon. They draw attention to how the primary focus of current literature on resistance to change is on the individual, which tends to promote a rather narrow view of resistance as something that occurs solely through the perceptions and behaviours of single isolated persons. Taking a view of resistance to organisational change as *socially constructed*, Ford et al. (2002) *shift the focus to the role of language and social interaction* in shaping negative background conversations and resistive attitudes and behaviours within specific change contexts.

As such, resistance is seen as borne out of how change is 'talked about in context'. In an organisational setting, different accounts or narratives of change within and across different parts of the organisation provide the linguistic backdrop and patterns of interaction which create and sustain different types of resistance to change. Ford et al. (2002) refer to these different accounts or narratives of change as background conversations. Ford et al. (2002) identify three main types of background conversations that produce three key types of resistance to change.

Background conversations for complacency

This type of conversation is grounded in past success – where one looks with uncritical satisfaction at past accomplishments as an excuse to maintain the status quo and downplay the importance of change as unnecessary, if not potentially dangerous. This type of resistance is typified by reactions such as:

- If it ain't broke, don't fix it.
- Why change when we are already doing it right.

Background conversations for resignation

By contrast, this type of conversation looks to past failure which provides the justification for resisting change on the basis that it will inevitably end up badly. Resignation is usually associated with negative feelings including discouragement, low self-esteem and self-efficacy, and apathy which are reflected in responses such as:

- Why change, we are no good at it.
- Why do it when you know you will fail.

Background conversations for cynicism

This type of conversation is also linked to past experiences of change. For example, it can relate to employees' doubt about the real motives of change agents as demonstrated by past behaviours – as reflected in comments such as:

- It's just old wine in new bottles.
- We all know who the real winners and losers are going to be.

The important points to be distilled from the above discussion are as follows:

i Resistance to change is not only 'embrained' and 'embodied' in individuals but is also situated within and across particular interacting stakeholder groups.
ii At the collective level, resistance is shaped by language in the form of background conversations which provide the justification for various types of resistive attitudes and behaviours.
iii Different types of background conversations can produce different types of resistance within or across different organisational groupings.

Illustrating resistance as a product of background conversations

We have developed a diagram in Figure 5.5 to illustrate these points and to foreground the type of systemic thinking which underpins the conception of resistance as a product of background conversations – and which sits well with our own commitment to systems thinking as one of the three pillars upon which this textbook rests (refer to Chapter 1).

As highlighted in Figure 5.5, as a larger system, the organisation is made up of a number of sub-systems (SS) which can stand for different departments, functions, branches, business units, etc. Different background conversations (BC) can be situated within a sub-system (such as BC3) giving rise to a particular type of resistance (RT3) which is restricted to that specific sub-system. However, background conversations can cut across different sub-systems (such as BC1, BC2 and BC4) to produce different types of collective resistance (such as RT1, RT2 and RT4). In such cases, resistance is dispersed across the organisation and involves different clusters of people working in different sub-systems but who may have participated in or been influenced by particular types of background conversations.

For example, BC1 in Figure 5.5 could stand for a background conversation for complacency within a large multinational company. As we can see, this background conversation spreads

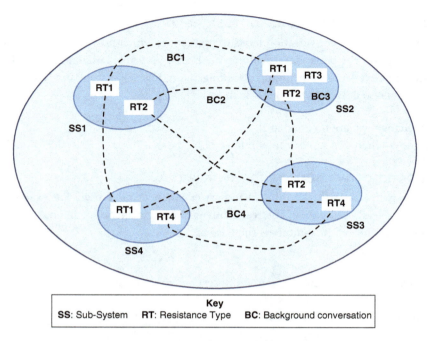

Figure 5.5 A systemic mapping of organisational resistance to change

across three sub-systems (SS1, SS2 and SS4) which, in this case, could be three business units located in three different countries. The spread of BC1 could have happened through various forms of online communication or through its replication based on the commonalities in the way employees talked about and resisted (RT1) change across the three business units.

Value of a social systemic conception of resistance to change

A social systemic conception of resistance to organisational change as the one described above not only draws attention to its complex and multidimensional nature but also points to the sheer difficulty of managing it, which makes it a real challenge for change agents. However, this does not mean that resistance to change should be ignored or dismissed altogether as unmanageable. A social systemic conception of resistance to organisational change has certain merits in that it:

- Allows for a deeper and more nuanced understanding of the tensions between individual and collective forms of resistance and of their compound effect on the change process.
- Can be used as an effective tool to map out the negative background conversations that serve to create and sustain different types of resistance across the organisation.
- Provides a framework for the development and diffusion of more positive background conversations that can help minimise the negative effects of resistance and muster ongoing stakeholder commitment throughout the change process.

1   Can you think of other types of background conversations that can lead to resistance to change?
2   In what ways can background conversations spread across an organisation?

5.6 Conceptual nugget: Managing resistance to change as dialogic practice

Ford et al. (2022) also see a form of democratic dialogue as an effective means for managing resistance to change as a socially constructed phenomenon. This once again resonates with another of the conceptual pillars that underpin this textbook and which calls for a dialogic approach to change management. We push our understanding of the term dialogic a little bit further here in support of how it can serve as a lever for managing resistance to change.

Managing resistance to change as dialogic practice carries the ideal of a democratic space to enable *free dialogue* between change agents and 'resistive groups' and warrants certain specific conditions, notably:

- A suspension of inequalities in power relations and the creation of a psychologically safe and socially empowering space for ongoing dialogue between change agents and resistive groups.
- A freezing of taken-for-granted assumptions, prejudices and ill-feelings towards the proposed change and an openness of mind as to why resistant groups might oppose it or have certain reservations about it.
- A willingness to listen to and give a voice to all 'participants-in-dialogue' to achieve shared understanding around the necessity and true purpose of the proposed change, its potential outcomes (whether desirable or unwanted) and its implications for all change stakeholders.
- An intent on nurturing 'change readiness', addressing divergent interests and integrating valuable alternative perspectives and positive contributions of resistive groups into the change agenda while constructing more positive background conversations around it – as opposed to harbouring a fixation on overcoming or indiscriminately dismissing all forms of resistance to change (Rafferty et al., 2013).

Furthermore, we want to stress the point that, to be effective, a dialogic approach to managing resistance to change should not be a one-off, cosmetic exercise but a continuous process of repeated dialogic acts – for resistance is usually not an isolated incident but can occur anywhere and at any time throughout the change process.

Deploying dialogic practice

Deploying dialogic practice as a means of managing resistance to change does not have to be overly complex but calls for a firm intent to commit the necessary resources to bring about the conditions described above – as modelled in Figure 5.6.

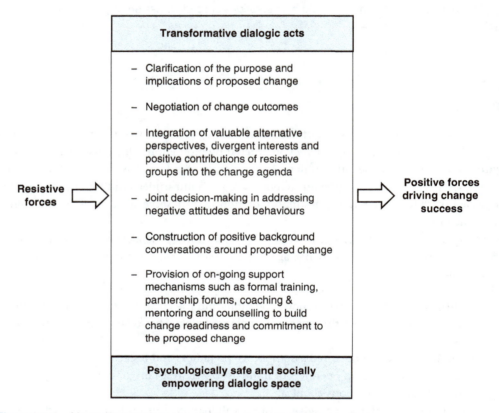

Figure 5.6 Managing resistance to change as dialogic practice

Our model places an emphasis on the transformative power of 'dialogic acts' that can effectively address potentially damaging resistive forces and 'modulate' them into positive forces for driving change. To this effect, the model draws attention to the following:

- The need for the creation and maintenance of a psychologically safe and socially empowering space for free dialogue between change agents and resistive groups.
- A battery of transformative on-going 'dialogic acts' designed to put a positive spin on managing resistance to change as a means to democratically deal with the divergent interests of resistive groups and incorporate their valuable perspectives and contributions into the change agenda.
- An organisational capability to address sources of resistance via on-going dialogic acts at both individual level (e.g. through mentoring and counselling) and collective level (e.g. through formal training and partnership forums) and to monitor the tensions

between the two levels to effectively tap into both the psychological and social factors underlying resistance to change, build change-readiness and commitment to change.

- An anticipation of positive outcomes that can drive change success in the form of shared understanding, negotiated change outcomes, unity of purpose, employee engagement, stakeholder commitment and a concerted approach to change implementation.

A legitimate expectation

We recognise the fact that *free dialogue* remains a tall order and could be dismissed as 'purely speculative' or 'utopian' – given the inherently 'undemocratic' context of many business organisations which are primarily driven by economic interests with little regard to the psycho-social and emotional dimensions of change. It is also understandable that the overwhelming pressure to expedite change outcomes is temptation enough to turn a blind eye to resistance in the hope that it will simply go away or be bulldozed over by the sheer momentum of change.

However, we contend that this is short-sighted and self-defeating. For if left unattended, resistance is likely to fester and spread across the organisation with harmful (and often irreversible) effects on the change outcomes. More importantly, we argue that *free dialogue is a legitimate expectation* of all change stakeholders, without which they would never be able to make meaningful sense of any change initiative, let alone commit to it. In this regard, we want to leave the reader with this final question as food for thought: *If not through dialogue, how else can change agents effectively manage resistance and muster the commitment of stakeholders to organisational change?*

REFLECTIVE EXERCISE

1   What are the conditions for managing resistance to change as dialogic practice?
2   Why can free dialogue be a tall order for many business organisations? However, why is it a legitimate expectation of stakeholders?

5.7 Key learning points

The following key learning points can be extracted from the preceding discussion.

1   The way people react to change is dependent on *both their natural psychological disposition and the nurturing socio-cultural factors* to which they are exposed over the course of their personal and working life.
2   Kirkpatrick's well-known typology of reactions to change identifies three basic types of reaction including negative, positive and neutral. Attention was drawn to the fact that *these different types are not fixed or static but evolve over time* – where the balance can tip towards any particular reaction over the course of the change implementation process.

3 The coping cycle is a stage model that charts the psychological responses which an individual typically displays when experiencing change. In its simplest form, the cycle includes the following key stages: *Denial, Defence, Discarding, Adaptation* and *Internalisation.* Individuals usually move along the coping cycle at their own pace and in their own particular way – making it difficult to generalise any evidence gathered through its application to the wider organisation. Importantly, *the coping cycle can be used as a change tool* to investigate the relationships between individual responses at each of its stages and other variables which can impact change success such as motivation, commitment, job engagement and performance.

4 Resistance can be defined as a refusal to accept the terms of a change initiative or an opposing force that acts to either slow down or even stop the flow of change. The most common types of resistance to organisational change include overt, covert, passive, active and adaptive resistance. Resistance to change is not always negative and can have a positive impact on the change agenda. The main causes underlying resistance to change range from conflicting interests and fear of the unknown through misunderstanding and lack of trust to perceived violation of the psychological contract and culture shock.

5 The notion of resistance to change as a social phenomenon shifts the focus to *the role of language and social interaction* in shaping resistive 'background conversations' and negative attitudes and behaviours within specific change contexts. The main types of negative background conversations identified by Ford et al. (2002) include *background conversations for complacency, resignation* and *cynicism*. From a systemic perspective, we have shown how the spread and diffusion of background conversations can be mapped out across the organisation.

6 Our conceptual nugget for this chapter entails the development of a model to enable an approach to *managing resistance to change as dialogic practice* – which warrants the creation and maintenance of a psychologically safe and socially empowering space for free dialogue between change agents and resistive groups and a battery of transformative *dialogic acts* designed to effectively address potentially damaging resistive forces and 'modulate' them into positive forces for driving change.

—END-OF-CHAPTER CASE STUDY 5.3—

Managing reactions to leadership and culture change at Henkel

Author: Dr Timur Erim

Introduction

Henkel is a German-based multinational chemical and consumer goods company head-quartered in Düsseldorf. Founded in 1876, the organisation has sustained more than 140 years of success on the back of its diversified portfolio, strong brands, innovations and technological applications. Apart from being the global market leader in the adhesives sector, Henkel also dominates the competitive landscape in the Laundry & Home Care, and Beauty Care sectors. In 2020, Henkel had a culturally diversified workforce of more than 52,000 globally and registered record sales of over 19 billion euros.

However, such success was not achieved overnight and Henkel had to embark on a major change initiative to make it happen. In 2018, management realised that the leadership principles that were put in place back in 2013 fell short of the expectations of the employees and posed a threat to the competitive bases of the company. There was a sense that there was a need to open up opportunities for greater employee collaboration across the entire organisation which was seen as critical to Henkel's success in the longer term – as evidenced by the following comment from one of the senior managers:

> We achieved a lot in the past. But to stay ahead in the future we at Henkel need to challenge the status quo and strive for more. We all need to open up and collaborate better.

This led to the establishment of *New Leadership Commitments* that entailed a reworking of Henkel's existing leadership principles and a transformation of the company's cultural value system and people management strategy.

New Leadership Commitments

The New Leadership Commitments (hereinafter NLC) were introduced in January 2019. Their overarching aim was to transform Henkel's leadership and culture in order to sustain its strong competitive position in rapidly changing markets and to enable employees to leverage their full potential and collaborate across the entire organisation within an environment characterised by trust and empowerment. Figure 5.7 below foregrounds the four main dimensions of the NLC.

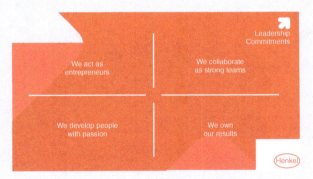

Figure 5.7 Henkel's New Leadership Commitments (NLC)

Source: Permission to use granted by Dr Timur Erim.

Management wanted to provide a framework to articulate in no uncertain terms the new behaviours that were now highly valued and that they believed would enable them to effectively address the current issues faced by the company whilst ensuring its future success. Rooted in an ethos of partnership and collaboration, the behaviours that account

(Continued)

for the four dimensions of the NLC were accompanied by *actionable dos and don'ts* to facilitate their translation into practice and embed them into the lived experiences of all organisational members – which is why it was made clear that the new desired behaviours were not only applicable to managers but to all of Henkel's employees. As such, they had to be continuously integrated into all HR processes, notably recruitment, onboarding, talent and performance management and people development.

The desired outcomes of the NLC were as follows:

i   To enable the company to become more entrepreneurial and enhance its performance across hyper-competitive markets.

ii To reform the perceived silo culture in parts of the organisation and stamp out the tendency towards conformity and micromanagement that had so far limited the possibilities for greater collaboration and team working across business units and functions.

iii To leverage the learning and development of employees so as to release their creative potential and entrepreneurial energy geared towards sustainable success.

Employee reactions to the NLC

Employees had different responses to the introduction of the NLC which resonated well with Kirkpatrick's threefold typology of reactions to change – as illustrated in Figure 5.8.

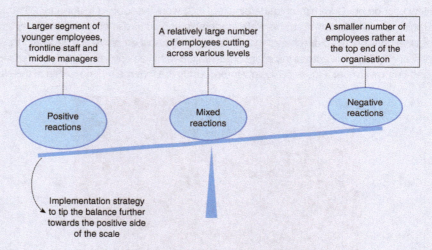

Figure 5.8   Spectrum of employee reactions to Henkel's NLC

1   *Positive reactions*: A large segment of the employee population consisting mainly of younger employees, staff with lower tenure jobs or little leadership responsibility together with a significant number of middle managers had a very positive initial reaction to the NLC. They felt that there was much to be gained from the shift to a more empowering and inclusive type of leadership and culture. This would enable the organisation to do away with the silo mentality and the propensity for

micromanagement and open up the possibility for more trusting and collaborative relationships, higher levels of employee autonomy, and greater ownership of change objectives.

2   *Mixed reactions*: A relatively large number of employees cutting across various hierarchical levels had mixed feelings about the NLC. This segment of employees were ambivalent regarding the feasibility of such a large change initiative which would take a lot of time to implement. While they viewed the intended outcomes of the NLC as appealing, they remained quite sceptical regarding the mindset of management which was perceived as firmly entrenched in old ways of working. They also expressed some doubt as to the ability of managers to drive the proposed change and bring it to successful completion.

3   *Negative reactions*: As in each larger company that undergoes a major change initiative, there were also a few signs of reservations regarding the NLC, despite the careful planning in which many stakeholders were actively involved across the entire organisation. Some of the employees questioned the actual need to focus on leadership and culture instead of focusing on business priorities. For this particular group of employees, the NLC would eradicate proven ways of doing things that had contributed to Henkel's success, which they found rather difficult to accept.

Managing reactions to the NLC

Despite the generally positive response to the NLC, management felt it was imperative to address any potential sources of resistance as this could adversely impact the implementation of the proposed change. A detailed implementation strategy was developed to tip the balance further towards the positive side of the scale – as highlighted in Figure 5.8.

The implementation strategy comprised three main axes:

1   *Communication road map*: A detailed 12-month communication roadmap targeted at all employees was designed to reinforce on a regular basis the necessity and potential benefits of the change initiative. The communication roadmap comprised not only face-to-face events and forums but also employed digital platforms such as the setting-up of an open online leadership content hub to foster dialogue and the sharing of best practice.

2   *Ongoing familiarisation*: It was very clear to management that more needed to be done to bring the NLC to life and increase the acceptance and commitment of all employees. Therefore, dedicated activation workshops were designed to enhance communication with employees and enable them to dive deeper into the meaning of the NLC and internalise its intended outcomes. The activation workshops targeted top management, management teams, production teams and all staff members.

3   *Day-to-day integration*: Employees would be able to use the actionable *do's and don'ts* related to each of the four dimensions of the NLC as a checklist to validate their behaviours and embed these within their daily routines. In addition, all employees had recourse to what was termed 'leadership hacks' that could be applied to both individuals and teams. 'Leadership hacks' are, in essence, tips and easy-to-implement

(Continued)

bite-sized information on how to challenge entrenched routines and work patterns and facilitate the embedding of the new behaviours associated with the NLC.

Three years after its launch, there is a general sense amongst organisational members that the core values of the NLC have become an integral part of the company's DNA and that the leadership process and cultural value system at Henkel have changed for the better. The determinant success factor in this case was that management was able to address employee reactions to change in a proactive and timely manner. This has not only served to generate and sustain a positive momentum to drive the organisation forward but has turned the NLC into a valuable blueprint for managing change in uncertain times – especially over the past couple of years when Henkel had to grapple with the challenges thrown up by the COVID-19 pandemic.

Conclusions

A number of key issues can be distilled from this case study. First, there is a need to manage employee reactions to change in a proactive and timely manner. Change agents were prompt to experiment with innovative ways to reinforce positive reactions and transform the potentially adverse effects of mixed and negative reactions into positive energy to sustain the momentum of change and achieve its intended outcomes. Second, there is great value in adopting a dialogical approach to managing reactions to change. Change agents deployed *activation workshops* to enhance communication with employees and clarify the meaning and intended outcomes of the NLC. Finally, managing reactions to change is a continuous exercise that has to be carried out throughout the change process. Change agents at Henkel used the *do's and don'ts* and *leadership hacks* on a regular basis to provide timely and easy-to-digest information and guidance on how to translate the NLC into practice and embed its principles and behaviours into daily work routines.

Questions

1   What were the key causes underlying the different types of employee reactions to the NLC at Henkel?
2   What were the main components of the implementation strategy for the NLC? To what extent were these effective?
3   In what way did change agents at Henkel adopt a dialogic approach to change?

5.8 Independent learning

Ford, J.D., Ford, L.W. and McNamara, R.T. (2002) 'Resistance and the background conversations of change', *Journal of Organizational Change Management*, 15(2), 105–121. We encourage you to read this article in full. This will enable you to further develop your understanding of background conversations and of the concept of resistance as a social systemic phenomenon.

Myers, P., Hulks, S. and Wiggins, L. (2012) *Organizational Change: Perspectives on Theory and Practice*. Oxford: Oxford University Press, Chapter 4: Emotions of change. An excellent discussion on the emotions of change as a vital yet often neglected dimension of organisational change which ties into some of the key issues addressed in this chapter. Also contains valuable alternative perspectives on the coping cycle and its practical application.

The Change Curve [video]: www.youtube.com/watch?v=YOul0fb3g0Q&t=403s. This eight-minute video presents another version of the coping cycle (which is also referred to as the change curve) and explains how, from a practitioner perspective, it can be used to manage emotional responses and accelerate the speed of change.

5.9 References

Amarantou, V., Kazakopoulou, S., Chatzoudes, D. and Chatzoglou, P. (2018) 'Resistance to change: An empirical investigation of its antecedents', *Journal of Organizational Change Management*, 31(2), 426–450.

Burnes, B. (2014) 'Understanding resistance to change – building on Coch and French', *Journal of Change Management*, 15(2), 1–25.

Carnall, C. (2003) *Managing Change in Organizations*, 4th edn. Harlow: Pearson Education.

Endrejat, P. C., Klonek, F. E., Müller-Frommeyer, L. C. and Kauffeld, S. (2020) 'Turning change resistance into readiness: How change agents' communication shapes recipient reactions', *European Management Journal*, 39(5), 595–604. [Online] Available at: https://doi.org/10.1016/j.emj.2020.11.004 (accessed 14 March 2023).

Ford, J. D., Ford, L. W. and McNamara, R. T. (2002) 'Resistance and the background conversations of change', *Journal of Organizational Change Management*, 15(2), 105–121.

Griep, Y. and Cooper, C. (eds) (2019) *Handbook of Research on the Psychological Contract at Work*. Cheltenham: Edward Elgar Publishing Limited.

Hotten, R. (2015) *Volkswagen: The Scandal Explained*. [Online] Available at: www.bbc.com/news/business-34324772 (accessed 15 March 2023).

Jacobs, D. and Kalbers, L. P. (2019) *The Volkswagen Diesel Emissions Scandal and Accountability*. [Online] Available at: www.cpajournal.com/2019/07/22/9187/ (accessed 15 March 2023).

Jung, J.C. and Park, S.B. (2017) 'Volkswagen's diesel emissions scandal ', *Thunderbird International Business Review*, 59(1), 127-137.

Kirkpatrick, D. L. (2001) *Managing Change Effectively: Approaches, Methods and Case Examples*. London: Routledge.

Knights, D. and Vurdubakis, T. (1994) 'Foucault, power, resistance and all that', in J. Jermier, D. Knights, W. Nord (eds), *Resistance and Power in Organizations*. London and New York: Routledge, pp. 167–198.

McDowell, E. and Hartmans, A. (2022) 'The rise and fall of Sears, once the largest and most powerful retailer in the world', *Business Insider*, January. [Online] Available at: www.businessinsider.com/rise-and-fall-of-sears-bankruptcy-store-closings?IR=T (accessed 1 March 2023).

Myers, P., Hulks, S. and Wiggins, L. (2012) *Organizational Change: Perspectives on Theory and Practice*. Oxford, GB: Oxford University Press.

Paton, R. A. and McCalman, J. (2015) *Change Management: A Guide to Effective Implementation*, 4th edn. London and Thousand Oaks: SAGE Publications.

Rafferty, A. E., Jimmieson, N. L. and Armenakis, A. A. (2013) 'Change readiness: A multilevel review', *Journal of Management*, 39(1), 110–135.

Scott, C.D. and Jaffe, D.T. (2006) *Change Management: Leading People through Organizational Transitions*, 3rd edn. USA, Seattle: Crisp Publications Inc.

Straatmann, T., Kohnke, O., Hattrup, K. and Mueller, K. (2016) 'Assessing employees' reactions to organizational change: An integrative framework of change-specific and psychological factors', *The Journal of Applied Behavioral Science*, 52(3), 265–295.

Unite (2021) *Heathrow Airport Braced for Fresh Strikes in 'Bitter' Fire and Rehire Dispute.* [Online] Available at: www.unitetheunion.org/news-events/news/2021/january/heathrow-airport-braced-for-fresh-strikes-in-bitter-fire-and-rehire-dispute/ (accessed 30 May 2021).

Vakola, M. (2016) 'The reasons behind change recipients' behavioral reactions: A longitudinal investigation', *Journal of Managerial Psychology*, 31(1), 202–215.

Wang, A. and Kebede, S. (2020) 'Assessing employees' reactions to organizational change', *Journal of Human Resource and Sustainability Studies*, 8(3), 274–293.

6

CULTURE CHANGE

Learning Outcomes

After completing this chapter, you should be able to:

- Gain an understanding of culture as a complex and multidimensional concept through the consideration of a range of alternative definitions and metaphors.
- Explain Schein's model of cultural layers and apply it to a real-life organisation.
- Critically examine Johnson and Scholes' cultural web and use it as an effective change tool to diagnose the current cultural status of an organisation and to frame culture change.
- Explain the meaning of organisational subcultures and appreciate their impact on culture change.
- Consider a range of strategies and tools for managing culture change that apply to different change contexts and objectives.
- Discuss the key dimensions of our dialogic model for effectively managing culture change and think about ways to translate it into practice.

6.1 Introduction

The purpose of this chapter is to help you develop a well-rounded understanding of the meaning of culture and provide you with an opportunity to experiment with a range of change tools to effectively manage it within the context of organisational change. The chapter begins with the consideration of a set of alternative definitions and metaphors of culture change, leading to a distillation of its key features as a complex and multidimensional concept. It then provides an overview of Schein's model of cultural layers with reference to a real-life organisation. The chapter proceeds to critically examine another popular model of organisational culture, Johnson and Scholes' cultural web, and shows how it can be turned into a practical tool to diagnose the current cultural status of an organisation and to frame culture change. In the same breath, some consideration is given to the meaning and underlying causes of organisational subcultures and to their impact on culture change. The chapter moves on to consider a range of change strategies and tools for managing organisational culture change that apply to different change contexts and objectives. The conceptual nugget for the chapter is presented in a final key section and entails the development of a dialogic model for managing culture change and elicits thinking about ways to effectively translate it into practice. The chapter concludes with an extraction of the key learning points arising from the preceding discussion and with a case study designed to illustrate and reinforce some of these key learning points.

6.2 The complex and multidimensional concept of culture

As a complex and multidimensional concept, culture carries many meanings and connotations which defies any single definition and makes it difficult to understand (Alvesson, 2013). When applied to organisational settings, it can become even more confusing as organisations are themselves difficult to define unambiguously. This is why many authors have had recourse to alternative definitions and metaphors to shed light on the complex nature of culture and explain its distinctive features from different angles and perspectives (Öcal, 2011). In the following section, we draw on various definitions and metaphors that have been used to make sense of culture as a complex concept – leading to a distillation of the key meanings that can be attached to it and to the consideration of their implications in the context of organisational change.

Defining culture

The literature contains some useful definitions of culture that draw attention to its basic characteristics and provide a good starting point for developing a sound understanding of the phenomenon (Baek et al., 2019). The Oxford Dictionary defines culture as the way of life of a certain group of people, relating to things such as language, customs, food, religion, music and architecture. For Schein (2017), **culture** is based on a set of assumptions that people hold and that find their expression in a shared system of beliefs, expectations and meanings. In more practical terms, culture is seen as the glue that binds people together and make them think and behave in certain preferred ways – contributing to some degree of stability and order, vital to proper social functioning.

Metaphors of culture

Metaphors are used in everyday life and in practically every single act of communication as they play a key role in the way we organise our thoughts, make sense of reality and justify our beliefs, decisions and behaviours (Morgan, 2006; Muthusamy, 2019). With regard to culture, metaphors provide a range of relatable ideas, images and representations to facilitate understanding of this complex concept which would have otherwise remained elusive and difficult to comprehend. Below are some of the most common metaphors that have been used to explain the meaning of culture.

Culture as a river

The metaphor of *culture as a river* compares culture to a stream of water flowing along a distinctive path and as being in a constant state of flux, evolving and always changing – which tends to go against the commonly held view of culture as rather static, deeply entrenched and very difficult to change. While it is true that – like the riverbed – certain features of culture (such as business missions, ethical principles and social commitments) can be relatively stable and enduring, they are not beyond change. Even riverbeds can take a different course following a major upheaval like an earthquake – just as some organisations might need to completely change their relatively stable cultural value system in the face of major upheavals in their immediate environments.

Other interesting insights generated by the metaphor of culture as a river that are worth mentioning include the following:

- Like a river which is life-giving and which at times displays incredible strength, culture is usually seen as the powerful and dynamic force that energises and drives an organisation forward.
- Like the river which follows a distinctive path, culture clears the way for a particular course of action an organisation must take to reach its chosen destination.
- A river can be both shallow and quite deep in places – just as there is a form of 'shallow culture' which is more visible and can be observed in routine practices and interactions, and a type of 'deep culture' that is well-entrenched and accessed only through in-depth, probing research.

However, the *culture as a river* metaphor can also carry some negative connotations. Rivers can have rapids where the water runs very fast and changes direction very suddenly, which makes them dangerous, if not deadly. Likewise, culture change can be at times overwhelming if it happens too fast and is forced upon people – where it can potentially 'drown' the individuality, creativity and commitment of organisational members.

Culture as software operating system

A software operating system is a set of programs, instructions and routines that enable the computer hardware to perform a specific set of tasks. When applied as a metaphor to organisational culture, it draws attention to the soft, human dimension of culture change and it conveys the idea of how culture can be used to programme the minds of organisational members and regulate their behaviours in line with the stated beliefs, values and mission of the organisation. However, the software metaphor is also a powerful reminder of how culture can be turned into an oppressive tool of mind control to force organisational members to 'conform and perform' in order to advance the sole interests of those in charge of the change process.

Culture as traffic signs

The primary purpose of traffic signs is to give instructions and warnings to regulate behaviours, maintain order and ensure the security of all road users. In essence, traffic signs inform road users about what is allowed, what is mandatory and what is outlawed. Traffic signs bring to attention the most visible aspects of culture. Like traffic signs, readily observable cultural objects such as symbols, dress codes, rituals, and policies and procedures aim to regulate the behaviours of organisational members and inculcate in them the 'right way of doing things around here' whilst providing a warning against what is prohibited or out of order. However, while 'cultural traffic signs' can contribute largely to the institutionalisation of preferred cultural values across the organisation, they tend to ignore the less visible yet potentially more influential aspects of culture – which are addressed in the following sub-section.

Culture as iceberg

The iceberg is perhaps one of the most common visual metaphors. In short, an iceberg is a relatively small piece of freshwater ice that floats freely in the open sea. When applied as a metaphor, the focus of attention is the proverbial 'tip of the iceberg' which is a powerful reminder of how the visible aspects of culture represent only a small part of a much bigger and more complex phenomenon – most of which remains invisible and inaccessible through surface level understanding. Therefore, the iceberg metaphor places an emphasis on the importance of 'the visibility factor' in cultural studies and on the need for a type of context-sensitive, probing research that can delve into the invisible and more influential elements of culture and enable a rich understanding of their impact on organisational practices and change processes.

REFLECTIVE EXERCISE

Skim read the sub-section on cultural metaphors and answer the following questions:

1   Why are metaphors useful in explaining the meaning of culture?
2   Which of the four cultural metaphors discussed above appeal to you the most? Why?
3   What are the limitations of your preferred cultural metaphor?

Distilling the key meanings of culture in an organisational change context

It is impossible to contain the full meaning of culture in a single, all-encompassing definition. We can however, in light of the alternative definitions and metaphors discussed above, distil the key meanings that can be attached to culture and consider how they apply to an organisational context – as follows:

- It refers to a way of life and doing things which are specific to an organisation as a discrete entity.

- It is based on a shared system of assumptions, values and beliefs that have a shaping influence on the way of thinking and behaviour of organisational members.
- It contributes to some degree of stability and order, vital to proper organisational functioning but is dynamic, evolving and open to change.
- It influences the mode of thinking of organisational members and regulates their behaviours in line with the organisation's core values and strategic imperatives.
- It consists of a visible dimension which is relatively easy to access and an invisible yet bigger and more influential dimension which can have a greater impact on organisational change and which needs to be accessed through immersive and probing research.
- It relates to the soft dimension of organisational change and as such, is the dynamic force that drives an organisation forward and sustains the motivation, creativity and commitment of its key stakeholders.
- Finally, it can potentially be turned into an oppressive tool to enforce conformity and drive performance in pursuit of the interests of dominant groups whilst suppressing critical reflection and creativity and preventing subordinate organisational members from making any real contribution to the change project.

PRACTICAL EXERCISE

To enable you to memorise some of the distinguishing features of organisational culture which were brought to light by the set of metaphors covered in this section, match the descriptions in the first column of Table 6.1 below with the appropriate metaphor.

Table 6.1 Matching distinguishing cultural features with relevant metaphors

Distinguishing features of culture	Metaphors
Portrays culture as a constant state of flux, evolving and always changing.	
Compares culture to a set of instructions to programme the minds of organisational members and regulate their behaviours.	
Places an emphasis on the need for a type of immersive research that can delve into the invisible and more influential elements of culture.	
Foregrounds culture as relating to the soft dimension of change.	
Represents culture as the dynamic force that drives an organisation forward.	
Is a powerful reminder of how the visible aspects of culture represent only a small part of a much bigger, more complex and mostly hidden phenomenon.	

(Continued)

Distinguishing features of culture	Metaphors
Draws attention to how culture change can be at times overwhelming and counterproductive if it happens too fast and is forced upon people.	
Contributes largely to the institutionalisation of preferred cultural values across the organisation.	
Places an emphasis on the need for probing research that can delve into the invisible and more influential elements of organisational culture.	
Elicits thinking about how culture can be used as an oppressive form of mind control.	

6.3 Layers of organisational culture

The notion of **cultural layers** originated from the work of psychologist Edgar Schein who developed a model of organisational culture comprising of three distinctive layers with different degrees of visibility: *artefacts*, *beliefs and values*, and *assumptions*. Table 6.2 below provides an overview of Schein's layers of organisational culture which are explained in more detail in the following discussion.

Table 6.2   Overview of Schein's layers of organisational culture

Key dimensions of Schein's model of cultural layers	Description	Visibility	Accessibility
Artefacts (Surface culture)	Concrete and obvious elements such as company logos, symbols, dress codes, office layouts.	High visibility	Easily observable but often need to be interpreted in context to be fully understood.
Beliefs and values (Shallow culture)	Conscious principles and standards of behaviour such as integrity, innovation, diversity, commitment, etc.	Medium visibility	Partially observable, need a greater level of awareness and have to be probed to access full meaning.
Basic underlying assumptions (Deep culture)	Mostly pre-conscious such as perceptions, feelings, philosophies and espoused theories that can have a greater causal impact on decision-making and action.	Low visibility	Mostly hidden and need to be accessed via immersive, context-sensitive and causally oriented research.

Artefacts

Artefacts make up the most visible layer of an organisation's culture and primarily refers to objects created by the organisation to inform or remind members of the meaning and purpose of its core cultural values. This particular cultural layer is often referred to as 'surface culture' because artefacts are readily observable and entail 'meaningful objects' such as company logos, symbols, uniforms and badges, office layouts, personal parking spaces, routine behaviours, gestures and product packaging. The primary purpose of artefacts is to provide an enabling structure for the desirable values, norms and behaviours that an organisation wants to promote. While artefacts are highly visible, they cannot always be taken at face value and have to be interpreted in their specific context to enable a full understanding of their meanings.

Beliefs and values

Beliefs and values entail a set of conscious principles and precepts usually passed on by earlier 'generations' of organisational members that define standards of behaviour or the 'right' way of doing things and conducting business. Beliefs and values include notions such as integrity, innovation, diversity and commitment which are outlined in policies and other documents designed to inculcate and reinforce desirable attitudes, behaviours and working practices. Beliefs and values are often referred to as 'shallow culture' because they are only partially visible, need a greater level of awareness and have to be probed in order to access their full meaning.

Basic underlying assumptions

Basic underlying assumptions form the least visible layer of organisational culture. They are mostly *pre-conscious* – i.e. they are primarily latent things that one is not actively thinking about, which jump to mind given the right trigger or when one is faced with particular situations. Basic underlying assumptions can include perceptions, feelings, philosophies and theories espoused by organisational members which consistently influence their decision-making and action. For example, top management may endorse the theory that *if you take care of your employees, they will take care of customers*, which will influence the way they exercise their duty of care towards employees. Basic underlying assumptions are often referred to as the 'deep culture' of the organisation because while they are mostly hidden and well-entrenched, they can have a greater causal effect on the change process and outcomes – and, as such, can only be accessed via immersive, context-sensitive, causally oriented research.

---CASE STUDY 6.1---

Mumbai Dabbawala: Culture as a lever for high-performance standards

Introduction

Mumbai Dabbawala is an Indian low-cost and extremely reliable food delivery service company that has been able to maintain the highest performance standards, not because of any reliance on high-tech support but solely due to its high commitment to its core values and traditions. Every single working day, about 5,000 delivery persons (*walas* in Hindi) organise and execute the delivery of around 200,000 lunchboxes (*dabbas* in Hindi) from people's homes located up to 70 km away from Mumbai to their offices in the city centre and back. Mumbai Dabbawala began its operations back in 1809 with a single customer. Nowadays, the organisation boasts of being able to maintain its high quality service at all times, even under extreme conditions such as periods of torrential rain, civil unrest and terrorist attacks.

Culture as the main driver of service quality

The 5,000-strong workforce of male delivery workers form a homogenous group of people and most of them come from the same village near Pune, a city 150 km away from Mumbai. They are organised in 200 largely autonomous, self-managing teams of 25 employees who are responsible for collecting, sorting, transporting and delivering the lunch boxes to their clients located all over Mumbai. Delivery workers are all dressed in white uniforms and wear traditional white *Gandhi caps* (a symbol of independence, self-reliance and pride) and use only bicycles and commuter trains as means of transportation which sets the pace for their daily work routines. Delivery workers have less than a minute to load lunch boxes on and off trains – an exercise which has to be on the clock and perfectly synchronised.

Mumbai Dabbawala considers its ability to 'deliver food on time, every time' as the driving force of the company. For the company, serving food to an office worker is 'the best charity' – in the same vein as delivering medicine to a sick person whose life is in danger, where mistakes and delay could be fatal and are therefore unacceptable. *Dabbawalas* usually serve the organisation their entire working lives, which has allowed them to internalise its core cultural values and traditions, which has in turn enabled them to forge strong bonds with their co-workers and customers and maintain such a high level of quality service over the years – with hardly any recourse to modern technology.

Sources: Dabbawala, 2022; Thomke, 2012

Questions

1   What can we learn from the above case study about the value of culture in driving organisational performance and delivering excellence in customer service?
2   Apply Schein's model of organisational culture discussed in this section to identify the different layers of culture underpinning Mumbai Dabbawala's business model.

6.4 The cultural web

The **cultural web** is another popular model – developed by Gerry Johnson and Kevan Scholes in 1992 – which, as will be shown later, can be used as an effective change tool to both analyse the current cultural status of an organisation and to frame culture change. As highlighted in Table 6.3, it consists of six interrelated dimensions – *stories, symbols, power structures, organisational structures, control systems* and *rituals and routines* – the combined effects of which contribute to the formation of the *paradigm*, the organisation's dominant culture (Johnson et al., 2012). We examine in some detail each dimension in what follows.

Table 6.3 Key dimensions of the cultural web

Cultural paradigm	
Stories	Transmitted in oral or written form and draw on past experiences and events to shape an organisation's ways of thinking and doing things.
Symbols	Form part of an organisation's artefacts and highly visible objects designed to promote its dominant cultural values and norms.
Power structures	Determine the way power and authority are distributed and exercised across an organisation.
Organisational structures	Determine the way work is configured in order to achieve the strategic goals and objectives of an organisation.
Control systems	Determine the way work processes and behaviours are monitored, evaluated, regulated and rewarded.
Routines and rituals	Routines refer to repetitive and automatic processes or activities that contribute to the stability and predictability of organisational practices. Rituals are consciously carried out to achieve a specific purpose or generate certain desirable outcomes.

Source: Johnson et al. (2012) [adapted]

Stories

Stories primarily draw on past experiences and events that have had a shaping influence on an organisation's ways of thinking and doing things and become an essential part of its 'cultural heritage'. Stories are transmitted in oral or written form and their main focus is usually on 'heroes', specific courses of actions, strategic decisions or achievements that have contributed to the success of the organisation. As narratives of choice, they carry key precepts and principles, moral values, examples of desirable behaviours and other prime motivators that define the organisation as a discrete entity and that management would like to inculcate in employees.

It is worth noting that stories will lose their shaping influence and become a source of employee distrust and dysfunctional relationships if the principles and behaviours they advocate are not aligned with actual, day-to-day behaviours and working practices. Change leaders and top management have to model the principles and behaviours idealised in stories and provide appropriate support mechanisms to translate them into practice across all organisational levels.

Symbols

As previously mentioned, **symbols** form part of an organisation's artefacts and are highly visible objects created to promote its dominant cultural values and norms. Symbols include things such as architectural designs, company logos and colours, dress codes, work arrangements, job titles, etc. They are in essence, visual representations of an organisation's dominant culture and serve as powerful *signifiers* for culturally influenced things such as the nature of working and power relationships, job-specific roles and responsibilities, and competitive positioning of the organisation within its particular industry and representation across the wider community. Like stories, symbols can take on 'distorted meanings' and become dysfunctional if there is a discrepancy between what they signify and actual behaviours and working practices.

Power structures

Power structures determine the way power and authority are distributed and exercised across the organisation. Hierarchical power structures serve to sustain unequal power relations between dominant and subordinate groups, centralised decision-making contained at the highest level of the organisation, top-down communication, close supervision and control, and formal working relationships – tending towards an autocratic, directive and conservative organisational culture.

Power structures that are more organic and flexible do not attach much importance to differences in power relations between dominant and subordinate groups. Such power structures are characterised by decentralised, shared decision-making, two-way communication channels, loose supervision and control, informal working relationships and are generally more accommodating of a more inclusive and collaborative approach to change – reflecting a more democratic, empowering and innovative organisational culture.

Organisational structures

Organisational structures determine the way work is configured in order to achieve the strategic goals and objectives of an organisation. Organisational structures are usually visually represented in charts and diagrams detailing the various levels and functions, roles and responsibilities, reporting lines and supervisory controls to coordinate processes and activities and optimise outputs.

There are many types of organisational structures which are inevitably related with the organisation's dominant culture, the most common ones being: *hierarchical structures* with several management layers, a strict chain of command and formal relationships and mechanistic ways of working; *flat structures* with few management layers, loose supervision, informal relationships and more organic and flexible ways of working; *matrix structures* with individual employees reporting to more than one supervisor or line manager, conducive to cross-functional and project-based teamwork; and *network structures* that prioritise informal and collaborative relationships and knowledge sharing both within and across organisations.

It is important to draw attention to the possibility of combining structures – e.g. organisations can combine hierarchical and matrix structures to maintain strict control over the production process whilst providing the support mechanisms for enabling collaborative teamwork in line with the organisation's innovative culture.

Control systems

Control systems determine the way work processes and behaviours are monitored, evaluated, regulated and rewarded – and can include financial systems, quality systems, training systems, performance management systems and reward systems. Control systems are critical to change success in that they enable change leaders to track progress at key milestones of the change process – by assessing learning and performance outcomes, conducting quality audits, rewarding 'change wins' and key contributions to the change initiative whilst keeping tabs on its financial viability. Tight, strong control systems tend to reflect core cultural values driven by performance outcomes and economic interests. On the other hand, loose, weak controls tend to reflect a collaborative and organic approach to change and a concern with the creation of both business and social values.

Routines and rituals

Routines are repetitive processes or activities that need to be carried out on a regular basis to ensure proper organisational functioning. Routines do not require a 'presence of mind' to be effectively performed – in other words, routines are an ordered sequence of activities that are generally repeatedly and automatically carried out without much thought but that contribute to the stability and predictability of organisational practices. Routines include things such as replying to emails as first order of the day, servicing production lines and machinery, doing quality checks before product deliveries, etc.

Like routines, **rituals** usually follow an ordered sequence of activities but they differ from routines in that they require 'a presence of mind' – i.e. they are consciously carried out to achieve a specific purpose which is to generate certain desirable outcomes. Rituals can include things such as formal meetings, daily 'pep talks', working lunches, award ceremonies, celebrations of outstanding performance and success – which are designed, among other things, to reinforce core cultural values, create a strong sense of belonging, build trusting relationships, and sustain employee engagement, commitment and performance levels. However, rituals can be perceived as pointless and stale if they are counterproductive and do not add value to the achievement of change objectives.

Cultural paradigm

As previously mentioned, the combined effects of the six interrelated dimensions explained above contribute to the formation of the organisation's **cultural paradigm** or *dominant culture* – a complex set of ideas, values, beliefs and assumptions that define an organisation's cultural identity and act as a perceptual filter in shaping its ways of thinking and doing things.

It is important at this point to reiterate the fact that the cultural web can be turned into an effective change tool to both analyse the current cultural status of an organisation and to frame culture change – a tool with which you will be able to experiment in the practical exercise.

6.5 Organisational subcultures

This section explains the meaning of organisational subcultures and identifies the key causes underlying them before considering the extent to which they can be regarded as good or bad.

Meaning of organisational subcultures

Organisational **subcultures** develop when groups of employees cluster around a set of values, beliefs and ways of doing things that deviate from the dominant culture – creating different degrees of 'cultural variance' across the organisation. Subcultures can emerge at different organisational levels – whether it be at functional level (e.g. marketing, HR), hierarchical level (e.g. middle managers), regional level (e.g. divisions located in different parts of the same country) and global (e.g. business units across different countries).

Causes underlying subcultures

There are many possible causes or reasons that underlie subcultures. However, generally speaking, subcultures tend to emerge in the following cases:

- When subculture groups subjectively interpret the organisation's dominant culture and attach meanings to it which digress from those intended by top management or change leaders – e.g. subjective interpretations of the meaning and extent of collaborative change.
- When subculture groups develop different values and assumptions by virtue of their specific roles or professional interests – e.g. IT engineers driven by 'technical solutions' at the expense of the ethical principles governing a duty of care to employees.
- When there is a disconnect between the core values endorsed in the organisation's 'cultural manifesto' and actual behaviours and working practices – e.g. top management and change leaders' failure to model the core cultural values driving a new change initiative.

Are organisational subcultures good or bad?

Organisational subcultures are not necessarily good or bad. It all depends on the extent to which they pose a threat to the change agenda and to the organisation's competitive position. Subcultures that are doggedly subversive, counterproductive and serve to maintain pockets of negative resistance across the organisation for no good business reasons except to 'sabotage' change efforts can be considered as 'inherently bad' – and therefore, potentially harmful and undesirable.

However subcultures can be positive and viewed as 'good' if they emerge from a genuine interest in the 'common good' and long-term success of the organisation – where, for example, they can provide valuable alternative perspectives that would have otherwise skipped the attention of change leaders and make positive contributions that can be integrated into the core cultural value system and change agenda of the organisation.

PRACTICAL EXERCISE

Turning the cultural web into a practical change tool for managing culture change

Table 6.4 shows you how the cultural web can be turned into a change tool to take stock of the current 'cultural status' of an organisation and, on the basis of the findings, develop appropriate recommendations to frame culture change.

The first column of the table shows you how each key dimension of the cultural web has been 'operationalised' into practical, bottom-line questions that will enable you to carry out a first-hand analysis of the dominant culture of your organisation or one which you have researched online. We have added another key dimension relating to organisational subcultures to augment the overall quality of your analysis.

Next, record your answers to the questions in column 1 in the second column under the heading 'findings' – which, when completed, will provide you with a sound understanding of the current organisational culture under scrutiny – *as it is now*.

Proceed to address the questions in column three to think about how the current organisational culture might be reinforced and improved – *as it could be in the future*. Jot down your answers to these questions under the column 'recommendations' and consider their practical implications in the final column of the table.

Once you have completed this exercise, it should enable you to map out the key differences between your organisation's culture *as it is now* and *as it could be in the future* and use your practical recommendations to develop an informed action plan for culture change.

(Continued)

Table 6.4 Turning the cultural web into an effective change tool

Key dimensions of the cultural web	Findings	Scope for change	Recommendations	Practical implications
Stories What kind of stories are currently being told across the organisation? What is their impact on organisational members?		Do we need to reframe or reject current stories? Do we need new stories?		
Symbols What are the key symbols in use? What is their impact on organisational behaviours and practices?		Which symbols do we need to keep and which ones do we need to drop? Do we need to create new symbols?		
Power structures Who has actual power and makes the strategic decisions? Are current power relations conducive to change success?		Do we need to change existing power relations and arrangements? If yes, what can be done to this effect?		
Organisational structures What type of structures are in place? Are these structures conducive to the achievement of strategic goals and objectives?		Do we need to change the current structures? Is there a possibility to combine structures?		
Control systems What types of controls are in place? Are these controls tight or loose?		Which controls need to be consolidated or recalibrated? Do we need new/additional controls?		

Key dimensions of the cultural web	Findings	Scope for change	Recommendations	Practical implications
Routines and rituals				
Which key routines keep the organisation going?		Is there need to improve or change existing routines?		
Which rituals are critical in the establishment of the organisation's core cultural values?		Are current rituals still vibrant or have they gone stale?		
		Is there need for new rituals?		
Cultural paradigm				
How would you describe the organisation's dominant culture?		Is there need to reinforce or change the organisation's dominant culture?		
Subcultures				
Are there any significant subcultures?		What can be done regarding good subcultures?		
Are they good or bad?		How do we cope with bad subcultures?		

6.6 Strategies for managing cultural change

There is a range of strategies that change leaders can deploy to effectively manage organisational culture change. Table 6.5 provides an overview of some of the most common approaches to managing culture change – which are detailed in the following discussion, drawing attention to the change situation to which they apply and, where appropriate, the methods and techniques to translate them into practice.

Table 6.5 Strategies for managing culture change

Enculturation	Acculturation	Assimilation	Integration	Separation
The process through which an individual or group learn and internalise the dominant culture of their own organisation.	The process of learning and incorporating the core cultural values of another organisation.	The process of abandoning one's own organisational culture to embrace that of another organisation.	The process of adopting the cultural values of another organisation, while maintaining one's own culture.	The maintenance of one's own culture with little interest in adopting the culture of another (partner) organisation.

Enculturation

Enculturation is the process by which an individual or a group of people internalise the dominant culture of their own organisation – i.e. make their own organisation's core values and behavioural norms an integral part of their inner being and mindset. Enculturation happens through learning and exposure to the shaping influence of more experienced organisational members who are often involved in the articulation and diffusion of the organisation's core cultural values and norms. Methods and techniques of enculturation can include both formal interventions such as onboarding and culture-focused training to educate and familiarise employees with desirable cultural values and behaviours or informal processes such as coaching and mentoring, shadowing more 'culturally tuned' members, teamwork and other collaborative activities.

Acculturation

The process of learning and incorporating the core cultural values of another organisation. This usually happens in the context of mergers and acquisitions and tends to be uni-directional – where, the 'weaker' business partner or acquired organisation is the one that has to learn and internalise the dominant culture of the 'stronger' business partner or acquiring organisation. **Acculturation** can be a source of 'cultural discomfort' and organisational dysfunction, and trigger negative reaction and resistance, especially if organisational members feel it is being imposed or forced upon them by a change in circumstances over which they have no or little control.

Assimilation

Assimilation is a process through which organisational members have to let go of their original culture to embrace that of another organisation. It can happen after prolonged periods of acculturation and organisational members come to the decision that adopting a different culture altogether is a greater match with the new strategic imperatives and business needs. Assimilation can exacerbate negative reactions and resistance in cases where organisational members feel that they have to abandon their own cherished beliefs and dilute their own cultural values while losing, in the process, their distinctive cultural identity.

Integration

Integration is usually seen as a positive approach to culture change. It involves a process whereby an organisation adopts the key elements of another organisation's culture while maintaining those of their own culture – especially in cases where two or more organisations decide to combine their respective cultural values in the hope that this will create a desirable form of 'cultural synergy'. Strategies for cultural integration can include all the methods and techniques used for processes of enculturation but need to factor in the need to achieve a balance in the development and practical application of newly integrated cultural value systems.

Separation

Cultural **separation** occurs when an organisation decides to maintain its own culture while having little interest in adopting the culture of another (partner) organisation. While cultural separation seems at face value negative and susceptible to culture clashes, it can work if partner organisations develop a mutual respect for each other's culture and can agree over the need to protect the practical boundaries within which their respective cultures can be applied to good effect.

─PRACTICAL EXERCISE─

Managing culture change in a merger situation

You work as a middle manager in a company that has recently merged with another company, which was up to now a major competitor. The top management teams of the merging companies have decided to follow the *cultural integration route* as all parties involved see a lot of value in retaining and combining the original core values and norms of each organisation. These core values and norms have already been identified and outlined in the broadest of terms under the heading 'cultural manifesto' in the merger documents which was duly approved by the new Board of Directors.

(Continued)

Since you have been heavily involved in the merging process from its very beginning, you have been tasked with the development of an action plan to effectively 'operationalise' or translate into practical terms the new cultural manifesto of the merged organisation in order to facilitate its organisation-wide implementation. While you do not have a lot of experience in managing culture change, you have decided that the best way to proceed is to draw an ordered list of activities that you need to carry out to successfully complete this task. You have already figured out that the first item on your list should be to gain a good understanding of the core values and norms outlined in the merger documents. *You now need to complete the list below.* The number of activities (N) to be included in the list is up to you – as long as it is logically sequenced and helps you progress towards the completion of the task that has been entrusted to you. Refer to Table 6.5 above and the discussion that follows to help you with this exercise.

Ordered list of activities

1   Consult the merger documents and extract the core values and norms of the newly merged organisation.

2

3

4

5

6

N

CASE STUDY 6.2

Aetna: Targeted culture change for a major turnaround

Introduction

Aetna is an American life insurance company that was founded in 1853 and offers a range of innovative products and services (such as medical and dental care, disability plans, and insurance and benefit schemes) to individuals, employers and healthcare professionals. At the turn of the 21st century, Aetna was going through a difficult phase. Its relationships with customers and healthcare professionals was rapidly deteriorating. Its reputation was being tarnished because of an increase in lawsuits and a nationwide reaction against healthcare and maintenance organisations which Aetna had supported. To make matters worse, the company was bleeding money and was losing around US$1 million a day as a result of a series of unfortunate acquisitions and inefficient, wasteful processes.

Culture-related problems

There was a growing sense amongst stakeholders that many of Aetna's problems were due to its overly conservative culture that had turned it into a complacent, insular, risk-averse company and oblivious to the mediocrity that had taken hold of the organisation. The prevailing psychological contract was based on the implicit understanding that the company would exercise a duty of care to employees as long as they got on with their jobs and did not rock the boat. A merger with another American low-cost healthcare provider with a far more competitive orientation lead to a major culture clash causing Aetna to become even more deeply entrenched in its conservative culture.

Targeted culture change

A new CEO was appointed to transform the company and turn it into a profitable business. What was particularly impressive was the new CEO's approach. He did not want to embark the company on a wholesale change initiative that could have caused a lot of discomfort and negative reactions. Instead of focusing on what was not working well, he decided to target and reinforce the company's 'cultural strengths'. With the help of the senior team, he consulted with employees at all levels to identify the key cultural strengths of the company. These cultural strengths included: a great sense of pride in the company's history, purpose and mission, a deep concern for customers, respect for colleagues and professional dedication.

Achieving a major turnaround

The new CEO implemented a change strategy dubbed *The New Aetna* – which was focused on the reinforcement and establishment of the company's cultural strengths identified in consultation with employees and which required 'small but significant' behavioural changes. A few years down the line, employees were reported as reenergised, enthusiastic and strongly committed to the company. This was reflected in Aetna's financial performance. By the mid-2000s the company was making around US$5 million a day, turning a US$300 million loss to a US$1.7 billion gain with its stock price climbing steadily, from US$5.84 to US$48.40 a share – a major turnaround achieved on the back of targeted culture change.

Source: Katzenbach et al. (2012) [adapted and modified]

Questions

1   What type of culture change strategy did the new CEO adopt to transform Aetna into a successful business? (Refer to Table 6.5 to frame your answer.)
2   Why do you think a targeted approach was seen as less risky than a wholesale approach to culture change?

6.7 Managing cultural diversity in an international context

With the increasing pace of globalisation, more and more organisations are expanding their operations across national borders and have to cope with greater cultural diversity (Hofstede Insights, 2019). While managing a culturally diverse organisation is in itself a tall order and is the subject of intensive research which is beyond the scope of this book, we want to keep the focus here on one of the most popular models that can be turned into a practical tool to manage cultural diversity in an international context: Hofstede's model of national cultural differences. Psychologist Geert Hofstede developed his model in the late 1970s. Since then the model has undergone considerable developments and refinements and has become a globally recognised tool for understanding and managing national cultural differences (Hofstede, 2022).

It has to be said that Hofstede's model has been criticised for lacking in empirical evidence, making sweeping generalisations and casting different nations into cultural stereotypes – which does not really apply in a globalised and rapidly changing world characterised by cultural exchange and diversity not only across but within national borders. However, the Hofstede model remains a valuable analytical tool that can be used as a steering device in managing cultural diversity. Table 6.6 presents an overview of the key dimensions of the Hofstede model and their organisational implications.

Table 6.6 A summary overview of Hofstede's model of national cultures

Key dimensions of Hofstede's model of national cultural differences	Description	Organisational implications
Power distance index – PDI	The extent to which unequal power distribution is accepted by those with less power. Examples: High PDI: Singapore, China Low PDI: US, Canada, Germany, Sweden	High PDI: Hierarchical structures, centralised decision-making, close supervision and tight control systems. Low PDI: Flatter structures, teamwork, decentralised decision-making, flexible working and greater delegation of responsibilities.
Individualism v. Collectivism – IDV	The extent to which emphasis is placed on individual rights and interests, or group cohesiveness and loyalty and collective achievements. Examples: High IDV: US, Australia, UK, France Low IDV: Singapore, China, Mexico	High IDV: Pursuit of self-interests, autonomy, focus on personal career progression. Low IDV: Importance attached to sense of community and belonging, teamwork, group harmony and organisational commitment.

Key dimensions of Hofstede's model of national cultural differences	Description	Organisational implications
Uncertainty avoidance index – UAI	The extent to which members of a particular culture feel threatened by uncertain, unknown situations. Examples: High UAI: Greece, Portugal and Japan Low UAI: Singapore, Jamaica, Denmark	High UAI: Strict policies and procedures, tight control systems and evaluative measures, risk aversion. Low UAI: Flexible policies and procedures, greater tolerance for ambiguity, propensity for risk-taking.
Masculinity v. Femininity – MAS	The extent to which importance is attached to differentiated gender roles and male-dominance traits. Examples: High MAS: Japan, China, US, India Low MAS: Sweden, Norway, Denmark	High MAS: Competitive stance and pursuit of economic success. Reward schemes based on assertiveness, performance, material gains and career progression. Low MAS: Preference for collaborative approach with a premium placed on trusting relationships, a duty of care and quality of life.
Long-term orientation v. Short-term orientation – LTO–STO	A long-term orientation (LTO) emphasises decisions and courses of action directed towards the future. A short-term orientation tends to focus on past experiences and present issues and concerns. Examples: LTO: Japan, China STO: US, Canada	LTO: Long-range planning, focus on survival and growth in the longer term, ecological concerns, driven by savings, and elimination of inefficiencies and waste, interest in sustainable futures. STO: Emphasis on learning from past success. current performance, quick wins and short-term gains.
Indulgence v. Restraint – IND	The extent to which a particular cultural group promotes or limits the gratification of human needs and respect their rights to happiness and an enjoyable life. Examples: High IND: US, Australia, Canada Low IND: Russia, China, Japan	High IND: Flexible policies promoting personal development, quality of working life and work–life balance, focus on job satisfaction and individual needs. Low IND: Strict policies and control systems to regulate behaviours in the interest of the organisation, focus on work commitment and delayed gratification in favour of common good.

As highlighted in Table 6.6, Hofstede's model comprises six key dimensions against which differences across national cultures can be identified. The table is largely descriptive and provides ample information on the meaning of each dimension, the measures employed within each dimension to identify national cultural differences with key examples, and the translation of such differences within organisational settings. It is therefore appropriate at this point to focus our attention on how Hofstede's model can be used as a powerful tool to manage cultural diversity in an international context and provide you with an opportunity to experiment with it in the next practical exercise.

PRACTICAL EXERCISE

Using Hofstede's model of national cultures as a change tool to manage cross-cultural teams

You work as a project manager for a multinational company headquartered in London and with several branches and business units in many countries including Sweden, France, Germany, Canada, China, India and Singapore. You have been asked to take charge of a new IT project that will last for about a year and involves managing a remotely located cross-cultural team including members from all the countries in which your company has a foothold. You are very much aware of the many pitfalls of managing people from different cultural backgrounds and expressed your concerns to one of your colleagues who has some experience in this area. He has advised you to use the Hofstede model of national cultural differences which he thinks can be an effective tool for managing cross-cultural teams. He has given you a copy of the framework he has been using in his international work project.

You now need to fill in the last two columns of Table 6.7 which will provide you with valuable insights into the key cultural characteristics of the international project team you will need to manage over the coming year and consider their implications for your approach to team management. Your colleague has already filled in the first row of the framework to provide you with an example of how to go about this task.

Table 6.7 Using Hofstede's model of national cultures as a change tool to manage cross-cultural teams

Key dimensions of Hofstede's model of national cultural differences	Evaluative measures	Cross-cultural team characteristics	Implications for team management
Power distance index	PDI: High v. Low	Team members from France, Germany, Canada and Sweden will tend to have a low PDI score while those from China, India and Singapore will tend towards a high PDI.	High PDI: Provide on-going support and encouragement, exercise close supervision, rely on formal rules, and provide explicit guidance and feedback on assigned tasks. Low PDI: exercise loose supervision, encourage open communication, involve in decision-making, delegate responsibilities.

Key dimensions of Hofstede's model of national cultural differences	Evaluative measures	Cross-cultural team characteristics	Implications for team management
Individualism v. Collectivism	IDV: High v. Low		
Uncertainty avoidance index	UAI: High v. Low		
Masculinity v. Femininity	MAS: High v. Low		
Long-term orientation v. Short-term orientation	LTO: STO:		
Indulgence v. Restraint	IND: High v. Low		

6.8 Conceptual nugget: A dialogic model for managing culture change

One of the most common reasons for change failure is the lack of proper communication throughout the culture change process (Oliver, 2010). Our conceptual nugget for this chapter aims to address this recurrent communication problem and entails the development of a *dialogic model for effectively managing culture change*. The model rests on a two-fold premise: (i) the need to locate culture change within an ongoing process of free and open dialogue as a means of increasing the likelihood of success, and (ii) the need to manage the meanings attached to culture change which is as important as managing the change itself. (We will further develop and reinforce this line of reasoning in Chapter 8 on communicating change.)

Our dialogic model is firmly grounded in *a system of meaning creation and action enabled by an ongoing process of free and open dialogue* – as illustrated in Figure 6.1. We proceed to briefly explain its key elements in the following discussion.

Shared understanding

The first stage of the model warrants the creation of an inclusive and empowering communication platform to enable a free process of collective sense making and meaning creation around the core cultural values and norms driving culture change. Following the premise underpinning our model, this is a necessary precondition for effectively managing the meaning of culture change beyond any doubt right from the start of the change process – which, we argue, is the only way to achieve shared understanding and consensus amongst key organisational stakeholders as to the scope, content and impact of the proposed culture change (Francis et al., 2013).

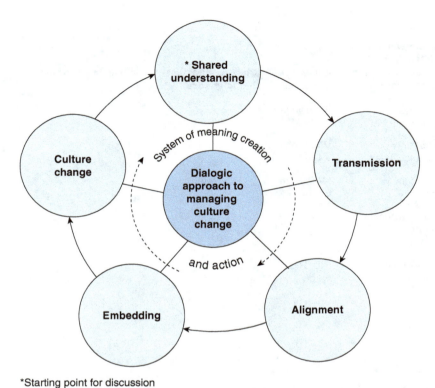

*Starting point for discussion

Figure 6.1 A dialogic model for managing culture change

Transmission

Change leaders also have to choose the right communication channels and media to transmit the new cultural values and norms across the organisation. There is need at this stage for a two-way communication system and appropriate feedback mechanisms to register stakeholder responses, views and lived experiences of the culture change.

Alignment

Another key principle of successful culture change is the ability to maintain an alignment between the core cultural values and the strategic objectives of the organisation – which, once again, is impossible without an ongoing dialogue between organisational members both across hierarchical and functional levels. It is worth noting in passing that maintaining culture-strategy alignment through ongoing dialogue can prove to be very effective in managing organisational subcultures – either to bring them in line with the core values of the organisation or integrate their alternative views and positive contributions into the organisation's dominant cultural value system.

Embedding

This particular stage of the model is focused on the discursive and behavioural aspects of culture change. It involves a back-and-forth movement between the dominant 'cultural talk' (i.e. the different texts and practices through which the organisation's culture is transmitted) and day-to-day behaviours to ensure consistency between the cultural values endorsed by the organisation and their translation into practice – leading, over time, to their institutionalisation or 'embedding' into the socio-cultural fabric and behavioural patterns of the organisation.

From a dialogic perspective, the embedding of cultural values involves an ability to both *talk the cultural talk* and *walk the cultural talk* – i.e. an ability to not only speak convincingly of the organisation's core cultural values but also model such values through everyday behaviours and practices to solidify and firmly establish the organisation's cultural value system.

Culture change

Our dialogic model also accounts for the fact that the cultural value system of an organisation is not fixed or determinate but dynamic, evolving and open to change. There is therefore a need to include in the model a final stage which accounts for that fact and keeps open the possibility for further cultural change – whether it be in the form of a refinement, renewal or radical transformation of the organisation's cultural value system in view of new strategic, social and ethical imperatives.

Undoubtedly, keeping open the possibility for culture change is impossible without ongoing dialogue and a free exchange of views and ideas among organisational stakeholders – which is why we see this important stage as a catalyst for ongoing culture change and sustained movement along the virtuous and never-ending cycle of meaning creation and action in which our model is grounded.

REFLECTIVE EXERCISE

1   Why is it as important to manage the meaning of change as it is to manage the change itself? Why is this even more important in the case of culture change?
2   Refer back to the dialogic model in Figure 6.1. Think about how you would apply the model in practice. To help you with this exercise, use Table 6.8 to organise your thoughts and do a list of activities you would need to carry out to optimise its practical application. Think also about the outcomes you would like to achieve at each stage and outline them in the last column of the table.

(Continued)

Table 6.8   Practical application of dialogic model

Key stages of dialogic model of culture change management	List of activities	Intended outcomes
Shared understanding		
Transmission		
Alignment		
Embedding		
Culture change		

6.9 Key learning points

The following key learning points have been covered in this chapter:

1   While organisational culture is too complex to be pinned by any single definition, there is considerable value in distilling its most distinctive features derived from *alternative definitions* and *metaphors* that can enable us to identify it as a unique concept and understand the multiple meanings that can be attached to it.

2   Schein's model of organisational culture consists of three distinctive yet interrelated layers with different levels of visibility and means of accessibility and includes: *artefacts, espoused values and beliefs*, and *basic underlying assumptions*.

3   Johnson and Scholes' *cultural web* consists of six interrelated dimensions: *stories, symbols, power structures, organisational structures, control systems* and *routines and rituals*. These six dimensions contribute to the formation of the *cultural paradigm* or what is commonly referred to as the dominant culture of the organisation. Importantly, the cultural web can be used as a valuable change tool to both analyse an organisation's current culture and frame culture change.

4   *Organisational subcultures* are groups of employees with shared values, viewpoints and interests that *deviate from the dominant culture*. Organisational subcultures are not necessarily good or bad. It all depends on the extent to which they pose a threat to or can positively contribute to the change success.

5   Strategies for managing culture change need to be adapted to specific change situations and include processes of *enculturation, acculturation, assimilation, integration and separation*. Moreover, Hofstede's model of national cultures which consists of six key dimensions – *power distance, individualism v. collectivism, uncertainty avoidance, masculinity v. femininity, long-term v. short-term orientation* and *indulgence v. restraint* – can be used as an effective change tool to manage cultural diversity in an international context.

6   Finally, our *dialogic model of culture change management* firmly grounds culture change in a *virtuous cycle of meaning creation and action* enabled by an *ongoing process of free and open dialogue*. Its key elements include *shared understanding, transmission, alignment,*

embedding and *culture change* – which are designed and sequenced in such a way as to increase the likelihood of culture change success and keep open the possibility for further culture change.

END-OF-CHAPTER CASE STUDY 6.3

Dutch bank ING: Clearing a cultural path for agile transformation

Introduction

ING (The Internationale Nederlanden Groep) is a Dutch bank with more than 58,000 employees serving 38 million customers in more than 40 countries. ING came about in 1991 from the merger of two insurance companies. Since then, ING has acquired multiple banks and insurance companies and established strong business partnerships with more than 100 financial technology firms – turning it, according to industry analysts, into one of the leading banks in Europe and an innovative pioneer of online banking.

However, ING soon realised that online banks were lagging behind other online businesses such as Amazon, Instagram and Facebook and could not deliver the same kind of customer service and user experience that these companies were able to offer, notably frictionless, speedy transactions and high-quality customer support services across a wide range of Internet connected and mobile devices. In 2015, ING launched a major change initiative to implement an agile business model that would enable it to quickly catch up with other high-performing online businesses and protect its position at the forefront of the banking industry as a prime innovator in technological application and the creation of customer value.

Implementing agile transformation via a culture shift

The implementation of an agile business model warranted a culture shift towards flexible collaboration and a reinforcement of ING's commitment to the development of innovative products and creating superior customer value. Hierarchical structures, tight control systems and rigid silo working had to make way for more fluid and dynamic, small, cross-functional, interdisciplinary and self-organising teams referred to as *squads* – which consisted of up to 9 members, including product designers, marketing specialists and IT engineers.

Squads added up to form larger units of around 150 employees, labelled as *tribes*. The new squads and tribes had to take ownership of product development and were entrusted with the responsibility to proactively demonstrate creativity and craftsmanship geared towards continuous improvement and the maximisation of customer value – which is at the core of ING's innovative and customer-centric culture. To establish this new cultural orientation across the organisation, some routines and control systems had to be changed – formal meetings, exhaustive resource and action planning and narrow supervisory control had to be abandoned in favour of more informal, trusting relationships, autonomous working, fast decision-making and proactive approaches to continuous process improvement. Training interventions and reward schemes were recalibrated with a focus on 'agile outputs' and the capability to optimise customer value while keeping in view ING's new strategic objectives.

(Continued)

Tearing down physical and psychological barriers

Top management decided that to ensure the successful implementation of its new agile business model, there was a need to tear down both the physical and psychological barriers between organisational members. This involved the creation of open offices and inclusive communication platforms to enable collective decision-making and collaboration both within and across squad teams and provide a safe and engaging workplace environment conducive to learning, knowledge sharing and creativity vital to the successful implementation of ING's agile business model.

Top management were also keen to lead by example and model the core values and behaviours that defined ING's new cultural orientation. They regularly attended daily stand-up meetings and conversations with employees to motivate them, check on their progress and tune into their concerns, needs and expectations. They set up feedback mechanisms as an integral part of ING communication strategy to take on board employee responses and suggestions with regard to new product development. In line with the new agile mindset, they also placed an emphasis on a 'fail-fast-move-on' attitude, which encourages employees to take risks, quickly move on from mistakes and failures and keep learning and experimenting to drive the organisation forward.

Conclusions

A number of key issues arise from this case study. First, there is need for a robust alignment between an organisation's core cultural values and strategic objectives to increase the likelihood of change success. At ING, changes to the structural arrangements and working practices were carried out in tandem with changes to the organisation's core values and behavioural patterns.

Second, there is need for the removal of all barriers that stand in the way of culture change. At ING, no efforts were spared to get rid of both the physical and psychological barriers that could potentially prevent the move towards agile working.

Third, there is need for change leaders to 'walk the cultural talk' to embed new cultural values. At ING, top management were keen to model the core values and behaviours as a way of motivating employees and integrating their views and learning into the development of new products in line with the organisation's innovative and customer-centric culture.

Finally, there is need for two-way communication and on-going dialogue between change leaders and employees in order to maintain the momentum of culture change and achieve the organisation's strategic objectives. At ING, top management maintained open, two-way communication channels with employees via daily conversations and stand-up meetings and set up feedback mechanisms as an integral part of its communicative practices to motivate employees and register their responses and suggestions with regard to new product development.

Sources: Barton et al. (2018); ING (2022a, 2022b)

Questions

1   How would you describe the new culture that management at ING wanted to establish in order to drive the move towards agile working?

2   Can you identify some of the elements of Johnson and Scholes's cultural web that had to be changed to implement and establish the new culture at ING?

3   Refer to the dialogic model of culture change management developed in this chapter. In what ways has each of its key stages been translated into practice at ING?

6.10 Independent learning

If you want to consolidate your understanding of culture change, you can access the following materials online:

Schein's 3 levels of organisational culture: www.youtube.com/watch?v=HM89E6ltVOg. This video provides you with an overview of Edgar Schein's Organisational Culture Model and shows a simple five-step process to apply it in organisations.

Cultural Web: www.youtube.com/watch?v=i9hVuurBvh4. Dr Mike Clayton talks about the components that make up an organisation's culture, based on Johnson and Scholes' Cultural Web model.

Organisational subcultures: www.youtube.com/watch?v=WoGn5gCCOUs. Annabelle Beckwith explains the meaning of subcultures within organisations.

Hofstede's six dimensions of organisational culture: www.youtube.com/watch?v=yKKruTRQ_2Acan. This video reviews Geert Hofstede's model which he developed with more than 110,000 employees from IBM based on a factor analysis. This model comprises six key dimensions against which differences across national cultures can be identified.

Transforming your company's culture: www.tonyrobbins.com/podcasts/episode-5/. In this podcast, Tony Robbins interviews Marissa Levin, CEO of Information Experts. Marissa Levin talks about the importance of transforming the company's culture by enlisting the engagement and commitment of employees in order to achieve organisational effectiveness and success.

6.11 References

Alvesson, M. (2013) *Understanding Organizational Culture*, 2nd edn. London: Sage Publications Ltd.

Baek, P., Chang, J. and Kim, T. (2019) 'Organizational culture now and going forward', *Journal of Organizational Change Management*, 32(6), 650–668.

Barton, D., Carey, D. and Charan, R. (2018) 'One bank's agile team experiment', *Harvard Business Review*, March–April, 59–61.

Dabbawala (2022) *Mumbai Dabbawala*. [Online] Available at: https://mumbaidabbawala.in/ (accessed 22 February 2023).

Francis, H. M., Ramdhony, A., Reddington, M. and Staines, H. (2013) 'Opening spaces for conversational practice: A conduit for effective engagement strategies and productive working arrangements', *International Journal of Human Resource Management*, 24(14), 2713–2740.

Hofstede, G. (2022) *The 6-D model of National Culture*. [Online] Available at: https://geerthofstede.com/culture-geert-hofstede-gert-jan-hofstede/6d-model-of-national-culture/ (accessed 25 February 2023).

Hofstede Insights (2019) *National Culture and Organizational Culture – How are They Different and How Do They Interconnect?* [Online] Available at: https://news.hofstede-insights.com/news/national-culture-and-organisational-culture-how-are-they-different (accessed 1 March 2023).

ING (2022a) *ING: About Us*. [Online] Available at: www.ing.com/About-us/Profile/ING-at-a-glance.htm (accessed 2 March 2023).

ING (2022b) *2021 Annual Report*. [Online] Available at: www.ing.com/About-us/Profile/Annual-reporting-suite/Annual-Report/2021-Annual-Report.htm (accessed 2 March 2023).

Johnson, G., Whittington, R. and Scholes, K. (2012) *Fundamentals of Strategy*. Harlow: Pearson Education.

Katzenbach, J. R., Steffen, I. and Kronley, C. (2012) 'Cultural change that sticks', *Harvard Business Review*. [Online] Available at: https://hbr.org/2012/07/cultural-change-that-sticks (accessed 1 March 2023).

Morgan, G. (2006) *Images of Organization* (updated edn). London: Sage Publications Ltd.

Muthusamy, S. K. (2019) 'Power of positive words: Communication, cognition and organizational transformation', *Journal of Organizational Change Management*, 32(1), 103–122.

Öcal, K. (2011) 'Evaluating organizational culture with metaphors', *African Journal of Business Management*, 5(3), 12882–12889.

Oliver, D. (2010) 'In search of the Holy Grail – internal communications and cultural change', *Journal of Change Management*, 1(2), pp.179–185.

Schein, E. H. with Schein, P. A. (2017) *Organizational Culture and Leadership*, 5th edn. New Jersey: John Wiley & Sons.

Thomke, S. H. (2012) 'Models of service excellence', *Harvard Business Review*. [Online] Available at: https://hbr.org/2012/11/mumbais-models-of-service-excellence (accessed 20 January 2023).

7
LEADING CHANGE

Learning Outcomes

After completing this chapter, you should be able to:

- Explain the meaning of leadership as a multidimensional, dynamic and emergent process.
- Gain an insight into the historical background of leadership and establish its links to the current conceptualisation of organisational change leadership.
- Draw the distinction between change leaders and change managers and appreciate their different yet complementary roles and responsibilities.
- Develop a sound understanding of a range of leadership theories and their practical implications with reference to relevant case examples.
- Discuss the key emergent concepts and challenges shaping contemporary approaches to leadership.
- Familiarise yourself with the concept of dialogic leadership that places an emphasis on the transformative role of open dialogue on the leadership process and that can be used as a lever for contemporary approaches to leadership.

7.1 Introduction

The purpose of this chapter is to enable you to develop a comprehensive understanding of organisational change leadership – from its historical roots in the wider leadership discourse through well-known leadership theories to key notions and challenges impacting contemporary leadership. The chapter begins by drawing attention to the multidimensional dynamic and emergent nature of leadership as a *process of becoming* and the need to resist all-encompassing definitions that attempt to 'pin down' its meaning. It then provides a brief historical overview of political leadership, establishing in the process important links to organisational change leadership. The chapter proceeds to revisit one of the most recurrent themes in the change literature regarding the differences between change leaders and change managers, leading to the development of an argument as to their distinctive yet complementary roles in the pursuit of change success. The chapter then critically examines in chronological order (from the early 1940s to date) some of the most prominent leadership theories to draw out their relevance to organisational change leadership and consider their practical implications with reference to appropriate case examples. Finally, our conceptual nugget presents our model of dialogic leadership and explains how it can serve as a lever for contemporary approaches to leadership. The chapter concludes with an outline of the key learning points arising from the preceding discussion and an end-of-chapter case study about Jeff Skoll, an exemplar of 21st leadership.

7.2 The meaning of leadership

A complex and multidimensional phenomenon

Leadership is usually seen as the holy grail of business and change success. It is therefore not surprising that it is still a great sales pitch across business schools and remains one of the most salient features of the literature on organisational change. However, the concept of leadership remains ill-defined, ambiguous and elusive. This is understandable given that the term refers to a multidimensional phenomenon that encompasses a complex mix of notions, ideals and behaviours. The difficulty in pinning down the concept of leadership is compounded by the fact that the meanings attached to it are filtered by different cultural values, social norms, perspectives and ideological commitments. Different people across different geographical and socio-cultural boundaries entertain different ideals and ideas about what leadership should be and what it should stand for.

Stogdill (1974), one of the leading proponents in the area, gives some credence to this. His oft-quoted remark is a constant reminder of the plethora of existing definitions of leadership: 'there are almost as many definitions of leadership as there are persons who may have attempted to define the concept' (ibid., p. 7). It would be fair to say that no change expert would dispute the fact that no single definition of leadership could ever capture all of its facets or decant its meaning into one all-encompassing statement. We also take the view that there would be little point in trying to do so. This would only serve to reify the phenomenon – i.e. rigidly fix its meaning with little regard to its evolving nature and scope for expanding our understanding of the leadership process in view of both current and future challenges and imperatives.

Leadership as a process of becoming

This is why, along with many other colleagues, we tend to resist all-encompassing definitions of leadership that attempt to fix its conceptual contours and claim to capture, once and for all, its essential meaning. We see leadership as a process of becoming – a multidimensional, dynamic and emergent process that can take on new dimensions and meanings together with the specific changing contexts in which it pans out. We therefore stay away from any specific definition of leadership that attempts to 'pin down' its meaning. We prefer here to 'talk about' leadership in a non-fixating way and in so doing, we review a wide range of meanings which have been attached to it in the course of its historical development and the contemporary issues and challenges that have shaped its meaning.

7.3 Leadership through the ages: Implications for organisational change leadership

So much ink has been spilled on the subject matter that no single treatise on leadership could ever hope to cover the multiplicity of ideas and images, propositions and prescriptions that have been woven around the phenomenon over the course of documented history. Here, we focus attention on some of the greatest leaders that have made their mark on the 'collective consciousness' and draw out their relevance to organisational change leadership.

Leaders from antiquity

From Ancient Greece, how many times have we been told the stories of much celebrated leaders such as Alexander the Great (356–323 BC) who was known for his military genius, motivational skills and love of knowledge or Pericles (494–429 BC), the great orator who contributed to the establishment of democracy in Athens. A few centuries later, Julius Caesar (100–44 BC) emerged as a controversial leader and first dictator of the Roman Empire who demonstrated his prowess and motivational skills on the battlefield. Julius Caesar is also remembered for his troubled relationship with Cleopatra who is herself one of the most famous female leaders in history and known for her charisma, 'quick strategic thinking' and ability to forge many political alliances to protect her interests and transform Egypt into one of the world's greatest kingdoms. The traits and skills possessed by these leaders – especially their practical intelligence, motivational skills, strategic mindset and ability to forge powerful alliances – are still some of the most valued leadership characteristics across modern-day organisations.

At the time when the Roman Empire had gained control over the Mediterranean region, Jesus Christ came onto the scene as perhaps the greatest leadership figure the world has ever witnessed. Putting religious beliefs aside, there is wide agreement among scholars that Jesus was outstanding as a visionary, charismatic and inspirational leader. As a person of complete integrity with a towering moral stature, he displayed a pattern of behaviour that was compassionate, motivating, forgiving and self-sacrificing – which, for many, makes him the archetype of the servant leader, the ramifications of which still have a significant bearing on current conceptualisations of change leadership and the nature of the leader–follower exchange relationship.

The Middle Ages

The Middle Ages (which lasted from the fall of the Roman Empire in 476 CE to around 1450 CE) produced outstanding leaders such as Wu Zetian (who ruled China from 690 to 705) and Charlemagne, King of the Franks (742–814). Wu Zetian was a well-educated, highly intelligent woman with exceptional skills in politics, strategic decision-making and the ability to surround herself with talented and competent people which, under her rule, helped China prosper, improve the quality of life of its population and expand its borders by conquering new lands.

For his part, Charlemagne is known as the humble, unpretentious yet extremely competent leader who contributed to important cultural and educational reforms in Europe which paved the way for the Renaissance across Europe, a buoyant period of European economic rebirth, cultural renewal and scientific exploration. What makes Charlemagne stand out as a leader is his love of learning and the investments he made in education throughout his kingdom. Moreover, he did not believe in 'micromanaging' but knew how to rely on those working under him to ensure the enforcement of the law and the proper administration of the courts. Leaders like Wu Zetian and Charlemagne embody key characteristics such as a strategic mindset, networking and talent management skills, and the ability to delegate responsibilities and work as part of a team – which are undisputedly timeless leadership qualities vital to change success.

Renaissance leaders

Sometimes referred to as the early modern era (lasting from around 1450 to the late 1700s), the Renaissance brought us Machiavelli (1469–1527 CE), a writer and political philosopher who outlined his own particular brand of 'leadership virtue' principally in his political treatise entitled *The Prince*. Machiavelli's notion of the virtuous leader is often interpreted as a demoralised version of leadership in which he condones deception, manipulation, corruption and other forms of unscrupulous acts as acceptable, if not desirable behaviours.

However, when cast in a more positive light from the perspective of Machiavelli's political realism, an effective leader is one who is able to take a pragmatic stance in protecting their power bases, making moral compromises and pursuing their interests in circumstances rife with conflicting interests, hardships and threats to their own survival – where managing power is the only way the virtuous leader can do any good (and keep doing it) in the real world. This speaks strongly to organisation change leaders who have to operate within a complex network of conflicting power relations and face increasing challenges in the form of fierce, relentless competitive pressures and immediate threats to the survival and continuity of their organisations (Cunha et al., 2013; Harris, 2010).

Another towering figure of the late Renaissance is Napoleon Bonaparte (1769–1821), the first Emperor of France. History shows that Napoleon was callous, cold and calculating in the way he staged a *coup d'état* to establish himself as a dictator and ordered numerous massacres and genocide-like atrocities of thousands outside of the battlefield – making him a *dealer in death*.

However, Napoleon is seen by many historians as a visionary master–organiser and military strategist who won an impressive number of battles and is often quoted as an inspirational, visionary leader and a *dealer in hope*, capable of motivating people and driving them towards a desirable future – a quality cherished by all change leaders.

Late modern leaders

Hitler is one of the most notorious political figures of the late modern era (early 1800–late 1940s). He capitalised on the economic turmoil, political infighting and popular discontent following the First World War to seize power in Germany beginning 1933. Master of propaganda and crowd conditioning, he excelled in the use of symbols and gestures, rituals and rallies to manipulate and deceive his countrymen and advance his nationalist–supremacist political agenda, which led to the genocide of millions of Jews. He was the typical narcissistic leader who loved being adulated by adoring crowds without in the least reciprocating their feelings. This particular form of malignant narcissism can be found in other tyrants and cult leaders around the world and reflects a dark, pathological form of transformational leadership which fetishises deceit and manipulation and perpetuates an abusive master–slave relationship which can lead to violence and deadly consequences. Hitler is an archetype of toxic leadership that can be used as a normative yardstick for sensitising organisational change leaders to the pitfalls of transformational leadership which any decent human being would want to avoid.

Fortunately, this particular era has also witnessed the emergence of a leader by the name of Mohandas Karamchand Gandhi (1915–1947) who reflected the more positive side of transformational leadership. Gandhi was a visionary, charismatic and inspirational leader who led India on a non-violent path towards independence which was achieved in 1947. He is well known for his belief that if people could change themselves, so would the world around them – a belief that carries the valuable precept that change leaders should themselves be open to change and do change *with* people and not *to* people.

Contemporary leaders

Another exceptional leader who emerged at the beginning of the contemporary era (1950s to date) is Martin Luther King who led the civil rights movement in the 1950s and 60s in the USA. He worked relentlessly towards racial justice and the social integration of black people in the USA despite being arrested, assaulted and put in jail on several occasions. Change leaders can certainly draw inspiration from his resilience, formidable public speaking skills and ability to develop a common vision and muster his followers' commitment to change by challenging them to question the current state of affairs and consider the possibility of a better future.

Nelson Mandela is also often cited as one of the most outstanding transformational leaders of the 20th century. After being jailed for 27 years for defying the apartheid system of racial segregation that prevailed in South Africa, he won the country's first democratic, multi-racial general election in 1994. Mandela is much revered for his humility, integrity, dignity and many other laudable traits. However, what perhaps defines him as a transformational leader is his ability for introspection and self-reflection through which he managed to *transform himself* into the type of empathic and forgiving leader that was needed to dismantle apartheid in a peaceful way and promote a politics of reconciliation that could pave the way towards a democratic society in South Africa. The ability to *look inwardly* and *change oneself* is no small feat and seen as one of the greatest qualities of a change leader.

Other leaders of the contemporary era that can inspire change leaders for different reasons include:

Indira Gandhi, who was the Prime minister of India for 18 years from 1966 to 1984. She is known for her strong will, courage, bold (albeit sometimes controversial) decisions and her political intransigence in pursuing courses of action that she felt was right for her country. While she never cast herself as a feminist, she fought in many ways for women's rights in a highly patriarchal society and shared with Margaret Thatcher, the first female prime minister in Britain, the 'dogged determination' to succeed in a male-dominated arena that characterised both Indian and British politics at the time. This elicits thinking about the role of gender in organisational change leadership – more specifically, the challenges women leaders face in terms of access and agency within the higher spheres of the organisation and the unique contribution they can bring to change initiatives.

Barack Obama, the first black president of the United States who was in office between 2009 and 2017 and who is seen by many as a modern-day role model for aspiring leaders. As the first black president of the United States, Barack Obama possessed a range of leadership traits and skills that are taught across business schools including well-honed oratorical skills, emotional intelligence, a professional code of ethics rooted in discipline and hard work, and a great sense of posterity demonstrated by his staunch commitment to the development of new leaders. He had an exceptional ability to not only face domestic challenges head-on but also to connect with other world leaders and governing bodies to consolidate the position of the United States within a network of agencies working towards global economic, social and environmental sustainability – an exemplar of the typical eco-leader who is both inward and outward looking and caring for both people and planet.

Finally, Angela Merkel, the first woman Chancellor of Germany who held office from 2005 to 2021 and who shares with Barack Obama the characteristics of the eco-leader. In this respect, she was adept at blending domestic and internal policies to spearhead important economic and social reforms in her own country whilst working relentlessly to strengthen international cooperation geared towards building a more politically stable, economically viable and environmentally friendly future – all of which are key concerns that have to be factored into the development of sustainable organisational change.

Some reflections on the links between political and organisational change leadership

First, the wider discourse on political leadership is very much *at the centre of our frame of reference* when we think and talk about leadership in the context of organisational change. This is because political leadership and organisation change leadership have a common denominator: they both involve the action of an individual with a distinguishing set of traits and skills leading other people towards a desired goal. While their respective domains of action are different, political leadership and organisational change leadership share the same 'essence'; and, as shown by the preceding discussion, the principles, ideals, concerns and of course pitfalls of political leadership are highly applicable to the context of organisational change – as will be made more explicit in the following sections.

Second, we have to bear in mind that the process of leadership can never be divorced from politics – irrespective of the context within which it unravels. Like political leaders, organisational change leaders have to protect their power bases, build effective coalitions, manage resistance and conflict, address the concerns and interests of different constituent groups and achieve shared understanding around their vision and strategic choices. In short, *organisational leadership is to a large extent political leadership.*

Third, by virtue of their status as *human beings leading other human beings*, both political and organisational change leaders have to develop people-oriented skills to achieve consensus around their vision, build a rapport with their followers and muster the commitment necessary to bring about successful change.

Fourth, the consideration of leadership from a political perspective, outwith organisational boundaries, allows for a greater analytical distancing that brings into sharper focus the *dark side of leadership* which tends to be brushed over in the change literature. All too often, the discussion of organisational leadership remains one-dimensional and tends to pay sole attention to the positive traits that a leader is expected to possess. The history of political leadership has shown that there are *both good and bad leaders* – which is equally true in the context of organisational change.

Fifth, the history of political leadership shows that both men and women have been effective leaders in the past, that there are currently effective leaders of both genders, and that it is more than likely that this will still be the case in the future. Hence, applying a gendered lens to change leadership that cast men and women leaders into rigid stereotypes under the assumption that they are naturally suited to different roles and responsibilities is, in our view, erroneous. As we shall argue in more detail later on, change leaders – whether they be men or women – should be judged on their performance and success achieved on their own terms and on the back of their own competences as effective leaders.

Finally, *political leadership has a shaping influence on organisational change leadership.* For example, even a cursory overview of contemporary leaders brings to attention the concerns surrounding sustainability that are at the forefront of their minds – concerns which have had spillover effects on organisational change leadership which is under greater pressure to find sustainable solutions in response to global economic, social and environmental challenges. We will revisit the notion of sustainable leadership when we consider modern-day approaches to leadership in a later section.

—REFLECTIVE EXERCISE—

Once again, skim read the historical overview of leadership presented in this section and answer the following questions:

1   Why is a reading of political leadership important to our understanding of organisational change leadership?
2   In your view, what are the most striking similarities between political leaders and organisational change leaders?
3   What are the key challenges facing both types of leadership?

7.4 Leaders v. managers

Before going any further, we need to revisit the change leaders v. change managers debate which is recurrent in the change literature and is always covered in some manner in change management modules. Table 7.1 below highlights the key differences between the two.

Table 7.1 The key differences between change leaders and managers

Leaders	Managers
Change leaders: *Doing the right things*	Change managers: *Doing things right*
• Create vision and set direction • Develop and communicate change strategy • Bring about conditions conducive to change • Inspire, influence and motivate followers • Build coalitions and trusting relationships geared towards change success • Operate mostly at a strategic level • Status bestowed upon by followers	• Set specific goals and objectives to ensure change implementation • Focus on planning, budgeting, organising and monitoring of appropriate resources and activities • Translate the change plan into action • Operate mostly at a tactical and operational levels • Allocated status which dictates relationship with subordinates

Change leaders are usually focused on *doing the right things* – i.e. their primary responsibility is to ensure that the organisation is doing what it is supposed to be doing. In this regard, change leaders are primarily concerned with creating a vision, setting a direction for the organisation, designing and communicating the change strategy and bringing about the conditions to ensure its effective implementation. Change leaders also share in large part the responsibility to address the 'softer dimension' of change and are as such expected to be people-oriented and sensitive to the psychological and emotional need of their subordinates. In this regard, good leaders are able to inspire, influence and motivate their followers. They also seek to build trusting relationships and strong coalitions with key organisational stakeholders to ensure the successful completion of change projects. Importantly, another defining characteristic of change leaders is that they operate at the strategic level in ensuring that the organisation is doing the right things and their status is usually 'bestowed upon them' by their followers without whom their role would be greatly diminished (Gill, 2002).

By contrast, change managers are mostly concerned about *doing things right*. As such, the main responsibility of change managers is to set specific goals and objectives that are aligned with those of the overall change strategy. Change managers are mostly concerned with the 'hard aspect' of change and are primarily focused on the more mundane tasks of planning, budgeting, organising and monitoring of resources and activities. To this end, change managers are deemed to be more transactional in their dealings with their subordinates and tend to relate to them in such a way as to increase the likelihood of successful change implementation.

As such, change managers are seen as restricted to a lower-level, tactical activity, the primary purpose of which is to implement change. Moreover, change managers have an 'allocated status' which reflects the fact that they have been assigned specific, 'concrete' roles and responsibilities to ensure the proper execution of the change plan (Hayes, 2021).

Reconciling the paradoxical tensions between the roles of change leaders and managers

While the distinction between change leaders and managers draws a valuable analytical (and functional) line between the two and reflects to a large extent current practices across real-life organisations, one may wonder whether such distinction is not too rigid and favours one role over the other. Leaders carry an aura around them and are often glamourised as the face of change – a high-profile, highly visible, person-centered and vital figure spearheading change initiatives which would be doomed to failure without it. Managers, on the other hand, are portrayed as confined to a back-end, mechanical role entangled in complexity and monotony that can be carried out by any reasonably trained yet expendable individual – i.e. one who is easily replaceable and hence not so vital to change success.

While these popular representations of leaders and managers hold partial truths, they do poor justice to the fact that both change leaders and change managers have a critical role to play in the pursuit of change success. Kotter (1990) argues in favour of placing leadership and management on an equal footing and assigning both roles equal value. He sees both roles as complementary and thus, interrelated and mutually reinforcing and beneficial in the pursuit of change success. Moreover, change managers are not necessarily more easily replaceable than leaders. Change leaders are on even more slippery ground than managers and their heads are often the first to roll in case of change failure.

Although the dichotomy between change leadership and management is certainly not a false one, it should not be pushed too far. Change leaders and managers do have overlapping responsibilities: to varying degrees, leaders have to hone their managerial skills to effectively manage their time, the people working in their immediate sphere of influence and the resources at their disposal. On the other hand, managers have to develop and deploy solid leadership skills when counselling, mentoring, motivating and harnessing the commitment of their direct reports to change initiatives.

The distinction between change leaders and change managers should not be rigidified to such an extent that both sets of activities and responsibilities are seen as totally separate and running parallel to each other. In actual practice, change leaders and change managers have to reconcile the **paradoxical tensions** between their two respective roles to achieve sustainable change success – where they have to work in collaboration to achieve a balance between the need for dynamic change and the need for relative stability to embed new working practices, the need to achieve short-term objectives while pursuing long-term goals, and the need to optimise operational efficiency while keeping the organisation on the right strategic path. In short, change leaders and change managers have to blend their distinctive yet complementary roles to achieve sustainable change success – and it is by effectively reconciling the paradoxical tensions between their respective roles that they can collaboratively help the *organisation do the right things right* and clear the path to change success (Berti and Cunha, 2022; Berti et al., 2021).

REFLECTIVE EXERCISE

1   What are your views on the distinction between change leaders and change managers?
2   In what ways do the roles of change leaders and change managers overlap?
3   Why do change leaders and change managers have to blend their respective roles to ensure sustainable change success?

7.5 Key leadership theories

In this section, we examine in chronological order the key leadership theories that are of particular relevance to organisational change. Table 7.2 presents a synopsis of the approaches that define the main eras of leadership theory which are detailed in the following discussion.

Table 7.2   Key eras of leadership theory

Eras of Leadership Theory	
Traits Approach	Dominant until late 1940s Focus on personality Main assumption: Leaders born not made
Styles Approach	Held sway between 1950–1970 Focus on leadership behaviours Main assumption: Leadership behaviours can be taught
Situational Approach	Popular in the 1980s Focus on context of leadership Main assumption: Effective leadership is dependent on the requirement of the situation
Transformational Approach	Became of particular interest in the 1990s Focus on leader–follower exchange relationship Main assumption: Transformation leadership is the primary driver of change and innovation

Eras of Leadership Theory	
Contemporary Approaches	Turn of the 21st century to date.
	Focus on leadership as a complex and multidimensional process
	Main assumption: Contemporary leadership is being shaped by intertwining global influences reflecting the most pressing concerns and challenges of the times.

Sources: Adapted from Bryman, A. (1996) 'Leadership in organizations', in S. R. Clegg, C. Hardy and W. R. Nord (eds), *Handbook of Organization Studies*. London: Sage Publications, pp. 276–292; Western, S. (2008) *Leadership: A Critical Text*. London: Sage Publications.

Traits theory

Traits theory was dominant in the 1940s and is built on the premise that some people possess certain genetically determined, clearly identifiable and relatively stable characteristics and qualities that enable them to be effective as leaders. At face value, traits theory seems to lend credence to the view that *leaders are born not made* – which once again, brings us back to the *nature v. nurture* debate discussed in Chapter 5 (see section on *A combination of psychological dispositions and socio-cultural factors*).

We will not re-engage with this debate at any length here. Suffice to say that we believe most people nowadays would agree that a more balanced conception of leadership is needed – one that goes beyond the dichotomous view of leaders as *either born or made*. It is undeniable that good leaders possess certain natural traits and genetic dispositions that distinguish them from others. However, like President Obama, we also endorse the view that leaders can and should be properly trained in order to acquire and develop the necessary knowledge, skills and behaviours without which they would not be able to operate effectively 'in context'.

Hence, for us, good leaders are *both born and made*. We push the envelope a little bit further to make the point that traits and training are locked in a virtuous cycle and can reinforce each other in a positive way – where, for example, individual traits can determine one's approach to training (e.g. logical, conscientious, goal-oriented approach to learning and development); and training can serve to consolidate existing traits or develop new ones (e.g. communication skills, self-reflection, integrity, resilience, etc.).

A non-exhaustive list of leadership traits

Table 7.3 contains a non-exhaustive list of some of the nuanced traits that effective change leaders are expected to possess partially in light of the overview of political leaders presented in the previous section. Importantly, it *reconciles to some extent the born or made dichotomy* and provides an indication of the areas in which they can receive appropriate training to consolidate existing traits and develop new ones.

Table 7.3 Change leaders as born *and* made

Change leaders as born *and* made	
Trait	**Training**
Personal Dispositions	Systems thinking
Ambitious but not ruthless	Strategic management
Intelligent but not pedantic	Company law
Visionary but grounded	IT
Motivated	Communication
Hard working and disciplined	Networking
Emotionally intelligent	Change management
Self-reflective	People management
Resilient and resolute	Diversity management
High tolerance for failure	Project management
Humble and teachable	Business ethics
	Corporate social responsibility
Professionalism	Critical thinking
Competent but not pretentious	Decision-making
Creative and able to think outside the box	Problem solving
Risk-taking but not reckless	Team working
Entrepreneurial	Motivation and engagement
Eloquent and communicative	Emotional intelligence, etc.
People–Social skills	
Charismatic but not deceptive	
Inspirational	
Socially engaged	
Non-narcissistic and empathic	
Non-manipulative and non-exploitive	
Take and delegate responsibility	
Motivational	
Democratic but impartial	
Collaborative and inclusive	
Compassionate and caring	
Ethical qualities	
Morally sound and ethical	
Ecological and philanthropic	
Demonstrate integrity	
Trustworthy	
Decent and respectable	
Forgiving	
Self-sacrificing	
Sense of posterity, etc.	

While no single leader is likely to possess all the traits mentioned in Table 7.3, we can think of a number of remarkable organisational leaders in whom some of these traits are more pronounced, depending on the sector in which they operate. For example, Elon Musk, the leader of Tesla and SpaceX, who has an IQ of 155, an extraordinary work ethic based on hard work, resilience, a commitment to continuous learning and a high tolerance for failure as a stepping-stone to success. As a celebrated entrepreneur, he is visionary and techno-savvy and sees the capacity for risk-taking, and coping with criticism as a means of survival and setting the tone for others to progress his company's mission.

There are many other renowned 21st century organisational leaders who share Elon Musk's admirable leadership qualities. To name but a few, Tim Cook, the highly successful CEO of Apple Company who is known for not only his humility and low-key approach but also for the value he places on collaboration and trusting relationships as a vehicle for creativity and innovation; Jeff Bezos, founder and CEO of the world's largest online retailer, Amazon, who, although autocratic at times, is transformational in the way he empowers his employees to take risks, commit to learning and experimentation, think outside the box and even embrace failure as a springboard for success. He is also interested in developing a philanthropic strategy that effectively combines *urgent business need* and *lasting social impact*.

PRACTICAL EXERCISE

Go online and find out more about successful 21st century organisational leaders. You can access valuable websites such as *Geeknack.com*, Centre for Management and Organisation Effectiveness (*CMOE.com*), *New York Times.com* and *Britannica.com*. Get the latest information on leaders such as:

- Elon Musk – Founder, CEO and Chief Engineer at SpaceX; CEO and Product Architect of Tesla, Inc.
- Dr Leila Fourie – CEO of the Johannesburg Stock Exchange.
- Sheryl Sandberg – Chief Operating Officer of Facebook, Inc. and founder of LeanIn.Org.
- Aloke Lohia – Founder and group CEO of Indorama Ventures Public Company Limited.
- Wang Wei – Founder and chairman of SF Express, a multinational delivery services and logistics company.
- Özlem Türeci – Co-founder of the biotechnology company BioNTech.
- Sanjiv Mehta – Chairman and managing director of Hindustan Unilever Limited.
- Mary Barra – CEO of General Motors.

Use the list in Table 7.3 to map out their traits and think about how these leaders are driving change in their respective organisations.

Criticisms

A number of criticisms have been leveled at traits theory. First, trait-spotting in great leaders tends to give primacy to the view that leaders are born with certain fixed characteristics whilst downplaying the importance of leadership training and development. Second, despite a lot of research in this area, the list of effective leadership traits is not exhaustive and remains difficult to prioritise; and no single leader could ever possess all the traits that are deemed desirable. Finally, as you will have certainly realised from doing the above practical exercise, by focusing on the personality of great leaders, traits theory pays little attention to the behaviours, context and nature of the leader–member exchange relationship – which the other leadership theories that are reviewed below have attempted to address (Stippler et al., 2011).

Styles theory

Styles theory held sway during the 1950s and the late 1960s. It is often viewed as a counterpoint to the primary focus of traits theory on the personal characteristics of the leader – with an emphasis on *leadership behaviours* as opposed to the personality of the leader. As such, styles theory shifts the focus from *being* (what a leader is) to *doing* (what a leader does) and is usually seen as a significant development in the conceptualisation of organisational leadership for the following reasons:

i   from a research perspective, leadership behaviours are more 'visible' than some of the more discrete traits and internal dispositions of leaders and are therefore seen as amenable to observation

ii   such behaviours can be taught and measured, lending credence to the assumption that leaders are not just *born* but also *made*.

Leadership styles continuums

There is a wide range of continuums of leadership styles that have been identified in the change literature. Table 7.4 below provides a summary overview of some of the most prominent ones.

Table 7.4   Prominent continuums of leadership styles

Continuums of leadership styles		
Autocratic		**Democratic**
Exploitive – – – – – – – – – – – – ➔ Benevolent – – – – – – – – – – – – – – ➔Empowering		
Paternalistic – – – – – – – – – – – ➔ Consultative – – – – – – – – – – – – – ➔Laissez-faire		
Leader control – – – – – – – – – ➔ Shared control – – – – – – – – – – – – ➔Group control		
Leader decides – – – – – ➔ Leader consults – – – – – ➔ Leader shares – – – – – ➔Leader delegates		
Telling – – – – – – – – ➔Selling – – – – – – – – ➔ Participating – – – – – – – ➔Delegating		
Controlling – – – – – – – – – ➔ Accommodating – – – – – – – – – – – – – ➔ Indifferent		

Sources: Adapted from Harbison, F. and Myers, C. A. (eds) (1959) Management in the Industrial World: An International Analysis. New York: McGraw-Hill; Hersey, P. and Blanchard, K. H. (1969) 'Life cycle theory of leadership', *Training and Development*, 23(5), 26–34; Tannenbaum, R. and Schmidt, W. H. (2009) How to Choose a Leadership Pattern. Boston, MA: Harvard Business Review Press; Vroom, V. H. (1974) 'Decision making and the leadership process', *Journal of Contemporary Business*, 3(4), 47–64.

Continuums of leadership styles vary between the two opposite poles of autocratic and democratic forms of leadership. Autocratic leadership tends towards exploitive, controlling and dictatorial leadership styles and is generally based on the assumption that human beings are inherently lazy, have a natural dislike for work and as a result, have to be closely supervised and work within strict parameters. Rewards for 'good behaviour' usually consist of 'hygienic factors' such as monetary rewards or performance-related payments while failure to abide by the rules or poor performance are met with sanctions and threats. Autocratic leadership has been severely criticised for creating a harsh and untrusting work climate which frustrates the possibility for effective teamwork, creativity and innovation.

By contrast, democratic leadership is grounded in the assumption that human beings enjoy work, are driven by a sense of purpose, and will naturally seek the opportunity to learn, self-develop and take responsibility in achieving the goals and objectives of the organisation. Democratic leaders display confidence in the ability of their subordinates and entrust them with tasks and projects through which they can demonstrate such ability. In this case, rewards for a job well done are not accounted for solely in monetary terms but can include due recognition for making a significant contribution to change success and the sense of belonging and achievement derived from it. It is not surprising why change experts tend to argue in favour of democratic leadership as a critical success factor for the establishment of an inclusive, collaborative and empowering work climate conducive to learning, creativity and innovative change.

A caveat regarding democratic leadership styles

A caveat is in order with regard to democratic leadership styles. As can be seen from Table 7.4, democratic leadership can lead to a *laissez-faire* (French for *leave alone*) or 'self-rule' work culture – where subordinates are given free rein to complete a task without any interference or guidance from the leader, and have complete autonomy in taking swift action at the 'point of need'. The downside to the *laissez-faire* leadership style is that subordinates are left without any direction, expertise and support in carrying out the work entrusted to them – and can often end up being the ones who have to take the blame in case of failure while not necessarily getting the whole credit in case of success.

This type of deliberate hands-off leadership approach is often seen as counterproductive as it can potentially result in employee demotivation, poor collaborative work and disengagement from the change process. While democratic leaders should trust and empower their subordinates – and certainly not micro-manage their work – they should also be able to provide the necessary guidance, resources and emotional support to ensure that the required change activities are completed on time and that the motivation and commitment for doing so are sustained throughout the change process.

Combining leadership styles

One possible solution to this problem is to combine leadership styles to achieve a much-needed balance between employee autonomy and the necessary material and psychological support to enable them to effectively contribute to change goals and objectives. A combination of leadership styles can allow for the integration of both a rational, task-oriented approach and an affective, relationship-oriented approach to change leadership – which are both vital to change success.

—CASE STUDY 7.1—

Eric Schmidt: Combining leadership styles to drive innovation at Google

Eric Schmidt is the CEO of Google and the driving force behind the company's extraordinary success. Schmidt joined Google in 2001 when it was a relatively small search engine company with only a few hundred employees. After a decade under Schmidt's leadership Google has been transformed into a massive Internet company with over 32,000 employees and offering more than 50 Internet services and products, from e-mail and online document creation to software for mobile phones and tablet computers.

Google's success is attributed in a large measure to Schmidt's ability to combine leadership styles to drive innovation. As a task-oriented leader, Schmidt provides organisational members with strategic direction, making sure that everybody knows *what* is to be done. As a relationship-oriented leader, Schmidt gives a voice and a high level of autonomy to all employees – where he encourages them to think independently, take ownership of their work, share their innovative ideas, and decide for themselves how to best implement the strategy set out by the leadership team. He makes it a point to spend time getting to know his best employees on a personal level and to generously reward high performance. As he has famously been reported to say: 'A leader can tell people *what* to do but he cannot tell them *how* to do it'.

Sources: Nguyen (2010); Feloni (2017)

Questions

Refer back to the different continuums of leadership styles in Table 7.4 and answer the following questions:

1   What different types of leadership style did the CEO manage to combine to drive innovation at Google?
2   What are the challenges involved in combining different leadership styles?

Situational leadership theory

Situational or contingency theory was popular in the 1980s. Mainly associated with the work of Fiedler (1967), its underlying assumption is that there is no one best way to lead and the leader can switch between styles to fit different situations. The choice of leadership style can be influenced by a multiplicity of contextual variables, including the following:

- The business context – e.g. the intensity of competitive rivalry or performance standards.
- The nature of the leader–member relationship – e.g. degree of loyalty of followers to leader or the level of maturity of the followers.
- The type of cultural climate – e.g. the core values and beliefs impacting working relationships.

- The task structure – the type of parameters or variety of procedures determining how tasks are to be carried out.
- Position power – the level of authority the leader has in rewarding or sanctioning their subordinates.
- The type of technology-in-use – e.g. the impact of communication technologies on work relationships (e.g. see Northouse, 2013).

The above variables are by no means exhaustive and one can think of many other configurations of contextual variables that can have a significant influence on the adoption of particular leadership styles. What is of particular importance here is to retain the fact that situational theory is driven by a notion of 'best-fit' and a concern to match the right leadership style to the right context.

Hersey and Blanchard: A reference point for situational leadership

We cannot talk about situational leadership without referring to the work of Hersey and Blanchard (1969). Their highly popular model of situational leadership identifies four main leadership styles that leaders can use depending on the levels of competence and commitment of their followers. For the sake of clarity, Figure 7.1 below presents a simplified version of their situational leadership model.

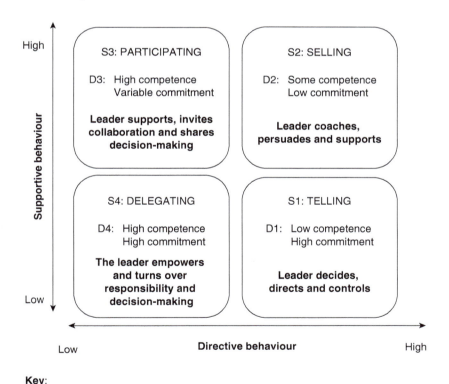

Key:
S: Style
D: Developmental level

Figure 7.1 Hersey and Blanchard's model of situational leadership

Telling (S1)

In this particular situation, the leader directs and *tells* their subordinates what to do and how to do it. This leadership style is particularly useful with novice employees with high commitment levels but lacking in competence and experience (D1). In this case, the leader decides what to do, gives precise instructions on how to do it, and takes control if the situation warrants it.

Selling (S2)

This is where the leader *sells* their ideas and decisions to followers who have some competence but lack commitment (D2). In this case, the leader adopts a coaching style to persuade, support and involve their subordinates in decision-making in order to boost their commitment.

Participating (S3)

In this case, the leader adopts a more collaborative style and allows their subordinates to have a more active *participative* role. This particular leadership style is appropriate for followers with high competence but with variable commitment (D3). By adopting this particular style, the leader shares responsibility and decision-making with their subordinates but also provides the extra support for those with lower levels of commitment and in need of encouragement.

Delegating (S4)

Here, the leader adopts a hands-off, empowering style and delegates responsibility and decision-making to his subordinates. This approach is best suited to followers with high levels of both competence and commitment (D4). In this case, the leader turns over responsibility for decision-making and implementation of organisational goals to their subordinates because they have complete trust in the latter's ability and commitment levels.

Criticisms

The Hersey and Blanchard model has also drawn some criticisms. First, it assumes a natural ability in leaders to seamlessly switch between styles in adapting to different situations – which, however, can be psychologically draining and stressful in the longer term. Moreover, the problem of having to switch between styles can be compounded by the possibility of *internal variance* – where *different* leadership styles have to be applied to meet the *different* needs of subordinates in the *same situation*. Second, switching between different leadership styles sometimes requires time or a period of adaptation – a luxury that many change leaders do not have when thrown in at the deep end when driving change and pressurised to meet tight deadlines. Finally, the onus placed on the leader to switch between styles obscures the possibility of changing the situation and the people within to fit the leader's preferred style – which in actuality can often be the case when a new leader is appointed to turn around an ailing company (Meirovich and Gu, 2015).

Using Hersey and Blanchard's model as a change tool

The following scenario provides you with an opportunity to try out the Hersey and Blanchard model of situational leadership as a change tool.

You work as a line manager for a large company which has recently gone through a major restructuring exercise. The rationale behind the change was to streamline existing processes to optimise their efficiency and to reduce costs to increase profitability and enable reinvestments in new business units as part of the company's new expansion strategy. The restructuring exercise involved several rounds of redundancy where many employees had to be laid off because of the need for a 'renewal of skills and competences' in view of the new change strategy.

To this effect, a number of new employees with specialist skills were hired and were deployed across newly formed teams. You have to lead one of these new teams which consists of 25 members. Team members now include: (i) experienced, highly competent employees who have been with the company for more than 15 years but whose commitment levels are at an all-time low, having gone through the 'trauma' of losing close colleagues following the redundancy, (ii) new employees with specialist skills with high levels of competence but low levels of commitment as they seem more interested in using their new roles at the company to gain work experience and build their own career portfolio, and (iii) new employees with variable levels of commitment but who will need to get a lot of training because of their lack of work experience.

Activity

In light of the above scenario, use the Hersey and Blanchard model of situational leadership (refer to Figure 7.1) to carry out the following activities:

1 Organise your team members into smaller groups according to their levels of competence and commitment.
2 Plot the smaller groups on the corresponding quadrants of Hersey and Blanchard's model.
3 Develop a plan of action as to how you will adjust your leadership style to match the needs of each of the groups you have identified.

Transformational leadership

The discourse of **transformational leadership** came to the fore in the 1990s and triggered a renewed interest in the dispositional traits of the leader. It wove together an idealised image of a type of leader endowed with exceptional qualities and one who would be able to successfully drive change in an increasingly competitive and unpredictable global business context. As such, the transformational leader is someone who is charismatic, inspirational, motivational and capable of transforming organisational reality and importantly, the people within it in pursuit of certain desired goals and objectives (Northouse, 2013).

Another theory closely associated with transformational leadership is the **Leader–Member–Exchange (LMX) theory**. LMX focuses on the quality of the *dyadic* (or two-way) relationship between a leader and their followers. In relation to transformational leadership, it promotes the view that transformational leaders can have a positive influence on the employee attitudes and behaviours vital to change success. A high-quality LMX is founded on mutual respect and trust and a positive emotional bond between the leader and the employee – resulting in greater employee satisfaction, sense of belonging, performance and commitment to change (Chaurasia and Shukla, 2013).

Transformational v. transactional leaders

Transformational leaders are often contrasted with *transactional leaders* (Yahaya and Ebrahim, 2016). As hinted above, transformational leaders are primarily concerned with change and innovation. To this end, they attach considerable importance to the LMX aimed at building trusting and empowering relationships, enabling employees to internalise change goals and objectives and sustain their motivation and commitment throughout the change process. They usually favour intrinsic motivating factors such as recognition, job satisfaction and enhanced opportunities for learning as key drivers of successful change.

By contrast, transactional leaders are mostly driven by short-term goals whilst showing a predilection for close supervision and control, stability and order, and clear policies and procedures designed to provide a robust structure for day-to-day operations. Transactional leaders do not tend to pay too much attention to the quality of the LMX. Their approach to leadership primarily rests on the assumption that people are not intrinsically motivated or naturally disposed to do anything without getting something in return. In this case, a more productive leader–member relationship should be in essence *transactional* – where roles and responsibilities are allocated through negotiation and bargaining and there is a reliance on 'hygiene' factors such as job security, compensation and fair reward systems to satisfy the basic needs of employees and drive performance. Understandably, **transactional leadership** is seen as defective and falling short of the principles for effective organisational change.

The dark side of transformational leadership

There is a potentially dark side to transformational leadership. Behind a charismatic front and seductive appeal, the transformational leader could be hiding narcissistic tendencies, selfish motives and dangerous ideologies that can be detrimental to those under their influence (Tourish, 2013). Cases about the abusive, fraudulent and even criminal behaviours of transformational leaders across various domains of human activity, whether it be business, political or religious, are numerous. While a more in-depth discussion of the dark side of transformational leadership is beyond the scope of this book, we just want to mention the fact here that, in an organisational change context, 'transformation leadership gone wrong' can entail a betrayal of the organisation's core values, the ruthless imposition of the leader's vision on other stakeholders, and the guiltless pursuit of the leader's self-interests with little concern for those of others. If left unbridled, transformational leadership can transform change initiatives into the 'ideological stronghold' of the narcissistic leader and irremediably lead to change failure if not to the demise of the organisation.

Organisational cynicism about change: A big problem for transformational leadership

Recent research into *Organisational Cynicism About Change* (OCAC) suggests that it poses a big problem for transformational leadership (Toheed et al., 2019). Transformational leaders seek to inspire, motivate and muster the commitment of organisational members to the desired change. However, OCAC can potentially frustrate the endeavours of transformational leaders. It can occur at any level of the organisation and entails a set of pessimistic beliefs and assumptions about the necessity of organisational change whilst casting serious doubt regarding the 'actual' motives and interests that underlie it.

Some of the causes of OCAC that relate directly to the transformational leader include amoral self-promotion, the pursuit of self-interest, abuse of power, manipulative tactics benefitting a select few at the expense of the larger stakeholder group, and follower perceptions of the leader as being incompetent, dishonest and untrustworthy.

So what can transformational leaders do about OCAC?

It has been suggested that transformational leaders can implement the following measures to minimise the negative effects of OCAC:

i   Ensure that the change message communicated to followers is crystal clear, coherent and authentic – i.e. that it translates the leader's authenticity, honesty and real motives.

ii   Develop a sound understanding of the situated nature of OCAC across organisational levels in order to identify and swiftly address their underlying causes.

iii Spare no efforts in making followers feel valued, competent and engaged with the change process.

iv   Adopt a participatory leadership style to enable greater employee involvement and contribution to the change initiative.

v   Put in place structures and control systems that set a limit on what the leader can do in view of agreed upon change goals and objectives and prevent 'slippages' towards the dark side of transformational leadership (e.g. see DeCelles et al., 2013; Gupta et al., 2021).

Research involving significant numbers of employees in the public sector and in the IT industry tend to suggest that an 'active orientation' towards positive interpersonal relations, and employee empowerment, participation and involvement in decision-making can mitigate the negative effects of OCAC as the unintended yet potentially harmful consequences of change (Brown and Cregan, 2008; Gupta et al., 2021). Thus, because OCAC is proving to be a key determinant of change success, transformational leaders can no longer ignore it but should learn to effectively manage it if they want to live up to their name.

7.6 Contemporary approaches to organisational change leadership

Figure 7.2 foregrounds the emerging notions of leadership that we think have had a significant influence on 21st century approaches to change leadership. We proceed to provide a brief explanation of each notion in the following discussion.

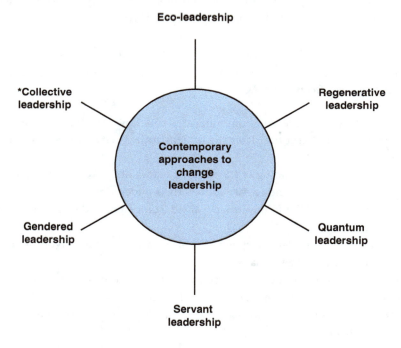

* Starting point of following discussion

Figure 7.2   Contemporary approaches to change leadership

Collective leadership

The notion of **collective leadership** brings to the fore the idea that in the real world leadership is *distributed* and *situated* – a fact which seems to have slipped the gaze of leadership analysts and which has been downplayed in academic literature with its primary focus, since the 1940s, on the leader and the context in which they operate (Bolden, 2011). Denis et al. (2001) have effectively addressed this loophole by issuing a powerful reminder of the fact that collective leadership has been hiding in plain sight – for in most domains of human activity involving large numbers of people, leadership (and the power that comes with it) is diffused across different levels. For example, in the domain of political democracy, the leader of the elected political party lead members of parliament who in turn act as leaders to local representatives who themselves have a leading role in defending the interests of the local constituents.

Similarly, within large organisational settings, leadership is usually distributed and situated at or across different levels: the Board of Directors, senior managers, middle managers, line managers, team leaders, project leaders, etc. – all of whom have leadership roles and responsibilities which are exercised to varying degrees and at different points of need. Denis et al. (2001) also portray collective leadership as a *constellation of leaders* to emphasise the fact that although the specific responsibilities of organisation leaders might differ, they have to work in concert and align their efforts to achieve a common goal. Finally, it is important to point out that the notion of leadership as the property of a collective, allows for a systemic understanding of the leadership process which is in line with our own approach to change management and which we believe is vital in building organisational capacity for change and sustaining its momentum towards the achievement of its desirable outcomes.

Eco-leadership

The concept of **eco-leadership** was coined by Simon Western (2008) to signal the emergence of a new leadership paradigm for 21st century organisations. Eco-leadership promotes a systemic approach to change, reengages leadership with its ethical responsibilities and effectively connects organisational change leadership with the wider discourse about climate change and sustainability.

First, in enabling a systemic approach to change, eco-leadership portrays the organisational leader as 'Janus-faced' – where the leader is both *inward-looking* by paying attention to the internal ecosystem of the organisation to ensure the proper functioning of its interrelated parts and *outward-looking* by keeping a watchful eye on and promptly responding to the key drivers of change within the external context within which the organisation operates. As such, the concept of eco-leadership promotes a holistic approach to change and casts a wider net on the abilities and responsibilities of the leader to drive change *within* the organisation and navigate the waves of change *outside* the organisation to ensure its survival and growth in the longer term.

Second, by re-engaging leadership with its ethical responsibilities, the concept of eco-leadership fosters an ethos of integrity, fairness and equity in the employment relationship and in the way the organisation conducts its business in view of the law and the normative expectations of its key stakeholders. In this respect, the eco-leader strives for ethical solutions and pursues courses of action geared towards a much-needed balance between the needs and interests of all stakeholders including employees, investors, suppliers, business partners, customers and the wider community.

Finally, eco-leadership places an emphasis on the good stewardship of the natural environment. It promotes the idea that business organisations have a symbiotic relationship with the natural environment and that such a relationship has to be preserved for the long-term survival and prosperity of both. The mandate of the eco-leader is therefore to champion modes of production that rely on cleaner sources of energy, aim to reduce the toxicity of waste materials and minimise the adverse effects of industrial carbon emissions.

Regenerative leadership

Regenerative leadership is seen by many as the new paradigm for 21st century change leaders and answer to the global challenges that they have to face: political extremism, wars and nuclear threats, social inequality, climate change, natural disasters and pandemics compounded by hyper-competitive and volatile markets, increasingly complex and unstable supply chains, heightened workplace stress levels, shifting stakeholder expectations and close scrutiny from environmental pressure groups. For proponents of regenerative leadership, the answer to these unprecedented challenges lies in a different approach to leadership that is 'life-giving and affirming' and that can potentially contribute to more sustainable and better futures for both businesses and societies across the world (Hutchins and Storm, 2019).

Regenerative leadership is founded on *biophilic* principles (i.e. principles rooted in literally, the love of life). This entails an ability of the leader to understand the full implications of their organisation as a 'living system' that is in a symbiotic relationship with the 'wider living ecosystem' in which it operates and to seek ways to preserve, enrich and ensure the sustainability of both living systems. As such, the regenerative leader shares some similarities with the eco-leader in that they both have an *inner* and *outer* approach to change. The *inner approach* is focused on strategic choices, work relationships and the development of a culture that aims to create inclusive, caring and empowering 'life-affirming conditions' in which the health and safety, developmental needs and overall quality of working life of organisational members can be effectively addressed. The *outer approach* is concerned with product offerings, the design of production processes, the management of the supply chains and the pursuit of collaborative partnerships to find innovative ways to sustain economic progress, bring about life-enriching social reforms and protect and preserve the natural environment as a living system upon which the survival of humankind and all other species on planet earth is dependent.

For its proponents, regenerative leadership goes beyond other 'mechanistic' conceptualisations of leadership in that it warrants a major 'shift of consciousness' – an altogether new mindset that embraces a move from life-destroying practices to 'working with life' to protect living systems upon which the survival and future of business and society are dependent.

Quantum leadership

Quantum leadership allows for an unusual yet insightful take on change leadership that draws on quantum physics. Simply put, quantum physics is the study of particles – tiny pieces of matter inside an atom which scientists believe make up everything in the universe. While particles and the so-called 'quantum world' are invisible to the naked eye, they have provided the scientific basis for the development of things that today form part of our daily lives such as computers, smartphones, LED lights, TVs and other electronic devices.

However, what is peculiar about particles is that they are extremely difficult to observe. It is a well-known fact that one cannot measure both the position and the speed of a particle at the same time. In fact, the very act of observing a particle can change it, making it impossible to predict its behaviour with any certainty. This has led to the formulation of the *uncertainty principle* that governs the behaviour of particles which is elusive, indeterminate and unpredictable (Zohar, 2022).

The application of the uncertainty principle to change leadership casts light on the increasingly uncertain, ambiguous and unpredictable business world that modern-day leaders have to grapple with. The 'quantum leader' is therefore one who is able to cope with uncertainty, has a high tolerance for ambiguity and complexity, and can easily adapt to fluctuations and even chaotic disruptions in their change situation. Moreover, quantum leaders are counterintuitive and are not afraid of challenging prevailing assumptions and bending the rules in seeking viable solutions to the problems arising from uncertain and unpredictable change situations.

To this effect, quantum leaders are welcoming of alternative views and perspectives, support continuous learning and experimentation, promote diversity and tend towards an inclusive and consultative leadership style in navigating the waves of uncertainty. Thus, quantum leaders are the antithesis of autocratic leaders and are highly conscious that constructive change in an increasingly uncertain and unpredictable business world is impossible without the commitment and the creative contributions of others.

Servant leadership

The concept of **servant leadership** is quite revolutionary in that it inverts the traditional power relations between the leader and their followers to place the leader in a 'lower position' of servant and whose primary role is to serve the ones they lead. While the concept of servant leader is not new and can be traced back to early Buddhism and Christianity, it gained traction in the 1970s following Greenleaf's (1970) essay on the subject and since then further conceptual developments in academic literature, the notion of the servant leader has still a lot of currency across modern-day leadership circles (Eva et al., 2019; Greenleaf, 1977, p. 13).

Servant leadership rests on the premise that decent human beings have a natural disposition to serve others and an effective leader is first and foremost a servant. The servant change leader *puts people first* and, moving away from command-and-control and transactional approaches to change, empowers employees to take ownership of the change initiative and share responsibility in leading it. As such, the servant leader demonstrates humility, empathy, integrity and advanced interpersonal skills through which he can develop trusting relationships with others, release their creative potential and do change *with them* in the pursuit of change goals and objectives.

While some might argue that the concept of servant leadership is not applicable to all types of organisations (the military being a case in point), it has proven to be a key determinant of higher performance and commitment to change across a wide range of industries. For advocates of servant leadership, someone can only become a good leader if they remain a servant and can reconcile with the paradox that leaders who can let go of power and control eventually have more of both over the change process (Tanno and Banner, 2018).

Gendered leadership

With more women taking on organisational leadership roles in the 21st century, there has been a growing interest in the role of gender in leadership. While there are many factors that can impact on the role of women leaders in modern-day organisations (e.g. nature of power relations, core cultural values, self-perception, individual expectations, etc.) what is of particular interest is the way a **gendered approach to leadership** has cast men and women into rather rigid (and often sexist) stereotypes that serve to perpetuate gender inequality and stifles forward thinking in this area (Appelbaum et al., 2019).

Male and female leaders are often judged against different criteria based on the assumption that they have fundamentally different natural dispositions and are best suited for different responsibilities and roles. Male leaders are generally seen as autocratic, individualistic, task-oriented, performance-driven, competitive and concerned with financial success. On the other hand, female leaders are assumed to be more democratic, communal, people-oriented and primarily concerned with social values and the quality of working life. The major drawback of this dichotomous approach to gender in leadership is that it tends to discriminate against women leaders – who are either assigned 'diminished leadership roles' in which they can only act in a 'supportive capacity' or have to display (often against their own core values and preferred leadership styles) masculine traits and behaviours so as to be favourably judged within male-dominated organisational cultures.

Although gender stereotyping is not something that can be easily eradicated, there is need for a move beyond a dichotomous mode of thinking towards the establishment of gender equality in change leadership – where the effectiveness of change leaders, irrespective of their gender or natural dispositions, is evaluated against their ability to play to their strengths and use their unique talents in appropriate contexts to bring about change success – whether it be in the form of financial performance, the creation of social value, the organisational environmental impact or ideally, a combination of all the aforementioned outcomes.

In our view, the contemporary approaches to leadership described above serve two key purposes: (i) they reaffirm the multidimensional and complex nature of change leadership and point to the increasing challenges contemporary leaders have to grapple with and (ii) they carry a wide range of intertwining views, commitments and principles that are shaping a global and evolving discourse around change leadership which reflects the most pressing concerns and challenges of the times.

—CASE STUDY 7.2—

The rise and fall of a world-class woman leader

Introduction

Olivia Lum is a well-known figure who went from rags to riches to become one of the most successful and respected leaders in South-East Asia until she recently landed her company in deep trouble following a series of bad decisions. Born in Malaysia, Olivia Lum became an orphan early in life and grew up with adoptive parents in very poor conditions with no access to proper sanitation or running water. However, her harsh childhood never dampened her resolve to turn her life around and never slip back into poverty. Even at a young age, she began to display some unique qualities that offered a glimpse into the type of business entrepreneur and leader she would become – and the very fact of her having no access to running water would later prove to be a determining factor in the development of her chosen business model.

A flair for business

While still in school Olivia Lum displayed a flair for business and was selling fruit on the streets to contribute to the family's expenses. At 16, she left for Singapore where she studied at the National University of Singapore and, in 1986, graduated with honours in applied chemistry. She then joined Glaxo Pharmaceuticals where she worked as a laboratory chemist for 3 years – during which time she realised that the lack of access to running water in certain South-East Asian countries presented a new business opportunity – a *sunrise business* as she called it. Lum left Glaxo in 1989 to set up Hydrochem and with the help of just two other staff members began selling water treatment systems in Singapore, Malaysia and Indonesia.

The business underwent rapid growth and soon after Lum assumed the role of CEO, her company name was changed to Hyflux, which provided solutions in seawater desalination, water recycling, wastewater treatment, and potable water treatment for both municipal and industrial markets. Hyflux quickly expanded its business to several other countries and regions including China, India, the Middle East, and North Africa.

An accomplished leader

Her leadership style was rooted in entrepreneurship and innovation and driven by hard work, a 'can-do spirit' and a 'boldness to dream'. She placed a premium on the integrity and efficiency of all her employees who she referred to as the 'ambassadors of the Singapore brand'. She also believed that an effective leader had to be able to communicate their vision

(Continued)

to their employees and inspire them to achieve their fullest potential. As a woman leader, she felt that more women had the capacity to become successful leaders, but a change of mindset was needed from all quarters to increase opportunities for women leaders – from schools to public and private institutions to family units and last but not least, with women themselves.

A series of bad business decisions

Olivia Lum was seen as one of the most successful women entrepreneurs in Singapore with a reported net worth of over US$325 million. Over the years, she also won several prestigious awards and was at one point a Nominated Member of Parliament. However, a series of bad business decisions led to her downfall following an attempt to expand her company's portfolio through an investment in a sea water desalination and electric power project. Stiff competition from rival companies and 'weaker-than-expected' electricity prices practically wiped out Hyflux's profits, leading the company to file for bankruptcy protection in 2018. Following a series of failed rescue deals and restructuring attempts, Hyflux went into liquidation in July 2021. To make matters worse, Olivia Lum was charged in court with disclosure-related offences and for intentionally failing to ensure her company's compliance with the law after the authorities launched a probe into Hyflux's disclosure, accounting and auditing issues. Lum, 61, is out on bail of S$100,000 but still faces a possible jail sentence and several years in prison.

Conclusions

Olivia Lum's rise and fall as an outstanding woman leader raises a number of key issues. First, Lum's success as a leader was achieved on the back of certain unique traits and talents that she developed over the years and on her ability to make the best of the opportunities that came her way, irrespective of her gender. Second, her effectiveness as an accomplished leader was rooted in gender-neutral principles and precepts such as the need to articulate and communicate a vision, inspire and motivate others and empower them in pursuit of clear goals and objectives. Third, Lum's personal experience draws attention to the fact there is still work to do to achieve greater gender equality in organisational leadership, warranting the need for a change in mindset and more support mechanisms to increase women's agency and access to leadership positions. Finally, the series of bad decisions that led to Lum's downfall cannot be unarguably attributed to her gender. Leaders succeed and fail on their own terms and merits – regardless of their gender.

Sources: *Leaders* (2012); Leong (2022)

Questions

1   What unique traits and talents did Olivia Lum possess as an outstanding leader?
2   Why are the principles underpinning her leadership effectiveness seen as 'gender-neutral'?
3   What can be done to increase women's agency and access to leadership positions in your own country?

7.7 Conceptual nugget: Dialogic leadership

In this last section, we introduce our conceptual nugget for this chapter: dialogic leadership. Our conceptualisation of dialogic leadership addresses contemporary issues in leadership and places an emphasis on the constitutive role of open dialogue and its transformative impact on the leadership process. Figure 7.3 below foregrounds its three key elements (*Talk – Reflection – Action*) which are discussed in more detail below.

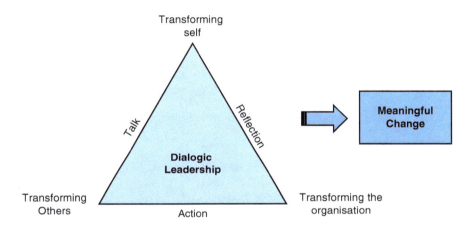

Figure 7.3 Key elements and transformative effects of dialogic leadership

Talk

As dialogic practice, leadership involves a twofold process: *talk with self* and *talk with others*. Mainstream theories of leadership such as traits, styles and situational theories do not pay much attention to the role of *talk* in the leadership process. For example, traits theory promotes a rather static image of the leader as possessing a stereotypical set of skills and attributes which they can apply to good effect on command – leaving little scope for leaders to question themselves, learn from others and grow into their roles. Likewise, styles and situational theories tend to portray leaders as equipped with some chameleonic ability to mechanically switch between a range of styles to fit the change context and the people within it – paying little attention to leadership learning and growth while perpetuating a view of leaders as doing change *to* people rather than *with* people which is however, a central theme in contemporary approaches to leadership.

Talking with self

Dialogic leadership locates language and *talk* at the core of the leadership process. *Talk with self* is in essence introspective – i.e. it is inward-looking and entails an ability of leaders to 'face themselves' and question their own modes of thought, values and motives and gauge their own feelings and desires in relation to the change they are leading. This exercise can be quite therapeutic in that it encourages change leaders to critically examine their authenticity and integrity and the extent to which their behaviours are aligned to their professed values and the change objectives of their organisation. *Self-talk* hinges on the ability of change leaders to *look inwardly* and transform themselves as they seek to transform others – which finds echo in the concepts of collective, servant, eco and gendered leadership but remains one of the biggest challenges facing change leaders.

The following are indicative of the type of introspective questions that dialogic leaders can ask themselves when engaging in *self-talk*:

Am I getting this right?

Do I really understand the implications of all my actions?

Are my behaviours in accord with my core values?

Am I being true to myself and others? Or am I being deceptive and manipulative?

Am I really enabling others and helping them contribute to the change?

Am I robbing others of their agency?

Am I driven by my own interests? Or do I have the interests of all at heart?

Talking with others

Talking with others has to do with the relational and interactive dimension of leadership. It is outward-looking and invites the leader to face others through repeated moments of free and open dialogue with key stakeholders. While continuous dialogue with others enables an inclusive and collaborative approach to change, it also serves the important function of developing a sense of belonging and solidarity and a shared understanding around the way forward from the vantage point of alternative perspectives and possibilities that would have otherwise slipped the gaze of the leader acting on their own.

Moreover, continuous dialogue with others allows for the creation of a strong coalition to drive and sustain the momentum of change, greater clarity in the distribution of respective roles and responsibilities, more objective evaluation of change progress and timely implementation of corrective measures. In this respect, dialogic leadership clears the path for contemporary approaches to leadership – notably collective, quantum and eco-leadership.

The following set of interactive questions provides the parameters for *talking with others*:

What are our change goals and objectives?

Has anything happened that warrants a change to our goals and objectives?

What have we done well so far? And how do we all benefit from this?

What went wrong?

How do we correct and learn from our mistakes?

What are our options moving forward? And what are the implications for our key stakeholders?

Reflection

Reflection is *contained* in the process of talking with *self* and with *others* and honestly answering the sets of questions listed above. By *talking with self*, the leader can critically reflect on their accomplishments and failings, their performance in delivering the organisation's strategic goals and objectives and on the nature of their relationship with organisational stakeholders – which can also lead to an assessment of their own learning and developmental needs. By *talking with others*, change leaders place themselves at the centre of an enabling network of relationships through which they can benefit from collective feedback, alternative assessment of the change situation, and a grounded understanding of the sentiments and expectations of stakeholders in relation to the change implementation and un/intended outcomes.

Even more importantly, this form of collective reflection and sense making can become a platform for problem solving, experimentation, out-of-the-box thinking, simulation modelling and other innovative ways of working together as a team that can generate effective solutions in an increasingly complex, competitive and unpredictable business world. Both self-reflection and collective reflection are critical to all the modern approaches to leadership discussed in the previous section – especially in the case of quantum and regenerative leadership, where respectively, the ability to cope with uncertainty and to generate 'life-affirming' and sustainable solutions are considered paramount.

Action

Action is also contained in talk. What is 'talked about' and 'reflected upon' at different levels of the organisation provides the framework for collective courses of action and processes of adaptation in the face of emerging threats and opportunities. In this regard, dialogic leaders cannot lead change from their ivory tower, expecting others to work for them but are called to 'walk the talk' and take an active part in the change process whilst modelling the behaviours they want to see in their followers.

In our dialogic model, change leaders are locked with their followers in a mutually beneficial process of dialogue, reflection and action to *transform themselves, others and the organisation* in order to bring about *meaningful change* and themselves *become* the change that they seek (Quinn et al., 2000). As eloquently put by Eriksen (2008, p. 622), 'meaningful organisational transformation does not occur without a corresponding self-transformation, most importantly of the individual leading the change'. In this respect, one can easily imagine the beneficial impact that dialogic leaders can have on contemporary leadership approaches such as servant and gendered leadership where the ability of leaders to transform themselves, others and the core cultural values of the organisation is a critical success factor.

Conclusions

In bringing this section to a close, we want to distil the purpose of our model of dialogic leadership: to foster a communicative mode of thought and action that tends towards the democratic and transformational end of the leadership styles spectrum and that can serve as a powerful lever for contemporary leadership approaches. We also want to give you, the reader, food for thought: much has been said about leadership as the Holy Grail of organisational change – something which is sought-after but which somehow remains just beyond our reach. But, to paraphrase Simon Western (2008), leadership as the Holy Grail of organisational change is to be found when we stop searching for it, when we strive forward to make it better and when we communicatively keep improving the systems, processes and behaviours underpinning it in response to the great challenges of the times.

REFLECTIVE EXERCISE

1   In what way can dialogic practice of the type described above serve as a lever for contemporary approaches to leadership? Refer to Figure 7.3 to frame your answer.
2   Can you think of some organisational barriers that can limit the possibility of dialogic leadership?

7.8 Key learning points

The following key learning points can be extracted from this chapter:

1   Leadership is a *multidimensional, complex and emergent process* that defies any single, all-encompassing definition and that can take on a wide range of meanings according to the changing contexts in which it unravels.
2   *Political leadership and organisational change leadership share the same essence* and, as such, the principles, ideals, concerns and of course pitfalls of political leadership are highly applicable to the process of organisational change leadership and exert a shaping influence on it.
3   Change leaders and change managers have to *reconcile the paradoxical tensions between their distinctive yet complementary roles* and have to work in collaboration in achieving a much needed balance between the need for dynamic change and relative stability, the need for achieving short-term objectives and pursuing long-term goals, and the need to optimise operational efficiency and keep the organisation on the right strategic path.
4   The key leadership theories that we have reviewed in this chapter include *traits, styles, situational* and *transformational leadership approaches to change*. While all these theories have strengths and weaknesses, they can inform the development of valuable tools to frame the leadership process in the context of organisational change.
5   Contemporary approaches to leadership identified in this chapter include: *collective, eco, regenerative, quantum, servant* and *gendered approaches* which serve two key purposes: (i) they reaffirm the multidimensional and complex nature of change leadership and point to the increasing pressures contemporary leaders have to grapple with and (ii) they carry a wide range of intertwining views, commitments and principles that are shaping a

global and evolving discourse around change leadership which reflects the most pressing concerns and challenges of the times.

6   Finally, our *dialogic model of leadership* places an emphasis on the transformative role of open dialogue in the leadership process and can serve as a powerful lever for contemporary approaches to leadership. It comprises three key elements (Talk – Reflection – Action) through which leaders can transform themselves, others and the organisation in the pursuit of sustainable change success.

—END-OF-CHAPTER CASE STUDY 7.3—

Jeff Skoll: An exemplar of 21st century leadership

Introduction

Jeff Skoll is a Canadian social entrepreneur, activist, filmmaker and philanthropist. He is also a self-made billionaire who made most of his fortune in his role as first president of auction platform eBay and further increased his wealth (which is estimated at more than 4.3 billion USD) through investments in high-profile companies such as PayPal, Skype and Groupon. As a committed social entrepreneur, he founded the Capricorn Investment Group, a private investment firm that invests in organisations that seek to have a positive impact on society while delivering strong financial returns.

Jeff Skoll has also proven himself to be a strong activist – especially as founder of Participant Media, a film production company that creates content intended to spur social change. As a philanthropist, Jeff Skoll has, through the Skoll Foundation, donated hundreds of millions of dollars to social entrepreneurs and organisations to address global health problems and provide life-saving treatments to millions of people around the world. In 2012, Jeff Skoll was appointed to the Order of Canada, one of the country's highest honours for his contributions to business and philanthropy. This was followed by other prestigious honours such as the Jefferson Award for the greatest public service by a private citizen and the Carnegie medal of philanthropy. With such an impressive portfolio, Jeff Skoll is viewed by many as the embodiment of the multifaceted leader and an exemplar of 21st century leadership.

An impressive ecosystem for large-scale social change

One of Jeff Skoll's most outstanding qualities is his ability to connect with and surround himself with the right kind of people to create an impressive ecosystem that is capable of juggling so many challenges on so many different fronts to bring about large-scale social change. With Participant Media, the Jeff Skoll group has produced a series of award-winning films (such as *An Inconvenient Truth, Roma, Syriana* and *Contagion*) that have served to raise global awareness around a range of social issues such as the plight of blue collar workers, sexism, oil politics, government corruption, war and terrorism, the dangers of global warming and the threat of pandemics which took on ominous proportions after the COVID-19 outbreak.

(Continued)

With the Skoll Foundation, Jeff Skoll has been able to bring together social entrepreneurs and innovators to effectively respond to the world's most pressing yet solvable problems and deploy tried and tested and cost-effective solutions on a global scale. For example, the Skoll Foundation actively supports *Eyelliance*, an organisation dedicated to the creation of a world in which 'all children and adults can have access to eye glasses where they live and learn'.

With his patronage of the Skoll Centre for Social Entrepreneurship (affiliated with Oxford University), Jeff Skoll has displayed a great sense of posterity by investing in the development of a new generation of social entrepreneurs who can pick up the torch and develop business models that can generate both economic and social value.

Leading change through conversational practice

An outstanding feature that typifies Jeff Skoll's leadership style is the way he leads change by being reflective and having open and honest conversations with others to transform himself and empower others in transforming social systems and bringing about large-scale social change. This is modelled in Figure 7.4 below.

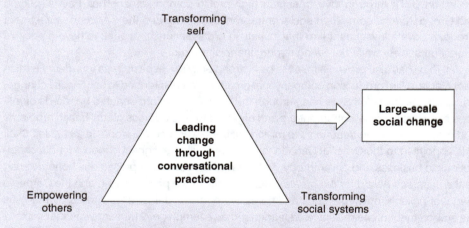

Figure 7.4 Leading change through conversational practice

Transforming self

Jeff Skoll is soft-spoken, humble and unassuming but is highly respected for coming across as being genuine, deeply reflective, resourceful and extremely successful as a business person and an agent of change. This is largely due to the fact that Jeff Skoll is bent on transforming himself into the type of leader that can help 'repair the planet' with the resources available to him. He is keen to share his stories and experiences, and conversations with others that have transformed him into a visionary, global leader who has been able to spearhead so many successful large-scale change initiatives.

Empowering others

Jeff Skoll also empowers others through 'honest dialogue' with key stakeholders as a means of 'expanding their horizons' and reaching consensus around what needs to be done to effectively achieve the intended outcomes. For example, the movies produced by Participant Media are the results of intense debate around their content which has to be intelligently designed, thought-provoking, attitude-changing and emotionally engaging so as to raise public awareness and ideally serve as a catalyst for social change. Another notable example is the way the Skoll Foundation is able to connect and provide a voice to a global network of social entrepreneurs and innovators who strive for transformational social change – whether it be through its annual conventions or free online platforms where potential change makers from around the world can exchange ideas and perspectives.

Transforming social systems

Transforming social systems on such a large scale rests largely on a commitment to free exchange of views and ideas and ongoing communication between the 'good people doing good things', the type of people Jeff Skoll likes to involve in his projects. In order to become effective agents of large-scale social change, key stakeholders have to become 'full participants-in-communication' to develop a shared understanding of the complex problems at hand and adopt a concerted approach to the deployment of proven, context-sensitive and scalable solutions and work towards the creation of a sustainable world in which 'peace and prosperity for all' can become a real possibility.

Conclusions

A number of key issues can be extracted from this case study. First, Jeff Skoll is an exemplar of 21st century leadership because he combines certain outstanding personal traits with an ability to operate within a global network of collaborators in pursuit of viable solutions to some of the most pressing problems of the times. Second, Jeff Skoll is the archetype of the multifaceted leader who can draw on a wide range of skills to successfully lead large-scale change and make a difference in so many domains of life and work. Finally, Jeff Skoll has made the dialogic principles of open and free conversations with key stakeholders as an integral part of his leadership approach to transform himself into an effective leader with global ambitions, empower others in bringing about transformational social change and transforming systems that can allow for proven, context-sensitive and scalable solutions to usher in a more sustainable and life-enriching world.

Sources: Antonucci (2012); Participant Media (2023); Skoll Foundation (2023)

Questions

1   What are the most salient personal traits that make Jeff Skoll an exemplar of 21st century leadership?
2   How would you describe his overall leadership style?
3   In what ways has Jeff Skoll proven himself to be a dialogic leader?

7.9 Independent learning

You can access the following sources to consolidate your knowledge of some of the key theories and concepts discussed in this chapter.

Watch this video clip on YouTube on the top 10 differences between leaders and managers from a practitioner perspective: www.youtube.com/watch?v=8ubRzzirRKs

You can learn more about the concept of eco-leadership by reading a PowerPoint presentation by Simon Western: www.slideshare.net/T_I_H_R/eco-leadership-2011

In this video clip, Giles Hutchins talks about the importance for regenerative leaders of developing a new regenerative consciousness: www.youtube.com/watch?v=kYm5KqU8th8

Listen to this podcast with Amy C. Edmondson as she talks about how to lead in times of absolute upheaval, which is very different from leading during everyday change: https://open.spotify.com/episode/3f585fJdK6aujb2tdC3FCd

7.10 References

Antonucci, M. (2012) 'Jeff Skoll's philanthropy focuses on world's biggest challenges', *Stanford Business Graduate School*, 24 October. [Online] Available at: www.gsb.stanford.edu/insights/jeff-skolls-philanthropy-focuses-worlds-biggest-challenges (accessed 5 February 2023).

Appelbaum, S., D'Antico, V. and Daoussis, C. (2019) 'Women as leaders the more things change, the more it's the same thing', *The International Journal of Management and Business*, 10(1), 24–38.

Berti, M. and Cunha, M. P. E. (2022) 'Paradox, dialectics or trade-offs? A double loop model of paradox', *Journal of Management Studies*. [Online] Available at: https://onlinelibrary.wiley.com/doi/epdf/10.1111/joms.12899?saml_referrer (accessed 13 March 2023).

Berti, M., Simpson, A., Cunha, M. P. E. and Clegg, S. R. (2021). *Elgar Introduction to Organizational Paradox Theory*. Cheltenham: Edward Elgar Publishing.

Bolden, R. (2011) 'Distributed leadership in organizations: A review of theory and research', *International Journal of Management Reviews*, 13(3), 251–269.

Brown, M. and Cregan, C. (2008) 'Organizational change cynicism: The role of employee involvement', *Human Resource Management*, 47(4), 667–686.

Bryman, A. (1996) 'Leadership in organizations', in S. R. Clegg, C. Hardy and W. R. Nord (eds), *Handbook of Organization Studies*. London: Sage Publications, pp.276–292.

Chaurasia, S. and Shukla, A. (2013) 'The influence of leader-member exchange relations on employee engagement and work role performance', *International Journal of Organization Theory*, 16(4), 465–493.

Cunha, M. P., Clegg, S. and Rego, A. (2013) 'Lessons for leaders: Positive organization studies meets Niccolò Machiavelli', *Leadership*, 9(4), 450–465.

DeCelles, K. A., Tesluk, P. E. and Taxman, F. S. (2013) 'A field investigation of multilevel cynicism toward change', *Organization Science*, 24(1), 154–171.

Denis, J-L., Lamothe, L. and Langley, A. (2001) 'The dynamics of collective leadership and strategic change in pluralistic organizations', *Academy of Management Journal*, 44(4), 809–837.

Eriksen, M. (2008) 'Leading adaptive organizational change: Self-reflexivity and self-transformation', *Journal of Organizational Change Management*, 21(5), 622–640.

Eva, N., Robin, M., Sendjaya, S., Dierendonck, D. V. and Liden R. C. (2019) 'Servant leadership: A systematic review and call for future research', *The Leadership Quarterly*, 30(1), 111–132.

Feloni, R. (2017) Google's Eric Schmidt on the decision making advice managers need to know [Online] Available at https://www.weforum.org/agenda/2017/06/googles-eric-schmidt-on-the-decision-making-advice-managers-need-to-know/ (Accessed 30 March 2023).

Fiedler, F. E. (1967) *A Theory of Leadership Effectiveness*. New York: McGraw-Hill.

Gill, R. (2002) 'Change management – or change leadership?', *Journal of Change Management*, 3(4), 307–318.

Greenleaf, R. K. (1977) *Servant Leadership: A Journey into the Nature of Legitimate Power and Greatness*. New York: Paulist Press.

Gupta, A., Goel, A. and Bande, B. (2021) 'Role of empowerment and interpersonal relations in reducing cynicism and politics among Indian IT workers', *Vision – The Journal of Business Perspective*, 1–9.

Harbison, F. and Myers, C. A. (eds) (1959) *Management in the Industrial World: An International Analysis*. New York: McGraw-Hill.

Harris, P. (2010) 'Machiavelli and the global compass: Ends and means in ethics and leadership', *Journal of Business Ethics*, 93(1), 131–138.

Hayes, J. (2021) *The Theory and Practice of Change Management*, 6th edn. London: Red Globe Press.

Hersey, P. and Blanchard, K. H. (1969) 'Life cycle theory of leadership', *Training and Development Journal*, 23(5), 26–34.

Hutchins, G. and Storm, L. (2019) *Regenerative Leadership: The DNA of Life-Affirming 21st Century Organizations*. UK: Wordzworth Publishing.

Kotter, J. P. (1990) *A Force For Change: How Leadership Differs from Management*. New York: Free Press.

Leaders (2012) 'The boldness to dream: An interview with Olivia Lum, Group President and Chief Executive Officer, Hyflux Ltd', *Leaders*, 35(1), 18–19. [Online] Available at: www.leadersmag.com/issues/2012.1_Jan/PDFs/LEADERS-Olivia-Lum-Hyflux-Ltd.pdf (accessed 22 March 2023).

Leong, G. (2022) 'Ex-Hyflux CEO Olivia Lum, ex-CFO and four others charged with violations of Securities and Futures Act', *The Straits Times*, 17 November. [Online] Available at: www.straitstimes.com/business/ex-hyflux-ceo-olivia-lum-ex-cfo-and-four-others-charged-for-violations-of-securities-and-futures-act (accessed 22 March 2023).

Meirovich, G. and Gu, J. (2015) 'Empirical and theoretical validity of Hersey-Blanchard's contingency model: A critical analysis', *The Journal of Applied Management and Entrepreneurship*, 20(3), 56–74.

Nguyen, H. (2010) 'Eric Schmidt – a legendary leader', *Business Review*, 1(6), 8-15.

Northouse, P. G. (2013) *Leadership: Theory and Practice*, 6th edn. Thousand Oaks, CA: Sage Publications.

Participant Media (2023) *Participant Media*. [Online] Available at: https://participant.com/action (Accessed 4 February 2023).

Quinn, R. E., Spreitzer, G. M. and Brown, M. V. (2000) 'Changing others through changing ourselves: The transformation of human systems', *Journal of Management Inquiry*, 9(2), 147–164.

Skoll Foundation (2023) *Skoll Foundation*. [Online] Available at: https://skoll.org (accessed 4 February 2023).

Stippler, M., Moore, S., Rosenthal, S. A. and Dörffer, T. (2011). *Leadership: Approaches, Developments, Trends*. Gütersloh: Verlag Bertelsmann Stiftung.

Stogdill, R. M. (1974) *Handbook of Leadership: A Survey of the Literature*. New York: Free Press.

Tannenbaum, R. and Schmidt, W. H. (2009) *How to Choose a Leadership Pattern*. Boston, MA: Harvard Business Review Press.

Tanno, J. P. and Banner, D. K. (2018) 'Servant leaders as change agents', *Journal of Social Change*, 10(1), 1–18.

Toheed, H., Turi, J. A. and Ramay, M. I. (2019) 'Exploring the consequences of organizational cynicism', *International Journal of European Studies*, 3(1), 1–7.

Tourish, D. (2013) *The Dark Side of Transformational Leadership: A Critical Perspective*. London: Routledge.

Vroom, V. H. (1974) 'Decision making and the leadership process', *Journal of Contemporary Business*, 3, 47–64.

Western, S. (2008) *Leadership: A Critical Text*. London: Sage Publications.

Yahaya, R. and Ebrahim, F. (2016) 'Leadership styles and organizational commitment: Literature review', *Journal of Management Development*, 35(2), 190–216.

Zohar, D. (2022) 'Twelve principles of quantum leadership', in D. Zohar, *Zero Distance*. Singapore: Palgrave Macmillan, pp. 137–146.

8

COMMUNICATING CHANGE

Learning Outcomes

After completing this chapter, you should be able to:

- Explain the meaning of communication in the context of organisational change in light of the historical development of human communication.
- Discuss the key features and limitations of Shannon and Weaver's model of communication in the context of organisational change.
- Consider the causes and effects of poor organisational communication.
- Discuss Clampitt et al.'s typology of communication strategies and apply it as a change (or diagnostic) tool.
- Evaluate a range of media that change leaders can employ to effectively communicate change.
- Explain the meaning of organisational silence and identify its key causes and consequences.
- Discuss the core components of a dialogic model for communicating change and appreciate its significance as a key determinant of sustainable change success.

8.1 Introduction

The purpose of this chapter is to consider the meaning and impact of communication in the context of organisational change and explore ways to deploy effective change communication strategies. The chapter begins by distilling the key features of human communication in light of its historical development and considering their implications in the context of organisational change. The chapter then revisits Shannon and Weaver's

(1949) popular model of communication as applied to the context of organisational change, drawing attention to its key features and limitations. The chapter proceeds to explain why organisations fare badly in communicating change with a focus on the key causes and consequences of poor organisational communication. The chapter moves on to provide a critical review of Clampitt et al.'s (2000) typology of communication strategies before showing how it can be used as a diagnostic tool to assess the effectiveness of communicative approaches in real-life change situations. It then carries out an assessment of a range of media that change leaders can employ to effectively communicate change before considering the notion of organisational silence, which is a primary concern for change leaders, to unpick its main causes and consequences. Finally, we present the conceptual nugget for this chapter which entails the development of a dialogic model for communicating change. The model places an emphasis on the vital role of language in shaping the communication process between change leaders and other change stakeholders and shows how such communication can be located at the centre of a democratic platform to enable a balanced approach to organisational change. The chapter concludes with an outline of the key learning points derived from the preceding discussion and an end-of-chapter case study reporting on how COVID-19 served as a catalyst for the deployment of a digital communication strategy across a global automotive company.

8.2 Human communication and organisational change

To take a leaf from Watzlawick et al.'s (1967, p. 49) book, the much celebrated *The Pragmatics of Human Communication*, human beings 'cannot *not* communicate', and all forms of communication – whether intentional or not – have 'message value'. It is a truism that, from time immemorial, communication has been a basic human need enabling people to express their thoughts and feelings, tell their stories and establish some sort of connection with their surroundings and communities. This is why human communication trails a long and rich history that no single narrative could ever hope to capture in full. For the sake of relevance, we brush over the history of human communication to then promptly consider its meaning in the context of organisational change.

From cave paintings to Internet postings

Communication as a basic human need

The cave paintings in Lascaux (located in Southwestern France) are considered one of the most amazing examples of how pre-historic *Homo sapiens* used their art as a form of communication to capture their experiences of the world around them. The interesting side story to this monumental discovery is how pre-historic artists used all sorts of natural pigments for their wall engravings, some of which had to be sourced hundreds of kilometres away and extracted from natural ores at very high temperatures (*World History Encyclopedia*, 2016). This showed the great lengths to which these pre-historic artists were willing to go to satisfy a 'primal' need:

communication – which if not properly addressed, is bound to adversely impact change initiatives.

The behavioural and relational aspects of communication

The need for human communication was not limited to visual art forms. Some of the earliest forms of human communication before written language include speech, hand gestures and body language, which people used to express their thoughts and feelings and exchange information. This points to the importance of the pragmatics of human communication: the non-verbal, behavioural and relational dimensions of communication which account in a large measure for its effectiveness and which cannot be ignored in the changing context of modern-day organisations.

The written form of communication

With the development of the cuneiform – the first known writing system used in ancient Middle East around the 4th century BCE, people started to use pictograms and numerals especially on clay to convey information. As the cuneiform became a universal medium of communication, it was used mainly for commerce. The written form of communication found its way to other media such as wood, stone, bone fragments, the Egyptian papyrus and eventually paper in China around 100 BCE which made an enormous contribution to the spread of knowledge, education and business (Britannica, 2021). Nowadays, written forms of communication are vital to change success as they give a sense of permanence to things and help 'solidify' the strategic intent, policies and procedures, and roles and responsibilities which have to be crystal clear if change plans are to be successfully implemented (Myers et al., 2012).

Remote forms of communication

With the expansion of commerce and international trade, the ability of people to communicate at a distance took on greater importance. Before the invention of the electric telegraph and the international Morse code in the 19th century, methods of remote communication were as varied as inventive. To transmit basic messages at long distances, people had recourse to visual signaling systems such as smoke signals, fires, flags, mechanical arms and later to 'mail systems' such as pigeon-posts and horse-and-rider relays which were increasingly used by businesses and newspapers.

Remote communication took on new proportions with the commercialisation of the radio and TV in the first half of the 20th century. This enabled mass communication on an unprecedented level, where a message could be broadcast to whole populations from a single station. This opened up greater opportunities for business on a global scale, enabling companies to expand their marketing strategies across national borders and enlarge their customer base – where communication became a key change variable in the pursuit of business growth and success.

Internet-based communication

The development of computer technology in the 1960s and its convergence with Internet and satellite technologies in the 1990s had another major impact on our way of life and importantly, on the way organisations started to conduct business via online platforms (Delone and McLean, 2004). Human communication is now supported by a wide array of digital platforms such as email, social media, web blogs, news groups, video streaming, cloud computing and mobile applications. Nowadays, more than half of the world population has access to the Internet and trillions of online interactions happen every second – a quantum leap in telecommunications that has produced an upsurge in e-commerce and has been the cornerstone of the commercial success of global companies such as Amazon, Apple, Facebook, Google and Netflix (Sharma and Aggarwal, 2019; Walton, 2012).

There is currently a lot of talk about the so-called **Internet of Things** – where people, machines and all sorts of electronic devices will be digitally interconnected and will wirelessly communicate with each other to revolutionise the way we work, purchase goods and services, develop relationships and entertain ourselves (Greencard, 2015). Governments, businesses and other institutions are actively looking into innovative ways to leverage these fast-paced developments in communication technologies to enhance performance and productivity and build new business models geared towards sustainable change.

In light of its historical development, it is undeniable that human communication has been a primary driver of both social and organisational change. From cave paintings to Internet postings, human communication has come a long way and its enabling technologies are taking organisations on a path where it will become more than ever a critical factor of change success.

Meaning of communication in the context of organisational change

In light of the brief historical overview of the development of human communication and its implications for organisational change, we can now distil its key meanings that will serve as a theoretical baseline for the following discussion.

1   Human communication is a basic 'primal need' which, if not properly addressed, is bound to have a negative effect on change initiatives.
2   The non-verbal, behavioural and relational dimensions of communication account largely for its effectiveness and cannot be ignored in the development of sound strategies for communicating change.
3   Written forms of communication are vital to change success as they give 'a sense of permanence to things' and help 'solidify' the strategic intent driving change and clarify the terms and conditions of its implementation.
4   Remote communication has opened up business opportunities on a global scale and as such, a key change variable in the pursuit of business growth and success.
5   Internet-based communication has revolutionised the way organisations conduct business and is now the cornerstone of commercial success and a primary lever for performance and productivity, and sustainable change.

—REFLECTIVE EXERCISE—

1   In light of the brief historical overview of human communication, what are the defining features of human communication?
2   What are their implications for organisational change?

8.3 Shannon and Weaver's model of communication

We revisit Shannon and Weaver's (1949) popular model of communication as a starting point for a discussion of the basic features of organisational change communication and draw attention to its limitations that warrant a more sophisticated approach to the phenomenon. Figure 8.1 presents an adapted version of Shannon and Weaver's model.

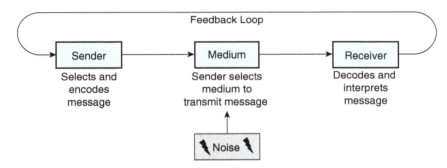

Figure 8.1   Shannon and Weaver's model of communication

Source: Adapted from Shannon, C. L. and Weaver, W. (1949) *The Mathematical Theory of Communication*. Urbana: University of Illinois Press.

Shannon and Weaver's model consists of the following key elements: the sender, the communication medium, the receiver, a feedback loop and noise.

Sender

Within the context of change, the sender is usually the agent leading the change. The sender decides about the content of the change message and encodes it – i.e. turns the change message into a form that can be transmitted and shared with other organisational members. This is a vital stage in the communication process as the message has to be crystal clear and expressed in a common language that is meaningful to all organisational members. A well-designed, clear and accessible change message plays a vital role in legitimising, and gaining stakeholder acceptance of, the proposed change. As is often said, the change message is as (if not more) important than the actual change.

Medium

The sender then has to decide about the medium or channel they will employ to transmit the change message. As previously mentioned, today there is a wide array of possible choices: organised events, face-to-face change forums, one-to-many online communication such as emails or intranet postings, interactive video conferencing, etc. Nowadays, most organisations would employ a range of communication channels to extend the 'reach' of the change message and ensure that it is fairly distributed among stakeholders and that they are rightly informed of the change situation and of its practical implications.

Receiver

The receiver of the change message has to decode and interpret it. In the context of change, the decoding process would involve unpacking the change message and understanding its actual meaning and implications. In an organisational setting, decoding can happen at an individual level (e.g. when reading a change message sent through personal email) or at a collective level (e.g. when participating in a change forum).

Feedback loop

The feedback loop is a mechanism which allows the receiver to respond to the message sent by the sender. If the delivery and decoding of the change message is asynchronous – i.e. if these two activities do not happen at the same time (e.g. if a change message is sent through an email), the feedback from the receiver is usually delayed. If the delivery and reception of the change message are synchronous (i.e. they happen at the same time as in the case of a participative forum) – the receiver can immediately provide their feedback. It has to be said that most change messages, because of their complex implications, cannot be taken at face value and neither do they always necessitate immediate feedback.

Noise

In the context of communicating change, noise refers to any unwanted forms of distortion, disruption or barriers that can have a negative effect on the change message and 'corrupt' its intended meaning. Noise can be of: (i) a *physical nature* (e.g. background or ambient sounds), (ii) a *semantic nature* (ambiguities and confusion over the meaning of the change message), (iii) a *psychological nature* (the mental or emotional state of both the sender and receiver), and (iv) a *socio-cultural nature* (prejudices, different values and expectations) – all of which can prevent shared understanding and consensus around the proposed change.

Criticisms

First, the Shannon and Weaver original model has been criticised for not doing justice to the role of the receiver in the communication process (Al-Fedaghi, 2012; Foulger, 2004). The receiver is cast in a rather passive role where all they can do is make sense of the sender's message as intended and provide the latter with an appropriate response. As such, the model does not leave much scope for a more proactive role on the part of the receiver and limits the possibility of their contributions to the framing of the change message.

Second, the model is focused on the process of communication and does not pay enough attention to the social context in which it plays out – obscuring the socio-cultural factors (such as power relations, core values and plurality of interests) that can have a significant impact on the quality and effectiveness of change communication.

Third, the model comes across as linear and one-dimensional and gives the impression that communication is limited to the interaction between a single sender and receiver. As such, it is of limited value to change situations which are plurivocal and shaped by multiple voices and a continuous and iterative process of interaction and negotiation between change stakeholders.

Finally, Shannon and Weaver's model tends to focus attention on the mechanics and technical aspects of communication to ensure the reliability of the communication medium and the 'semantic accuracy' or the meaning of the message 'as intended'. It, however, pays scant attention to the *pragmatics of human communication* – or as previously explained, the non-verbal, behavioural and relational dimensions of communication which account largely for its effectiveness, especially in the context of change.

In the final section of this chapter, our conceptual nugget entails the development of a dialogic model which effectively addresses all of the above issues.

—REFLECTIVE EXERCISE—

1   What are the implications of each of the key components of Shannon and Weaver's model to communicating organisational change?
2   What are the key criticisms that have been levelled at it?

8.4 Why do organisations fare badly in communicating change?

As aptly remarked by Myers et al. (2012), while the importance of communication as a key determinant of change success is a widely recognised fact, research in the area suggests that it remains poorly managed and a stumbling block for change agents. A Grossman survey of 400 companies, each employing around 100,000 employees, reports an average loss of more than US$62 million per company because of the inadequacy of communication both between management and employees and amongst employees (SHRM Org, 2016) – which points to the magnitude of the problem of poor communication, which can be exacerbated in the context of change.

Causes and consequences of poor organisational communication

The causes underlying poor communication can be deeply entrenched, inter-connected and lead to unfortunate (and sometimes irreversible) consequences. Figure 8.2 below provides a broad overview of the main causes of poor organisational communication and their potential consequences.

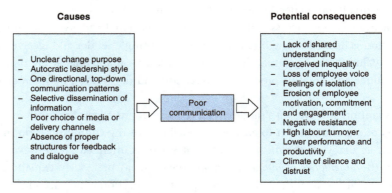

Causes

- Unclear change purpose
- Autocratic leadership style
- One directional, top-down communication patterns
- Selective dissemination of information
- Poor choice of media or delivery channels
- Absence of proper structures for feedback and dialogue

Poor communication

Potential consequences

- Lack of shared understanding
- Perceived inequality
- Loss of employee voice
- Feelings of isolation
- Erosion of employee motivation, commitment and engagement
- Negative resistance
- High labour turnover
- Lower performance and productivity
- Climate of silence and distrust

Figure 8.2 Causes and consequences of poor organisational communication

Causes of poor communication

The box on left side of Figure 8.2 presents a list of possible causes that seem to be persistent across change contexts. One of the most commonly cited reasons for poor communication is the lack of clarity of the purpose of change – which might arise from the fact that change leaders are themselves uncertain about what they are trying to do and are unable to construct a clear, consistent and compelling change message.

An autocratic leadership style is another common reason for poor change communication. Leaders who force change upon others do not generally see the need to explain, let alone justify their change agenda. As a result, their change messages tend to be one-directional and top-down with little scope for input from those operating at the bottom of the organisational hierarchy. Needless to say, such communication patterns usually serve to reaffirm the oppressive culture that autocratic leadership tends to perpetuate.

The **selective dissemination of information** is yet another feature of autocratic leadership. This is when change leaders choose to filter the content of the communication message based on the assumption that its recipients do not have to be privy to the full details of the proposed change – because they are either not capable of fully understanding the rationale underpinning it or making any valuable contribution to it. It could also be that certain information which change agents perceive as potentially damaging to themselves is screened out of the change messages targeted at subordinate groups of employees – which usually results in an imbalance in the dissemination of change information, where different organisational members end up with different 'versions' of the change initiative, resulting in confusion and mistrust.

Poor communication can also be the result of an inadequate choice of media or channels – where change messages are not delivered in the right format, through the right channel and at the right time. For example, posting a generic change message on the company intranet that is buried under a mass of unrelated information is unlikely to get the attention or interest of its target recipients. The absence of proper structures and procedures for dialogue and feedback is also symptomatic of a poor communication strategy – where there is no inbuilt capacity for shared understanding and negotiated meaning around the proposed change.

As can be easily inferred from the above discussion, the reasons underlying poor communication are often interconnected and form a complex causal web that is difficult to disentangle in practice. For example, autocratic change leaders will favour a top-down approach to change, disseminate information to a select few who share their interests and discard the possibility of opening direct lines of communication with employees as a means of avoiding negative feedback or resistance and strapping a protective belt around their own interests.

Consequences of poor communication

The box on the right side of Figure 8.2 contains a list of the potential consequences of poor communication:

- A lack of transparency and shared understanding around the purpose of change.
- Perceived inequality in access to information vital to effective change implementation.
- Loss of **employee voice** by being denied access to the decision-making process relating to important change issues and courses of action which might have a significant impact on the quality of work life and their career prospects.
- Feelings of isolation resulting from employees' perception that they are not treated as valued members of the organisation which can in turn cause high levels of anxiety and emotional distress.
- Erosion of employee motivation, commitment and engagement that can trigger negative forms of resistance to change, lead to high labour turnover and have an irreversible impact on overall performance and productivity.
- A climate of silence where employees in turn withhold potentially valuable information that could affect the change initiative primarily because of their distrust in change agents. Organisational silence is a complex phenomenon that is given a deeper treatment in a later section.

The potential consequences of poor communication described above are also interconnected and difficult to isolate in practice. However, the most important point here is that if persistent, the negative consequences of poor communication can easily spin out of control and prove extremely costly to both employees and the organisation – and should therefore not be treated lightly.

—CASE STUDY 8.1—

Nike: Showing agility in tackling a communication crisis

As one of the most powerful brands and the most successful producer and seller of athletic footwear, clothing and equipment, Nike needs no introduction. The company is renowned for its high-quality products but even more so for its creative marketing strategy which aims to establish a connection and a durable relationship with its target customers which is based on the notions of 'emotional branding' and 'product intimacy' – where customers develop an attachment with the brand and a deep liking for the utility and quality of the product with less concern for its price.

While Nike is able to effectively communicate and connect with its customers, it recently faced a major internal communication crisis which showed that this was not the case with regard to its employees. In 2018, Nike's female employees spoke out against the company's patriarchal, male-dominated and toxic culture that condoned workplace harassment and discrimination and a leadership team that was out of reach and out of touch with what was happening. A 'renegade survey' was undertaken by a group of employees to expose and confirm this state of affairs, the findings of which were then forwarded to the company's CEO. The survey revealed, among other things, a general lack of trust in HR, limited scope for bottom-up communication and a leadership team who claimed to be unaware of the situation.

Nike took swift measures to address this internal communication crisis including firing top executives who were held accountable, conducting mandatory training for managers and commissioning a comprehensive review of its HR procedures and internal communication structures to enable a move towards a more open and inclusive culture. It seems that the gravity of the situation left Nike with no other choice than to show some agility in tackling this internal communication crisis head-on. Nike would have landed itself in an 'ironic situation' if its highly reputed ability to communicate and connect with its customers did not apply to its employees.

Source: Slotosch (2021)

Questions

1   What were the causes that led to the internal communication crisis at Nike?
2   What lessons are to be learned from the way Nike addressed this problem?

8.5 Clampitt et al.'s typology of communication strategies

While change agents cannot communicate everything to everybody all the time (Myers et al., 2012), choices have to be made in relation to what should be communicated, when and at what level of detail. Clampitt et al.'s (2000) typology maps out five key different communication strategies along two key axes: communication effectiveness and amount of information transferred – as shown in Figure 8.3. In the following discussion, we provide a brief explanation of each of these strategies, starting from the bottom left and moving in a clockwise direction.

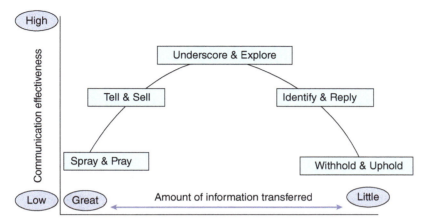

Figure 8.3 Clampitt et al.'s (2000) typology of communication strategies

Source: Clampitt, P. G., DeKoch, R.. J. and Cashman, T. (2000) 'A strategy for communicating about uncertainty', *Academy of Management Executive*, 14(4), 41–57. Reproduced with permission.

Spray and pray

As the term suggests, the **spray and pray** communication strategy involves throwing all the available information relating to change at employees in the hope that they will be able to find their way through it and make sense of the meaning of the change initiative. One might argue that it is a form of distributive justice – where everybody gets access to the same quantity and quality of information. However, such a 'scattergun approach' tends to end in a 'hit or miss' outcome. While some employees might be able to make some sense out of the information that is 'showered upon them', this might not be the case for those who do not have the baseline skills or pre-requisite knowledge to do so.

Moreover, for a change message to be effectively communicated it needs to be 'pre-interpreted' – i.e. it has to reflect the sender's own interpretation and sense making of the change situation and encoded in a language which the receiver can easily understand – which is hardly possible with the *spray and pray* approach. While having some semblance of a democratic approach to change communication, the *spray and pray* strategy betrays a lack of effective change leadership and does not have any real 'communicative intent' – leaving stakeholders second guessing, confused and disengaged from the change process.

Tell and sell

The **tell and sell** communication strategy is rooted in an autocratic leadership approach to change. In this case, the change message is pre-determined and pre-scripted – i.e. it contains the strategic choices that have already been decided upon by change leaders and details in no uncertain terms the manner in which such choices are to be implemented. The most important function of the change message is to promote the desired outcomes and potential benefits of the change plan to employees in the hope that they will endorse it and commit to its pre-set goals and objectives.

The flip side of the *tell and sell* strategy is that it casts the recipients of the change message in a passive role – with very little or no scope for their input and contribution to the change initiative. It can be seen as driven by the implicit assumption that the change leaders know best and that employees just have to follow their directions. This can create a work climate that is not conducive to employee motivation, learning and creativity – thus preventing the organisation from leveraging its talent pool to optimise change outputs.

Underscore and explore

The **underscore and explore** strategy can be seen as the most desirable approach to change communication and reflects a more democratic and participatory leadership style. In this case, the change message contains only a broad outline of the change strategy which provides the parameters for employee input while leaving some scope for feedback and input on how to best implement the change plan. As such, the *underscore and explore* strategy allows for dialogue and employee participation – albeit contained within asymmetrical power relations and leadership control of the change process.

One might contend that this particular approach to communicating change can be time-consuming and resource intensive and therefore not applicable to all change situations – especially those requiring an executive decision and swift action as a means of survival or for seizing unique business opportunities. However, one cannot underestimate the vital importance of inclusive dialogue and participation in change management. In the final section of this chapter, we consider the implications of the concept of dialogic communication which seeks to go beyond the constraints of the *underscore and explore* strategy to propose a mode of communication in which change leaders and their followers can operate as co-participants-in-communication and co-shapers of change.

Identify and reply

The **identify and reply** strategy focuses on obtaining feedback from employees and addressing issues and concerns arising from the change initiative from their perspective. In that sense, the *identify and reply* strategy is to some extent participatory and draws on the empathic and listening skills of change leaders, giving employees a voice and the opportunity to feel valued and an integral part of the change process.

However, the *identify and reply* strategy is based on the assumption that all employees have a genuine interest in the change initiative and have the knowledge and capacity to make a significant contribution to it – an assumption which might not necessarily be the case. Moreover, if change leaders engage in such participative forums with employees as a cosmetic exercise, then not much good can be expected from the *identify and reply* strategy.

Withhold and uphold

This is perhaps the least effective of the communication strategies in Clampitt et al.'s typology. It combines very little information sharing with very little effort to engage employees. The change message in this case is minimalist – i.e. it contains only a broad outline of the proposed change and contains basic information deemed sufficient to get employees on board the change programme, leaving out the more 'strategic' details to the care of the leadership team. A **withhold and uphold** strategy tends towards the autocratic end of the leadership styles spectrum – where the change leaders drive the change without feeling the need to consult with other organisational members.

Various reasons could underlie the *withhold and uphold* approach to communicating change. For instance, change leaders might entertain the view that employees do not have much to contribute to the change programme and are therefore not worth the trouble of spending extra time and resources on any extended forms of information exchange or protracted consultation. Other possible reasons could include change leaders' fear of negative feedback from employees, their lack of confidence in their own ability or more alarmingly, their unbridled ambition to pursue their own interests without opposition. In whichever way one looks at it, the *withhold and uphold* strategy is counterproductive and oblivious to the fact that organisational change without proper communication is simply unsustainable.

CASE STUDY 8.2

Atlassian: Driving change through a suite of collaborative software products

Applying Clampitt et al.'s typology of communication strategies as a diagnostic tool

Introduction

Atlassian is an Australian company committed to delivering high-quality, high-security yet user-friendly collaborative software products. Founded in 2002, it has 7,000 employees and its flagship products include Jira, Confluence, Bitbucket, and Trello, which are designed to help teams manage projects, track tasks and collaborate effectively, all of which are critical to change success. Atlassian also provides a wealth of resources and support services to ensure that its 200,000+ customers get the most out of its products – in line with its mission which is to revolutionise the way people work by enabling teams to unleash their full potential and empowering individuals to contribute to the process of change.

A philosophy of open work

Atlassian promotes a philosophy of 'open work' which is grounded in a culture of transparency, trust and inclusivity designed to bring out the best in employees to tackle a never-ending

(Continued)

stream of complex challenges. Atlassian believes that its philosophy of open work can serve as a compass for effective change – in that it encourages IT-enabled teams to operate in an open workspace, participate in daily stand-ups, and maintain transparency when sharing information. The company reinforces its philosophy of open work through communication channels such as town hall meetings, team updates and training sessions, as well as using its own collaborative tools to share information and provide feedback in real time.

An enabling structure for change

The collaborative software produced by Atlassian also provides an enabling structure for change. In this regard, it includes powerful features that can be used to streamline project management, identify problems, track progress, document activities and capture valuable knowledge in the process of software development. Moreover, Atlassian collaborative tools can be customised to meet specific team needs and can be integrated with other popular tools to expand their functionality to enhance communication and optimise team productivity whilst reducing administrative overheads.

Going viral

Atlassian's philosophy of 'open work' is going viral as more and more companies across the globe are adopting its approach to teamwork and using its products to leverage their change initiatives.

Sources: Atlassian (2023)

Questions

Use Clampitt et al.'s typology of communication strategies as a diagnostic tool to assess Atlassian's approach to change.

1   Which one of the different types of communication strategies identified by Clampitt et al. best describes Atlassian's approach to change?
2   In what ways does the collaborative software developed by Atlassian enable effective change communication?
3   Are there any drawbacks to a reliance on technology for communicating change?

8.6 Choosing the right medium for communicating change

In this section, we consider the range of media that change leaders can employ to communicate change. Nowadays, the continuing convergence of information and communication technologies and their rapid uptake across organisations means that change leaders have access to a wider array of media – whether it be digital, print or those requiring a physical presence – through which they can communicate with organisational stakeholders throughout the change process.

The richness of communication media

Communication media can be differentiated according to their 'richness' (Ishii et al., 2019; Lee and Borah, 2020) and media richness is determined by the following criteria:

- The extent to which a particular medium can support interaction.
- The number of cues – i.e. signals or prompts to guide understanding or elicit particular responses.
- The level of detail contained in the information conveyed.
- The opportunity for immediate responses and feedback.
- The degree of personalisation or 'tailoring' of the message to meet the needs of its recipients.

Assessing the richness of communication media

Another more sophisticated way of assessing communication media is to cross-reference their *richness* against their *level of interactivity* – as shown in Figure 8.4.

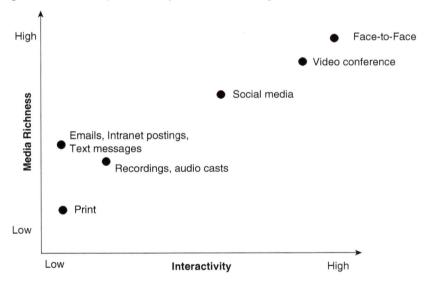

Figure 8.4 Media richness and level of interactivity of organisational communication media

Print

Printed messages score low on both media richness and level of interactivity. Print media can be put to good effect as 'lean' forms of communication such as newsletters, bite-sized reports and updates on change progress. However, they are not the best choice if used on their own for major events like launching the change initiative or making announcements that relate to major issues that can have considerable impact on the change process and that warrant negotiation or joint decision-making.

Audio and Internet-based messages

Recording and audio casts are moderately rich in that they contain vocal and emotional cues that can add to the personalisation, authenticity and trustworthiness of the change message and the one delivering it. However, they rate relatively low on interactivity as they do not support interaction or immediate feedback – although they do allow for asynchronous responses to change messages – i.e. delayed responses happening at some point after the delivery of the change message. Similarly, emails and intranet postings are moderately rich but relatively low on interactivity, and responses to change messages using such media tend to be asynchronous. However they can contain certain features (e.g. video clips, podcasts) that add to the richness of change messages.

Social media

Social media is a collective term for Internet communication platforms that enable the sharing of information and multimedia contents across virtual networks and communities. As such, they score relatively high on both richness and interactivity. In the context of organisational change, they can provide a democratic and informative platform where 'anyone can say anything' and feel part of the change process. However, social media is exposed to noise of a semantic nature, where it can become a carrier of half-truths, fake news and inflammatory comments that can quickly 'go viral' and run out of control – leading to a loss of meaning around the intended change and of trust in the competence or integrity of change leaders.

Video conferencing and face-to-face communication

Video conferencing and face-to-face communication rate high on both *richness* and *interactivity* and are better 'conduits' for a two-way communication in real time between change stakeholders, which is conducive to dialogue, negotiation of meaning and joint decision-making. However, video conferencing is subject to the whims of the technology upon which it is dependent, while face-to-face communication can lose its effectiveness if it is used to reinforce the power inequality between change leaders and their subordinates or as a show of force to impose pre-determined change objectives upon the latter.

The more important point to remember here is that communication media are not intrinsically good or bad and there is no failsafe recipe for their effective use. The choice of media should be based on the extent to which they are 'fit for purpose' and in keeping with the timings and desired outcomes of change communication. Moreover, the choice of communication media does not have to be limited by an 'either–or' approach. Change leaders, as is increasingly the case, can combine media and use them simultaneously or in a chosen sequence in response to the needs of their target audiences.

---PRACTICAL EXERCISE---

Go online and find out more about the communication tools and media that large IT-driven companies are deploying for enabling collaboration, joint decision-making, team working and employee engagement. Use a search engine to look at the communication tools used by the companies listed in the left-hand column of Table 8.1 and outline your findings in the right-hand column.

Table 8.1   Key features of communication tools used by large IT-driven companies

Company	Key features
IBM's *Connection Engagement Suite*	
Google's *Happeo*	
Amazon's *Chime*	
BT's *Facebook Workplace*	

8.7 Organisational silence

As mentioned in the previous section, we consider it necessary to give some space to the notion of **organisational silence** as it is a primary cause of change failure and therefore a cause for concern. Organisational silence is a systemic, collective-level phenomenon that entails the 'widespread withholding of information about potential problems or issues from employees' (Morrison and Milliken, 2000, p. 706). While a more detailed treatment of organisational silence is beyond the scope of this book, we want to draw attention to its main causes and consequences – as highlighted in Figure 8.5.

As shown in Figure 8.5, we prefer to conceptualise the factors leading to organisational silence as a complex web of causal influences arising from the negative relational dynamics between change leaders and employees (highlighted in the left-hand box). As the causal influences identified here are largely descriptive, we will not explain their meaning in any more detail. However, we want to draw attention to the fact that these causal influences tend to be mutually reinforcing and their combined effects can serve to erect a formidable communication barrier between change leaders and employees, leading to systemic silence – an organisation-wide, collective phenomenon, where employees withhold information about change problems which are dismissed as undiscussables – things that should not be discussed or talked about for fear of reprisal (Morrison and Milliken, 2000).

The right-hand box in Figure 8.5 lists some of the negative consequences of organisational silence. Once again, these will not be expounded here but suffice to say that organisational silence can have an extremely demoralising and damaging effect on the employment relationship and on change outcomes. This is why it should be a primary concern of change leaders; and, in our view, the only way to 'break' organisational silence is to adopt a more democratic, inclusive and empowering change communication model – which is addressed in the following section.

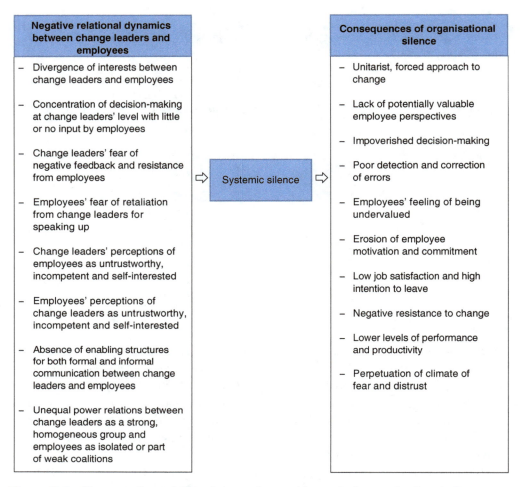

Figure 8.5 The negative relational dynamics and impact of organisational silence

Source: Adapted from Morrison, E. W. and Milliken, F. J. (2000) 'Organizational silence: A barrier to change and development in a pluralistic world', *Academy of Management Review*, 25(4), 706–725.

8.8 Conceptual nugget: A dialogic model for communicating change

In this final section, we present our conceptual nugget for this chapter which entails the development of a dialogic model for communicating change – in line with the conceptual pillar underpinning this part of the book. Our dialogic model aims to address the limitations of Shannon and Weaver's communication model and is rooted in three robust communication theories which account for its legitimacy:

i   Habermas' **theory of communicative action** which views language as a medium of unrestrained communication and action and develops the notion of an ideal speech situation – a democratic space which is placed under the binding principle of free dialogue and which warrants a suspension of power inequalities to enable a collaborative process of interpretation and deliberation through which 'participants-in-communication' can achieve shared understanding and coordinate their actions (Habermas, 1987).

ii   Watzlavik's **pragmatics of human communication** which focuses on the non-verbal, relational and behavioural aspects of human communication which account for a large part to sense making and interpretation. It also calls to attention the role of 'punctuation' or sequencing of communication flows in reinforcing meaning and building positive relationships. Moreover, it underlines the importance of pragmatic competences and skills in safeguarding the democratic principle underpinning open dialogue between participants-in-communication (Watzlawick et al., 1967).

iii   Fairclough's **discourse theory** which promotes the notion of language as a form of social practice and having a shaping influence on power relations, collective sense making and ideological commitments that provide the justification for chosen courses of action. Discourse theory also reinforces a view of dialogue as 'a cooperative conversation between equals' with equal communicative rights and obligations – where matters of status have been set aside to enable the creation of a democratic, negotiated and plurivocal order of discourse that can provide the justification for collective choices and courses of action (e.g. see Fairclough, 1995, pp. 46–70).

In light of the above discussion, Figure 8.6 presents our dialogic framework which consists of the following core components: *Creation of meaning, Extraction of meaning, Negotiation of meaning and Shared meaning.*

Creation of meaning

The process of meaning creation in a change context normally begins with change leaders – who in this case act as the senders of the change message. It is important to note upfront that the 'crafting of the change message' already involves a *cooperative process of deliberation* and a *first layer of interpretation*. By addressing a set of practical bottom-line questions (in the left-hand box of the model) change leaders first have to make sense of the change situation which is influenced by their own assumptions, experiences and values. They then have to reach some sort of consensus about the purpose, scope, resource implications and intended outcomes of the proposed change. Finally, they have to translate what has been agreed upon into a 'communicable' change message – i.e. one that is clear, coherent and couched in a language that its recipients will easily understand (Grice, 1991).

We also want to draw attention to how language fulfils two important functions in the framing of change messages. First, as discussed in Chapter 7, one of the most important responsibilities of change leaders is to persuade, inspire, motivate and muster the commitment of key stakeholders. To this effect, the change message needs to have a soft *affective, emotional dimension* – where change leaders can have recourse to a rich repertoire of emotionally charged forms of expression in

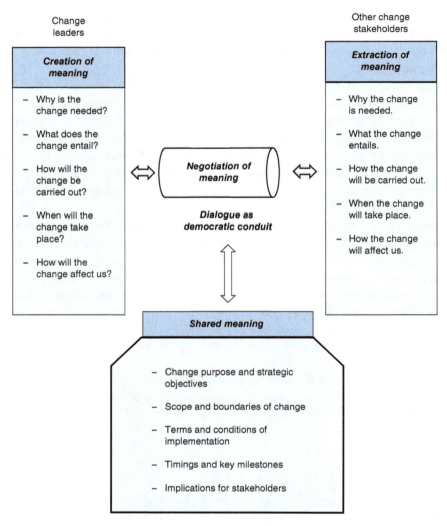

Figure 8.6 A dialogic framework for change communication

the construction of the change message to elicit a favourable response from its recipients. These can include metaphors, stories and catchphrases to, for example, convince stakeholders of the necessity of change, revive the core values of the organisation, sell the benefits of change or build employee commitment (e.g. see Palmer and Dunford, 1996; Smollan, 2014).

Second, an effective change message is also grounded in the real world and has a *functional, instrumental dimension*. This is where change leaders need to use a form of plain, down-to-earth type of language – a 'business speak' that includes familiar terms (e.g. strategic goals, return on investment, shareholder value, production capacity, profit margins) and which, along with well-placed statistics and charts, aims to demonstrate the rationality and economic viability of the proposed change.

Creating a meaningful change message is therefore not an afterthought or just an ad hoc exercise that change leaders can expedite. Effective change messages are *pre-interpreted* and *borne out of a collaborative process* of deep reflection and sense making amongst change leaders – which is key to the 'ideological positioning' of the proposed change as a promising course of action and one that is worth pursuing (Fairclough, 1995; Habermas, 1987).

Extraction of meaning

Once the change message is delivered to its intended recipients (in this case the other change stakeholders), it goes through another interpretive layer as they try to make sense of its content and extract the meaning that it carries. The *conversion of the bottom-line questions* (in the left-hand box of the model) *into simple statements* (in the right-hand box of Figure 8.6) points to the process of interpretation through which the recipients have extracted and made sense of the meanings contained in the change message – *as intended*.

Two key issues have to be taken into consideration here. First, for the meanings contained in the change message to be received as intended, the change message has to be *semantically accurate* – i.e. it has to be free from 'semantic noise' or any kind of linguistic ambiguities that could corrupt its true meanings and confuse the recipients – reinforcing the need for the change message to be couched in a clear, coherent and common language that is easy to understand by all parties involved. Second, the accuracy of a change message is no guarantee of its *acceptance and internalisation* by its recipients. For a change message to be accepted and owned by all key change stakeholders, it has to be filtered through a cooperative process of interpretation and deliberation between change leaders and other stakeholders as equals – with equal communicative rights and obligations and with an equal chance of having their needs and interests factored into the change agenda. In other words, the meanings attached to the proposed change have to be *negotiated* if it is to be widely accepted and internalised by key stakeholder groups.

Negotiation of meaning

We locate the process of meaning negotiation at the centre of a democratic communication platform akin to Habermas' notion of the *ideal speech situation* – one which calls for a suspension of power inequalities, a freezing of taken-for-granted assumptions and a 'putting out of play of all motives except that of a willingness to come to a [shared] understanding around the proposed change' (McCarthy, 1988, p. xiv). We also draw on the *conduit metaphor*, a recurrent theme in communication theory, and 'plug it' at the core of our dialogic model.

The conduit metaphor is a figure of speech which was identified by American linguist Michael Reddy to explain how language functions as an enabling channel to carry meaning and enable people to interact and share their beliefs, ideas and viewpoints (Reddy, 1979). We emphasise the democratic orientation of the conduit metaphor to show how *dialogue as a democratic conduit* can open up the possibility for free, open dialogue between change leaders and other change stakeholders to enable a balanced approach to collective sense making and the negotiation of meaning around the proposed change. The metaphor of *democratic dialogue as conduit* is therefore used here as a firm reminder of the reconciliatory power of language and how it can be used for accommodating alternative perspectives and key change stakeholders' needs and for resolving potential conflicts of interest – which is, in any case, a precondition for stakeholder buy-in and long-term commitment to the change programme.

It is important to note that the effectiveness of democratic dialogue is to a large extent dependent upon the *pragmatic competence* of participants-in-communication – which refers to the development of 'democratic communication skills' of all those involved in the negotiation process, geared towards building positive behaviours and relationships: eloquence or ability to speak in a persuasive manner about one's views and interests, active listening skills to demonstrate interest in alternative perspectives, turn-taking to demonstrate mutual respect in communication exchanges, adherence to social norms in the use of body language and other pertinent rules of engagement to facilitate free, open dialogue. Pragmatic competence is a critical element of the meaning negotiation process – for, to paraphrase Watzlavick, the process of negotiation cannot be divorced from the relational context in which it is played out and upon which it is largely dependent (Habermas, 1987; Watzlavik et al., 1967).

Shared meaning

Shared meaning around the proposed change is the desirable outcome of our dialogic model. It can be seen as a function of both the effectiveness of the change message itself and of the quality of the interpretation and negotiation it has elicited. It paves the way for consensus and closure around the purpose, scope, implementation, timing and implications of the proposed change. In this respect, shared meaning represents the *collective ideological commitments* of all change stakeholders and a commonly approved *order of discourse* that integrates a plurality of perspectives and interests – and that provides the legitimacy for a concerted approach to change and an effective coordination of action in the pursuit of common change goals and objectives (Fairclough, 1995; Habermas, 1987).

Importantly, we want to stress upon the fact that *shared meaning is not a fixed order of discourse* but one that should remain open to on-going rounds of interpretation and negotiation in view of emerging issues and challenges or new strategic imperatives. Moreover, this ties in nicely with Watzlavick's notion of *punctuation or sequencing* of the flow of communication – which calls for repeated dialogic moments as a means of reinforcing initial meanings of change, attaching new meanings to it, and building positive and trusting relationships to sustain the momentum of change.

Finally, we realise that our dialogic model for communicating change could be dismissed by some as purely speculative and even 'counterfactual' – in that it is rarely, if ever, found in practice. However, to take a leaf out of Habermas' book, we contend that it is grounded in sound communication theories and principles and a 'legitimate anticipation' of change stakeholders – for it holds the promise of far more positive communicative and relational dynamics as a key determinant of sustainable change success.

REFLECTIVE EXERCISE

Look back at the key elements of our dialogic model for communicating change in Figure 8.6 and answer the following questions:

1 Why is it important for change leaders to be able to answer the questions in the left box before communicating the change message?
2 Why is negotiation an important condition for the acceptance and internalisation of the change message by other change stakeholders?

3   What are the key skills that both change leaders and other stakeholders need to develop to be effective participants-in-dialogue?

Think also about how the dialogic model developed in this chapter could be used to support the work of change consultants in the area of change communication.

8.9 Key learning points

1   Human communication is a *basic need* which, if not properly addressed, is bound to have a negative effect on change initiatives. Its *non-verbal, relational and behavioural dimensions* account largely for its effectiveness. There are different forms of communication – written, verbal, remote, and Internet-based – which can be put to good use in driving and sustaining change success.

2   Shannon and Weaver's model of communication consists of the following key elements: the *sender*, the communication *medium*, the *receiver*, a *feedback loop* and *noise*. While it is a good starting point for a discussion of the basic features of organisational change communication, it has certain limitations – notably its scant attention to the context and to the relational and behavioural dimensions of communication – which makes it inappropriate for a more robust approach to communicating organisational change.

3   The causes underlying poor communication can be deeply entrenched and inter-connected and have adverse consequences. Causes of poor communication include an unclear change purpose, an autocratic leadership style, top-down communication patterns, selective dissemination of information, poor choice of communication media and the absence of structures for dialogue. The consequences of poor communication are also interconnected and include, among other things, a lack of shared understanding, perceived inequality, feelings of isolation, erosion of employee motivation, commitment and engagement, lower performance levels and a climate of silence and distrust.

4   Clampitt et al.'s typology of communication strategies identifies five key approaches to communicating change along the two key axes of communication effectiveness and amount of information transferred, including: *spray and pray, tell and sell, underscore and explore, identify and reply*, and *withhold and uphold*. The least effective communication strategy is *withhold and uphold* which combines very little information sharing with very little effort to engage employees. *Underscore and explore* seems to be the most effective strategy as it allows for employee participation and dialogue, albeit contained within asymmetrical power relations and leadership control of the change process.

5   Communication media can be differentiated according to their *richness* and *level of interactivity* and include print, audio and Internet-based messages, social media, video conferencing and face-to-face communication. While all these communication media have their uses and limitations, the more important point is that communication media are not intrinsically good or bad and there is no failsafe recipe for their effective use. The choice of media should be based on the extent to which they are fit for purpose and in keeping with the timings and desired outcomes of change communication.

6   *Organisational silence* is a systemic, collective-level phenomenon that entails the widespread withholding of information about potential problems or issues by employees. It is conceptualised in this book as a complex web of causal influences arising from the *negative relational dynamics between change leaders and employees*. These causal influences include, among other things: divergence of interests between change leaders and employees, change leaders' fear of negative feedback, employees' fear of retaliation, change leaders' and employees' perceptions of each other as untrustworthy, incompetent and self-interested, and the absence of enabling communication structures. The adverse consequences of organisational silence include: a lack of alternative perspectives, impoverished decision-making, erosion of employee motivation and commitment, lower performance levels and the perpetuation of a climate of fear and distrust.

7   Our dialogic model for communicating change is rooted in Habermas' theory of communicative action, Watzlavik's pragmatics of human communication and Fairclough's discourse theory. It places an emphasis on the vital role of language in shaping the communication process between change leaders and other change stakeholders and consists of the following core components: *Creation of meaning, Extraction of meaning, Negotiation of meaning* and *Shared meaning*. The model shows how such communication process can be located at the centre of a democratic platform to *open up the possibility for free, open dialogue* between change leaders and other change stakeholders and enable a balanced approach to collective sense making, the negotiation of meaning and shared understanding around change initiatives. Importantly, the model takes account of the *behavioural and relational aspects of human communication* and draws attention to the *communication skills and other pertinent rules of engagement* critical to the democratic process of deliberation and negotiation of meaning. Finally, we stress the fact that the model is not static but remains *open to on-going rounds of interpretation and negotiation* as a means of reinforcing initial meanings or attaching new meanings to change initiatives and building positive and trusting relationships to sustain the momentum of change.

—END-OF-CHAPTER CASE STUDY 8.3—

AutoCo: COVID-19 as a catalyst for digital communication strategy

Introduction

AutoCo is a multinational automotive firm headquartered in Germany, with subsidiaries in Europe, Asia, Africa and Latin America. AutoCo gradually extended its core activities of commercial vehicle manufacturing and sales to include the provision of integrated transport solutions on a global scale. It targets premium niche markets with annual sales exceeding 10 billion euros and an internationally based workforce of around 40,000. AutoCo is currently undergoing the largest transformation in its history in response to the mega trends of *electrification, automation* and *digitalisation* which are having a major impact on the automotive industry and demand bold investments in new technologies and capabilities. This company-wide transformational change is primarily driven by the need to cut costs and entails a range of measures, including headcount reductions, production facility closures and business process restructuring.

The impact of COVID-19 on AutoCo's communication strategy

With the transformational change underway, AutoCo was still struggling to shift a deeply entrenched culture characterised by rigid hierarchies and an excessive focus on presenteeism (the practice of privileging physical presence or spending more time than required in the workplace, in order to appear to be working hard *rather* than focusing on performance outcomes and productivity). As a result, the communication strategy at AutoCo was primarily based on face-to-face interaction and mostly contained within the physical boundaries of the organisation. However, the arrival of the COVID-19 pandemic proved to be a catalyst for leveraging the company's digital communication platform which had up to then remained dormant.

Literally overnight, digital communication became the new norm. Employees had to work and collaborate via virtual platforms across hierarchical levels, functional areas and national borders. To the surprise of both management and staff, this proved to be more effective than face-to-face interaction and traditional forms of working that typified the company before it was hit by the pandemic. With digital communication now in a phase of active experimentation across the organisation, many stakeholders are beginning to ask the burning questions:

1 Is digital communication the new normal?
2 Is it here to stay?

Modelling the COVID-19-induced digitalisation of AutoCo's communication strategy

Figure 8.7 charts the digitalisation of AutoCo's communication process which was triggered by COVID-19. It shows how the company effected a fast-track move from *analogue communication* (which is taken here to mean face-to-face interaction requiring a physical presence) that prevailed before COVID-19 to one that incorporates a digital component, highlighting the positive impact this had on the effectiveness of the communicative process. Importantly, it draws attention to how the new digital mode of communication served to challenge the existing hierarchical structure and cultural value system which typified the organisation before the COVID-19 pandemic. Finally, it keeps in the foreground the question that is still preoccupying stakeholders regarding the role of digital communication in the future.

(Continued)

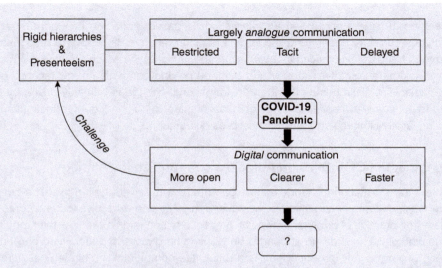

Figure 8.7 COVID-19-induced digitalisation of AutoCo's communication strategy

Communication before the pandemic

Before COVID-19, the analogue form of communication at AutoCo could be described as *restricted, tacit* and *delayed. Restricted* communication meant that access to information and knowledge transfer was determined by rank and status which is typical of German automotive companies where hierarchies tend to be quite rigid. As a result, higher-level staff were able to obtain and act on vital information that lower-level staff could not access, which was detrimental to the latter's performance and development. Restricted communication and knowledge transfer were also a function of geographical location both within and across national boundaries. Employees who were 'physically distant' from a vital source of information could not access it even if such information was key to the successful completion of their tasks.

Knowledge transfer had so far remained largely *tacit* – i.e. contained within 'insider' groups and informal personal networks, couched in technical jargon, never explicitly documented and selectively distributed across the organisation without any clear purpose or the possibility of tracking its impact on current processes and practices. Moreover, the impact of information that was distributed across the organisation was *delayed* and had a 'lagged effect' – i.e. its intended outcomes were extremely slow, sporadic and inconsistent. Thus, the analogue form of communication at AutoCo had, albeit unintentionally, brought about a type of subjectively biased filter mechanism and selective dissemination of information which was having an adverse effect on both individual and organisational performance.

Communication post COVID-19

As the COVID-19 pandemic spread across Europe in Spring 2020, AutoCo had no choice but to emulate its industry rivals by implementing a remote working policy for an undefined period – something which was up until then unthinkable given the company's entrenched culture of presenteeism. This new policy made good on the company's digital communication platform which had been in place for more than a decade to allow staff to work remotely 1–2 days per week at the discretion of their managers. To the surprise of many, digital communication soon showed itself to be much *more open, clearer* and *faster*.

More open communication meant that interaction across the organisation was not limited anymore by 'physical presence' or status but was extended to all employees irrespective of geographical location, rank or job title. As a result, the very nature of the communication process at AutoCo was evolving towards the more democratic end of the spectrum. Unlike the physical layout in board and staff meetings which tend to reinforce unequal power relations and stifle free exchange of information, employees felt that communicating online via a screen was like participating in a 'round table', where everybody was on an equal footing and could freely express their views and opinions.

Change messages were much *clearer*. Staff were better able to make sense of the corporate decisions, strategic choices and policy development that related to the transformational change the organisation was going through. From a knowledge transfer perspective, staff were having a much better deal. They were able to readily access technical experts and other professionals with specialist knowledge to keep abreast of the latest developments relevant to their work, get timely help and support in addressing emerging problems and implement best practices in line with the change goals and objectives.

Finally, digital communication was much *faster* and significantly increased the pace of information and knowledge transfer across the organisation. Employees could access a wide range of digital formats – whether it be emails, intranet postings, chat rooms, video conferencing, podcasts and webcasting of key events and forums – depending on the purpose and urgency of the information and knowledge required to perform their tasks.

It soon came to management's attention that not all employees were up to speed with the use of online communication platforms and that there was a need for targeted training in this area which is now at the top of the company's change agenda. However, as AutoCo is still coming to terms with the adverse impact that COVID-19 has had on the industry, the burning question remains as to whether digital communication is the *new normal* or whether top management will revert to the old ways of working and communicating rooted in presenteeism and hierarchical relationships once the worst of the pandemic is past.

Conclusions

A number of key issues emerge from this case study. First, what started out as a transformational change driven by cost-cutting measures at AutoCo turned into an organisation-wide culture change brought about by COVID-19, which triggered the sudden actioning of the digital component of its communication strategy that until then had remained dormant. Second, in this particular case, digital communication served as a lever for culture change in that it enabled AutoCo to democratise its communicative process towards more open, flexible and inclusive forms of dissemination of information and knowledge transfer across the organisation. Finally, like other organisations that had to grapple with the new business reality brought

(Continued)

about by COVID-19, AutoCo will soon find itself at a crossroads where it will have to decide how it is going to manage the new ways of working enabled by digital communication and sustain the culture change that was practically forced upon it by the pandemic.

Questions

1   Why do you think AutoCo never capitalised on its investment in digital communication until the outbreak of COVID-19?
2   What are the benefits of digital communication as compared to analogue communication?
3   Moving forward, how should AutoCo manage its communication strategy to tackle future challenges related to or similar to COVID-19?

8.11 Independent learning

Shannon and Weaver's model of communication: www.youtube.com/watch?v=OY1JsGFZprc (Communication coach Alex Lyon); www.youtube.com/watch?v=xuJKEqiv0XQ (St Paul University). For a bite-sized introduction to the original Shannon and Weaver model which explains its key elements and considers its merits and limitations, watch these short video clips.

Clampitt et al.'s Five communication strategies: www.jstor.org/stable/4165684. You can read a free excerpt of Clampitt et al.'s article via this link to get a sense of the context in which it was written. You should be able to get access to the full article through your university library services.

Poor communication and organisational silence: www.youtube.com/watch?v=5NpZPg5hV9E&t=11s. Watch this short video clip which gives an overview of some of the adverse effects of employee silence.

Using the power of conversations to influence change: www.enclaria.com/2014/05/15/interview-using-the-power-of-conversations-to-influence-change/. In this podcast Ankit Patel, managing partner of The Lean Way Consulting, discusses how to tap into the natural information flows in an organisation to influence change.

8.12 References

Atlassian (2023) *Atlassian*. [Online] Available at: www.atlassian.com/ (accessed 30 March 2023).

Al-Fedaghi, S. (2012) 'A conceptual foundation for the Shannon-Weaver model of communication', *International Journal of Soft Computing*, 7(1), 12–19.

Britannica (2021) *Cuneiform Writing System*. [Online] Available at: www.britannica.com/topic/cuneiform (accessed 25 August 2022).

Clampitt, P. G., DeKoch, R. J. and Cashman, T. (2000) 'A strategy for communicating about uncertainty', *Academy of Management Executive*, 14(4), 41–57.

Delone, W. H. and McLean, E. R. (2004) 'Measuring e-commerce success: Applying the DeLone & McLean information systems success model', *International Journal of Electronic Commerce*, 9(1), 31–47.

Fairclough, N. (1995) *Critical Discourse Analysis*. London: Longman.

Foulger, D. (2004) *Models of the Communication Process*. [Online] Available at: http://davis.foulger.info/research/unifiedModelOfCommunication.htm (accessed 18 October 2022).

Greencard, S. (2015) *The Internet of Things*. Cambridge, MA: MIT.

Grice, P. (1991) *Studies in the Way of Words*. London: Harvard University Press.

Habermas, J. (1987) *The Theory of Communicative Action: The Critique of Functionalist Reason*, vol. *2*. Cambridge: Polity Press.

Ishii, K., Lyons, M. M. and Carr, S. A. (2019) 'Revisiting media richness theory for today and future', *Human Behavior and Emerging Technologies*, *1*(2), 124–131.

Lee, D. K. L. and Borah, P. (2020) 'Self-presentation on Instagram and friendship development among young adults: A moderated mediation model of media richness, perceived functionality, and openness', *Computers in Human Behavior*, *103*, 57–66.

McCarthy, T. (1988) 'Translator's introduction', in J. Habermas, *Legitimation Crisis*. Cambridge: Polity Press, pp. vii–xxiv.

Morrison, E. W. and Milliken, F. J. (2000) 'Organizational silence: A barrier to change and development in a pluralistic world', *Academy of Management Review*, *25*(4), 706–725.

Myers, P., Hulks, S. and Wiggins, L. (2012) *Organizational Change: Perspectives on Theory and Practice*. Oxford: Oxford University Press.

Palmer, I. and Dunford, R. (1996) 'Conflicting uses of metaphors: Reconceptualizing their use in the field of organizational change', *Academy of Management Review*, *21*(3), 691–717.

Reddy, M. J. (1979) 'The conduit metaphor: A case of frame conflict in our language about language', in A. Ortony (ed.) (1993) *Metaphor and Thought*, 2nd edn. Cambridge: Cambridge University Press, pp. 164–201.

Shannon, C. L. and Weaver, W. (1949) *The Mathematical Theory of Communication*. Urbana: University of Illinois Press.

Sharma, H. and Aggarwal, A. G. (2019) 'Finding determinants of e-commerce success: a PLS-SEM approach', *Journal of Advances in Management Research*, *16*(4), 453-471.

SHRM Org (2016) *The Cost of Poor Communications: A Business Rationale for the Communications Competency*. [Online] Available at: www.shrm.org/resourcesandtools/hr-topics/organizational-and-employee-development/pages/the-cost-of-poor-communication.aspx (accessed 30 August 2022).

Slotosch, A. (2021) *5 Business Communication Failure Examples and How to Avoid Them*. [Online] Available at: www.beekeeper.io/blog/3-internal-communication-failures-that-turned-into-pr-disasters/ (accessed 30 August 2022).

Smollan, R. (2014) 'The emotional dimensions of metaphors of change', *Journal of Managerial Psychology*, *29*(7), 794–807.

Walton, N. (2012) '"Four-closure": How Amazon, Apple, Facebook & Google are driving business model innovation', *Chinese Business Review*, *11*(11), 981–988.

Watzlawick, P., Bavelas, J. B. and Jackson, D. D. (1967) *Pragmatics of Human Communication: A Study of Interactional Patterns, Pathologies and Paradoxes*. London: W. W. Norton & Co, Inc.

World History Encyclopedia (2016) *Lascaux Cave*. [Online] Available at: www.worldhistory.org/Lascaux_Cave/ (accessed 23 August 2022).

PART III

A PROCESSUAL APPROACH TO CHANGE

9

IMPLEMENTING CHANGE

Learning Outcomes

After completing this chapter, you should be able to:

- Draw the distinction between directed and facilitated approaches to change implementation.
- Critically discuss the core principles and limitations of a set of change implementation methods (BPR, Lean and Six Sigma) and experiment with some of their most widely used tools.
- Consider the key differences and commonalities between Lean and Six Sigma and explain how combining the two (LSS) can have synergistic effects and leverage the change implementation process.
- Use a filtering device to facilitate the selection of appropriate change implementation methods.

9.1 Introduction

The purpose of this chapter is to help you develop an understanding of some of the most common methods, tools and techniques that change leaders can employ to implement change and effectively translate their change plan into practice. The chapter begins by drawing the distinction between directed and facilitated approaches to change implementation to foreground their key features and limitations and argue in favour of a reconciliatory approach in which both approaches can be combined in effective ways to meet the needs and interests of both organisation and employees. The chapter then presents a critical evaluation of three popular change implementation methods: Business Process Reengineering, Lean and Six Sigma, to consider their core principles and potential drawbacks and provide you with an opportunity to experiment with some of the popular tools associated with each method. The chapter moves on to consider the differences and commonalities between Lean and Six Sigma and shows how combining the two change implementation methods (into what has been referred to as Lean–Six Sigma or LSS) can have synergistic effects and enable a greater balance between organisational and employee needs. The chapter then presents our conceptual nugget which involves the development of a filtering device which can prove valuable in the selection of appropriate change implementation methods. The chapter concludes with a summary of key learning points and a case study focusing on the Toyota Production System as an exemplar of effective Lean implementation.

9.2 Approaches to change implementation

Myers et al. (2012) do an excellent job in drawing the distinction between a *directed* and a *facilitated* approach to organisational change. In this section, we will consider the main features and potential drawbacks of each approach in line with the topics that have been covered so far.

Directed change implementation

Directed change implementation is generally viewed as the hard approach, where it is led from the top and driven by economic interests – entailing in many cases drastic cost-cutting measures such as process streamlining, downsizing, or mergers and acquisitions which are designed to eliminate waste and inefficiencies or optimise productivity and profitability. However, the pursuit of purely economic interests is often detrimental to the actual needs and interests of employees and can lead to their resistance and disengagement (see Chapter 5).

Directed change implementation is usually the upshot of a planned approach to strategic change – where it is used as a means of translating into practice pre-determined change goals and objectives within the strict parameters set out by change leaders. In this respect, directed change implementation lends itself to an *autocratic leadership style* where change is primarily 'forced from above' and imposed on organisational members by change leaders (see Chapter 7). It is also consistent with a *Tell and Sell* or a *Withhold and Uphold* communication strategy, where employees are cast into a passive role and involved in the change process only on a 'need to know and do' basis (see Chapter 8).

Moreover, the general view arising from the literature is that directed change is best suited to situations in which the organisation has to deal with a crisis or seize unique business opportunities – where swift executive decisions are called for and there is little time for debate or negotiation about the terms and conditions of change implementation. For instance, an ailing company might find itself in a situation where it has to swiftly merge with or acquire another company without any meaningful consultation with employees to fend off the possibility of a hostile takeover, reverse the effects of previous poor management or even exploit the resources of its new strategic partner to enter new markets. We will refine all these points when we consider the different types of interventions for implementing change in the following sections.

Facilitated change implementation

Facilitated change implementation, on the other hand, can be seen as a soft, more people-oriented approach to change – where, as the term suggests, change leaders adopt a more *democratic and participatory style* to facilitate employee involvement in decision-making whilst providing them with an opportunity to contribute to the intended change and shape to some extent its implementation. This particular approach fits with an *Underscore and Explore* and ideally a *dialogic* communication strategy where change leaders are keen to enter into an on-going dialogue with employees and draw on their talent to optimise the execution and outputs of the change initiative (see Chapter 8).

It is also important to note that facilitated change implementation is amenable to *emergent strategic change* (see Chapter 3) – where continuous employee involvement and contribution to the change process can become an integral part of the organisation's capability to effectively respond to the unforeseen challenges and opportunities arising from its specific change context. In this regard, facilitated implementation fosters an organic, inside-out approach to change where it enables employees to not only internalise the change goals and objectives and perform optimally to them but also empowers them to think and learn independently and as a group to creatively contribute to the change efforts.

However, in line with what was discussed in Chapter 3, planned and emergent change are intertwined in real change situations – and so are directed and facilitated change implementation. Myers et al. (2012, p. 195) aptly remark that 'in reality, there is not necessarily a sharp dividing line between directed and facilitated approaches [to change]'. We are in agreement with their view. On the one hand, we place an emphasis on the responsibility of change agents to provide strong visible leadership and a clear direction for change, and on the other hand, we contend that a directed approach to change implementation should not prevent the possibility for continuous employee involvement and participation in the change initiative.

Reconciling directed and facilitated change implementation

We therefore favour the reconciliatory perspective in which direction and facilitation are combined in effective ways to meet the interests of both organisation and employees at the point of need throughout the change process. There are situations which call for swift executive decisions and directed change implementation with hardly any time for deep consultation as a means of ensuring the survival of the organisation and seizing growth opportunities that would otherwise slip out of reach. However, the general approach to change implementation (especially in the case of radical change requiring a cultural shift and long-term employee commitment) should be one that fosters inclusivity, dialogue and collaboration through which a healthy balance between organisational and individual needs and interests can be achieved.

---PRACTICAL EXERCISE---

We have mentioned in the preceding discussion the case of mergers and acquisitions (M&A) that can sometimes justify a directed approach to change implementation. More and more companies are pursuing this route as a means of ensuring business survival, continuity and growth.

Activity

Go online to find out more about some of the high-profile M&A which have happened over the past two years and think about the following:

- The factors that led to the merger or acquisition.
- The dominant approach – whether directed or facilitated – adopted during the implementation phase of the merger or acquisition.
- Whether there were any attempts to integrate elements of both directed and facilitated approaches to change implementation.

9.3 Methods of change implementation

There are many different methods that can be used to effectively implement change. For the sake of brevity, we focus here on three popular change implementation methods that have received, over the past few decades, particular attention in the change management literature: Business Process Reengineering, Lean and Six Sigma.

Business Process Reengineering

Business Process Reengineering (BPR) came to the fore in the early 1990s on the back of the work of its leading proponents – notably, Davenport (1993); (Davenport and Short, 1990); Hammer (1990); and Hammer and Champy (2001). Unequivocally, BPR is a 'rapid and radical' change intervention – where, to use some of the buzz words that have been woven around it, the primary aim is to enable a 'radical redesign' of current business processes in order to achieve 'dramatic improvements' in terms of performance, productivity and quality, keeping in view the needs and satisfaction of target customers. While a more detailed discussion of BPR is beyond the scope of this textbook, we shall briefly discuss what we consider to be some of its essential features and drawbacks as a change intervention.

Figure 9.1 is a representation of the basic functional areas that account for an organisation's value chain and that can become the target of BPR. It is not meant to cover all the possible processes and sub-processes of an organisation as these can vary across sectors and are often described under different labels. Its main purpose here is to provide a broad framework for considering the key principles and features of BPR which are detailed in the following discussion.

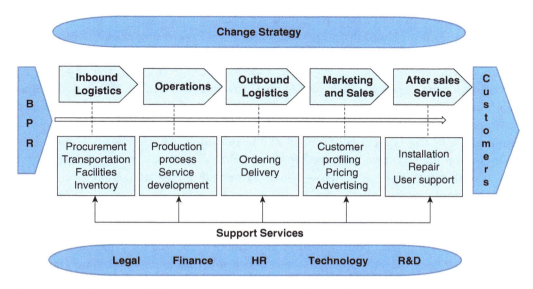

Figure 9.1 Applying BPR to the key processes of the value chain

Source used to build framework: Adapted from Porter, M. E. (1985) *The Competitive Advantage: Creating and Sustaining Superior Performance*. New York: Free Press.

Systemic approach to change

First of all, BPR warrants a *systemic approach to change* and entails a wholesale, enterprise-wide re-creation of the organisation's processes. As such, implementing BPR calls for a cross-functional perspective and an understanding of how the processes and sub-processes that underpin the organisation's value chain are interconnected and have a mutual bearing on each other. For example, streamlining the processes for procurement and stock control can lead to the removal of bottlenecks in the production process and a reduction in the delay between the ordering and delivery of goods and services to customers.

For its main proponents, a fragmented, localised and piecemeal approach to process redesign is unlikely to generate the 'dramatic improvements' that have been touted as the major strength of BPR (Hammer and Champy, 2001). What is therefore required is the elimination of waste and inefficiencies across *all* the functional areas that account for the organisation's value chain (as illustrated in Figure 9.1) in order to optimise its overall performance and productivity.

BPR is scalable

Also, it is important to note that BPR is scalable. In other words, once successfully tried and tested in one part of the organisation, BPR interventions can be transposed to its other parts (such as different branches or strategic business units) – either simultaneously or at different points in time depending on feasibility and the ability of the organisation to 'absorb' the disruption that BPR can cause to current business practices.

Myers et al. (2012) provide an excellent example of how BPR interventions can be scaled out to the wider organisation – that of Cigna, an international health insurance provider. Cigna started its BPR intervention with the downsizing of one of its divisions. Over the following 18 months, Cigna extended the reengineering exercise across functional areas with the establishment of cross-functional service teams and a team-based reward system. The organisation registered a dramatic improvement in the underwriting procedure for the approval of insurance policies (from two weeks to 15 minutes). Cigna then implemented BPR in other parts of the organisation with varying degrees of success in which top management buy-in and employee commitment seemed to have played a prominent role. Cigna eventually applied BPR in two other countries where it conducted business. Top management soon realised the cultural adjustments that were needed for BPR to work across national borders – which, as we will discuss later, is far from being a straightforward process.

Alignment with business strategy

One of the most important principles underpinning BPR is the need for *a tight alignment with the business strategy*. The success of BPR is seen as dependent upon a sound business rationale and clear strategic goals and objectives. Doing BPR for its own sake or to just mirror industry practice is symptomatic of a lack of strong leadership and strategic direction – without which it can disrupt already productive processes beyond repair whilst leaving the organisation in complete disarray. For this reason, mapping, diagnosis and selection of processes to be reengineered should always be kept in line with the mission and overarching strategic goals and objectives of the change programme.

Sarker and Lee (1999) provide some critical insights into the 'failings' of top management leadership as one of the key issues that contributed to BPR failure at TELECO, a US telecommunications company. Such 'failings' included, among other things: an inability to communicate a clear vision, non-participation in the BPR implementation phase, and poor communication with the BPR team leaders. Similar research conducted in other regions around the world – such as Africa, Asia and the Middle East – point to the same factors associated with poor leadership as a major cause of BPR failure (Virzi, 2019).

Radical and rapid

The rhetoric around BPR leaves no doubt as to its mode of execution. The now famous catchphrase taken from the title of Hammer's 1990 article on BPR which appeared in the *Harvard Business Review* journal says it all: *Don't automate, obliterate*. BPR is not meant to be incremental and gradual. As that title suggests, BPR is not about automating old processes which can more than likely result in an escalation of their existing flaws and inefficiencies. BPR is *radical* and recommends the complete destruction of old processes that do not add value and their replacement with new ones that can correct past mistakes and generate the much talked about 'dramatic improvements' in terms of cost, productivity and quality (Hammer and Champy, 2001).

BPR is also meant to be *rapid* in that it does not recommend excessive planning, prolonged experimentation or lengthy adaptation periods. The diagnosis and redesign of existing core processes should be swift and cut across the value chain in a timely fashion to allow for a speedy optimisation of the organisation's overall performance and the consolidation of its competitive position. In his 1990 Harvard article, Hammer cites, among others, the example of Ford automotive company which reengineered its old accounts payable process that was labour-intensive, error-prone and inconsistent. The company established an 'invoiceless' purchasing process supported by new computer systems – whereby it achieved a 75% reduction in headcount whilst benefiting from a much more streamlined, accurate and faster account payable process.

Customer centric

One of the key performance outcomes for BPR is a significant improvement in customer service. In BPR, processes are compressed, silos are broken down, parallel functional activities are linked, and employees are upskilled to not only achieve major cost reductions but even more importantly, to maximise customer service in terms of quality, value for money, speed of delivery, after-sales support, etc. This is why *customers* are foregrounded in Figure 9.1 as the end target of BPR interventions that cut across the organisation's value chain.

For example, Airbnb (an American company which operates an online marketplace for homestays, lodging, holiday rentals and other tourism activities) recently had to carry out a complete redesign of their product development process. This led to the integration of the separate systems and the creation of a single digital environment which enabled designers, researchers and front-line staff to synchronise their activities and collaborate in real time to deliver high-quality products to customers in a more consistent and timely fashion. In so doing, Airbnb effectively applied the BPR principles of centralising dispersed resources and reorganising processes, not around discrete tasks, but around performance outcomes – which in this case was to generate quality and value in view of customer needs and satisfaction (Antin, n.d.; Magátová, 2020a).

Technology-driven

All the advocates of BPR would agree that the role of technology in BPR has to be made clear. Technology deployment for its own sake is certainly not endorsed by BPR agents. In BPR technology is an *enabler* and a vital means to an end – which is the optimisation of performance and productivity in line with the business model and strategic goals and objectives of the organisation (Davenport, 1993). Moreover, as highlighted in Figure 9.1, technology is but one component of the support services that need to be in place to enable the effective implementation of BPR. Technology is meant to be harnessed alongside other support services (HR, Finance, Legal, R&D, IT, etc.) to allow for integrative solutions and a concerted approach to new ways of working or the production of new products and services that an organisation wants to bring to market.

For example, Wal-Mart, the American multinational retail corporation, deployed an IT system that connects all retail locations, distribution warehouses and suppliers to enable frontline decision-making at point of need, eliminate unnecessary distribution steps and improve customer service (Attaran, 2003).

Criticisms of BPR
Old wine in new bottles?

Critics have questioned whether BPR is really a novel concept or should be exposed as yet another instance of the proverbial 'old wine in new bottles'. The fact is that the notion of process redesign and improvement is certainly not new and can easily be traced back in management theory to leading figures such as Frederick Taylor (1856–1915) and Henry Ford (1863–1947). Both Taylor and Ford are famous for their application of scientific principles which aimed to find the one best way to do a job including rigorous analysis, simplification and standardisation of work processes in order to minimise production costs and maximise efficiency, quality and customer satisfaction – which are some of the most valued objectives of BPR. So for some, BPR is nothing more than a re-articulation of well-established principles, albeit packaged in more modern language.

An autocratic leadership style

Critics have also drawn attention to the type of autocratic leadership style that BPR seems to condone. As recommended by Hammer and Champy (2001), BPR should be driven by top management who are deemed to have the necessary strategic mindset and cross-functional perspective for a holistic, wholesale approach to process redesign. Leaders in the context of BPR have been compared to 'tsars' which for many does not really paint a desirable picture of effective leadership – as tsars were the archetype of the supreme male monarch with utmost power who did not have to answer to anybody and had the final say in all matters. This stands in stark contrast with the type of democratic leadership that, as discussed in Chapter 7, befits modern-day organisations. It goes without saying that the type of autocratic leadership and centralised mode of governance that BPR seems to endorse leaves very little scope for employee involvement and participation – which can potentially lead to employee alienation, resistance and disengagement.

Insensitive to culture

BPR has also been criticised for being rather insensitive to the shift in culture that it calls for – where employees are often coerced into adopting new ways of thinking and working and sometimes have to go against their own core values to satisfy the economic interests of top management – a situation where they feel they have little to gain – if not more work and stress. Culture change takes time and effort and is likely to be out of sync with the rapid pace of change that is warranted by BPR. Therefore, it is felt that greater attention should be given to the cultural dimension of BPR – where employees may not be given the necessary time and support for making the required cultural adjustments and coping with the (potentially overwhelming) disruptions that BPR can bring about.

One size fits all?

BPR has often been touted as the answer to all process-related problems with the implicit assumption that it is applicable to all organisations, irrespective of size. However, research into effective BPR implementation has been mostly focused on large organisations with little attention to how it applies to SMEs. The fact is that BPR can be quite resource-intensive, requiring large investments in technology deployment, major restructuring, re-training of staff, etc., which are beyond the financial limits and developmental capacity of small and even medium-sized enterprises. Moreover, BPR often involves large-scale downsizing and redundancies which are hardly applicable to small and micro businesses.

This, however, does not mean that BPR is totally inapplicable to SMES. Although SMEs have limited resources and contend with different business dynamics, they do play a major part in the economic development of many countries and often have to compete against large organisations. Recent research suggests that BPR is as applicable to SMEs as it is to large organisations (Kenneth et al., 2018; Şerban, 2015). The same principles of effective BPR (e.g. optimisation of process efficiency, cost reductions, knowledge and skills assessment, effective communication, leveraging technology, etc.) equally apply to both large-scale organisations and SMEs – except for the fact that BPR interventions have to be 'scaled down' in view of the specific contexts and needs of SMEs (Aziz, 2019).

A rhetoric for legitimising a managerialist agenda

There has been a sober warning about the possibility of BPR being co-opted by change agents to pursue their own managerialist agenda and economic interests at the expense of employees – where the BPR rhetoric provides the legitimacy for downsizing, redundancies and other unilateral decisions that are potentially detrimental to employees (e.g. see Davenport, 1995). However, the 'radical' in BPR does not have to equate with 'ruthlessness' and a total neglect of the human dimension of change. As we have repeatedly argued in this textbook, showing a disregard for the human dimension of organisational change is showing a lack of understanding of the importance of employee commitment and engagement as a critical success factor for sustainable change – and BPR is no exception.

REFLECTIVE EXERCISE

1. What are the main benefits of BPR?
2. What are the main criticisms that have been directed at BPR?
3. Under what conditions is BPR applicable to SMEs?

CASE STUDY 9.1

T-Mobile: Re-engineering from the perspective of the customer

Introduction

T-Mobile is a wireless network operator headquartered in the US with more than 100 million subscribers. Recently, the company faced a major challenge with regard to its existing customer service: outdated service contracts, excess roaming fees and limited data allowances were stacked against the customer. Thus, from the customer point of view, management came to the realisation that the whole system was broken. Moreover, management had to decide whether to adhere to industry standards which measured performance from an organisational perspective and placed an emphasis on speed of service at the lowest possible cost; or to create a completely new service process from the perspective of the customer that placed a premium on perceived value and the extent to which it would 'keep customers happy' – which after all, was always T-Mobile's primary goal.

A radical redesign of customer service processes

T-Mobile opted for a radical redesign of its customer service processes by:

- Setting up self-service portals through which customers themselves could carry out basic transactional tasks such as checking their balance or changing their addresses – with significant gains in terms of both expediency and convenience.
- Developing a Team of Experts model which was referred to as TEX. The TEX model entailed the establishment of cross-functional groups of knowledge workers who serve specific markets and who are able to solve complex customer problems 'from start to finish' – without in most cases having to transfer customers to tech specialists and 'plug' them into long phone queues for indefinite (and frustrating) periods of time.

Applying BPR principles

The creation of a new customer service process at T-Mobile followed two key BPR principles:

1 *Let those who use the output of the process perform the process* – in this case, dedicated teams of highly trained experts are the ones responsible for the outcomes of the customer service process. As such, they are placed in direct contact with customers and are held accountable in 'making customers happy'.
2 *Shift the decision point to where the work is performed and build control into the process* – relocating authority and decision-making to the point of customer need, make the entire process shorter yet stronger whilst allowing those performing the work to have greater control and impact on customer service outcomes.

Conclusions

By re-engineering its service process from the perspective of the customer, T-Mobile was able to go beyond industry standards to provide visionary leadership in customer service and enhance its overall performance. In more concrete terms, since implementing its new re-engineering measures in 2018, the company achieved, among other key performance indicators, a 71% decrease in transferred customer calls, 25% drop in post-paid customer churn and a 56% increase in Net Promoter Score.

Sources: Magátová (2020b); T-Mobile (2021)

Questions

1   Why did T-Mobile opt for a radical redesign of its customer service processes?
2   Which BPR principles underpinned this exercise?
3   From an employee perspective, what challenges might have arisen from T-Mobiles' BPR intervention despite the positive spin of the account presented in the case study?

PRACTICAL EXERCISE

Using process mapping as a BPR tool

The first key step in BPR is **process mapping** to analyse and select the core processes to be redesigned. A process map visually represents a sequence of activities or tasks that are meant to transform an input into a desired output. Its main purpose is to diagnose inefficiencies or waste in the process under consideration and find ways to improve it. The example in Figure 9.2 is a high-level process map for purchasing a particular component part to sustain the production line of a manufacturing company.

Pay attention to the sequence of activities and decision points that cut across the different departments identified in the process map in order to gain a quick, first-hand understanding of the process as a whole and then answer the following questions.

Questions

1   What, according to you, are the most obvious sources of inefficiencies in the procurement process?
    (Tip: think in terms of the number of employees needed to complete the process, time wasted between tasks, possible blockages that might slow down the completion of the process, etc.).
2   How could technology be applied to redesign and improve the procurement process as a whole?

Activity

Draw a new map to illustrate how you have redesigned the procurement process – highlighting the critical points where dramatic improvements have been achieved.

(Continued)

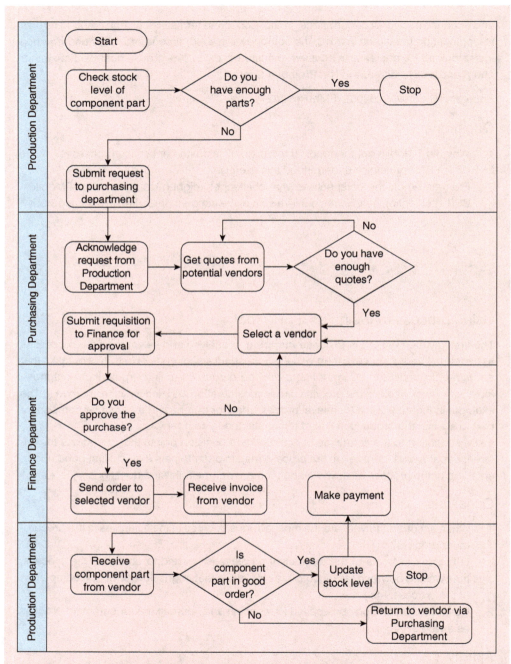

Figure 9.2 Process map for procuring a component part for a production department

Lean

A change method or philosophy?

The term Lean was coined in 1988 by John Krafcik, a leading figure in the automotive industry and former lean production researcher and consultant at MIT. Lean thinking and principles were defined in more explicit terms by Womack and colleagues in the early 1990s, who used it to describe a production system that is free of waste and inefficiencies and functions optimally to turn out goods and services to the highest standards in line with customer needs and demands (Womack et al., 1990). Hayes (2021) draws attention to the interesting question as to whether Lean is a change method or a philosophy. It seems both views hold water.

As a method, Lean can be viewed as a set of tools and techniques designed to improve existing processes or create new ones, the ultimate goal of which is to eliminate waste and maximise the efficiency of specific production processes. As a philosophy, Lean is a set of overarching principles that warrants a systemic and cross-functional perspective and seeks to transform the whole organisation into a lean enterprise and demonstrate a continuous commitment to quality improvement in the pursuit of optimal efficiency, performance and productivity.

Historical background

Lean can also be traced back to Taylorism and Fordism and shares with BPR a primary focus on the maximisation of efficiency and the standardisation of mass production. However, what is particularly relevant here is that with the emergence of global markets and increasing variation in customer demands, companies could not limit themselves anymore to the large-scale production of generic goods for mass consumption. There was a need for a new type of production system that could accommodate different tastes, preferences and lifestyles and enable companies to develop different product lines in line with customer demand.

This ushered in a new era in manufacturing which was referred to as Post-Fordism. While it is generally thought to have begun in the early 1970s, Post-Fordism was characterised by a move away from the mass production of identical products to a more flexible and specialised mode of 'small batch production' that could manufacture more diverse and differentiated products in response to customer demand (Jessop, 2021). Small batch production was greatly aided by computerised logistics and flexible automated systems, where inventory control was tightly connected to the production process – allowing for the transfer of the right quantity of component parts at the right time to the right place on automated production lines, which themselves could be swiftly adjusted to manufacture small batches of differentiated products according to customer demand.

This type of flexible specialised batch production led by customer demand allowed for a significant reduction in the risk of over or underproduction and inventory costs and economies of scope where costs can be lowered by manufacturing differentiated goods using the same automated systems and production lines. In this respect, the key features of the Post-Fordist mode of production could be construed as the prefiguration of Lean principles as defined by Womack and Jones in the mid-1990s.

Principles of Lean management

Figure 9.3 highlights the five core principles of Lean as defined by Womack and Jones (1996) which are addressed in turn in the following discussion.

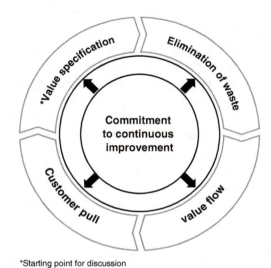

*Starting point for discussion

Figure 9.3 Core principles of Lean management

Source: Adapted from Womack, J. P. and Jones, D. T. (1996) *Lean Thinking: Banish Waste and Create Wealth in Your Corporation*. London: Simon & Schuster.

Value specification

The specification of value is considered as the first step in the implementation of Lean initiatives. In Lean, the specification of value is to be conducted from the perspective of the customer. While Womack and Jones (1996) place, in no uncertain terms, an emphasis on the primary objective of Lean as the capacity to do 'more with less' (less waste of resources, less human effort, less time, less space, etc.), they also underline the fact that all value-creating activities associated with Lean should be driven by the customer. Therefore, value specification calls for two-way communication between the organisation and its customers in an attempt to understand their specific needs and demands. This harks back to the Post-Fordist focus on the manufacture of small batches of differentiated products according to customer wants and preferences.

Elimination of waste

The next key step is to identify the avoidable sources of waste in the production process in order to eliminate them. To this effect, Lean experts have recourse to a technique often referred to as Value Stream Mapping (VSM). VSM is a form of flowchart that is used to diagnose sources of inefficiencies and waste along the value chain underpinning each specific product that the organisation wants to bring to market – from procurement and production through marketing and sales to delivery and after-sales service.

For example, VSM can be used to identify sources of waste causing unnecessary waiting times for component parts and excess inventories, adjust poorly calibrated assembly lines and match customer demand with production outputs. Thus, VSM can allow for a holistic approach to the elimination of waste – where all identifiable and avoidable sources of waste and non-value adding activities can be simultaneously exposed and eliminated, leading to a synergistic and positive overall impact on the net efficiency of the organisation's value chain.

Value flow

Once waste has been eliminated, there is a need to establish a continuous, smooth and efficient flow between the value-creating activities for each specific product. For example, this can entail a recalibration of existing production machinery or the installation of new equipment and tools to speed up the production process or the batch manufacturing of new products with differentiated features. It is worth noting that, unlike BPR which focuses on processes internal to the organisation, Lean initiatives can cross over organisational boundaries to include external stakeholders operating both at the upstream and downstream portions of the value chain.

For example, 'upstream' suppliers of component parts can collaborate on the Lean initiative of a client organisation by eliminating waste from their own production process to enhance the quality of their products and ensure that such products are transported to the assembly line of the client organisation in a timely fashion – thereby having a synergistic effect on the latter's Lean outputs. Downstream efficiencies can be achieved by for example, outsourcing after-sales services to an external partner that can be integrated into a company's Lean initiative – where, by streamlining its own processes for handling customer queries and complaints, the external partner can effectively contribute to the Lean initiative of the client organisation.

Customer pull

In Lean, activities along the value chain should be pulled downstream by customers. According to this particular Lean principle, instead of producing goods that are then 'pushed' to customers based on market predictions, *nothing should be produced until the customer demands it*. Customer demand sets the production process in motion which causes value-creating activities to 'cascade up' the value chain – from customer order to production of finished goods to purchase of component parts from suppliers. As opposed to mass or even batch production respectively, Lean advocates a Just-in-Time (JIT) mode of production – where customer demand dictates the order and volume of production and inventory levels which are restocked only as and when required.

Commitment to continuous improvement

Although Lean can be implemented as a RIE (Rapid Intervention Event spanning over a few weeks), it is founded upon a commitment to continuous improvement. For Womack and Jones (1996), Lean should not be regarded as a one-off intervention but an unending pursuit of perfection and consolidation of value-creating activities. It is for this reason that we have located this fifth principle at the centre of Figure 9.3 – where the commitment to continuous improvement continually feeds into the remaining value-creating activities of Lean which are themselves locked in a virtuous cycle.

This commitment to continuous improvement is often referred to in the literature as *Kaizen* – which is a Japanese term that can be roughly translated as 'changing for the better' as a gradual and systematic process and that requires the sustained input of all employees. As a *Kaizen* initiative, Lean fosters the development of quality circles (comprising of Lean experts and trained staff with different disciplinary backgrounds) that seek to engage, equip and empower all those involved in the quest for continuous improvement. In the end-of-chapter case study on the Toyota Production System, we shall consider other Japanese terms with which Lean practitioners have become familiar and which are now an integral part of the Lean lexicon.

Criticisms of Lean

Many criticisms have been directed at Lean despite the reporting of numerous 'success stories' across various industries. We briefly consider some of the most pointed criticisms in what follows.

Failure to deliver on promises

Survey-based research reports that many companies that have embarked on Lean initiatives have struggled to achieve the intended outcomes – especially with regard to cost-cutting and improvement of process efficiency which were well below expectations (Radnor et al., 2011). Moreover, there is significant variance in approaches and performance outcomes both within and across industries, which makes it impossible to develop commonly agreed performance standards and pass judgement on what can be actually considered 'Lean success' (Shah and Ward, 2007).

Failure to effectively manage culture change

Initial gains of Lean tend to be short-lived with companies reverting to old ways of working and 'pre-Lean' performance after a relatively short period of time. Lean is complex, costly, difficult to implement and demands long-term commitment – and as such, is likely to disappoint if it is not accompanied by the appropriate 'cultural adjustment'. Effectively managing culture in a Lean context means getting rid of old ways of working, establishing new core values and modelling new behaviours infused by Lean precepts and principles – and failure to do so is unlikely to lead to sustainable Lean success.

Lack of visible and engaged leadership

Lean initiatives are also unlikely to succeed if there is a lack of visible and engaged leadership. If change leaders only impose Lean on the organisation from the comfort of their ivory tower without participating fully in the process, it is unlikely that employees will endorse and commit to it. Leading Lean from a distance only serves to sap employee commitment and engagement, and goes against its collaborative ethos.

Lack of focus on employees

Lean is known for being waste-centric, number-centric and customer-centric but not so much employee-centric. In other words, Lean places a premium on the elimination of waste in production processes, the tracking of performance based on facts and statistical data, and the optimisation of customer satisfaction as one of its most desirable outcomes. However, when it comes to employees, Lean tends to fall short of expectations. Lean tends towards strict work parameters, close supervision, rigorous controls and high performance targets – which can leave employees stuck in repetitive, boring and overly-demanding jobs that can in turn lead to high levels of stress and an erosion of employee commitment in the longer term. Thus, if the people dimension of Lean is not properly addressed, it can be potentially dehumanising.

Low applicability to SMEs

Finally, we want to point out that, like BPR, the applicability of Lean to small organisations can be called into question. Arguably, BPR (which some might contend does not require the type of long-term commitment and investments warranted by Lean) can be seen as more flexible and easier to scale down than Lean to suit the needs of SMEs. However, while research into the applicability of Lean to SMEs is still limited, a review of the literature in this area suggests that Lean can be adapted to all types of companies and industries that aim to increase their competitiveness. In fact, there is an argument that because they are smaller and more agile, SMEs are better able to adapt Lean implementation to suit their particular needs – where, however, some of the key contextual factors to be considered include: top management buy-in, cultural orientation, ability to influence supplier and customer relationships, commitment to long-term survival and profitability, availability of sufficient funding, employee professionalism, technologies-in-use, etc. (Alkhoraif et al., 2019).

REFLECTIVE EXERCISE

1   Why is a commitment to continuous improvement of vital importance in Lean implementation?
2   What are the most important contextual factors impacting successful Lean implementation?
3   Do you think Lean is applicable to SMEs?

PRACTICAL EXERCISE

Experimenting with Value Stream Mapping

Value Stream Mapping (VSM) is a valuable visual tool that can be used to identify process inefficiencies and areas for improvement – leading to better products and services and greater customer satisfaction. The exercise below provides you with an opportunity to apply VSM to the context of a fictitious small business to enable you to get a sense of its effectiveness and appreciate how it can be of value to small businesses. Read the scenario below and carry out the activity that follows.

(Continued)

You are a consultant hired by the manager of a small restaurant offering Chinese dishes. The restaurant has one cashier, four back-of-house staff and seven waiters serving at its 50 tables. Over the past few months, the manager has noticed a steep decline in customers. Even the 'regulars' do not come in as often as they used to. The manager wants you to find out the causes underlying this situation so they may take remedial action.

You have decided to use VSM to map out the process underlying the customer dining experience to: (i) identify problem areas and (ii) find out where improvements can be made to increase customer satisfaction.

To carry out this exercise, you had to enlist the help of the manager and chief waitress and interview a number of customers. This enabled you to map out the key stages of the customer dining experience – from customers being allocated tables to the waiter bringing ordered dishes to the table. This also allowed you to gather some valuable information which you needed to carry out the VSM exercise including waiting times, processing times, and error and dissatisfaction rates.

Figure 9.4 maps out the key stages of the customer dining experience (in the top row) and the problems you have identified (in the second row). You now need to think about effective ways to address the problems you have identified and fill in the last row of the diagram – which you will then use to explain your findings and present your recommendations for improving the overall customer dining experience to the manager.

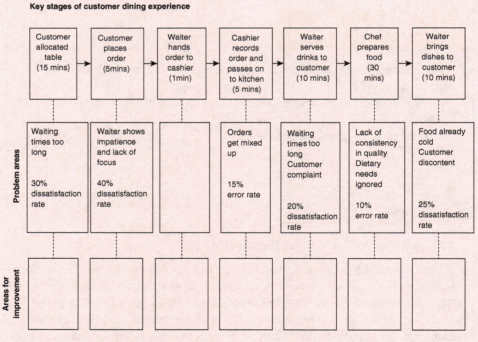

Figure 9.4   Application of VSM

Six Sigma

We now proceed to consider another popular change tool for process improvement and quality management: Six Sigma. This was developed by American engineers Bill Smith and Mikel Harry when they worked for Motorola in 1986.

The meaning of Six Sigma

The term Sigma (σ) is a Greek term used in statistics to measure the standard deviation from the mean in a normal distribution – which, as illustrated in Figure 9.5, is represented by a bell-shaped curve.

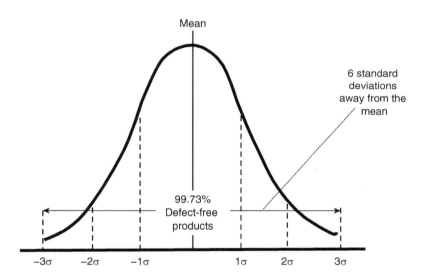

Figure 9.5   Six Sigma performance and quality standards

From Figure 9.5, we can see that one Sigma (σ) is equal to 1 standard deviation. Therefore, Six Sigma represents 6 standard deviations away from the mean, three above and three below. With regard to a production process, these limits (which are set by customer requirements) specify the defect rate for a given product. Without getting into the actual calculations, for every million items manufactured, there should be only 3.4 defective products and 99.73% of the rest of the products should be error-free or without defects. This allows for a very narrow margin of error and sets performance and quality standards to near perfection.

Core principles of Six Sigma

Figure 9.6 highlights the core principles of Six Sigma which are briefly explained in the following discussion.

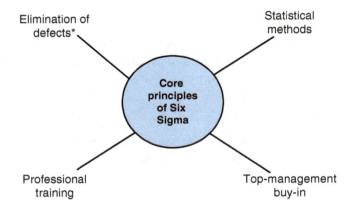

*Starting point for discussion

Figure 9.6 Core principles of Six Sigma

Elimination of defects

As mentioned above, Six Sigma is uncompromising with regard to its low tolerance for errors and pursuit of perfection. Therefore, its primary focus is on the elimination of defects and their root causes to ensure the highest quality standards as per customer requirements and expectations.

Statistical methods

Six Sigma is heavily reliant on statistical methods and measures to maintain process efficiency, high quality standards and customer satisfaction – where decision-making, evaluation and corrective measures are based on hard, verifiable statistical data.

Top management buy-in

As in BPR and Lean, top management buy-in and visible, engaged leadership in facilitating access to the necessary resources and sustaining the momentum of Six Sigma is seen as critical to its long-term success.

Professional training

The effective implementation of Six Sigma rests on the enabling and mentoring roles and responsibilities of Six Sigma champions. However, one of Six Sigma's defining features with regard to professional training is that it is grounded in a form of 'certified training' which follows a ranking borrowed from martial arts (master black belts, black belts, green belts and yellow belts) to denote the level of expertise and progress along the Six Sigma career paths of all those involved in the project.

Six Sigma methodology

In line with its core principles, Six Sigma implementation follows a five-step approach which is often referred to as DMAIC – as shown in Figure 9.7.

Figure 9.7 The Six Sigma DMAIC process

Define

This first step involves key activities such as: making a business case for the Six Sigma project, establishing strategic goals and objectives, specifying customer requirements, assessing the financial impact of the project, developing an action plan and forming the team that will be responsible for the implementation of the project.

Measure

The next step in the DMAIC process is taking stock of the performance and capability of the current production process – through auditing exercises such as collecting process data, documenting what works and identifying defects.

Analyse

As previously mentioned, Six Sigma gives primacy to statistical methods and the third step in the DMAIC process is to use appropriate statistical tools and graphical analysis to identify the root causes of defects and other process issues.

Improve

The fourth step in the DMAIC process is to make improvements to the current process by piloting, implementing and evaluating solutions – which, if effective, can then be scaled out across the organisation.

Control

This final step translates Six Sigma's commitment to high quality standards and is designed to maintain and monitor process performance, avoid degradation and pursue perfection.

Criticisms of Six Sigma

Six Sigma has also been the target of criticism, especially following a decline in its application by the late 2000s. While Six Sigma shares most of the potential pitfalls of BPR and Lean, for the sake of brevity we focus here only on the main criticisms that have been directed at it.

Nothing more than a statistical tool?

One of the main arguments against Six Sigma is that it is actually nothing more than a statistical tool essentially designed to maximise performance, productivity and profit. As such, it is primarily a tactical tool that should be in the service of strategy and not the other way around – for, with the type of heavy investments (in terms of both resources and effort) that Six Sigma calls for, it can potentially override the actual strategy and business imperatives of an organisation, leading to a dilution of its core values and mission.

Detrimental to employees

Like BPR and Lean, Six Sigma can be detrimental to employees' interest and well-being. Myers et al. (2012) provide a real-life example of how the rigid application of Six Sigma at a large US-based home-improvement company enabled an extraordinary rise in performance and productivity but also resulted in a dramatic drop in staff morale. There are also cases where Six Sigma can lead to downsizing, forced redundancies or a restructuring of working relationships that are most detrimental to employees (e.g. see Hindo, 2007). By 'letting the stats do the talking', Six Sigma can potentially deprive employees of a voice, sap their commitment to the organisation and prove to be untenable in the longer term.

A regimented approach to training and professional development

Another criticism that is usually laid at the door of Six Sigma is its regimented approach to training and professional development. Employees involved in Six Sigma initiatives are trained within its rigid, statistical parameters – which might not be that appealing to those who are not statistically inclined and whose talents might not be put to good use. Moreover, the martial arts ranking which defines the Six Sigma career path locks employees into a narrow, competitive and rigid hierarchy which can stifle their creativity and prevent them from exploring the possibility of enlarging their learning and career pathways.

CASE STUDY 9.2

Bosch Connected Industry: Taking Six Sigma to a new level through digital technology

Applying the Six Sigma DMAIC process

Introduction

Bosch Connected Industry (BCI) is the software house of German giant Bosch which provides innovative solutions for digitalising and optimising the efficiency of manufacturing and logistic processes. The flagship product of BCI is the Nexeed Industrial Application System (NIAS) which draws on cutting-edge technologies (such as artificial intelligence, cloud computing and the Industrial Internet of Things) to offer bespoke and highly flexible applications designed to automate manufacturing processes, optimise operating efficiency and reduce costs whilst developing products and services to the highest quality standards.

Digitalising Six Sigma

One of the most outstanding features of NIAS is that it is firmly grounded in the principles of Six Sigma, which it takes to a new level through digital technology. NIAS is highly flexible, accessible and user-friendly. It enables companies to employ a range of easy-to-operate visualisation tools to: (i) analyse and monitor the full production cycle, from the creation of the product to its delivery, (ii) detect errors or any step in the production process that falls outside of the specified tolerance range and identify their underlying causes, (iii) take swift corrective action to prevent inefficiencies and waste, and (iv) measure performance in line with high quality standards.

Keeping processes under control

By increasing transparency in the production process, NIAS makes it easier to keep processes under control. With its user-friendly cockpit, NIAS allows for live process data monitoring, where engineers can quickly identify and address variables which may be causing problems and even detect errors before they occur with its patented predictive maintenance functions.

A commitment to continuous improvement

BCI believes that NIAS can empower manufacturing companies to proactively manage their production and logistics processes and demonstrate a commitment to continuous improvement. Importantly, the in-built flexibility and user-friendliness of NIAS means that it can be easily customised to suit the diverse needs of manufacturing companies – even SMEs for which a full-blown approach to Six Sigma might prove untenable.

Source: Bosch Connected Industry (2023)

Activity

- Apply Six Sigma's five-step DMAIC methodology as described in this section to NIAS. Use each of the five steps to evaluate the extent to which the DMAIC methodology enables the deployment of Six Sigma principles across manufacturing companies.

9.4 Combining Lean with Six Sigma: LSS

Most experts would agree that while Lean and Six Sigma are different concepts, there is a strong affinity between the two. In this section we discuss how Lean and Six Sigma have been combined into what is viewed as a more encompassing and comprehensive concept, which is now referred to as Lean Six Sigma (LSS) (Antony et al., 2021; Kenton, 2021). Figure 9.8 high-lights the main differences between Lean and Six Sigma and importantly, maps the key features of LSS that lie at their intersection.

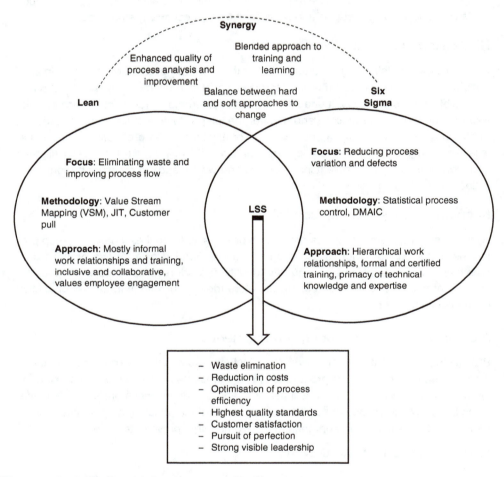

Figure 9.8 LSS: Combining Lean and Six Sigma

Differences

Since both Lean and Six Sigma have already been explained in some detail in this chapter, it is sufficient at this point to distil their key features in order to draw out their differences. As highlighted in Figure 9.8, Lean primarily focuses on the elimination of waste and on improving process flow. Lean attaches great importance to the use of process mapping (VSM) and visual displays to identify process issues and address their root causes. It also has recourse to procedures such as JIT and Customer Pull to optimise process efficiency and customer satisfaction. The overall approach to Lean is mostly informal and ad hoc yet collaborative and inclusive – whether it be training or problem solving, where a premium is placed on employee commitment and engagement which are consistently rewarded.

By contrast, the primary focus of Six Sigma is on the reduction of variance and defects in the production process. As explained earlier, Six Sigma relies on quantifiable measures, statistical analysis (e.g. means and variance, hypothesis testing, control charts, etc.) and on the DMAIC process to reduce the probability of defects to an almost insignificant level, maximise process efficiency and build products to the highest quality standards. To this effect, Six Sigma adopts a highly structured and formal approach to training and professional development but tends to pay less attention than Lean to individual learning, creativity and contribution to the change initiative – although its proponents might argue to the contrary.

Commonalities

The intersection of the Venn diagram in Figure 9.8 foregrounds the commonalities between Lean and Six Sigma. They are both driven by a primary concern to eliminate waste (defects are, after all, a form of waste), reduce production costs and optimise process efficiency and productivity. They both aim to achieve the highest quality standards in line with customer demands and expectations. Importantly, they are both guided by a commitment to continuous improvement and the pursuit of perfection as a means of sustaining quality enhancements, avoiding process degradation, increasing customer satisfaction and staying ahead of the competition. Finally, like any other change initiative, both Lean and Six Sigma need strong visible leadership to foster employee commitment and engagement and maintain the momentum of change in the longer term.

The synergistic effect of LSS

Combining Lean and Six Sigma (LSS) can have synergistic effects and yield outputs that are greater than the sum of their separate outputs. While the benefits of LSS can be discussed in finer detail, we have only space here to develop the following key points:

- First, the combination of Lean's visual mapping techniques and Six Sigma's statistical tools can enhance the quality of the diagnosis and elimination of the root causes of waste and defects.
- Second, the possibilities for process improvement and flexibility can be significantly enlarged via the integration of the key elements of Lean's JIT and Six Sigma's DMAIC.
- Third, the blending of Six Sigma's formal approach to training and Lean's mostly ad hoc, informal mode of learning can provide both a solid structure for professional development and access to collaborative networks and learning groups that are vital to creativity and innovation and a commitment to continuous improvement that typifies both change implementation methods.
- Lastly, and perhaps more importantly, LSS can allow for a much-needed balance between the hard and soft approaches to change implementation. Lean's greater

attention to people issues and endorsement of empowering working relationships can provide a healthy counterbalance to Six Sigma's primary focus on business process improvement and the achievement of corporate goals and objectives. Thus, LSS can enable some sort of equilibrium between organisational and employee needs – without which no change initiative would prove sustainable.

PRACTICAL EXERCISE

In light of the above discussion, carry out a comparative analysis of Lean, Six Sigma and LSS along the dimensions listed in the first column of the Table 9.1. Use the other cells to structure your analysis.

Table 9.1 Comparative analysis of Lean, Six Sigma and LSS

Dimensions	Lean	Six Sigma	LSS
Definition			
Methodology			
Intended outcomes			
Limitations			

9.5 Conceptual Nugget: A filtering device for selecting change implementation methods

Amid all the hype and criticism, choosing the right change implementation method can be quite challenging. Therefore, our conceptual nugget for this chapter consists of the development of a filtering device which can prove valuable in selecting the appropriate change implementation method. As illustrated in Figure 9.9, our filtering device comprises five layers which are briefly described in the following discussion.

Alignment with business strategy

In choosing the right change implementation method, change leaders need to ensure that it is aligned with the company's business strategy. As previously discussed, the substantial investments and efforts that the change implementation methods reviewed in this chapter call for can result in a loss of focus on the actual strategic goals and objectives, which should remain the overriding concern of change leaders. Therefore, the strategic goals and objectives of the company should guide the choice of the change implementation method – not the other way round.

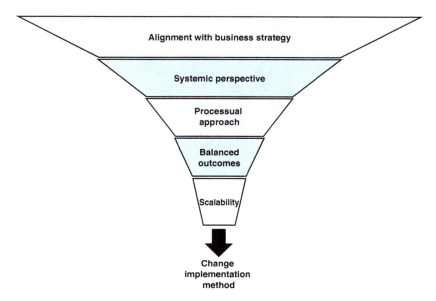

Figure 9.9 Filtering device for selecting change implementation methods

Systemic perspective

A good change implementation method is underpinned by a systemic perspective – i.e. one that allows for a holistic, cross-functional understanding of how it will impact the whole organisation. As such, a good change implementation method allows change leaders to track and monitor the various activities that it entails across different functional areas, understand how these activities are interconnected and, importantly, how their combined effects contribute to the successful achievement of the organisation's strategic goals and objectives.

Processual approach

Effective change implementation is not a one-off event but an on-going process. The selection of a good change implementation method has to take account of whether it has 'factored in' a progression pathway with clear milestones and evaluative measures, allows for long-range planning and places an emphasis on the need for a commitment to continuous improvement.

Balanced outcomes

A good change implementation method is not skewed in favour of top management and detrimental to employees. In this regard, the choice of a change implementation method should attach equal importance to the needs and interests of all change stakeholders and aim for outcomes that reflect a much-needed balance between performance and developmental objectives, business and ethical imperatives, and organisational and individual well-being.

Scalability

A good change implementation method should be scalable. As recent research suggests, popular change implementation methods like the ones discussed in this chapter are, to varying degrees, applicable to organisations of all sizes – insofar as such methods can be 'scaled up or down' to meet their diverse business needs and interests.

9.6 Key learning points

The key learning points arising from this chapter include the following:

1   Approaches to change implementation can be either *directed* or *facilitated*. Directed change implementation follows a hard, planned approach to change and is mostly led from the top with a primary focus on the pursuit of economic interests. Facilitated change implementation represents a softer approach that is more responsive to emergent change, promotes a participatory leadership style and fosters employee involvement in decision-making. Importantly, it is possible to reconcile both approaches to enable a healthy balance between organisational and employee needs and interests.

2   The primary aim of BPR is a rapid and radical redesign of current business *processes* to enable dramatic improvements in terms of performance, productivity and customer service. The key features of BPR include: a systemic and scalable approach to change, a tight alignment with business strategy, a primary focus on customers and the use of technology as an enabler of process redesign. BPR has been criticised, among other things, for condoning an autocratic leadership style, paying scant attention to culture, being inapplicable to SMEs, and legitimising the pursuit of a managerialist agenda.

3   Lean is underpinned by five core principles: (i) the specification of value from the perspective of the customer, (ii) the identification and elimination of waste via value stream mapping and other visual techniques, (iii) the establishment of a smooth and continuous flow across the organisation's value-creating activities, (iv) the production of finished products in line with customer demand, and (v) a commitment to continuous improvement. Lean has been criticised for its failure to deliver on promises and effectively manage culture change, a lack of visible, engaged leadership and focus on employees, and its low applicability to SMEs.

4   Six Sigma is driven by the following core principles: (i) a primary focus on the elimination of product defects and their root causes, (ii) a reliance on statistics to achieve and maintain process efficiency, (iii) top-management buy-in to provide visible and empowering leadership, and (iv) certified training and professional development. In line with its core principles, Six Sigma implementation follows a five-step methodology which is often referred to as *DMAIC* (Define – Measure – Analyse – Improve – Control). Six Sigma has been criticised for being nothing more than a statistical tool, detrimental to employees, and for its regimented approach to training and professional development.

5   While Lean and Six Sigma are different concepts, there is a strong affinity between the two. Importantly, the combination of Lean and Six Sigma into LSS can have synergistic

effects and yield outputs that are greater than the sum of their separate parts – especially with regard to the quality of process analysis and improvement, a blended approach to training and professional development and a greater balance between hard and soft approaches to change implementation.

6   The conceptual nugget for this chapter involves the development of a filtering device designed to help change leaders choose the right change implementation method that best suits the needs of their organisation. It consists of five key layers: alignment with business strategy, systemic perspective, processual approach, balanced outcomes and scalability.

—END-OF-CHAPTER CASE STUDY 9.3—

The Toyota Production System: An exemplar of Lean implementation

Introduction

One cannot talk about Lean without referring to the Toyota Production System (TPS) which is an exemplar of successful Lean implementation. The TPS is often described as an elegant socio-technical system that effectively combines sound people management practices with creative technology application to manufacture the best quality products at the lowest possible cost in line with customer demand. It was developed by industrial engineers Taiichi Ohno and Eiji Toyoda between 1948 and 1975 and is seen by many as the precursor of the Lean management principles.

TPS: An integrated socio-technical system

Figure 9.10 presents a diagram of the TPS as an integrated socio-technical system, which will be explained along its three main axes: Production process, Management practices and Lean outputs.

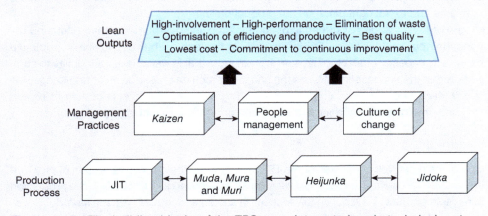

Figure 9.10   The building blocks of the TPS as an integrated socio-technical system

(Continued)

Production process

JIT

The TPS was actually referred to as Just-in-time (or JIT) production in the early days of the Toyota Company and is considered a foundational element of Lean. At Toyota, JIT is a term used to describe *a production system that flows continuously and that makes only what is needed, only when it is needed and only in the right amount needed*. As such, JIT significantly reduces the possibility of overproduction by aligning the manufacturing of Toyota's vehicles to customer demand. JIT also enables greater inventory control and more effective management of storage space – where stocks of component parts are kept to a bare minimum and replenished only as required by the production line and according to the volume of customer orders.

Muda, Mura and Muri

One of the key objectives of the TPS is to eliminate all sources of avoidable waste. At Toyota, the elimination of waste is achieved around the following three Japanese concepts: *Muda, Mura* and *Muri*.

Muda refers to anything that can be considered wasteful and that does not add any value to the end product the customer is willing to pay for. *Muda* includes such things as time wasted between tasks, excessive movement of machine or people on the production line, overproduction, over-processing of component parts needed for the final product, large buffer inventories that hold up capital and take up storage space, and product defects.

Mura refers to any form of irregularity or abnormality in the production process. For example, *Mura* happens when there is a marked difference in the capacity of workstations that a Toyota product has to go through before it is completed and ready to be delivered to the customer. This can result in overproduction at the station with greater capacity and a bottleneck at the lower-performing workstation – leading in turn to interruptions and idle time at other stations further down the production line. JIT can significantly reduce the risk of *Mura* by regulating the flow of the right component parts, in the right quantity, at the right time and to the right place on the production line.

Muri carries the idea of someone or something being overburdened and operating beyond their power or capacity. For instance, *Muri* can occur when a machine is employed beyond its capacity or an employee is given a quota that is well above their ability to complete within the set deadline. *Muri* is the cause of machine breakdowns or unmanageable stress levels in overworked employees – leading to costly disruptions of the production flow and employee disengagement which can prove unsustainable in the longer term.

Heijunka

One of the most salient features of the TPS is Heijunka. The closest translation of the word into English is *levelling*. In essence, *Heijunka* is a scheduling tool for levelling the production of multiple products in response to variations in customer demand. As a multi-product levelling tool, Heijunka sequences the production process in such a way as to balance out both the type and volume of each product to be manufactured over a set time frame. *Heijunka* has enabled the Toyota Company to effectively apply an important Lean principle, which is *customer-pull production* – where production is driven and sequenced by patterns of customer demand and the actual number of sales orders. Moreover, *Heijunka* works in tandem with JIT to reduce both inventory requirements and the risk of overproduction.

Jidoka

Jidoka is another foundational element of the TPS. The term was coined by Toyota itself and can be translated as 'intelligent automation with a human touch'. *Jidoka* is a visual quality control system that makes problems visible so that they can be addressed at source before the completion of the final product – thus allowing for the rapid identification and correction of production problems and avoiding waste arising from the need to scrap or rework defective finished products.

Management practices

Kaizen

Within TPS, great importance is given to Kaizen principles. Kaizen means *change for the better* and advocates the continuous improvement of the production process. At Toyota, this means continually looking for ways to swiftly attend to production problems and product defects (*Jidoka*), improve the efficiency of production levelling (*Heijunka*), and eliminate sources of waste (*Muda, Mura* and *Muri*) so as to optimise customer satisfaction and consolidate competitive advantage. Importantly, for *Kaizen* to work, there is need for the engagement of all those involved in the production process – and, at Toyota, every single employee, irrespective of designation or status, is held equally responsible for contributing to the continuous improvement of the TPS.

People management

At Toyota, people management is encapsulated in *The Toyota Way* which is based on an ethos of respect for people, discipline and teamwork which are vital to the proper working of the TPS. Employees working on the production line are schooled in the core principles of Lean and *Kaizen* and are empowered to rigorously apply such principles throughout the TPS. They are actively involved in problem solving and are rewarded for making any significant contribution to the continuous improvement of the TPS.

Culture of change

Managers and leaders at Toyota seek to instil in all employees a 'culture of change' which they see as one of the main strengths of the TPS. Employees are alerted to the danger of being 'hostage to routine' and enjoined to remain 'open to change' as a precondition for enacting Toyota's commitment to continuous change. The company is always looking for ways – via R&D, technology development and innovative employee-led solutions – to make incremental yet constructive change. The culture of change that drives the TPS forward also allows for the consolidation and stabilisation of the Lean principles that underpin it while encouraging the continuous pursuit of perfection as a way of making the lives of both employees and customers better.

(Continued)

Conclusions

The success of the TPS lies in the unique way the Toyota company has been able to apply Lean principles and adapt it to suit its particular needs. These Lean principles include high-commitment and high involvement of all those involved in the process, a systematic and concerted approach to the elimination of waste and the optimisation of efficiency, the production of best quality vehicles at the lowest possible costs, and a commitment to the continuous improvement of the TPS rooted in core values that benefit both employees and customers. The TPS remains an exemplar of Lean implementation. It has become a global benchmark for not only the automotive industry but has also been applied to a range of diverse industries such as finance, healthcare, retailing, mining and the police force.

Sources: Morgan (2015); SixSigma.us (2017)

Activity

Go online and find out more about the Japanese concepts mentioned in the case study: *Muda, Mura* and *Muri, Heijunka, Jidoka* and *Kaizen*.

Research organisational examples of TPS-inspired Lean implementation across the industries mentioned in the concluding section of the case study.

Once you have completed the online exercise, answer the following questions:

1   What are the building blocks of the TPS?
2   What are the key TPS-inspired Lean principles that are applicable to other industries and organisations?
3   What management practices are critical to the long-term success of a Lean initiative such as the TPS?

9.7 Independent learning

Lean, Six Sigma and LSS: read Antony et al. (2021) 'An evaluation of Lean and Six Sigma methodologies in the National Health Service', which contains a critical review of these change methods and includes an excellent comparative analysis of Lean, Six Sigma and LSS. It is presented in tabular form and is very easy to follow. Full reference details are included in the reference list.

The Toyota Production System (TPS): www.youtube.com/watch?v=wk-Mz_4Rzx0. Access the link to watch an interview with Luis Almeida, manager of the TPS group of trainers at Toyota, and Larry Edwards, one of Toyota's certified TPS trainers. Both of these highly experienced practitioners provide some valuable insights into the application and potential benefits of TPS and unpick its key elements – all of which serve to illuminate the end-of-chapter case study.

9.8 References

Alkhoraif, A., Rashid, H. and McLaughlin, P. (2019) 'Lean implementation in small and medium enterprises: Literature review', *Operations Research Perspectives*, 6. [Online] Available at: www.sciencedirect.com/science/article/pii/S2214716018301659 (accessed 4 January 2023).

Antin, J. (n.d.) *From the Ground Up*. [Online] Available at: https://airbnb.design/from-the-ground-up/ (accessed 12 March 2023).

Antony, J., Lancastle, J., McDermott, O., Bhat, S., Parida, R. and Cudney, E. A. (2021) 'An evaluation of Lean and Six Sigma methodologies in the National Health Service', *International Journal of Quality & Reliability Management*, 40(1), 25–52.

Attaran, M. (2003) 'Information technology and business – process redesign', *Business Process Management Journal*, 9(4), 440–458.

Aziz, W. A. (2019) 'Business Process Reengineering impact on SMEs operations: Evidences from GCC region', *International Journal of Services and Operations Management*, 33(4), 545–562.

Bosch Connected Industry (2023) *Nexeed Industrial Application System*. [Online] Available at: www.bosch-connected-industry.com/de/de/nexeed-portfolio/nexeed-industrial-application-system (accessed 7 April 2023).

Davenport, T. H. (1993) *Process Innovation: Reengineering Work through Information Technology*. Boston, MA: Harvard Business School Press.

Davenport, T. H. (1995) *Reengineering – The Fad that Forgot People*. [Online] Available at: https://web.archive.org/web/20071107044721/http:/www.rotman.utoronto.ca/~evans/teach363/fastco/reengin.htm (accessed 3 November 2022).

Davenport T. H. and Short J. E. (1990) 'The new industrial engineering: Information technology and business process redesign', *Sloan Management Review*, 31(4), 11–27.

Hammer, M. (1990) 'Reengineering work: Don't automate, obliterate', *Harvard Business Review*, July–August, 104–112.

Hammer, M. and Champy, J. (2001) *Reengineering the Corporation: A Manifesto for Business Revolution*, fully revised and updated. New York: HarperCollins.

Hayes, J. (2021) *The Theory and Practice of Change Management*, 6th edn. London: Red Globe Press.

Hindo, B. (2007) *At 3M, a Struggle Between Efficiency and Creativity*. [Online] Available at: www.bloomberg.com/news/articles/2007-06-10/at-3m-a-struggle-between-efficiency-and-creativity (accessed 3 November 2022).

Jessop, B. (2021) *Post-Fordism*. [Online] Available at: www.britannica.com/topic/Fordism#ref309455 (accessed 3 November 2011).

Kenneth, N., Enefaa, T. and Deedam, F. B. (2018) 'Applying Business Process Reengineering to small and medium scale enterprises (SMEs) in the developing world', *European Journal of Computer Science and Information Technology*, 6(1), 10–22.

Kenton, W. (2021) *Lean Six Sigma*. [Online] Available at: www.investopedia.com/terms/l/lean-six-sigma.asp (accessed 10 May 2022).

Magátová, M. (2020a) *How Airbnb Reengineered the Product Development Process*. [Online] Available at: https://medium.com/minit-process-mining/3-business-process-reengineering-examples-airbnb-t-mobile-ford-motor-company-success-stories-8d3132df1c75 (accessed 10 November 2022).

Magátová, M. (2020b) *T-Mobile Becomes Un-Carrier by Reinventing Customer Service Process.* [Online] Available at: https://medium.com/minit-process-mining/3-business-process-reengineering-examples-airbnb-t-mobile-ford-motor-company-success-stories-8d3132df1c75 (accessed 10 November 2022).

Morgan, R. (2015) *Why the Toyota Production System Isn't Just for Auto Manufacturers.* [Online] Available at: www.bizjournals.com/bizjournals/how-to/growth-strategies/2015/08/toyota-production-system-not-just-for-manufacturer.html (accessed 3 March 2023).

Myers, P., Hulks, S. and Wiggins, L. (2012) *Organizational Change: Perspectives on Theory and Practice.* Oxford: Oxford University Press.

Porter, M. E. (1985) The Competitive Advantage: Creating and Sustaining Superior Performance. NY: Free Press.

Radnor, Z., Holweg, M. and Waring, J. (2011) 'Lean in healthcare: The unfilled promise?', *Social Science & Medicine*, 74(3), 364–371.

Sarker, S. and Lee, A. S. (1999) 'IT-enabled organizational transformation: A case study of BPR failure at TELECO', *The Journal of Strategic Information Systems*, 8(1), 83–103. [Online] Available at: www.sciencedirect.com/science/article/pii/S0963868799000153 (accessed 20 November 2022).

Şerban, A. I. (2015) '*Business Process Reengineering on SME's: Evidence from Romanian SME's*', *Proceedings of the 9th International Management Conference "Management and Innovation for Competitive Advantage"*, 5–6 November, Bucharest, Romania.

Shah, R. and Ward, P. T. (2007) 'Defining and developing measures of Lean production', *Journal of Operations Management*, 25(4), 785–805.

SixSigma.us (2017) *The Toyota Production System (TPS) – The Making of a Post war Automotive Star.* [Online] Available at: www.6sigma.us/six-sigma-articles/tps-making-of-post-war-automotive-star/ (accessed 15 March 2023).

T-Mobile (2021) *Experience Radically Reinvented Customer Service.* [Online] Available at: www.t-mobile.com/business/solutions/visit-our-team-of-experts (accessed 11 November 2022).

Virzi, K. (2019) 'Examining the success and failure factors of Business Process Reengineering in Africa, Asia, the Middle East, and North America: A literature review', *Open Access Library Journal*, s(9). [Online] Available at: www.scirp.org/journal/paperinformation. aspx?paperid=95298 (accessed 31 October 2022).

Womack, J. P. and Jones, D. T. (1996) *Lean Thinking: Banish Waste and Create Wealth in Your Corporation.* London: Simon & Schuster.

Womack, J. P., Jones, D. T. and Roos, D. (1990) *Machine that Changed the World.* New York: Rawson Associates.

10

EVALUATING CHANGE

Learning Outcomes

After completing this chapter, you should be able to:

- Explain the meaning and purpose of evaluation in the context of organisational change.
- Discuss the key features of a process model of change evaluation and apply it in practice.
- Unpack the key dimensions of the BSC and take stock of the criticisms that have been directed at it.
- Consider the various evaluative tools SMEs can employ to monitor and improve their business processes and performance.
- Outline the key principles underpinning a critical approach to change evaluation.

10.1 Introduction

The aim of this chapter is to help you develop a sound understanding of the evaluation of organisational change. The chapter begins by explaining the meaning and purpose of evaluation in the context of organisational change, arguing in favour of a processual approach to change evaluation. A model is then developed to discuss the key stages and features of a processual approach to change evaluation. The chapter moves on to show how this process model of change evaluation can be effectively operationalised and applied in practice. The chapter then critically examines one of the most widely used evaluation tools, the Balance Scorecard, to explain its key dimensions and draw attention to the criticisms that have been levelled against it. The chapter proceeds to consider the different evaluative tools SMEs can employ to monitor and improve their business processes and performance. In the final section, we present our conceptual nugget for this chapter which advocates a critical approach to change evaluation and proposes a set of principles to that effect. The chapter concludes with a summary of key learning points and an end-of-chapter case study which focuses on how the TATA Motors Group expanded its application of the BSC in pursuit of sustainable value creation.

10.2 Evaluation in the context of organisational change

Meaning of change evaluation

Most dictionary definitions of evaluation can be distilled into the following statement: a process of making a judgement about something in order to determine its significance, worth or value (e.g. Collins Dictionaries, 2022). Common synonyms of the word evaluation itself include appraise, assess, rate and estimate. When applied to the context of organisational change, evaluation can be defined in generic terms as:

> A process designed to determine the value of a change project against a set of indicators such as performance, intended outcomes and impact in order to improve its overall effectiveness.

While we will be unpicking this definition of evaluation in the following sections, we first want to make an important point in line with one of the conceptual pillars that underpin this textbook: *change evaluation is a process*. Effective change evaluation is not a one-off, ad hoc exercise that is carried out in a haphazard and untimely manner with no follow-up action. Neither should it be seen as just a post hoc event – and conducted as a purely cosmetic exercise only *after* the completion of the change project with no real impact on the change outcomes or on future change projects.

A process model of change evaluation

In treating change evaluation as a process, one has to see it as an integral component of the change plan and as happening *before, throughout* and *after* the change implementation. Figure 10.1 presents a model of change evaluation which maps out one possible approach to change evaluation as an activity which spans the whole change process.

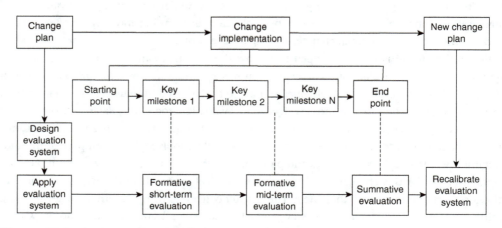

Figure 10.1   A process model of change evaluation

Designing an effective evaluation system

Starting on the left-hand side of Figure 10.1, the model places an emphasis on how the design of an effective change evaluation system should be derived from the change plan and tightly aligned with the strategic goals and objectives of the organisation. This is a vital exercise that should be carried out *before* the actual change implementation as it provides a robust framework for systematically tracking change progress *throughout* the implementation process in a timely manner and for assessing the overall impact of the change project *after* its completion whilst setting the stage for further change.

A phased approach to change evaluation

Once the change implementation is set in motion, a phased approach can be adopted to change evaluation – where different types of evaluation including different types of measures can be applied at different key milestones of the change. For example, a formative short-term evaluation employing both quantitative and qualitative measures can allow for an early assessment of change progress against the set objectives and the identification of 'quick wins' which can have a positive impact on stakeholder commitment and the momentum of change.

Formative evaluations can be carried out at other key milestones of the change implementation process (Key milestones 2 to N) with a mid-term evaluation in between. This can allow for further confirmation of change wins and, if need be, corrective measures to keep the change project on track in case of digression from the original change plan or emerging challenges that necessitate its modification. Once the change project is completed, a summative evaluation needs to be carried out. This is a final and comprehensive assessment of the completed change project in light of its initial goals and objectives – which can lead to a consolidation or recalibration of the overall evaluation system in view of the possibility of a new change plan.

A strategic tool

A process model of change evaluation as the one developed in Figure 10.1 is not a mere tactical tool designed only to demonstrate compliance with business auditing standards to escape the stakeholder scrutiny. In fact, it can be used as a powerful strategic tool to ensure the effective implementation of the change project and the achievement of its strategic goals and objectives from which it is derived and which can serve as a lever for further change and the development of new business models and strategies.

A multidimensional research tool

The model can also frame the development of a multidimensional research tool in that it allows for a combination of various types of investigative instruments which can effectively address both the hard and soft dimensions of change – where, for example 'hard' quantitative measures such as questionnaire surveys can be used to assess financial performance or productivity and 'soft' qualitative measures such as individual interviews and focus groups can provide valuable insights into critical success factors like employee engagement or customer satisfaction (Kaplan and Norton, 1992).

Evidence-based change management

Importantly, a process model of evaluation allows for 'evidence-based change management' where triangulated evidence consistently gathered at key stages of the change process from different stakeholder perspectives can enable change leaders to make more informed decisions and rationally justify their chosen courses of action. In this regard, evidence-based change management can prove to be a strong catalyst for team working and collaborative partnerships which are vital to long-term change success.

Strong leadership

Lastly, the process model of evaluation calls for strong leadership, of the type that fosters open and honest communication and demonstrates the following: a firm commitment to change evaluation, a readiness to objectively take on board stakeholder feedback, and a willingness to *act on* change evaluation outcomes – whether it be in the form of corrective measures, investments in training or strategy reorientation.

REFLECTIVE EXERCISE

Review the above sections and answer the following questions:

1   Why should evaluation be an integral part of the change plan?
2   What are the purposes of formative evaluation and summative evaluation?
3   What are the key features of a process approach to change evaluation?

10.3 Operationalising a process model of change evaluation

Table 10.1 shows how the process model of change evaluation presented in Figure 10.1 can be operationalised into a practical framework that can be appropriated, customised and selectively applied to context, depending on specific business needs. Since it is largely descriptive, we will only highlight its main features in the following discussion.

First, the operational framework in Table 10.1 provides an indication of how the different phases of the change evaluation process model can be deconstructed into finer details to facilitate its practical application. To this effect, it provides valuable pointers regarding the timings (*When?*), the various activities (*What?*), the measuring tools (*How?*), the responsibilities (*Who?*) and the intended outcomes (*To what effect?*) that have to be taken into consideration to ensure the effective application of the change evaluation system.

Second, it includes a wide range of activities which can enable a multidimensional and robust approach to change evaluation. Of course, all these activities do not indiscriminately

Table 10.1 An operational framework for a processual approach to change evaluation

Evaluation phases (When?)	An operational framework for change evaluation			
	Activities (What?)	Evaluative measures (How?)	Responsibilities (Who?)	Intended Outcomes (To what effect?)
Pre-change evaluation	- Assess feasibility of new change project - Assess impact and risks of proposed change - Gauge change readiness of key stakeholders - Develop evaluation system	- Environment diagnostic and benchmarking tools - Resource audit - Attitude surveys and focus groups	- Change leaders - Functional managers - Risk managers - Technical specialists - Evaluation experts	- Rationalisation of change goals and objectives - Indication of stakeholder consensus, readiness for change and support - Authorisation of change implementation - Evaluation system aligned with change goals and objectives
Change implementation evaluation	Conduct formative evaluations at key milestones to: - Track progress - Detect digressions from original change plan - Identify internal errors and sources of inefficiency and other implementation failures - Assess impact on value chain activities - Record short-term gains/ losses - Identify emerging external challenges and opportunities - Recalibrate evaluation system if necessary	- Financial performance ratios - Social and environmental impact metrics - Performance appraisals of employees, machines and equipment against set KPIs - Surveys, interviews, focus groups, observation targeting employees, customers, business partners, etc. - Environment diagnostic and benchmarking tools	- Change leaders - Designated data collectors and analysts - Evaluation experts - Functional managers - Technical specialists	- Interim assessment of financial, social and environmental impact of change project - Interim assessment of value-chain activities - Identification of problems to be solved and areas for improvement - Analysis of training and learning needs - Registration (and rewarding) of short-term wins - Confirmation/ change of strategic course of action - Recalibration of evaluation system

(Continued)

Table 10.1   (Continued)

	An operational framework for change evaluation			
Post-change evaluation	Conduct summative evaluation to: - Assess impact of change project against initial (and emergent) strategic goals and objectives - Assess impact on value chain activities - Identify critical success/failure factors (CSFs – CFFs)	- Financial performance ratios (e.g. Return on Investment, profitability, market value ratios) - Social and environmental impact metrics (e.g. impact on quality of life, public value, carbon emissions, energy efficiency, etc.) - Comparative resource audit and value-chain analysis - Cumulative performance appraisals of employees, machines and equipment against set KPIs (e.g. production capacity, equipment maintenance, employee engagement, customer satisfaction, etc.) - Large-scale surveys, interviews, focus groups targeting employees, customers, business partners, etc.	- Change leaders - Designated data collectors - Functional managers - Evaluation experts - Technical specialists	- Achievement of initial (and emergent) strategic goals and objectives - Final assessment of financial, social and environmental impact of change project - Final assessment of value-chain activities - Final performance appraisal of employees, machines and equipment - Registration (and rewarding) of overall change wins - Identification of CSFs and CFFs as a baseline for further change - Recalibration/ replacement of evaluation system

apply to all organisations. Change agents can 'pick and choose' the activities that best suit their needs at each phase of the change evaluation process.

Third, the same principle of selection applies to the battery of measures listed in the framework and change agents can choose the research instruments that best suit their needs. However, the more important point here is that a processual approach to change evaluation allows for:

i   multiple levels of analysis (individual – group – organisational),
ii   triangulation of both quantitative and qualitative data (e.g. surveys, focus groups, interviews) and
iii   a multilayered impact assessment (financial – social – environmental) – all of which can enable a context-sensitive, meaning-rich and in-depth evaluation of change initiatives. Examples of broad performance metrics/indicators are included in the framework but these need to be further detailed in context in line with specific business needs.

Fourth, the operational framework opens up the possibility for strong leadership and a stakeholder approach to change evaluation by:

i   highlighting the responsibility of change leaders to be involved throughout the evaluation process and
ii   identifying the key agents who can be involved at each phase of the change evaluation process and whose support or expertise can be drawn upon as and when required.

Finally, the operational framework allows for the development and application of a flexible evaluation system which can be recalibrated, modified or even replaced in response to new concerns, challenges or emergent strategic imperatives. Importantly, this makes change evaluation less susceptible to path dependency where an organisation may persistently use a particular evaluation system and refuse to change it, even if a new strategic course of action warrants it or better, cost effective alternatives are available (Choi, 2014).

PRACTICAL EXERCISE

You are an evaluator working for a renowned consultancy firm. Your firm has been hired by a medium-sized manufacturing company of wood furniture to develop an *effective evaluation system* for the change initiative which will be deployed in a few months' time. The company specialises in the production of household furniture (beds, cabinets, tables, chests of drawers, etc.) and employs around 600 people. Management have decided to expand the business which will involve a major restructuring to reorganise activities around product lines and the creation of two new off-site divisions to manufacture outdoor furniture, wooden doors and window frames. The restructuring will require the recruitment of 50 more staff. The company will also need to access additional suppliers, invest in new

(Continued)

machinery and equipment, and review its delivery and marketing services as it intends to sell its products to customers residing in neighbouring countries.

Activity

Your manager has asked you to develop a robust yet practical evaluation system for this new client. To carry out this exercise, you will need to use the operational framework in Table 10.1 as a baseline template to develop a customised evaluation system, tailored to the needs of the client.

As a starting point, you can 'pick and choose' the elements which you think are the most relevant to the client's particular change situation and work your way across Table 10.2. You can then refine your recommendations as per the specific needs of the client.

Table 10.2 Evaluation system for household furniture company

Valuation phases (When?)	Activities (What?)	Evaluative measures (How?)	Responsibilities (Who?)	Intended Outcomes (To what effect?)
Pre-change evaluation				
Change implementation evaluation				
Post-change evaluation				

10.4 The Balanced Scorecard

In this section, we consider in some detail the Balanced Scorecard (BSC), a popular evaluative tool devised by Kaplan and Norton in the early 1990s. As will be explained more fully in the following discussion, it is highly accommodating of a processual approach to change evaluation. It is also a multidimensional evaluative tool in that it integrates multiple perspectives and measures to enable a comprehensive and continuous assessment of change. Figure 10.2 presents an adapted version of the BSC which is used to frame the discussion that follows.

The first feature that stands out from Figure 10.2 is the multidimensional nature of the BSC. One of Kaplan and Norton's (1996a; 1996b) overriding concerns in developing this evaluative framework was to enable organisations to move away from a one-dimensional and reductive approach to change evaluation (which tends to focus exclusively on the economic dimension of change) and pay greater attention to all key activities that can have a significant bearing on the intended outcomes and long-term success of change. To this effect, the BSC integrates four key interdependent dimensions that are tightly aligned to the organisation's core values, vision and strategy and that change agents have to monitor consistently and simultaneously to ensure the successful completion and sustainability of change projects (Balanced Scorecard Institute, 2022). These four dimensions are explained below.

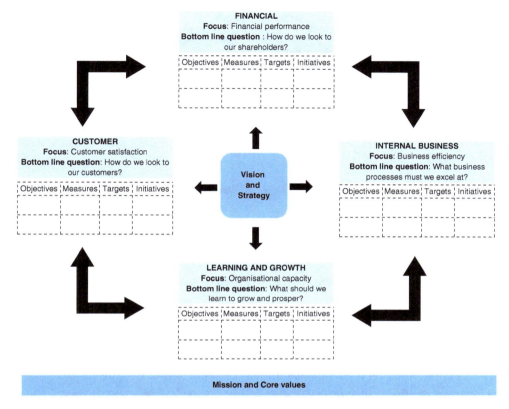

Figure 10.2 Key dimensions of the Balanced Scorecard

Source: Adapted from Kaplan, R. S. and Norton, D. P. (1996a) *The Balanced Scorecard: Translating Strategy into Action*. Boston: Harvard Business School Press; Kaplan, R. S. and Norton, D. P. (1996b) 'Using the balanced scorecard as a strategic management system', *Harvard Business Review*, 74(1), 75–85.

The financial dimension

The primary focus of this particular dimension of the BSC is on the financial performance of the organisation in view of the proposed change. The bottom line question that change agents need to grapple with here is: *How do we look to our shareholders?* In other words, change agents have to figure out what needs to be done to demonstrate to those who have invested in the company the financial viability of the proposed change. One of the great strengths of the BSC is that it warrants 'concrete measures' for each of its key dimensions – i.e. it calls for the use of tangible key performance indicators and metrics against which change can be measured in quantifiable terms in line with the strategic objectives of the change project. In this regard, the BSC can be particularly useful in demonstrating progress, which makes it particularly appealing to practitioners.

Table 10.3 provides a simplified example of a financial performance metric following the decision of a company to increase its profitability within the next financial year.

Table 10.3 Example of financial performance metric

Objective	Measures	Targets (this year)	Initiatives
Increase profitability by 7% by end of financial year	Sales revenue	↑ 5%	Penetrate new international markets
	Expenses and taxes	↓ 2%	Improve sales and marketing training programme
	Net profit	↑ 7%	Implement tighter accounting system
			Weekly monitoring of accounts

What is particularly important here is not the actual figures but the alignment between the set objective and the measures, targets and initiatives that have to be developed in specific terms to enable (weekly) progress monitoring towards its effective achievement.

The customer dimension

The focus of the customer dimension is firmly on customer satisfaction. In this case, the bottom line question which drives evaluation efforts is: *How do we look to our customers?* Change agents need here to get a sense of how customers perceive the organisation with regard to the quality of the products/services on offer and what can be done to monitor and maximise customer satisfaction against measures defined by the customer. Table 10.4 provides an example of what a company could do to increase customer satisfaction.

Table 10.4 Example of customer satisfaction metric

Objective	Measures	Targets (this year)	Initiatives
Increase customer satisfaction by 3%	Customer satisfaction index	↑ 3%	Upgrade product quality specifications
	Market share index	↑ 5%	Implement new customer relationship programme
	Customer retention	100%	Monthly monitoring of market share and customer retention

In this case, the positive upshot of the desired increase in customer satisfaction is a corresponding increase in market share and an optimisation of customer retention which is monitored here on a monthly basis.

The internal business dimension

The focus here is on business efficiency and the bottom line question: *What business processes must we excel at?* Change agents are concerned in this case with how to optimise the efficiency of internal processes across functional areas in order to achieve the organisation's vision and strategy. Table 10.5 contains an example of a manufacturing company aiming to improve the efficiency of its production process.

Table 10.5 Example of business processes metric

Objective	Measures	Targets (this year)	Initiatives
Improve the overall efficiency of the production process	Cycle time	↓ 3%	Implement Lean Six Sigma (LSS) manufacturing
	Unit cost	↓ 2%	
	Defects rate	< 1%	Monthly monitoring against LSS standards
	End-user experience	> 95%	

The measures used in this case are just indicative and could include a far wider range of variables. However, those included are just a reminder of the primary purpose of the LSS intervention used here – which is the pursuit of near zero product defects and the optimisation of end-user experience (refer to chapter 9 for a more detailed discussion of LSS).

Learning and growth dimension

The focus of this final dimension of the BSC is on building organisational capacity for learning and growth, and the bottom line question in this case is: *What should we learn to grow and prosper?* The primary concern of change agents here is how to bring about and sustain the conditions for learning, knowledge transfer and employee engagement in order to continuously create value and improve the capacity for innovative change as a means of ensuring sustainable business growth and prosperity. Table 10.6 provides an example of the measures, targets and initiatives that change agents can employ to this end.

Table 10.6 Example of learning and growth metric

Objective	Measures	Targets (this year)	Initiatives
Enhance organisational capacity for learning and growth	Training effectiveness as perceived by employees	> 90%	Develop training content in line with change strategy
	Employee development plans in place	100%	Roll out new coaching and mentoring scheme in support of employee development
	Employee engagement with technology	↑ 25%	Create an IT learning centre
	Employee involvement in teamwork and communities of practice	70%	Develop a policy for company-wide support of teamwork and communities of practice

Once again, the measures included here are just indicative of the wider range of activities that change agents can bring into play to optimise organisational capacity for learning and growth. Importantly, this dimension can be much more difficult to assess given that some of the measures (e.g. training effectiveness) are dependent on individual perceptions and susceptible to subjective bias, which calls into question their reliability. This is addressed in more depth in the following sub-section.

PRACTICAL EXERCISE

Go online to find examples of how companies from different sectors have applied the BSC. You could draw on examples from the IT, manufacturing, healthcare and government sectors. For all your chosen companies, use Table 10.7 below to map out the primary purpose driving the adoption of the BSC and outline the main emphasis across each of its key dimensions. We have included Apple as an example to provide you with an indication of how to carry out this exercise.

Table 10.7 Application of the BSC across sectors

Company/ Sector	Primary purpose of BSC	Financial	Customer	Internal business	Learning and growth
Apple – IT	The BSC used primarily as a planning device to expand the company's vision and strategy beyond solely economic interests	Emphasis on shareholder value and investments in business creation and development	Emphasis on customer satisfaction and tracking new market segments	Emphasis on core competencies underpinning user-friendly interfaces, software architecture and distribution systems	Emphasis on employee attitudes gauged through more frequent surveys and clear communication of results

Criticisms of the BSC

Like all other change evaluation methods, the BSC is not impervious to criticisms (Awadallah and Allam, 2015). We briefly discuss the criticisms below.

Resource intensive

As can be easily deduced from the preceding discussion, the BSC is resource-intensive and can be a very costly exercise. It requires considerable investments in terms of time, labour and data processing. Even in its initial stages, a BSC intervention can become so complex and overwhelming that change agents can 'get bogged down in the details' and quickly lose sight of the actual change goals and objectives. Thus, by virtue of its complexity and resource-intensity, the BSC can become an end-in-itself and trump strategy.

Elusive measures

It is generally recognised that there is limited guidance on how to apply the measures and access the information that is needed for the BSC to work properly. While some of the 'hard' performance indicators included in the BSC (such as financial measures, machine efficiency and defects rate) are relatively easier to compute, intangible performance indicators (such as training effectiveness, employee engagement and customer satisfaction) are liable to subjective bias and perceptual filters, and call into question the reliability and validity of the BSC outputs – and, importantly, their effectiveness in supporting informed decision-making and strategic choices.

One-sided focus

The BSC tends to have a one-sided focus on the positives which is underpinned by a tacit assumption that things such as operational efficiency, customer satisfaction, financial success and the capacity to learn and grow follow a straightforward input–output process. However, such pursuits have to contend with problems and challenges which can be very difficult to overcome. For example, financial performance is dependent on external factors which are all too often beyond the control of change agents; markets are not uniform and the variety of customer needs and preferences and the different ways they interact with a company's products and services are hard to tap into, let alone quantify; and the necessary conditions for learning and growth can be impacted by many adverse factors (employee resistance and disengagement, turnover and erosion of expertise, etc.) – all of which are major barriers that stand in the way of the practical application of the BSC but which tend to be obscured in the narratives that have been spun around it.

REFLECTIVE EXERCISE

In light of the above discussion and the practical exercise you have carried out:

1   What are the key advantages of using the BSC?
2   What are its limitations?
3   What can an organisation that is already using the BSC do to get greater value from it?

10.5 Change evaluation in SMEs

Defining SMEs

Small and Medium Enterprises (SMEs) have been described as the vital engine that is powering economic development, employment and trade across the globe (World Bank, 2023). While defining SMEs is problematic because of their sheer diversity, the most common criteria used to describe them are the number of people they employ and their turnover. In European countries, very small businesses with less than 10 employees and a turnover not exceeding €2 million are usually referred to as micro businesses. Companies employing between 10 and less than 50 staff with a turnover of up to €10 million are considered as small enterprises while those with 50 and less than 250 employees and a turnover of up to €50 million are seen as medium-sized enterprises (European Commission, 2023).

However, whichever scale is used to define SMEs, they do share certain characteristics which set them apart, especially when compared to larger businesses: limited access to capital and funding, limited resources, lower economies of scale, more restricted knowledge bases and access to external expertise, lower capacity for dealing with technological disruptions, lower resilience and ability to 'absorb' the adverse effects of external environmental forces such as economic downturns, natural disasters and, as recently witnessed, pandemics (Bank One, 2022; Faye and Goldblum, 2022).

SMEs and change evaluation

Given their vital contribution to the economy, governments and business communities have a keen interest in how SMEs monitor their performance and manage change within increasingly dynamic business environments, where they often have to compete against larger companies with greater resources and market power. Research in this area shows that SMEs are actively involved in monitoring their performance and some are already applying the BSC as their main evaluative tool – and evidence suggests that there is a positive relationship between the application of the BSC and performance improvement (e.g. see Abdallah et al., 2015; Dudic et al., 2020).

However, the application of the BSC in SMEs seems to be more focused on financial performance and current issues (Malagueño et al., 2018) pointing to a need for opening up the scope of the BSC application to pay greater attention to its other key dimensions and address long-term performance and sustainability issues (ibid.). Given their limited resources, SMEs are more likely to implement a scaled-down version of the BSC according to their most pressing business needs and strategic objectives.

Moreover, there are less expensive and easier-to-implement evaluation methods that SMEs can employ to enable an economical and focused approach to measuring and improving performance. For example, they can draw on a limited set of both quantitative and qualitative indicators to measure processes and outcomes that have a direct impact on their bottom lines (e.g. revenue growth, return on investment, profit margins, employee engagement, customer satisfaction, etc.).

SMEs can also have recourse to valuable visualisation techniques such as process mapping, value-stream mapping, culture mapping, technology mapping and different types of flow-charts and business canvases to diagnose and resolve problems, innovate and add value to their current processes and identify new business opportunities (Futcher, 2020). Finally, SMEs can now access inexpensive and customisable online evaluative tools to assess and improve their processes and performance and effectively manage change – as exemplified by the following two mini-case studies.

CASE STUDY 10.1

Amazon QuickSight: Scaling business intelligence for SMEs

Introduction

Amazon QuickSight (AQS), provided by Amazon Web Services is a scalable cloud-based business intelligence service that offers cost-effective solutions for monitoring, improving and predicting performance. AQS is particularly suitable for Small and Medium-sized Enterprises (SMEs) as it offers a pay-per-session pricing model, enabling small businesses to access advanced data analytics capabilities without incurring any major expenses or investing in additional infrastructure. AQS enables users to access various sources of stored data and create interactive dashboards and reports easily without the need for specialised training or highly developed technical skills. The AQS service also includes a powerful toolkit for data visualisation, ad-hoc analysis, reporting and predictive analytics which SMEs can easily access to improve operations and decision-making.

Accessing AQS

To get started, a user has to simply sign up for an account on the AQS website or through the Amazon Web Services Management Console. The user then gets access to a variety of video tutorials on how to connect with the data, create dashboards and datasets, and engage with the key features of AQS. There is a free one-month trial period which allows users to assess the suitability of the service in view of their own business needs.

Performing data queries in natural language with Q

AQS includes a natural language processing feature called *Q* which allows users to perform data queries in plain language and get easy-to-understand responses supported by visual data display such as graphs, charts and plots. For example, a user could ask 'What is our profit margin for financial year x?'. A graph would instantly show the profit margin for that year and enable the user to correlate the answer with other performance indicators such as customer satisfaction and retention. *Q* uses machine learning algorithms to interpret the meaning of questions and connect to data sources to provide consistent answers to a particular question even when it is phrased differently – which can be quite useful

(Continued)

when data is shared among organisational members with different functional expertise who may use different business jargons when addressing a particular issue.

Predicting performance

AQS can be combined with Amazon SageMaker Canvas to make 'performance predictions' from thousands of documents, images, textual and numerical data in minutes. To this effect, users have ready access to a range of analytical tools and custom models (e.g. sentiment analysis, object detection, document analysis, regression analysis, etc.) that can be used for statistical modelling, performance predictions and business forecasting.

Conclusion

AQS is a prime example of the type of affordable and scalable online evaluative tools that SMEs can employ to monitor, improve and predict their performance and develop the business intelligence they need to effectively manage change. While online evaluative systems such as AQS are certainly not the definitive evaluative solution for SMEs, they do allow for a level of autonomy and customisation that SMEs might find particularly appealing, given their limited resources and lack of access to the type of specialist knowledge and expertise required by enterprise-wide and resource-intensive interventions like BPR.

Source: Amazon Web Services (2023)

Questions

1   Do you think online evaluative tools are applicable to all SMEs?
2   Which basic skills are required to engage with such tools?

CASE STUDY 10.2

Evaluating change in a micro business

Introduction

Ferienwohnung Thiele (FeWoT) is a small family-run apartment rental business located in a residential area in a small spa town in Lower Franconia, Germany. The region is well known for its breathtaking mountain ranges, luxuriant vineyards and charming towns which are the main attractions for mostly domestic tourists seeking peace and quiet and an encounter with nature. Since its inception in April 2022, the owners of FeWoT have been looking for cost-effective ways to gradually grow their business by expanding customer reach, streamlining the booking process and providing a personalised and high-quality accommodation to all their customers.

Partnering with Booking.com

Following the advice from the Local Destination Management Organisation (which promotes local tourism and supports hospitality businesses), the owners of FeWoT got their business listed on Booking.com, a global platform accessed by millions of people seeking accommodation worldwide. Booking.com invests heavily in online advertising via various channels such as search engines, social media and email to increase their visibility and optimise the operations of their listed partners on a commission basis. After just a few weeks, the occupancy rates at FeWoT shot up to 70%, which is well above the average for this type of business.

Staying on top of things with Booking.com's online evaluation tool

To stay on top of things, FeWoT made extensive use of Booking.com's online evaluation tool which provides access to real-time data on booking performance and customer satisfaction together with a wealth of data on competitive pricing and customer behavioural patterns. Booking.com's evaluative tool enabled FeWoT to gain a better understanding of customer needs and preferences, optimise its pricing strategies and improve customer experience. Moreover, FeWoT benefits largely from Booking.com's Opportunity Centre which provides valuable advice on things such as how to increase business visibility, improve performance, maximise revenues and deploy sustainable strategies based on tangible performance metrics and machine learning algorithms that can uncover hidden patterns in available data to predict performance outcomes.

Conclusion

The case of FeWoT is quite insightful as it bears witness to how micro businesses with very limited resources can draw on inexpensive online evaluative systems of partnering organisations to drive change geared towards improved business performance and sustainable growth.

Source: Booking.com (2023)

Questions

1   Why is evaluation critical to change success, irrespective of business size?
2   In what ways are online evaluation tools helping micro businesses such as FeWoT to optimise their performance and build their competitive advantage?

10.6 Conceptual nugget: A critical approach to change evaluation

In light of what has been covered in this chapter, our conceptual nugget advocates a critical approach to change evaluation. A critical approach in this case means one that is reflective, based on informed decision-making and alert to the potential pitfalls of change evaluation. Figure 10.3 presents six key principles for a critical approach to change evaluation. Each of these principles is succinctly explained in the following discussion.

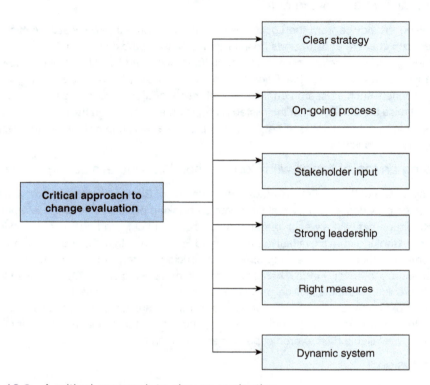

Figure 10.3 A critical approach to change evaluation

Clear strategy

First and foremost, there is a need for the development of a clear strategy for change evaluation that is tightly aligned with the business needs and strategic objectives of the organisation. This is where change agents have to identify and prioritise the key dimensions and elements that need to be included in the change evaluation system. This is an important exercise for, as the saying goes: *what gets measured gets done*. What is included in the change evaluation strategy will inevitably act as a perceptual filter and have a shaping influence on how the evaluation is carried out and how its outputs are used to justify certain preferred courses of action.

On-going process

We reinforce a view of change evaluation not as a one-off event but as an on-going activity that is carried out throughout the change process – and which, as already explained in this chapter, has to start even before the change implementation with a pre-evaluation analysis and the development of a sound change evaluation system. A process approach to change evaluation also has to account for both short-term and mid-term formative evaluations which can in turn inform long-term summative evaluations and serve as a springboard for further change – thus establishing a sense of continuity in the evaluation process and a cumulative and deepening understanding of the change progress.

Stakeholder input

An effective change evaluation system should reflect the input of all key stakeholders. The situated knowledge and functional expertise of organisational members together with the perspectives of customers, consultants and other external business partners can prove to be of vital importance in not only the design and application of the chosen evaluation system but also in the interpretation of its outputs, follow-up action and the assessment of its overall impact on the organisation. In any case, stakeholder input should be seen as a precondition for reaching consensus on the appropriateness and purpose of change evaluation and upholding the commitment of all those involved in the process.

Strong leadership

As for any other activity that can have a significant impact on the organisation's bottom lines, change evaluation warrants total buy-in on the part of change leaders – demonstrated by a willingness to actively support and participate in evaluation throughout the change process. An absence of strong leadership in change evaluation inevitably leads to a loss of commitment and to the disengagement of other key stakeholders together with an erosion of the capacity to take follow-up action as and when necessary. Change evaluation which is not followed by timely follow-up action is a pointless exercise.

Right measures

Choosing the right measures and investigative instruments to carry out the change evaluation is another key determinant of success. However, this is not a straightforward process. As previously discussed, change agents should be aware of the limitations of their chosen measures and research instruments and of their impact on the validity, reliability and overall credibility of evaluation outputs. Thus, obtaining precise, unequivocal data is a constant challenge in change evaluation. Therefore, acceptable levels of credibility and margins of error have to be factored into the selection and administration of evaluative measures and investigative instruments.

Dynamic system

A change evaluation system has to remain dynamic, flexible and open-ended – where it allows for timely changes in the use of methods, measures and investigative instruments in view of new challenges and strategic imperatives or in response to regular assessments of the effectiveness of the change evaluation system itself. A failure to consistently 'evaluate the change evaluation system' makes it liable to path dependency – where, as previously explained, an organisation may persist in the use of a change evaluation system even when it is ineffective and resource-draining and does not add any value to the change initiative.

REFLECTIVE EXERCISE

1   What are the key principles of a critical approach to change evaluation?
2   What are the challenges associated with each of those principles?

10.7 Key learning points

The key learning points arising from this chapter include:

1   In the context of organisational change, evaluation refers to a *process* designed to determine the *value of a change project* against a set of indicators such as performance, intended outcomes and impact in order to *improve its overall effectiveness*.

2   A process model of change evaluation provides a robust framework for systematically tracking change progress throughout the implementation process. It allows *for a phased approach to change evaluation* including *formative evaluations* carried out at key milestones of the change implementation process and a *summative evaluation* once the change has been completed. It can also be used as a *strategic tool* to ensure the effective achievement of strategic objectives whilst serving as a lever for further strategic change. It also accommodates various types of both quantitative and qualitative measures that address both the *hard* and *soft dimensions* of change. Moreover, it allows for an evidence-based approach to change management that calls for strong leadership and a firm commitment to change evaluation. Importantly, it was shown how it can be *operationalised* and *applied in practice*.

3   The Balanced Scorecard (BSC) is a popular evaluative tool consisting of four key interdependent dimensions that are tightly aligned to the organisation's core values, vision and strategy: *financial, customer, internal business* and *learning and growth*. The great strength of the BSC is that each of its key dimensions can easily be broken into *concrete measures, targets* and *initiatives* to allow for a systematic and multidimensional evaluation of change initiatives. The criticisms that have been leveled at the BSC include the fact that it is a resource-intensive and costly exercise, it provides limited guidance on how to apply the measures and access the information that is needed for it to work properly, and it also tends to have a *one-sided focus on the positives* while obscuring the challenges that stand in the way of its practical application.

4   Given their limited resources, SMEs are more likely to implement a *scaled down version of the BSC* according to their most pressing business needs and strategic objectives. Moreover, there are less expensive and easier-to-implement evaluation methods that SMEs can employ to enable an economical and focused approach to measuring and improving performance: *basic quantitative and qualitative indicators* (e.g. return on investment, profit margins, employee engagement, customer satisfaction), *visualisation techniques* (e.g. process mapping, value-stream mapping and different types of flowcharts), and inexpensive, customisable *online evaluative tools*.

5   Finally, our conceptual nugget for this chapter advocates a critical approach to change evaluation, which is reflective, based on informed decision-making and alert to the potential pitfalls of change evaluation. To this effect, it outlines six key principles underlining the need for: a *clear strategy*, a view of change evaluation as an *on-going process, stakeholder input, strong leadership, right measures* and a *dynamic* evaluation system.

---END-OF-CHAPTER CASE STUDY 10.3---

TATA Motors Group: Expanding the Balanced Scorecard in pursuit of sustainable value creation

Introduction

Established in 1945, the Tata Motors Group (TMG) forms part of the larger TATA Group which is headquartered in Mumbai, India. TMG builds a wide range of both commercial and passenger vehicles and provides innovative automotive solutions to meet customer needs and plays a leading role in 'bringing forth the future of mobility'. With a business portfolio of about USD 37 billion, TMG employs around 52,000 people dedicated to the design, production and sales of over one million vehicles annually across 125 countries.

In the early 2000s TMG applied the Balanced Scorecard (BSC) as an evaluative tool to turn around its 'financially stressed' commercial vehicles business in India and to ensure the successful integration of the newly acquired Korean commercial vehicle maker Daewoo. Ten years later, TMG expanded the way it was using the BSC to align it with its new strategic orientation. This warranted a move away from a sole focus on financial performance to incorporate evaluative measures that also accounted for how TMG was performing on the social and environmental fronts.

Going beyond profits

Following increasing lobbying from regulatory bodies and pressure groups, the Indian Parliament passed a new law in 2018 to ensure that publicly listed companies like TMG endorsed the so-called 'triple bottom lines'. This was to force them to consider the impact

(Continued)

of their business activities on the economy, society and the natural environment, on which they had to report in their annual reports. As a result, TMG needed to find ways to abide by this new business law. TMG decided to expand its use of the BSC to enable it to 'go beyond profits' and assess its overall performance against not only economic but also social and environmental indicators. Figure 10.4 provides a visual representation of the changes made to TMG's original approach to the BSC.

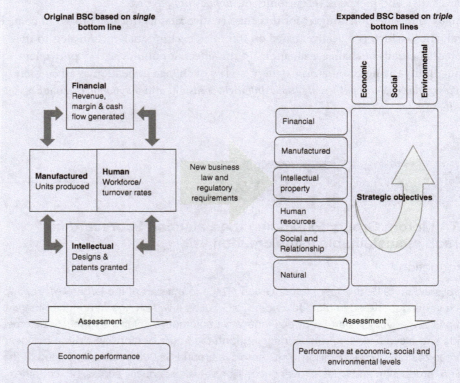

Figure 10.4 Tata Motors' expansion of the BSC

Mapping out TMG's strategic objectives against triple bottom lines

In mapping out its strategic objectives against the new BSC based on 'the triple bottom lines', TMG focused its efforts on six interconnected performance areas, or what were referred as 'capitals' – for which it formulated a set of 12 strategic objectives that are underpinned by a reconfiguration of the company's mission, vision and value system. The company's *mission* is to 'innovate mobility solutions with passion to enhance the quality of life'; its vision is to 'become the most aspirational Indian automotive brand by 2024'; and its value system includes corporate principles such as operational excellence, commitment to innovation, teamwork and collaboration, talent management, customer focus, technological development, a culture of safety and diversity, and capability to respond to climate change. Figure 10.5 highlights the key elements of this mapping exercise.

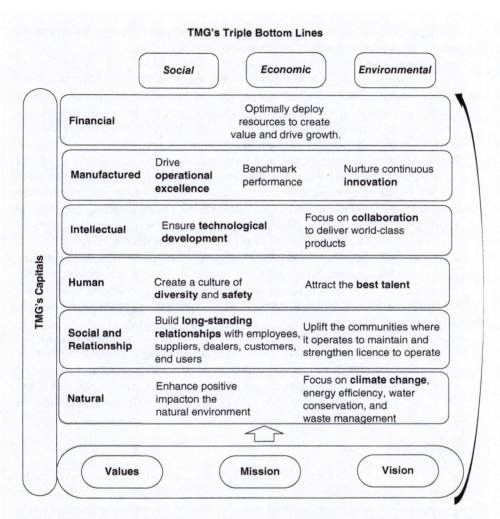

TMG's Triple Bottom Lines

	Social	Economic	Environmental
Financial	Optimally deploy resources to create value and drive growth.		
Manufactured	Drive **operational excellence**	Benchmark performance	Nurture continuous **innovation**
Intellectual	Ensure **technological development**		Focus on **collaboration** to deliver world-class products
Human	Create a culture of **diversity** and **safety**	Attract the **best talent**	
Social and Relationship	Build **long-standing relationships** with employees, suppliers, dealers, customers, end users	Uplift the communities where it operates to maintain and strengthen licence to operate	
Natural	Enhance positive impacton the natural environment	Focus on **climate change**, energy efficiency, water conservation, and waste management	

TMG's Capitals

Values　　　Mission　　　Vision

Figure 10.5 Map of TMG's strategic objectives against its triple bottom lines

Source: Adapted from Kaplan, R. S. and McMillan, D. (2021) 'Reimagining the Balanced Scorecard for the ESG Era', *Harvard Business Review* [Online]. Available at https://hbr.org/2021/02/reimagining-the-balanced-scorecard-for-the-esg-era.

Financial Capital focuses on finding the optimal balance between meeting short-term obligations and making long-term investments. For example, TMG has put in place a 'Business Agility Plan' to enable it to flexibly adjust prices, production capacities and inventory levels to maintain financial stability in times of high inflation or supply chain disruptions – thus optimising resource allocation and production outputs as short-term measures whilst keeping in view the long-term goals of the organisation. *Manufactured Capital* is about maximising the efficiency of TMG's operations by exploring and exploiting innovative approaches from within and outside the company. For example, TMG has recourse to a business process modelling platform (named *pFirst*) that has led to several hundred BOT-enabled process improvements to maximise production outputs and customer service.

Intellectual Capital refers to TMG's capability to turn knowledge (such as patented designs, marketing data) into effective business solutions. By way of example, TMG leveraged its engineering and sales data, and market knowledge to develop *Fleet Edge* – a connected vehicle management platform designed to help fleet managers in the planning, tracking and performance analysis of their commercial vehicles as a means of optimising fleet performance and minimising costs.

Human Capital relates to the challenge of creating a safe and healthy work environment and promoting a culture of inclusivity and diversity to ensure employee commitment to the company's strategic objectives whilst attracting the best talent. In hunting for new talent, TMG has launched in partnership with reputed private technical institutes the *Learn & Earn Scheme* which enables young people to learn and get valuable hands-on experience in the automotive trade while receiving a stipend for their services.

Social and Relationship Capital aims at forging bonds between TMG and its diverse group of stakeholders, such as employees, suppliers, and customers and the wider community. For instance, in 2022, the company worked with local governments in six Indian states to ensure effective communication and implementation of government welfare and financial schemes.

Natural Capital is concerned with efforts to reduce, if not eliminate, the negative impact that TMG's operations might have on the natural environment and the earth's finite resources. To this end, TMG has launched a series of initiatives, notably the recycling and renewal of groundwater used in its production processes, investments in wind and solar energies and special projects for refurbishing spare parts to reduce the company's carbon footprint.

Conclusions

A number of key issues arise from TMG's application of the BSC. First, it points to the flexibility of the BSC which can be reconfigured and consolidated to accommodate the strategic imperatives of an organisation. Second, it shows how investments at the social and environmental levels of the 'triple bottom line' do not have to be at the expense of an organisation's financial performance. In fact, activities carried out at all three levels of the 'triple bottom line' can be mutually reinforcing and serve, in synergistic fashion, to augment the overall quality of an organisation's business strategy and create sustainable value. Finally, it draws attention to the importance of consistent evaluative measures in driving forward change initiatives.

Sources: Kaplan and McMillan (2021); Kaplan and Norton (1992); Makhijani and Creelman (2008); Tata Motors (2022)

Questions

1   What are the key factors that led to an expansion of the BSC at TMG?
2   What lessons can be learned from TMG's application of the BSC as a strategic tool?
3   What is the role of evaluation in driving change?

10.8 Independent learning

The Balanced Scorecard: https://hbr.org/1992/01/the-balanced-scorecard-measures-that-drive-performance-2. Read Kaplan and Norton's seminal article which first appeared in the *Harvard Business Review*.

Interview with Bob Kaplan: www.youtube.com/watch?v=oNy8kupW8oI. This short video includes a discussion of the BSC with one of its key proponents Bob Kaplan.

An introduction to the BSC: www.youtube.com/watch?v=M_IlOlywryw. An excellent visual summary explaining the BSC and how it relates to business.

www.youtube.com/watch?v=cG9OO7KpSKs; www.youtube.com/watch?v=9V6u1qtsHaA: Watch these short video clips on what to consider when planning an evaluation, and some of the evaluation tools and approaches used in organisational settings.

10.9 References

Abdallah, A., Hegazy, I. R. and Amin, H. (2015) *An Investigation of the Effects of Balanced Scorecard (BSC) Implementation on Small and Medium Sized Enterprises (SMEs) Performance: Quantitative and Qualitative Approaches (A Case of Egypt)*. [Online] Available at: https://papers.ssrn.com/sol3/papers.cfm?abstract_id=3154266 (accessed 14 April 2023).

Amazon Web Services (2023) *Amazon QuickSight: Unified Business Intelligence at Hyperscale*. [Online] Available at: https://aws.amazon.com/quicksight/ (accessed 12 April 2023).

Awadallah, E. A. and Allam, A. (2015) 'A critique of the Balanced Scorecard as a performance measurement tool', *International Journal of Business and Social Science*, 6(7), 91–99.

Balanced Scorecard Institute (2022) *The Four Perspectives of the Balanced Scorecard*. [Online] Available at: https://balancedscorecard.org/bsc-basics/articles-videos/the-four-perspectives-of-the-balanced-scorecard/ (accessed 26 January 2023).

Bank One (2022) *How SMEs in Mauritius are Crucial to Building Back Better in the New Normal*. [Online] Available at: https://bankone.mu/en/how-smes-in-mauritius-are-crucial-tobuilding-back-better-in-the-new-normal/ (accessed 15 April 2023).

Booking.com (2023) *The Opportunity Centre*. [Online] Available at: https://partner.booking.com/en-gb/help/growing-your-business/increase-revenue/opportunity-centre (accessed 12 April 2023).

Choi, S. (2014) 'Path dependency and organizational change', *International Journal of Business Management and Research*, 4(1), 89–96.

Collins Dictionaries (2022) *Evaluate*. [Online] Available at: www.collinsdictionary.com/dictionary/english-thesaurus/evaluate#evaluate__1 (accessed 28 January 2023).

Dudic, Z., Dudic, B., Gregus, M., Novackova, D. and Djakovic, I. (2020) 'The innovativeness and usage of the Balanced Scorecard Model in SMEs', *Sustainability*, 12(8). [Online] Available at: https://www.mdpi.com/2071-1050/12/8/3221 (accessed 14 April 2023).

European Commission (2023) *SME Definition*. [Online] Available at: https://single-market-economy.ec.europa.eu/smes/sme-definition_en (accessed 10 April 2023).

Faye, I. and Goldblum, D. (2022) *Quest to Better Understand the Relationship between SME Finance and Job Creation: Insights from New Report*. [Online] Available at: https://blogs.worldbank.org/psd/quest-better-understand-relationship-between-sme-finance-and-job-creation-insights-new-report (accessed 15 April 2023).

Futcher, C. (2020) *How to Measure Change Management Effectiveness: Metrics, Tools & Processes*. [Online] Available at: https://info.cavendishwood.com/blog/how-to-measure-change-management-effectiveness-metrics-tools-processes (accessed 1 February 2023).

Kaplan, R. S. and McMillan, D. (2021) 'Reimagining the Balanced Scorecard for the ESG Era', *Harvard Business Review*. [Online] Available at: https://hbr.org/2021/02/reimagining-the-balanced-scorecard-for-the-esg-era (accessed 10 April 2023).

Kaplan, R. S. and Norton, D. P. (1992) 'The balanced scorecard: Measures that drive performance', *Harvard Business Review*, 70(1), 71–79.

Kaplan, R. S. and Norton, D. P. (1996a) *The Balanced Scorecard: Translating Strategy into Action*. Boston: Harvard Business School Press.

Kaplan, R. S. and Norton, D. P. (1996b) 'Using the balanced scorecard as a strategic management system', *Harvard Business Review*, 74(1), 75–85.

Makhijani, N. and Creelman, J. (2008) 'How leading organisations successfully implement corporate strategy with the balanced scorecard', *The OTI Thought Leadership Series*, 1(1).

Malagueño, R., Lopez-Valeiras, E. and Gomez-Conde, J. (2018) 'Balanced scorecard in SMEs: Effects on innovation and financial performance', *Small Business Economics*, 51, 221–244.

Tata Motors (2022) *TATA Motors 77th Integrated Annual Report 2021–22*. [Online] Available at: www.tatamotors.com/wp-content/uploads/2022/06/annual-report-2021-22.pdf (accessed 26 February 2023).

World Bank (2023) *Small and Medium Enterprises (SMEs) Finance*. [Online] Available at: https://www.worldbank.org/en/topic/smefinance (accessed 14 April 2023).

11

SUSTAINING CHANGE

Learning Outcomes

After completing this chapter, you should be able to:

- Develop a nuanced understanding of the notions of change sustainability and sustaining change and how to translate them into practice.
- Consider how the public discourse of sustainability has served to legitimise a multidimensional approach to organisational sustainability.
- Gain an understanding of how sustainability can be embedded into an organisation's value chain and discuss the key principles underpinning such an exercise.
- Consider a range of strategies that can be employed for effectively sustaining change.
- Appreciate how the seven-step framework developed in this chapter can be used as a practical guide to successfully sustain organisational change.

11.1 Introduction

The purpose of this chapter is to help you develop a sound understanding of the meanings and links between the discrete notions of change sustainability and sustaining change and what organisations can do to effectively translate both into practice. The chapter begins by drawing the distinction between change sustainability and sustaining change to foreground the inherent tension that lies at the core of change sustainability and underline the practical orientation of the process of sustaining change. The chapter then considers the impact of the wider public discourse of sustainability on business organisations and how it has served to legitimate a multidimensional approach to organisational sustainability. The chapter proceeds to show how sustainability can be embedded into an organisation's value chain, placing an emphasis on the key principles underpinning such an exercise. The chapter moves on to con-sider a range of practically oriented strategies that can be employed to sustain change, outlining their key features and purpose, methodologies and implications for sustaining change. The final section presents the conceptual nugget for this chapter which, in light of the preceding discussion, entails the development of a seven-step framework that provides concrete guidance on how to successfully sustain organisational change. The chapter concludes with a summary of the key learning points and a case study focusing on the application of simulation modelling as a driver of sustainability in a German multinational company operating in the building materials industry.

11.2 On change sustainability and sustaining change

The meanings attached to the discrete notions of change sustainability and sustaining change differ across contexts or domains of human activity and the links between the two tends to remain tenuous and ambiguous. For the sake of simplicity, we draw a fine line between the two concepts which we set out as a basic foundation for the following discussion.

Change sustainability

Most dictionary definitions of sustainability refer to it in the broadest of terms as to 'the ability to be maintained, upheld or supported, or to the capability of functioning or being continued at a certain level over time' (e.g. Cambridge Dictionary, 2022; Macmillan Dictionary, 2022). When applied to the context of organisational change, the term sustainability refers *to the ability of an organisation to maintain certain new processes, activities or ways of working to achieve certain desired outcomes over a specific period of time*. In this regard, sustainability implies a condition and includes a temporal element – i.e. *an ability to embed and stabilise new ways of working* over a specific length of time in order to achieve particular (and pre-determined) objectives.

However, this definition could be viewed as one-dimensional in that it reduces the meaning of sustainability to an ability to maintain and stabilise new ways of working – where the pursuit of sustainability can potentially lead to a 'freezing' or rigidifying of the organisation into a new status quo and to the creation of a situation where making more change becomes difficult, if not impossible. In short, if the meaning of sustainability is reduced to an ability to maintain and stabilise new ways of working, it can work against the possibility for further change.

Change sustainability could be interpreted as *the ability to sustain change* and keep the organisation in a 'state of unfreezing' – where on-going efforts are made to keep the organisation *open* to change and continuous improvement. From this particular perspective, change sustainability is primarily concerned with *maintaining the momentum of change* and *upholding the possibility* for further change. This is a view of change sustainability that tends to resonate more with those organisations that operate in fast-paced and hypercompetitive business contexts and that have to regularly undergo significant change in order to ensure their survival, continuity and growth (Struckman, 2021).

Reconciling inherent tensions

The fact is that in actual practice, organisations have to *grapple with and reconcile the inherent tensions that lie at the core of change sustainability* – where they have to both maintain and stabilise new ways of working for a set period in order to reap the desired benefits and continuously pursue performance improvements and implement innovative business models to stay ahead of the competition in their respective industries. For example, global IT company Apple (which is renowned for its capacity for rapid innovation) endeavours to effectively stabilise functional activities to optimise the production and delivery of new products and services. On the other hand, the company fosters cross-functional learning, knowledge transfer, and collaborative teamwork to continuously drive innovative change and the development of new products and services to sustain competitive advantage and business growth (Podolny and Hansen, 2020). As exemplified by Apple, we need to underline the fact that change sustainability is *contingent* – i.e. the way organisations reconcile the inherent tensions of change sustainability is dependent on their specific context and unique business needs.

Sustaining change

From our perspective, sustaining change is a *more practically oriented process* designed to optimise the ability of an organisation to manage sustainable change. As such, sustaining change involves a series of deliberate, *proactive steps* and responsibilities designed to optimise an organisation's ability to: (i) *embed and stabilise new ways of working* to achieve particular change objectives and (ii) *maintain the momentum of change* in the pursuit of continuous performance improvement and competitive advantage. Sustaining change is dependent upon a range of contextual factors and commitments which we will consider in more detail in the final section of this chapter.

—REFLECTIVE EXERCISE—

In light of the discussion in the above section, answer the questions below and carry out the exercise that follows.

1   What are the two key meanings that can be attached to the notion of change sustainability?
2   How can organisations reconcile the inherent tensions in pursuing change sustainability?
3   What is the difference between change sustainability and sustaining change?

11.3 The impact of the public discourse of sustainability on business organisations

It is now an established fact in the change literature that organisations do not operate in a vacuum but are in a symbiotic relationship with their external environment – where the way they interact with each other can be mutually reinforcing and beneficial. It is therefore important to consider how the increasing influential wider public discourse on sustainability has had a shaping influence on business organisations – and how business organisations are in return changing their understanding of and approach to sustainability to ensure good stewardship of their operating environments upon which their long-term survival and success depend.

Historical roots

The historical roots of the public discourse on sustainability can be traced back to environmental pressure groups and activists in the 1960s which began to make their voices heard on a much larger scale (Millar et al., 2012). More than a decade later, the first international conference on sustainability which was held in Stockholm in 1972, and the UN-commissioned Brundtland report which was put together later in 1987 brought the issue of sustainability into mainstream thinking and the public domain – touting it as a major concern that could seriously threaten the common future of planet Earth and the people within it (World Commission on Environment and Development, 1987). One of the most salient features of the Bruntland Report is how it has influenced global understanding of sustainability as a type of 'progress that meets the needs of the present without compromising the ability of future generations to meet their own needs' (ibid., pp. 489–490).

Impact on business organisations

This defining feature of sustainability has been criticised for being too broad, idealistic, disconnected with reality and a catalyst for disagreement (how can we even think about the needs of future generations when the current needs of so many people across the globe are barely met?) (e.g. see Daly, 1996). It did, however, serve as a starting point for an informed debate about how the sole pursuit of economic interests and production growth can rapidly sap the capacity of the natural environment to absorb the resulting pollution and to regenerate itself – leading to an increased pressure on business organisations to rethink and expand their approach to the issue of sustainability.

A multidimensional approach to managing change sustainability

Organisations began to endorse the now widely-held view that progress towards a more promising future requires a multidimensional understanding of sustainability in which attention is paid to social, environmental and cultural issues along with economic interests (Applebaum et al., 2016) – where economic viability, protection of the natural environment, social responsibility and enabling cultural value systems that support sustainable change are seen as interdependent, mutually reinforcing and are given equal weight in the move towards a more sustainable future. The diagram in Figure 11.1 below brings to attention the four dimensions of sustainability as a multidimensional concept and provides the parameters for a discussion of their implications for business organisations.

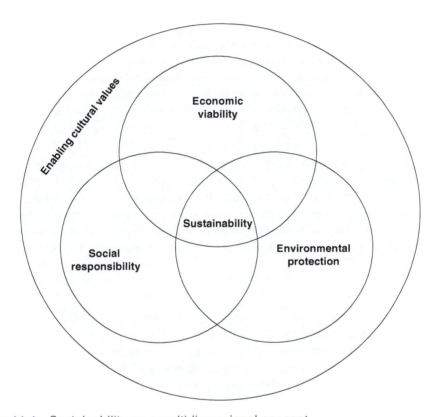

Figure 11.1   Sustainability as a multidimensional concept

Sources: Purvis et al. (2018); World Commission on Environment and Development (1987)

Economic viability

It is an undisputable fact that for any venture or project to be sustainable, it has to be economically viable – i.e. there is need to ensure that the costs and risks do not outweigh the benefits and that the financial returns and profits are high enough for it to survive and prosper in the longer term. Thus, from a sustainability standpoint, economic viability is a legitimate concern and has to be considered a strategic imperative – as long as it is not exploitive and achieved at the expense of less powerful stakeholder groups and the natural environment. To work towards sustainable economic viability, organisations have to pay close attention to issues such as cost effectiveness, the optimisation of productivity and profit, and savings or investments to ensure business continuity and, if desirable, growth.

Social responsibility

The social dimension of sustainability aims to achieve a desirable balance between economic interests and social responsibility. This means giving more weight to stakeholder engagement and integrating social values and objectives into business models and strategies. Nowadays, business organisations are much more conscious of the importance of creating social value and are taking a leading role in making a contribution to the well-being and quality of life of their stakeholders and to society at large. This can involve deploying HR policies that aim to foster caring and empowering working relationships in line with the principles of social justice and equity or abiding by the law and ethical standards when it comes to the rights, safety and expectations of customers and business partners.

In addition, many organisations are going beyond the law to demonstrate greater social responsibility by sponsoring charities or engaging in benevolent community projects that aim to alleviate extreme poverty and reduce 'social deficits' like unemployment and unequal access to education and healthcare. In making a strong case for the creation of social value, Porter and Kramer (2011) cite multiple examples of success stories. For instance, Cisco (a US technology company that sells networking products) which has, since its inception, provided free training to more than 5.5 million young people in 165 countries and as a result, managed to strengthen relations with business partners and governments around the world to significantly increase its global customer base – demonstrating in the process that being socially responsible does not necessarily involve a trade-off between the creation of economic value and social value and that businesses can generate profits from championing social causes.

Environmental protection

The environmental dimension of sustainability enjoins business organisations to 'go green' and demonstrate better stewardship of the natural environment whilst proactively contributing to its preservation, especially for the benefit of future generations. Environmental sustainability calls for closer monitoring of the polluting and destructive effects of business activities on the earth's natural ecosystems and taking swift corrective measures to maintain their regenerative capacity and ensure the survival of all the species which inhabit them.

Such measures can include reducing carbon emissions and waste resulting from the production process, investing in renewable energy and green technology, the timely replenishing of the natural resources used in manufacturing, and the development of biodegradable and responsibly sourced products in an attempt to preserve the biodiversity and regeneration of natural habitats (Spacey, 2019).

Enabling cultural values

This fourth dimension of sustainability calls for a shift in beliefs and core values 'in the way of doing things' – whereby sustainability issues and concerns are incorporated into business models, modes of governance and working practices across the whole organisation. This warrants a holistic understanding of how the three other dimensions of sustainability discussed above are interdependent, mutually beneficial and locked in a virtuous cycle – where economic success, social progress and good stewardship of the natural environment go hand-in-hand and serve to reinforce each other.

Once again, skim read and reflect on the key issues arising from the preceding discussion and answer the following questions:

1   What are key dimensions of the concept of sustainability?
2   What challenges might business organisations have to face in adopting a multidimensional approach to sustainability?

11.4 Embedding sustainability in the value chain

Grappling with the multiple dimensions of sustainability can be a real challenge as it involves a wide array of variables that can prove quite difficult to manage. Moreover, for a multidimensional approach to sustainability to work, there is need for a type of radical, mindset-altering type of change that requires a major adjustment in the core values, strategic orientation and (often well-entrenched) operations to which few organisations are willing or even able to commit (e.g. see Adams and McNicholas, 2007).

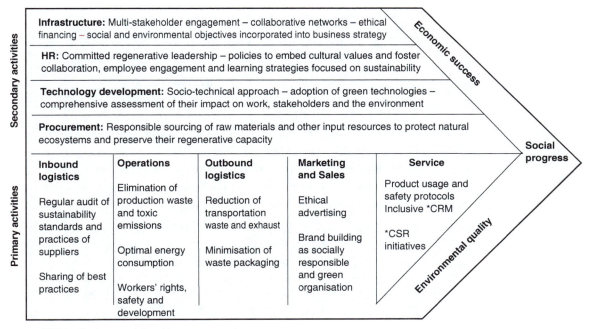

*CRM – Customer relationship management
*CSR – Corporate social responsibility

Figure 11.2   Embedding sustainability in the value chain

Source: Adapted from Porter, M. E. (1985) *The Competitive Advantage: Creating and Sustaining Superior Performance*. New York: Free Press.

However, sustainability is now considered a strategic imperative and a policy matter that organisations cannot ignore. Recent studies in the area suggest that organisations – whether it be commercial enterprises or those operating in the public sector – are proactively taking steps to move towards a *More Sustainability Oriented State* (MSOS) (e.g. see Adams and McNicholas, 2007; Lozano, 2018; Lozano and Garcia, 2020). Such a move requires a holistic approach whereby sustainability issues and concerns can be incorporated into the organisation's value chain, as shown in Figure 11.2.

Figure 11.2 is a modification of Porter's notion of the value chain which he first introduced in 1985 in his book on creating and achieving competitive advantage. As can be seen from the figure, the value chain consists of multiple stages and a set of interrelated activities through which a company creates value in manufacturing a product or performing a service for its target customers.

The value chain includes five primary activities:

- Inbound logistics: the management of raw materials and other 'input resources' from external suppliers.

- Operations: production processes that transform input resources into products and services that are valued by customers and that are designed to generate a profit.

- Outbound logistics: the delivery of products and services to customers through various transportation methods.

- Marketing and sales: activities such as advertising, brand-building, sales of goods and services.

- *Service*: activities such as after-sales service, product support and building long-term relationships with the customer base.

Secondary activities have a vital role in supporting primary activities. They include:

- *Infrastructure*: the mode of governance, structures, relational networks, financial commitments, quality standards that provide the foundation for all work activities, production process and engagement with stakeholders.

- *HR*: the effective management of human capital including activities such as employee training and engagement, supporting learning and knowledge transfer and upholding the core values of the organisation.

- *Technology development*: activities relating to the application of current and new technologies, research and development and IT management.

- *Procurement*: activities including purchasing of materials from external suppliers, managing supplier relationships and negotiating prices to achieve cost effectiveness.

A recalibration of value chain activities

As previously mentioned, what has been done in Figure 11.2 is a recalibration of the various activities described above to embed sustainability issues and concerns into the value chain and make them an integral part of the work routines and day-to-day processes and practices of an organisation. As Figure 11.2 is largely descriptive, we will focus here on the key principles that underpin it.

A holistic approach

Sustainability change warrants a holistic, system-wide approach – calling for a planned integration of social and environmental objectives into the business strategy and a robust alignment between the primary and secondary activities relating to sustainability. There is also a need for clear linkages between the various stages and elements of the production process, keeping in mind the triple bottom lines of economic success, social progress and environmental quality.

A democratic mode of governance

Sustainability change calls for an essentially democratic mode of governance that engages multiple stakeholders, facilitates open communication, and creates an inclusive and empowering space for partnerships and collaborative projects to maintain change momentum towards a more sustainable future for both the organisation and the community it serves.

A humanistic perspective

Sustainability change success is very much dependent on a humanistic perspective which supports the principles of humanism and exercises a duty of care to human beings, giving prime importance to their well-being, development and flourishing. In this case, this means effectively addressing the human dimension of the value chain and doing everything in one's power to support, motivate and empower stakeholders to effectively contribute to sustainability initiatives (Stoughton and Ludema, 2012).

A socio-technical approach

Sustainability change warrants a socio-technical approach demonstrated by the adoption of green technologies moderated by a comprehensive assessment of their potential impact on things such as job security, the effectiveness of the human–machine interface, the quality of working life, product/service delivery and consumption patterns, the health and safety of customers and of the wider public, and the preservation of the natural environment.

A commitment to continuous improvement

Finally, sustainability change calls for a commitment to continuous improvement across the value chain – which is vital to the maintenance of a healthy balance between the desired economic, social and environmental outcomes over time. To this effect, change leaders and managers need to proactively seek ways to enhance the sustainability elements and systems in the value chain (identified in Figure 11.2) and consolidate the links between them. It is by being embedded into the value chain on a continuous basis that sustainability can become etched into the organisation's DNA and an integral part of organisational change management.

—CASE STUDY 11.1—

IKEA: A trendsetter in sustainability change

Introduction

While some business leaders might see sustainability as a drain on resources, contributing very little to the bottom line and so hardly worth the investment, IKEA is taking a leading role in embedding sustainability in its value chain as a major driver of competitive advantage and long-term business success. IKEA is a Swedish multinational conglomerate offering a wide range of furniture, housing, food and other homeware products in more than 455 stores worldwide. However, the company is best known for its flat-pack, ready-to-assemble furniture which is its trademark and which is defined by its modern look, simplicity, affordable cost and eco-friendly features.

Sustainability as an integral part of IKEA's value chain

Over the past decade, the organisation has found a way to leverage sustainability across its value chain which is closely monitored by its Strategic Sustainability Council. At the production stage of its value chain, IKEA's products are designed to be both affordable and environmentally friendly. For example, the company uses particle boards (an alternative to solid wood which is manufactured from wood chips and synthetic resin) to not only reduce production costs but also to reduce deforestation and its negative impact on ecosystems and climate change.

With regard to upstream value chain activities, IKEA sources its materials only from suppliers who are committed to sustainability and demonstrate good stewardship of the environment. In the same spirit, IKEA has set in motion a supplier programme which will enable its 1,600 suppliers to use renewable electricity for their own production processes. This is in sync with IKEA's long-term sustainability strategy which aims by 2030 to transform the organisation into an 'energy-independent, circular business built on clean, renewable energy and regenerative resources' (Asad, 2021, p. 1).

IKEA also pays close attention to downstream value chain activities to find innovative ways to drive its sustainability strategy. For example, the company has eliminated packaging for many of its products and encourages its customers to pick up their purchases themselves (and where possible, using public transport) to reduce manufacturing waste and curb carbon emissions caused by shipping and heavy transport vehicles. IKEA has also been quite inventive in exercising a duty of care towards its customers. The company has expanded its product portfolio to offer 'flat-pack' houses and apartments at affordable prices for first-time buyers and solar panel systems to promote a clean, emissions-free and renewable energy source whilst making healthy and sustainable living more attractive and accessible.

Moreover, IKEA stores have play areas supervised by dedicated staff where parents can safely drop off their children while they are doing their shopping. More recently, during the COVID-19 pandemic, IKEA set up new services such as 'drive-through click-and-collect' and contactless deliveries for safer shopping. The company also launched a 'renewed' version of its '**augmented reality**' app (originally introduced in 2017) in France and the Netherlands in early 2019 before rolling it out globally to all its markets. The 'renewed' app enables customers using an Android or IOS device to visualise how IKEA products would fit into their homes and, unlike the original app, allows them to order their chosen items through that app without having to visit any store.

Conclusion

IKEA can be considered a real trendsetter in leveraging the value chain for effective sustainability change. Importantly, the company has shown how this can be achieved through the development of eco-friendly production processes, collaborative partnerships, customer-oriented technological applications and growth strategies that aim to create not only business value but also social and environmental value – which is why IKEA can be cited as an exemplar of sustainability change and a source of inspiration for other companies worldwide.

Sources: Asad (2021); Ikea (2022); Kaye (2013); Serafeim (2020)

Questions

1   Why do you think IKEA chose to go down the sustainability route instead of pursuing a strategy solely focused on economic success?
2   How did IKEA manage to link activities across its value chain to effectively implement its sustainability agenda?
3   Do you think every company has to make sustainability an integral part of their change strategy?

11.5 Strategies for sustaining change

As explained in the introductory section, sustaining change has more to do with practical steps to optimise an organisation's ability to both *embed and stabilise* new ways of working and *sustain change* in the pursuit of continuous performance improvement and competitive advantage. In this section we consider a range of change strategies that can be employed to sustain change. While a more detailed discussion of the change strategies considered below is beyond the scope of this textbook, we will, for the sake of brevity and relevance, keep the focus on their most salient features that make them amenable to sustaining change. Table 11.1 provides a broad overview of the change strategies which are explained in more detail in the following discussion.

Table 11.1 Strategies for sustaining change

Strategies for sustaining change	Key features and purposes	Methodology	Implications for sustaining change
Action Research	- Participatory process of inquiry (involving collaboration between professional researchers and active participants of client organisation) - Aims to generate practical solutions to pressing problems to benefit organisations and wider communities.	*Key stages:* - Problem identification - Problem diagnosis - Action planning - Implementation - Evaluation	- Robust understanding of pressing problems impacting organisational capacity to sustain change. - Collaborative approach to the development of practical solutions. - Stakeholder commitment and ownership of activities designed to sustain change.
Appreciative Inquiry	- Collaborative approach to change - Focuses on best practices and positive, life-enriching properties of the organisation.	*4D Model:* - Discover - Dream - Design - Deploy	- Focus on best practices across the value chain to enable a positive approach to sustaining change. - Facilitation of participation and dialogue to achieve consensus and embed best practices. - Collective learning and experimentation to leverage creativity and innovation and demonstrate commitment to continuous improvement.
Communities of Practice	- Informal groups of employees bound by shared interest and expertise - Focus on collaborative problem-solving, professional development and practical solutions.	*Key steps:* - Define domain of interest - Maintain enabling conditions for collective learning - Apply learning to real-life situations - Evaluate practical impact of learning	- Empowering platform for professional development and building organisational capacity for sustaining change. - Cross-functional expertise and linkages between value chain activities to allow for concerted approach to sustaining change. - Proactive support of learning and creativity, enhanced employee engagement and commitment vital to continuous performance improvement.

Strategies for sustaining change	Key features and purposes	Methodology	Implications for sustaining change
Simulation Modelling	- Enables an in-depth causal analysis of the organisation as a complex system - Allows for collaborative, experimental approach to learning and strategic change	*Key phases:* - Modelling - Simulation - Evaluation	- Systemic approach to sustaining change. - Safe environment for experimentation with alternative scenarios and strategic options to sustain change progress. - Collaborative approach to learning to leverage knowledge base and muster employee commitment to change. - More productive and innovative ways of working to sustain performance improvements and change progress.

Action research

Action Research (hereinafter, AR) was developed in the 1940s by Kurt Lewin. It involves a participatory process of inquiry (usually with professional researchers and active participants of the client organisation) that aims to generate practical solutions to 'issues of pressing concern' that can have a significant impact on organisational processes and performance (Reason and Bradbury, 2001, p. 1).

The methodology used in AR involves the following key stages:

i   *Problem identification* – collaboration between researcher and active participants of the client organisation to identify pressing problems and their focal points.
ii *Problem diagnosis* – use of sound research methods to identify causes underlying identified problems and formulate practical solutions.
iii *Action planning* – development of an action plan to implement practical solution.
iv *Implementation of action plan* – execution of action plan.
v   *Evaluation* – assessment of progress at key milestones of the implementation, leading to next cycle of AR (Hayes, 2021).

Implications for sustaining change

AR combines research expertise and insider knowledge and draws on sound research methods to:

i   Enable a robust understanding of the root causes of problems that can potentially constrain organisational capacity for sustaining change.
ii Allow for a collaborative approach to the development of practical solutions that reflect stakeholder input and are enriched by multiple perspectives.
iii Serve, by virtue of its participative nature, to build stakeholder commitment and promote greater ownership of activities designed to sustain change.

Appreciative inquiry

Appreciative Inquiry (hereinafter, AI) emerged from the collaborative work between the department of organisational behaviour at Case Western Reserve University and a healthcare organisation in Cleveland, Ohio (Bushe, 2012). While AI was at first simply viewed as a research method, it is now widely acknowledged as a proper process model for transformational change.

Instead of dwelling on the negative, dysfunctional and deficient aspects of organisational practice, AI gives primacy to a form of participative inquiry that focuses on the positive and life-enriching properties of the organisation. To this effect, AI advocates an approach to change through which the organisation can appreciate itself as a positive, affirmative force for change and investigate ways to leverage what it does best to re-imagine and re-construct a better future – hence, the term *appreciative inquiry* (e.g. see Cooperrider et al., 1995; Elliott, 1999).

Although there is some variation in ways to translate AI into practice, the initial methodology designed by its leading proponents – the 4-D model – includes the following steps:

i   *Discover*: identifying the current organisational practices that work well and that can be extrapolated to build a more positive and promising future.
ii *Dream*: envisioning (through sharing both past and present success stories and positive experiences) what would work well in the future and tracing the path for an ideal future state for the organisation.
iii *Design*: co-constructing the future through dialogue and achieving consensus around a plan to deliver the dream.
iv *Deploy*: implementing the design through collective learning and experimentation.

(Bushe, 2012; Cooperrider and Srivastva, 1987)

Implications for sustaining change

With regard to sustaining change AI can enable a qualitative, collaborative investigation to:

i   Focus on the best practices across the organisation's value chain and enable a positive approach to sustaining change.
ii Facilitate participation and dialogue as a means of achieving consensus and engaging employees in embedding best practices and sustaining the momentum of change.
iii Foster collective learning and experimentation to leverage creativity and innovation and translate into practice a commitment to continuous improvement.

Communities of practice

Communities of Practice (hereinafter, CoPs) has been defined as 'groups of people [who are] informally bound together by shared expertise and passion for a joint enterprise' and who are committed to practical outcomes (Wenger and Snyder, 2000, p. 139). The main characteristics of CoP include the following:

i   Members of a CoP are brought together by a common interest in a particular domain of knowledge or area of organisational functioning to which they feel they can make a contribution whilst progressing their own learning and development (Lave and Wenger, 1991).
ii Although informal and not subject to close supervision, CoPs nevertheless need full management support and access to appropriate resources.
iii Participation in CoPs is mainly through self-selection, where members usually join the group or are brought into the fold by another member based on their interests or learning needs. CoPs are also open to external stakeholders, especially those whose specialist knowledge is of particular relevance to the community's domain of interest.
iv CoPs do not have to be conducted face-to-face as they can be carried out online or through a hybrid mix of both forms of interaction to accommodate office-based, remotely located and mobile members (Kietzman et al., 2013).

v   CoPs are meant to be organic and free-flowing in order to provide a psychologically safe and mutually supportive space for knowledge exchange and social learning.

Given their highly informal nature, CoPs tend to follow the steps outlined below to optimise their effectiveness:

i   Define the domain of interest and clarify the scope of activities, learning objectives and practical outcomes.

ii   Maintain enabling conditions for collective learning and a collaborative approach to problem solving, professional development and the generation of creative practical solutions.

iii   Apply learning to real-life situations.

iv   Develop soft yet compelling evaluative measures to demonstrate practical impact of learning at individual, functional and organisational levels.

(Wenger and Snyder, 2000)

Implications for sustaining change

CoPs can be powerful tools for sustaining change in that:

i   They provide an empowering platform for professional development and building skills and competences that can augment the organisation's capacity for sustaining change.

ii   They can serve to break down organisational silos, combine expertise from across functional areas and bridge value chain activities to allow for a concerted approach to problem solving and the development of practical solutions that can in turn serve to sustain the momentum of change.

iii   They proactively support learning and creativity whilst enhancing employee engagement and commitment which is vital to continuous performance improvement.

CASE STUDY 11.2

GSK Consumer Healthcare: Exploring the possibility of a Community of Practice in sustaining innovative change

Introduction

In 2019, GlaxoSmithKline (GSK) and Pfizer merged their customer healthcare divisions to create the world's largest consumer healthcare company – operating under the name GSK Consumer Healthcare (GSKCH). As a newly merged company, GSKCH has an impressive product portfolio combining well-known brands such as Sensodyne, Voltaren, Advil and Centrum which have leadership market positions in oral health, pain relief and vitamins. GSKCH has 25,000 associates working in over 100 countries and its strategic objective is to drive growth with a focus on core products in key markets and putting customers at the heart of the company's operating model.

Community of Practice in a chaotic situation

COVID-19 ushered in a chaotic situation for GSKCH and members of the newly merged organisation who had to work remotely were not able to meet face-to-face. Project managers typically have a scientific background and have considerable experience in R&D activities relating to clinical issues, supply chain management, legal matters, marketing, team working and managing people at various organisational levels. Therefore, the role of project managers was seen as critical to the successful implementation of GSKCH's growth strategy. One of the senior directors of GSKCH put forward a proposal to create a virtual Community of Practice for R&D project managers which would enable them to look beyond the chaotic situation brought about by COVID-19 and adopt a collaborative approach to sustaining innovative change and driving the organisation towards its strategic goals.

A self-organising global community of project managers

The purpose of the Community of Practice was clear and straightforward: to bring together a self-organising band of R&D project managers from around the world in an informal, safe and empowering virtual space – where they could 'establish a team identity, share the passion for their work and participate in an exchange of skills to build capability, reduce frustration and improve motivation' (Cairns-Lee and Turpin, 2022, pp. 7–8). The Community of Practice would also serve to break down silos and overcome cultural differences whilst creating a team spirit among project managers vital to collaborative learning, problem solving and generating practical solutions.

Mixed reactions

The decision to set up a Community of Practice for global R&D project managers was met with mixed reactions. Some of them thought that setting up a community of practice was a good idea but not a top priority, given the many other challenges facing the company. Others found the 'softer aspects' of Communities of Practice valuable in enabling colleagues to meet, share experiences and contribute to the formation of a positive culture. Many of the project managers showed no particular reaction and their silence was difficult to interpret. Moreover, the challenges of having to work from home because of COVID-19 with little organisational support whilst struggling to strike a balance between work commitments and family life were proving to be too overwhelming for project managers to fully engage in a Community of Practice.

Conclusions

GSKCH's attempt to build a Community of Practice brings to attention an important issue. While there seems to be an increasing recognition of the potential benefits of Communities of Practice in sustaining innovative change, there are some significant structural and social barriers that stand in the way of its effective implementation. Even if the situation at GSKCH was at the time compounded by the COVID-19 outbreak, the case study suggests

(Continued)

that there are still some potential pitfalls that change agents have to contend with when implementing communities of practice – even in a post-COVID world as businesses begin to adjust to the 'new normal'.

Questions

1   What was the rationale underpinning the proposal to build a Community of Practice for R&D project managers at GSKCH?
2   How did the project managers react to the proposal?
3   What do you think are the potential pitfalls that change agents have to contend with when implementing Communities of Practice?

Simulation modelling

Simulation modelling (hereinafter, SM) originated from the work of renowned American systems scientist Jay Wright Forrester in the late 1950s (Größler et al., 2008). A key tool used in computer-assisted systems analysis and design, SM can be construed as a stand-alone process requiring a clear set of principles and steps that can enable an in-depth analysis of a complex system and causal relationships between its interrelated parts (e.g. see Fowler, 2003; Sterman, 2001). As such, SM can enable the following:

i   A robust analysis of the causal relationships between the key variables of a system which are necessary for its proper functioning – which in the case of an organisation-as-system can include, among other things, strategic objectives, environmental factors, available resources, production processes, technological applications, employee relations, customer base, business partnerships, etc.

ii   An experimental approach to change in a safe, virtual environment – where change agents can employ a range of appropriate simulation software to try and test their business models and predict the outcomes of change strategies before deploying them in real-life situations.

iii   A solid evidential base for informed decision-making and strategic choices. The predictive features of SM means that it can be used in scenario planning to consider the outcomes of alternative strategic routes and get a sense of where such routes might lead to in the foreseeable future.

iv   A collaborative approach to change, drawing on the combined knowledge and expertise of participants across functional areas.

v   An experimental approach to learning through trial and error, learning and unlearning, and the exploration of more productive and innovative ways of working.

The process of SM involves the following key phases:

i   *Modelling*: selecting participants with specialist expertise and identification of key variables to be 'input' into the simulation model.
ii *Simulation*: running of simulation, allowing for the testing of alternative strategic choices and courses of action.
iii *Evaluation*: assessing simulation outputs to validate or adjust simulation model in view of desired outcomes.

(See Luna-Reyes et al., 2006; Rouwette et al., 2000).

Implications for sustaining change

SM can act as a lever for sustaining change in that:

i   It allows for a systemic approach to change – enabling an in-depth understanding of the complex web of variables and causal relationships that underlie the change process and can have a significant influence on its outcomes.
ii It provides a safe environment for experimenting with alternative scenarios and strategic options that can clear a progression path for change and increase the likelihood of achieving its desired outcomes.
iii Like the other strategies for sustaining change discussed above, it enables a collaborative approach to learning and experimentation as a means of leveraging the knowledge base of the organisation whilst mustering employee commitment to change goals and objectives.
iv It can generate more productive and innovative ways of working to sustain performance improvements and change progress.

PRACTICAL EXERCISE

Read through this section and fill in Table 11.2 to compare and contrast the key features of the change strategies considered in this chapter which will help you appreciate their similarities and differences.

Table 11.2 Comparative analysis of change strategies for sustaining change

Key feature	Action Research	Appreciative Inquiry	Communities of Practice	Simulation Modelling
Approach to change				
Nature of participation				
Approach to problem diagnosis				
Technological support				

(Continued)

Key feature	Action Research	Appreciative Inquiry	Communities of Practice	Simulation Modelling
Commitment to practical outcomes				
Approach to evaluation				
Impact on sustaining change				

11.6 Conceptual nugget: A seven-step practical framework for sustaining change

In light of what has been covered in the preceding discussion, our conceptual nugget for this chapter entails the development of a seven-step practical framework for sustaining change – which is presented in Table 11.3 below. The key features of the framework and the principles regarding its application are explained in the following discussion.

Table 11.3 Seven-step practical framework for sustaining change

Seven-step practical framework for sustaining change	
1. Plan for sustaining change	- Connect with the wider sustainability discourse and reach consensus on organisational bottom lines - Develop an actionable plan for sustaining change as an integral part of change strategy - Identify potential threats to sustaining change - Commit resources to sustaining change
2. Take ownership of the process for sustaining change	Change leaders to: - Demonstrate commitment to sustaining change - Role-model behaviours to drive change forward and prevent regression to old ways of doing things - Build powerful coalitions to sustain the momentum of change
3. Evaluate change progress	- Adopt a collaborative approach to evaluating change - Conduct evaluation at regular intervals and different levels of analysis with appropriate evaluative tools and measures - Identify success and positive results in line with strategic goals and objectives - Identify failures and analyse their root causes - Identify key performance indicators and best practices to sustain performance improvement

Seven-step practical framework for sustaining change	
4. Communicate change progress	- Communicate change progress clearly and widely on a continuous basis - Make evaluation outputs visible via effective channels and media - Ensure transparency in reporting both successes and failures - Encourage employee feedback and participation in making sense of evaluation outputs as a catalyst for follow-up action
5. Manage emergent resistance	Line managers and supervisors to: - Manage fear, anxiety, cynicism and other sources of stress and discomfort arising from the implementation of the change initiative - Provide coaching, mentoring, counselling and other appropriate support mechanisms to help employees adapt to new ways of working and performance standards - Draw on good experiences and 'change wins' to increase employee motivation and engagement and uphold performance levels
6. Build capacity for sustaining change	- Develop plan and commit resources for further change - Provide training and mentorship to build skills and competences and enable continuous performance improvement - Foster employee self-development and ownership of change - Establish collaborative partnerships to harness learning, creativity and innovation in order to sustain change
7. Establish a sustainability culture	- Define success and reward change wins - Develop ability to learn from mistakes and failures - Embed best practices and habits for sustaining change as the 'new normal' - Establish a commitment to sustaining change as one of the core values of the organisation

Since the framework in Table 11.3 is largely descriptive in terms of activities involved at each of its key steps, we will focus here on its key features and the principles underpinning it.

Connecting with the public discourse on sustainability

First, the framework locates the organisation within its external environment and connects the planning stage of the process for sustaining change with the wider public discourse on sustainability – where change leaders have to reach consensus on its impact on organisational bottom lines and make an informed decision about the type of activities that will need to be sustained with regard to the organisation's responsibilities in creating economic, social and environmental value.

Planning and taking ownership

The framework also underlines the importance of developing a clear, actionable plan for sustaining change *prior to* its implementation and pitches this particular activity as an integral part of the change strategy. It also leaves no doubt as to the responsibility of change leaders to take ownership of the process for sustaining change and prevent the loss of change gains and regression to old ways of working or what has been referred to as change decay.

Adopting a collaborative approach to evaluating change progress

The framework reinforces the need for a collaborative and level-of-analysis approach to evaluating change progress – with an emphasis on the need to choose the right evaluative tools and measures, objectively take stock of successes and failures, and identify key performance indicators and best practices to sustain performance improvement.

Treating communication as king

The framework treats communication as king in the process of sustaining change – underlining the need for clear, organisation-wide and two-way communication via effective channels between change leaders and employees. It also advocates honesty and transparency in the reporting of both successes and failures as a precondition for effective follow-up action – whether it be rewarding and consolidating change 'wins' or taking timely corrective measures.

Managing emergent resistance and building capacity for sustaining change

The framework places the onus on line managers and supervisors to manage emergent forms of resistance – i.e. those arising from the process of sustaining change itself and which could not necessarily have been anticipated at the planning stage, as a means of upholding employee motivation, commitment and performance levels. It also stresses the importance of building organisational capacity for sustaining change through the provision of appropriate training, collaborative partnerships and other learning support mechanisms to foster employee self-development and ownership of change, and harness creativity and innovation in driving change.

Establishing a sustainability culture

The framework calls to the attention of change leaders the importance of establishing a sustainability culture by integrating sustainability issues and concerns into the organisation's everyday routines and activities and embedding best practices and habits for sustaining change as the norm. It also calls for the need to clearly define and reward success and develop an ability to learn from mistakes and failures as a form of resilience which is vital in sustaining the momentum of change. Lastly, establishing a sustainability culture warrants a change in not only structures and processes but also a shift in the predominant mode of thinking and behaviour that translate a commitment to sustaining change as one of the core values of the organisation.

Reconciling tensions

Finally, the framework speaks to the ability of the organisation in sustaining change to reconcile the tensions between the need to embed and stabilise new ways of working over a set period of time to reap the intended benefits of change and the need to continuously pursue performance improvements and sustain competitive advantage – an exercise which, it has to be said, is contingent and therefore dependent upon the variables at play within the specific context of the organisation.

CASE STUDY 11.3

Sustaining change: Tata Steel's Shikhar25 programme

Applying the seven-step practical framework for sustaining change

Introduction

Tata Steel Limited (TSL), founded in 1907 in Jamshedpur, India is the tenth largest steel producer in the world. The company has a consolidated turnover of US $32,836 million and employs over 65,000 people across five continents (2022). While TSL sources its raw materials from India and Canada, its manufacturing and downstream activities are spread across India, the UK, the Netherlands and Thailand. In 2014, when global steel prices fell by 30%, Tata Steel's profits went down by approximately 25%, prompting the company to launch an ambitious change programme, called Shikhar25.

Thinking beyond short-term fixes

While recognising the fact that the industry in which it operates has its ups and downs, top management felt it was time for the company to shape its own destiny and build the capacity to enhance and sustain TSL's profitability. Top management's priority was to steer clear of quick, short-term fixes and Shikhar25 was touted as a form of transformational change that would require a radical reorganisation of working practices and that would be driven by clear targets and evaluative measures focusing on quality improvements, cost reductions, process efficiency and sustainable profits.

Implementing Shikhar25

To ensure the success of Shikhar25, top management wanted every employee across the company to be actively involved in its implementation. Emphasis was placed on the need for everybody to own and drive the change initiative to effectively achieve the desired outcomes.

This is because top management realised that for Shikhar25 to work, they would need to loosen supervisory control, increase employee autonomy and establish a mode of governance that prioritised action over monitoring.

Effective communication was also seen as critical to the success of Shikhar25. To this effect, Impact Centres were set up in each operating unit, led by the unit's head. These

(Continued)

centres allowed middle managers to set their own goals, make decisions, and monitor progress, rather than rely on directives from top management. To facilitate yet ensure the quality of decision-making at point of need, the company adopted a colour-coded, *stage-gate system* – where every key decision and change-related project had to progress through each of the stages, namely, ideation, implementation, promoting efficient execution and impact tracking.

Planning for the long term

To facilitate innovative projects in the future, top management think it is important to further develop capability for change management at senior management level – especially with regard to risk taking, motivating employees and coping with failures. Much thought is also being given to how to sustain the creation of generated value by upskilling the entire workforce and providing them with further training in digital technologies such as AI and machine learning which they have already started to use during the implementation of Shikhar25.

TSL is also experimenting with **digital twin technology** which allows for the digital replication of real-world physical objects like products, processes and systems for practical purposes such as running simulations, monitoring and maintenance, and process integration. Digital twin technology will enable shop floor managers and operators to not only monitor and improve TSL's manufacturing processes but also predict product performance and train young engineers – as a way of enhancing TSL's digital capabilities in view of its commitment to continuous improvement and sustainable profitability.

Source: Narendran and Ganeriwalla (2020)

Activity

Apply the seven-step framework in Table 11.3 to assess TSL's approach to sustaining change. Use Table 11.4 to record the details of your assessment against each of the seven steps of the framework.

Table 11.4 Assessment of TSL's approach to sustaining change

Assessing TSL's approach to sustaining change	
1. Plan for sustaining change	
2. Take ownership of the process for sustaining change	
3. Evaluate change progress	
4. Communicate change progress	
5. Manage emergent resistance	
6. Build capacity for sustaining change	
7. Establish a sustainability culture	

11.7 Key learning points

The key learning points arising from this chapter are as follows:

1   In managing sustainable change, organisations have to reconcile the inherent tensions that lie at the core of change sustainability, where they have to both *maintain and stabilise* new ways of working for a set period of time in order to reap the desired benefits and *continuously pursue* performance improvements and innovation to stay ahead of the competition in their respective industries. Sustaining change, on the other hand, is a *practically oriented process* which involves a series of deliberate, *proactive steps* and responsibilities designed to optimise an organisation's ability for effectively managing sustainable change.

2   The *wider public discourse* on sustainability has had a *shaping influence* on business organisations, leading to a multidimensional approach to managing change sustainability – where *economic viability, social responsibility, protection of the natural environment*, and the *enabling cultural value systems* that support sustainable change are seen as interdependent, mutually reinforcing and given equal weight in the move towards a more sustainable future.

3   To become a more sustainability-oriented business organisations need to *recalibrate their value-chain activities* to make sustainability issues and concerns an integral part of their work routines and day-to-day processes and practices. The key principles underpinning this exercise include: the need for a *holistic, system-wide approach*, a *democratic mode of governance*, a *humanistic perspective*, a *socio-technical perspective* and a *commitment to continuous improvement*.

4   The strategies for 'sustaining sustainability change' that were considered in this chapter include: *action research, appreciative inquiry, communities of practice* and *simulation modelling*. Attention was given to their respective key features and purposes, methodology and how they can serve as a lever for a collaborative, creative and proactive approach to sustaining change.

5   Finally, the conceptual nugget for this chapter entails the development of a framework which consists of a set of seven practical and proactive steps to effectively sustain change. The key principles underpinning it include: a need to *connect change efforts* with the *wider public discourse on sustainability*; the need for an *actionable plan for sustaining change* and for *change leaders to take ownership* of the process for sustaining change; the need for a *collaborative approach to evaluation*; the need for *effective communication* in the reporting of change progress; the need to *manage emergent resistance* and *building capacity for sustaining change*; the need to *establish a sustainability culture* and to effectively *reconcile the tensions* arising from the necessity of stabilising new ways of working and pursuing continuous performance improvements and competitive advantage.

Simulation modelling as a driver of sustainability change at BuildCo

Introduction

BuildCo is a multi-billion-dollar business operating in the building materials industry. Over the past two decades, the company has grown substantially through numerous acquisitions. It now employs around 40,000 people with production facilities and large sales networks on every continent. Its pole position in many segments of the building materials market (such as drywalls, insulation or ceilings) has allowed BuildCo to command premium prices and realise considerable profit margins, resulting in rapid growth and the consolidation of its position as a global market leader. Alongside its success in the building materials industry, BuildCo has capitalised on the growing global demand for new energy-efficient housing and flexible commercial spaces, which have become a popular alternative to traditional buildings that are heavily reliant on the large-scale extraction (and depletion) of natural resources and low-cost, non-renewable energies.

Emergence of sustainability as a strategic priority

Recently, incorporating sustainability into the strategic agenda has become a priority for BuildCo. The key external factors triggering this change in strategic orientation include:

i   Solid evidence of the 'hidden costs' and environmental impact of traditional construction methods which can have a negative bearing on the economic interests of key industry players.

ii   An increasing demand for greener and more socially inclusive housing conditions – especially from younger generations who have a sharp 'ecological conscience' having been sensitised from an early age, primarily through social media, to the importance of being more socially and environmentally responsible.

iii   A push by governments and other pressure groups towards sustainable development with an emphasis on energy efficiency and renewal, the protection of natural resources and the adoption of greener technologies.

These external drivers of change were compounded by the sharp rise in oil and gas price levels because of the war in Ukraine which has dramatically affected the energy-intensive building materials industry's cost structures. Despite its strong past performance and success, the time seems ripe for BuildCo to recalibrate its strategy to effectively respond to these external change drivers and demonstrate a commitment to sustainability change to retain its competitive position as a market leader and ensure the company's future success.

A multidimensional approach to sustainability change

BuildCo is becoming increasingly aware of the need for a multidimensional approach to sustainability change and for significant investments in each of its key dimensions: **environmental protection**, **social responsibility** and **economic viability**. Figure 11.3 maps out the interrelationships between these key dimensions and the potential impact of their combined effects on the effectiveness of sustainability change at BuildCo.

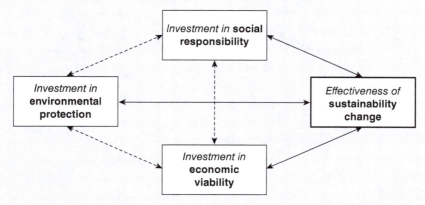

Figure 11.3 Mapping out the multidimensional approach to sustainability change at BuildCo

BuildCo's investment in *environmental protection* is to enable the redesign of its entire production process – from planning and design through operations to marketing and delivery – the aim of which is to allow for a shift to renewable energies, recycled products and a reduction of toxic waste.

The company's investment in *social responsibility* is focused on the provision of training programmes for all employees, the development of collaborative partnerships with local communities, and the promotion of learning, creativity and innovation to drive sustainability change that can benefit all key stakeholders and society at large.

In terms of investment in *economic viability*, BuildCo aims for a complete revision of its value chain activities to eliminate sources of waste, reduce operation costs and optimise efficiency, performance and productivity. To this effect, BuildCo digitalised its entire value chain through the application of a new Building Information Management System (BIMS) which is designed to rationalise the procurement of eco-friendly materials, adopt an innovative yet inexpensive approach to product design and manufacturing through the use of 3-D modelling tools, and streamline delivery and after-sales services.

Simulation modelling as a driver of sustainability change

Ensuring that these investments have a positive long-term impact remains a major challenge – and this is why BuildCo has decided to have recourse to simulation modelling (SM), which involves a three-phase process: *modelling*, *simulation* and *evaluation*.

The modelling phase

The modelling phase entails the creation of a simulation model, as shown in the stock and flow diagram in Figure 11.4.

(Continued)

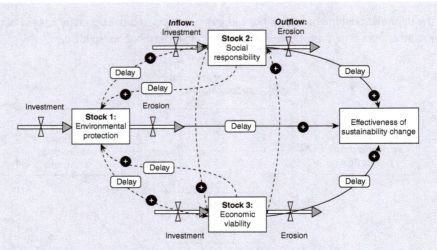

Figure 11.4 Stock and flow diagram representing dimensions of BuildCo's sustainability strategy

The primary goal of the simulation model is to optimise the effectiveness of sustainability change at BuildCo. The three main interdependent variables factored into the model were the investments made in *environmental protection*, *social responsibility* and *economic viability* – which in practice are usually referred to as stocks and can be measured in quantitative terms (such as percentages and monetary values). Stocks are not fixed but are subject to change over time, just like a stock in a warehouse. These changes are called flows.

There are two types of flows which both affect the level of a stock:

i   *Inflows* (in this case investments) are decided internally by change agents and refer to tangible resources (e.g. people, machines, facilities, etc.) and intangible resources (e.g. money, time, attention, processes, information technology, etc.) allocated to the sustainability change project.

ii *Outflows* (or *erosions*) happen when stocks are used up or become outdated because of external factors such as new environmental standards or technological advances.

If the inflows exceed the outflows, the stock level increases and if the outflows exceed the inflows, the stock level decreases. The links between the stocks are **feedback loops** and can be either positive (+) or negative (-). When the relationship between stocks is positive, they have an additive and mutually beneficial influence on each other. When the relationship between stocks is negative, they have a subtractive and mutually detrimental influence on each other.

Lastly, the simulation model accounts for *delay* which is common in practice. Delay refers to a time gap between an inflow or investment and the expected change in stock level. For example (with regard to *Stock 1*, in Figure 11.4) – a training programme on how to optimise energy consumption and environmental protection might take weeks or months to generate a noticeable improvement in production efficiency, performance and productivity, causing a delay in the registration of its impact on *Stock 3*, economic viability.

Simulation

Simulations can be run based on a set of different investment choices over set time frames. Figure 11.5 shows the outputs of a simulation modelling exercise involving three possible scenarios spanning over five years for sustainable change at BuildCo (actual computations have been left out for ease of understanding).

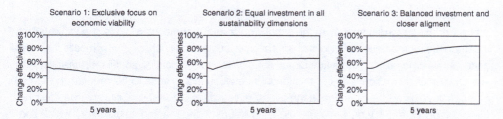

Figure 11.5   Outputs of simulation exercise for sustainable change at BuildCo

Scenario 1: Exclusive focus on economic viability

If BuildCo invests solely in economic viability, the simulation model shows how sustainability effectiveness would stagnate and diminish over time. Even if the investment levels in the economic viability stock were much higher than its erosion rate, a lack of investment in the other two stocks (social responsibility and environmental protection) would delay the expected benefits and keep the overall effectiveness of the sustainability change initiative well below 60%.

Scenario 2: Equal investment in all sustainability dimensions

If BuildCo equally spreads investments across all three dimensions of economic validity, social responsibility and environmental protection, this would result in a decrease in erosion and delay, and a gradual yet steady increase in the overall effectiveness of sustainability change.

Scenario 3: Closer alignment between investments and business strategy

Spreading investments equally across all three stocks but also maintaining a closer alignment between the activities under each stock and with the broader strategic objectives of the organisation would have an even greater impact on the overall effectiveness of sustainability change which would rise well above 80%.

Evaluation

After analysing the SM exercise, it became clear to change agents at BuildCo that an exclusive focus on only one dimension of sustainability change (in this case economic viability, which is all too often top management's overriding concern) would negatively impact the other two dimensions of social responsibility and environmental protection which would become susceptible to rapid erosion.

Moreover, as seen in all three scenarios in Figure 11.5, the initial dip in the overall effectiveness of sustainability change is followed by a strong growth rate if investments are kept

(Continued)

steady across all three stocks impacting sustainability change – which means that an initial delay before registering any increase in sustainability change effectiveness can be considered normal. In addition, the growth rate is higher if adequate action is taken to ensure a close alignment between the sustainability change initiative and the organisation's broader strategic objectives.

Conclusions

A number of key issues arise from the simulation exercise carried out in this case study. First, it demonstrates the need for a holistic approach to sustainability change which calls for a balance of investments in all three key dimensions of economic viability, social responsibility and environmental protection – as the relationship between them tends to be mutually beneficial and can have an additive impact on the overall effectiveness of sustainability change. Second, there is typically a delay between making an investment and reaping its benefits – which suggests that change agents need to look beyond initial setbacks or quick wins and take the long-range view when managing sustainability change. Finally, one cannot underestimate the importance of a robust alignment between sustainability change efforts and the organisation's strategic objectives as a key determinant of longer-term growth and success.

Questions

1   What are the key external factors impacting sustainability change at BuildCo?
2   What were the main phases of the simulation modelling exercise designed to drive sustainability change at BuildCo?
3   What were the key outputs of each phase?
4   What key principles for effectively managing sustainability change can be derived from the BuildCo case study?

11.8 Independent learning

Please access the links below for short videos on the strategies for sustaining change discussed in this chapter.

Action Research: www.youtube.com/watch?v=rAlNCm9iisU
Appreciative Inquiry: www.youtube.com/watch?v=l3RjC5vllZ4
Communities of practice (CoPs): www.youtube.com/watch?v=ao5qRFOepOE
Simulation modelling: www.youtube.com/watch?v=-6qlX_ihOwQ

11.9 References

Adams, C. A. and McNicholas, P. (2007) 'Making a difference: Sustainability reporting, accountability and organisational change', *Accounting, Auditing and Accountability Journal*, 20(3), 382–402.

Applebaum, S., Calgano, R., Magarelli, S. M. and Saliba, M. (2016) 'A relationship between corporate sustainability and organizational change (Part One)', *Industrial and Commercial Training*, 48(1), 16–23.

Asad, H. (2021) *IKEA Accelerates Suppliers' Shift to 100% Renewables*. [Online] Available at: www.environmentalleader.com/2021/06/ikea-accelerates-suppliers-shift-to-100-renewables/ (accessed 17 February 2023).

Bushe, G. (2012) 'Foundations of Appreciative Inquiry: History, criticism and potential', *AI Practitioner*, 14(1), 1–13. [Online] Available at: http://www.gervasebushe.ca/Foundations_AI.pdf (accessed 10 January 2023).

Cairns-Lee, H. and Turpin, D. (2022) 'GSK Consumer Healthcare: Building Communities of Practice to drive post merger innovation', *International Institute for Management Development*. [Online] Available at: https://www.thecasecentre.org/products/view?id=183039

Cambridge Dictionary (2022) *Sustainability*. [Online] Available at: https://dictionary.cambridge.org/dictionary/english/sustainability (accessed 1 February 2023).

Cooperrider, D. and Srivastva, S. (1987) 'Appreciative inquiry in organizational life', in R. Woodman and W. Pasmore (eds), *Research in Organizational Change and Development*, Vol.1. Bingley: Emerald Publishing, pp. 129–169.

Cooperrider, D. L., Barrett, F. and Srivastva, S. (1995) 'Social construction and appreciative inquiry: A journey in organizational theory', in D. Hosking, P. Dachler and K. Gergen (eds), *Management and Organization: Relational Alternatives to Individualism*. Avebury: Ashgate Publishing, pp. 157–200.

Daly, H. (1996) *Beyond Growth: The Economics of Sustainable Development*. Boxton, MA: Beacon Press.

Elliott, C. (1999) *Locating the Energy for Change: An Introduction to Appreciative Inquiry*. Canada: International Institute for Sustainable Development.

Fowler, A. (2003) 'Systems modelling, simulation, and the dynamics of strategy', *Journal of Business Research*, 56(2), 135–144.

Größler, A., Thun, J-H. and Milling, P. M. (2008) 'System dynamics as a structural theory in operations management', *Production and Operations Management*, 17(3), 373–384.

Hayes, J. (2021) *The Theory and Practice of Change Management*, 6th edn. London: Red Globe Press.

IKEA (2022) *FY21 Sustainability Highlights*. [Online] Available at: https://gbl-sc9u2-prd-cdn.azureedge.net/-/media/aboutikea/newsroom/publications/documents/ikea-sustainability-report-fy21.pdf (accessed 17 January 2023).

Kaye, L. (2013) *IKEA and Kingfisher Pledge Ambitious 'Net Positive' Agendas, But Can They Work?* [Online] Available at: https://sustainablebrands.com/read/supply-chain/ikea-and-kingfisher-pledge-ambitious-net-positive-agendas-but-can-they-work (accessed 23 February 2023).

Kietzmann, J., Plangger, K., Eaton, B., Heilgenberg, K., Pitt, L. and Berthon, P. (2013) 'Mobility at work: A typology of mobile communities of practice and contextual ambidexterity', *Journal of Strategic Information Systems*, 3(4), 282–297.

Lave, J. and Wenger, E. (1991) *Situated Learning: Legitimate Peripheral Participation*. Cambridge: Cambridge University Press.

Lozano, R. (2018) 'Sustainable business models: Providing a more holistic perspective', *Business Strategy and the Environment*, 27(8), 1159–1166.

Lozano, R. and Garcia, I. (2020) 'Scrutinizing sustainability change and its institutionalization in organizations', *Frontiers in Sustainability*, 1, 1–16. [Online] Available at: www.frontiersin.org/articles/10.3389/frsus. 2020.00001/full (accessed 2 February 2023).

Luna-Reyes, L. F., Martinez-Moyano, I. J., Pardo, T. A., Cresswell, A. M., Andersen, D. F. and Richardson, G. P. (2006) 'Anatomy of a group model-building intervention: Building dynamic theory from case study research', *System Dynamics Review*, *22*(4), 291–320.

Macmillan Dictionary (2022) *Sustainability*. [Online] Available at: www.macmillandictionary.com/dictionary/british/sustainability (accessed 13 February 2023).

Millar, C., Hind, P. and Magala, S. (2012) 'Sustainability and the need for change: Organizational change and transformation vision', *Journal of Organizational Change Management*, 25(4), 489–500.

Narendran, T. V. and Ganeriwalla, A. (2020) *Forging Sustainable Change at Tata Steel*. [Online] Available at: www.bcg.com/publications/2020/forging-sustainable-change-at-tata-steel (accessed 22 March 2023).

Podolny, M. and Hansen, M. T. (2020) 'How Apple is organized for innovation', *Harvard Business Review*. [Online] Available at: https://hbr.org/2020/11/how-apple-is-organized-for-innovation (accessed 13 February 2023).

Porter, M. E. (1985) *The Competitive Advantage: Creating and Sustaining Superior Performance*. New York: Free Press.

Porter, M. E. and Kramer, M. R. (2011) 'Creating shared value: How to reinvent capitalism and unleash a wave of innovation and growth', *Harvard Business Review*, 89(1–2), 62–77.

Purvis, B., Mao, Y. and Robinson, D. (2018) 'Three pillars of sustainability: In search of conceptual origins', *Sustainability Science*, 14(3), 681–695.

Reason, P. and Bradbury, H. (eds) (2001) *Handbook of Action Research: Participative Inquiry and Practice*. London: SAGE Publications.

Rouwette, E. A. J. A., Vennix, J. A. M. and Thijssen, C. M. (2000) 'Group model building: A decision room approach', *Simulation & Gaming*, 31(3), 359–379.

Serafeim, G. (2020) 'Social-impact efforts that create real value', *Harvard Business Review*, September–October. [Online] Available at: https://hbr.org/2020/09/social-impact-efforts-that-create-real-value (accessed 2 February 2023).

Spacey, J. (2019) *13 Examples of a Green Industry*. [Online] Available at: https://simplicable.com/new/green-industry (accessed 17 January 2023).

Sterman, J. D. (2001) 'System dynamics modeling: Tools for learning in a complex world', *California Management Review*, 43(4), 8–25.

Stoughton, A. M. and Ludema, J. (2012) 'The driving forces of sustainability', *Journal of Organizational Change Management*, 25(4), 501–517.

Struckman, C. (2021) *Sustaining the Fast Pace of Digital Business Transformation*. [Online] Available at: https://businesschief.com/digital-strategy/sustaining-fast-pace-digital-business-transformation (accessed 1 February 2023).

Wenger, E. C. and Snyder, W. M. (2000) 'Communities of Practice: The organizational frontier', *Harvard Business Review*, 78, 139–145.

World Commission on Environment and Development (1987) *Our Common Future*. [Online] Available at: www.are.admin.ch/are/en/home/media/publications/sustainable-development/brundtland-report.html (accessed 2 January 2023).

12

CONCLUSIONS

12.1 Introduction

This final chapter begins with a brief discussion of how the aim and objectives of this textbook set out in the introductory chapter have been achieved. It then provides a summary of the conceptual nuggets arising from each of the key topics covered in this textbook that represent its unique contribution to OCM. The concluding section brings this textbook to a close with some remarks on its contribution to OCM as a discrete field of research and practice.

12.2 Achievement of aim and objectives

Our aim in writing this textbook was to provide an alternative perspective on Organisational Change Management (OCM) that can advance student understanding of this discrete field of research and practice. Our key objectives were as follows:

- To capture the essence of OCM.
- To provide an alternative perspective on OCM as a distinctive field of research and practice.
- To address the emerging trends and contemporary issues in OCM.
- To inform the practice of OCM.
- To meet the learning needs of students on both undergraduate and postgraduate business and management programmes.

Capturing the essence of OCM

It was not our intention to provide an exhaustive text that would include everything that could be possibly subsumed under OCM. One of our particular interests was to *capture the essence* of OCM by bringing together in a particular order a set of key topics that would: (i) facilitate introduction to the field for those who are not already familiar with it, (ii) enable a holistic understanding of OCM and critical reflection on its key features and objectives, and (iii) provide students with a springboard for further learning.

Providing an alternative perspective on OCM

We also wanted to provide an alternative perspective on OCM that could add to its already rich landscape. To this end we developed a conceptual framework consisting of three foundational pillars: *Systemic*, *Dialogic* and *Processual* approaches to organisational change. This conceptual framework provided the parameters for a reframing of OCM along key dimensions that in our view, account for its overarching principles – especially a dialogic approach to change which is critical to change success but which has not been foregrounded in this particular way in other texts.

Addressing emerging trends and contemporary issues in OCM

We wanted this textbook to reflect the 'spirit of the times' and take stock of the key trends and contemporary issues in OCM. In this regard, we have devoted ample space in each chapter to identify such trends and issues and consider their implications for OCM in key areas such as strategy, business modelling, leadership, culture, communication, evaluation and sustainability. Importantly, the conceptual nuggets at the end of each chapter have provided unique insights and valuable guidelines as to how to effectively address the key challenges and opportunities arising from the global context of modern-day organisations.

Informing OCM practice

A pressing concern in writing this textbook was to avoid being overly prescriptive as OCM is not an exact science. While we do subscribe to certain precepts and principles in relation to OCM (as in the conceptual pillars underpinning this work) it was not our intention to create yet another 'dogma of change' or provide recipes for change success. However, we encourage the reader to critically assess the value of theories, models and tools discussed in this textbook before applying them in practice in line with the specific context and perceived needs of their organisation – which can increase the likelihood of change success.

Meeting the learning needs of students

From a learning perspective, we have adopted a multi-modal pedagogy (involving a blend of different modes of imparting knowledge) and a facilitative approach to learning. To this effect, we have drawn on a wide range of media and resources to enrich the learning experience of students and to construct a scaffolding for further independent, self-directed learning. As explained in the introductory chapter, we advocate connectivism as an important part of the learning process in the digital age – and we encourage students to 'connect and combine' what they have learned in this textbook with other learning materials to expand and consolidate their knowledge of OCM. While the independent learning section at the end of each chapter can be a good starting point for further learning, we also urge students to join online platforms and communities that provide a safe space for ongoing knowledge sharing and collaborative learning – where they can get access to a diversity of perspectives as they develop their own views and values in relation to OCM.

12.3 Summary review of conceptual nuggets

We have recourse here to a 'tree infographic' to highlight in a sequential and easy-to-understand manner the conceptual nuggets arising from each substantial chapter of the textbook. We then provide a summary of each conceptual nugget that you can use for revision and as a springboard for further learning and research.

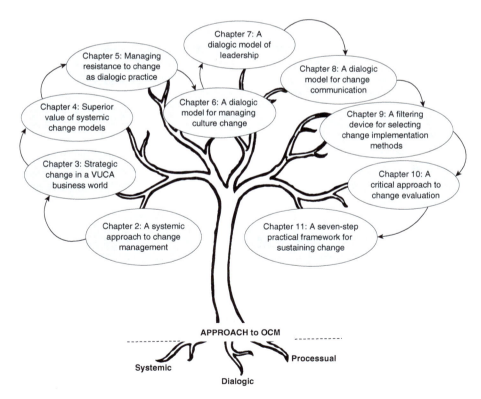

Figure 12.1   Tree infographic: Key conceptual nuggets

Chapter 2: A systemic approach to change management

We advocated a systemic approach to change management which views the organisation as *a complex ecosystem* and locates it *as a living organism* within its external environment with which it has a dynamic and symbiotic relationship. A systemic approach to change management also pays attention to the internal environment of the organisation and how its interrelated sub-systems and processes are purposefully configured and interact to create collective value that may be of benefit to all key stakeholders.

We also considered the key benefits and limitations of such an approach to change management, which are summarised below.

The key benefits of systemic change include:

i   A *multi-level and complex understanding* of the key environmental forces impacting an organisation undergoing change.
ii *Informed decision-making* as to how the interrelated sub-systems and processes can be reconfigured to generate greater collective value.
iii An *in-depth analysis* of the complex web of causal relationships that underlie the change process via different forms of causal modelling.
iv A *deeper understanding* of the relationship between incremental and transformational change that goes beyond a dichotomous mode of thinking showing how both types of change can happen simultaneously.

A systemic approach to change also has some limitations, the most obvious ones being:

i   The complex and esoteric nature of systems theory makes it unappealing to practitioners.
ii The fact that systemic change can be resource intensive and expensive which makes it difficult to get top-management buy-in and access to sufficient funding.
iii The lack of necessary competences and technical expertise to effectively engage in a systemic change.
iv A lack of evidence of success in this area means that a lot of organisations would be unwilling to invest in and experiment with systemic change management.

We did make the remark that the benefits of systemic change far outweigh its limitations. We also underlined the need to make the concept of systemic change more accessible to practitioners, raise awareness about its potential benefits, stimulate investments in training and development and encourage wider experimentation in this area.

Chapter 3: Leading strategic change in a VUCA business world

We demonstrated how the notion of the VUCA (*Volatile, Uncertain, Complex and Ambiguous*) business world can be turned into a powerful analytical framework and effectively complement other well-known diagnostic tools such as the PESTLE and SWOT analyses to frame strategic change in an increasingly unstable and unpredictable global business context. We have also considered the implications of leading strategic change in a VUCA business world to draw attention to:

i   How the notion of the VUCA business world serves to reinforce Quinn's and Mintzberg's conceptualisation of strategy as *a mix of planned and emergent change*.
ii How it calls for a type of *business acumen rooted in systems practice* – where change agents have to develop their ability to manage their organisations as complex adaptive systems and gain an understanding of the complex web of causal relationships underlying it.
iii How it requires a departure from traditional, top-down leadership to a special *brand of democratic leadership* that promotes collaboration, fosters organisation-wide commitment and empowers change stakeholders whilst releasing their leadership potential in the pursuit of competitive advantage and strategic success.
iv How it acts as a catalyst for experimental learning which is characterised by a high tolerance for mistakes, a focus on creativity and innovation, and a virtuous cycle of learning and unlearning, practical application and evaluation that can drive the organisation forward in an increasingly uncertain and unpredictable business environment.

Chapter 4: Superior value of systemic change models

We drew an important distinction between linear and systemic change models. Linear change models are mostly descriptive and project an image of organisational change as a neat step-by-step process which hardly accounts for its complexity and a sound understanding of the many interdependent variables at play within a change situation. By contrast, systemic models have superior value in that they enable a holistic, multidimensional and context-sensitive approach to organisational change that accounts for its complexity and specificity. Moreover, they have a high explanatory power, allowing for a robust analysis of the causal relationships between the interconnected parts of the organisation and are action oriented as they can be turned into an effective tool to frame informed courses of action geared towards the achievement of change objectives.

Chapter 5: Managing resistance as dialogic practice

We have proposed a way of managing resistance to change as *dialogic practice* – which carries the ideal of a safe and empowering space to enable free dialogue between change agents and organisational stakeholders and which could become a valuable platform for identifying the key sources of resistance to change and attending to them in a timely fashion. Dialogic practice warrants:

i   A suspension of inequalities in power relations amongst organisational stakeholders.
ii A freezing of taken-for-granted assumptions, prejudices and ill feelings towards the proposed change.

iii A willingness to listen to the voices of all 'participants-in-dialogue' and to reach a shared understanding around the necessity, purpose, intended outcomes and implications of change.

We have made the important point that for dialogic practice to be effective, it should not be a one-off, cosmetic exercise but a continuous sequence of 'repeated dialogic moments' that have to take place throughout the change process. We have also shown how the *force-field analysis* can be adapted for managing resistance to change as dialogic practice by:

i Enabling a holistic, collaborative and psychologically safe approach to addressing sources of resistance at both individual and collective levels.
ii Providing the parameters for considering the different types and effects of resistance and finding ways to counteract them while promoting more positive attitudes and behaviours across the change context.

Chapter 6: A dialogic model for managing culture change

Our conceptual nugget for Chapter 6 entailed the development of a dialogic model for effectively managing culture change. The dialogic model is firmly grounded in a system of meaning creation and action enabled by an ongoing process of free and open dialogue and consists of the following key elements:

i *Shared understanding*: A free process of collective sense making and meaning creation and reaching consensus around the core cultural values and norms driving culture change.
ii *Transmission*: The selection of the right channels and media and a two-way communication system to transmit the new cultural values and norms across the organisation.
iii *Alignment*: The ability, via on-going, free dialogue, to maintain robust links between the core cultural values and strategic objectives and effectively manage subcultures.
iv *Embedding*: To ensure consistency between the cultural values endorsed by the organisation and their translation into practice – leading, over time, to the institutionalisation of such values across the organisation.
v *Culture change*: To keep open the possibility for further cultural change – whether it be in the form of a refinement, renewal or radical transformation of the organisation's culture value system in view of new strategic, social and ethical imperatives.

Chapter 7: A dialogic model of leadership

In line with our commitment to dialogic practice, we developed a *dialogic model of leadership* that places an emphasis on the transformative role of open dialogue on the leadership process and can serve as a powerful lever for contemporary approaches to leadership. The model comprises three key elements: *Talk*, *Reflection* and *Action*.

Talk involves a twofold process:

i   'talk with self' which is inward-looking and entails an ability of leaders to 'face themselves' and question their own modes of thought, values and motives in relation to the change they are leading; and

ii   'talk with others' which is outward-looking and invites the leader to 'face others' through repeated moments of free dialogue with key stakeholders as a means of enabling a collaborative approach and building a strong coalition to sustain the momentum of change.

Reflection warrants an ability of the leader to think critically about their own accomplishments and failings and assess their own learning and developmental needs. It also places change leaders at the centre of an empowering network of relationships to enable collective reflection, sense making and problem solving.

Action is contained in talk – as what is 'talked about' provides a framework for specific courses of action and a process of strategic adaptation in the face of emerging threats and opportunities. Importantly, action enjoins leaders to 'walk the talk' and model the behaviours they want to see in their followers.

Chapter 8: Dialogic model for change communication

We developed a dialogic model for communicating change which is rooted in Habermas' *theory of communicative action*, Watzlavik's *pragmatics of human communication* and Fairclough's *discourse theory* and places an emphasis on the vital role of language in shaping the communication process between change leaders and other change stakeholders. The models consist of the following core components:

i   *Creation of meaning* – which involves a cooperative process of deliberation and interpretation among change leaders, leading to the crafting of a clear, coherent and accessible message that includes both an affective and a functional dimension.

ii   *Extraction of meaning* – which entails another layer of interpretation by the other change stakeholders as they try to make sense of its content and extract the meaning of the change message, which needs to be accurate and subject to a process of negotiation if it is to be widely accepted and internalised by key stakeholder groups.

iii *Negotiation of meaning* – which draws on the metaphor of dialogue as a democratic conduit to open up the possibility for free, open dialogue between change leaders and other change stakeholders and enable a balanced approach to collective sense making and the negotiation of meaning around the proposed change. Emphasis is also placed on the importance of democratic communication skills which is a precondition for building positive behaviours and relationships.

iv *Shared meaning* – which is the desirable outcome of our dialogic model and which can be seen as a function of both the effectiveness of the change message itself and of the quality of the interpretation and negotiation it has elicited. Moreover, shared meaning represents the collective ideological commitments of all change stakeholders that integrates a plurality of perspectives and interests and that provides the legitimacy for a concerted approach to change and an effective coordination of action towards common change goals and objectives.

Finally, attention was drawn to the fact that shared meaning is not a fixed order of discourse but calls for 'repeated dialogic moments' and an effective sequencing of the flow of communication between change leaders and other stakeholders – as a means of reinforcing initial meanings of change, attaching new meanings to it, and building positive and trusting relationships to sustain the momentum of change.

Chapter 9: A filtering device for selecting change implementation methods

Choosing the right change implementation method can be a daunting prospect. We therefore developed a filtering device that can facilitate the selection of the right change implementation method. Our filtering device consists of five layers:

i *Alignment with business strategy*: to underline the fact that the strategic goals and objectives of the organisation should guide the choice of the change implementation method – and not the other way round.
ii *Systemic perspective*: to allow for a holistic, cross-functional understanding of how the chosen change implementation method will impact the whole organisation.
iii *Processual approach*: to take into account that change implementation is an on-going process warranting a method with clear milestones and evaluative measures that allows for long-range planning and supports a commitment to continuous improvement.
iv *Balanced outcomes*: to effectively address the needs and interests of all change stakeholders and enable a balance between performance and developmental objectives, business and ethical imperatives, and organisational and individual well-being.
v *Scalability*: to assess the extent to which the chosen change implementation method can be scaled up or down to meet the specific needs of the organisation.

Chapter 10: A critical approach to change evaluation

We advocated a critical approach to change evaluation which is reflective, based on informed decision-making and alert to the potential pitfalls of change evaluation. To this effect we developed six key principles underlining the need for:

i A clear change evaluation strategy that is tightly aligned with the business needs and strategic objectives of the organisation – where change agents have to identify and prioritise the key dimensions and elements that have to be included in the change evaluation system.

ii   The reinforcement of a view of change as an on-going activity that is carried out throughout the change process – accounting for both short-term and mid-term formative evaluations which can in turn inform long-term summative evaluations and serve as a springboard for further change.

iii   The input of all key change stakeholders that is of vital importance to not only the design and application of the chosen evaluation system but also in the interpretation of its outputs, follow-up action and the assessment of its overall organisational impact.

iv   Strong leadership warranting a total buy-in on the part of change leaders and demonstrated by a willingness to actively support and participate in evaluation throughout the change process.

v   The right choice of measures and investigative instruments which is a key determinant of change success – bearing in mind their limitations and impact on the overall credibility of the evaluation outputs and the challenge of obtaining precise, unequivocal data.

vi   A dynamic, flexible and open-ended change evaluation system – so that it can allow timely changes in the use of methods, measures and investigative instruments in view of new challenges and strategic imperatives or in response to regular assessments of the effectiveness of the change evaluation system itself.

Chapter 11: A seven-step framework for sustaining change

We developed a seven-step practical framework for sustaining change which is underpinned by the following key principles:

i   *Connecting with the public discourse on sustainability*: Underlining the need to connect the planning stage of the process for sustaining change with the wider public discourse on sustainability to reach consensus on its impact on organisational bottom lines and responsibilities in creating economic, social and environmental value.

ii   *Planning and taking ownership*: Drawing attention to the importance of a clear, actionable plan for sustaining change and the need for change leaders to take ownership of the process for sustaining change to prevent regression to old ways of working and change decay.

iii   *Adopting a collaborative approach to evaluating change progress*: Reinforcing the value of a collaborative and level-of-analysis approach to evaluating change progress – with an emphasis on choosing the right measures, objectively reporting successes and failures, and identifying key performance indicators and best practices to sustain performance improvement.

iv   *Treating communication as king*: Highlighting the need for clear, organisation-wide and two-way communication via effective channels between change leaders and employees whilst advocating honesty and transparency in the reporting of both successes and failures as a precondition for effective follow-up action.

v   *Managing emergent resistance and building capacity for sustaining change*: Placing an onus on change leaders to effectively manage resistance arising from the process of sustaining change as a means of upholding employee motivation, commitment and performance levels. Stressing the importance of building organisational capacity for sustaining change through training, collaborative partnerships and other learning support mechanisms to foster employee self-development and harness creativity and innovation in driving change.

vi *Establishing a sustainability culture*: Calling attention to the importance of establishing a sustainability culture by integrating sustainability issues and concerns into organisational routines, embedding best practices and habits for sustaining change as the norm, rewarding success and developing an ability to learn from mistakes and failures. An emphasis is also placed on the need for a shift in the predominant mode of thinking and behaviour that translate a commitment to sustaining change as one of the core values of the organisation.

vii *Reconciling tensions*: Emphasising the organisation's ability to reconcile the tensions between the need to stabilise new ways of working over a set period of time to reap intended benefits of change and the need to continuously pursue performance improvements and sustain competitive advantage.

REFLECTIVE EXERCISE

1   Select, from the above summary review, three conceptual nuggets that appeal to you the most.
2   To what extent do you think they resonate with modern-day organisations? What would be the barriers standing in the way of their practical application?
3   What steps are you going to take to further develop your knowledge about them?

12.4   Concluding remarks

We now want to close this book with some parting comments with regard to the future of OCM.

We see OCM as a fluid, dynamic and evolving field of research and practice embarked on a continuous journey of experimental learning and self-discovery. From this particular vantage point, OCM is naturally open to new ideas, images and perspectives in response to the challenges and opportunities thrown up by an increasingly volatile and unpredictable global business context. In offering an alternative perspective on OCM, it is our hope that this textbook will elicit thinking about different ways of teaching and practising organisational change management, enlarge the scope of OCM activities and open up various lines of inquiry that can keep this discrete field of research and practice vibrant and forward-looking.

GLOSSARY

Acculturation The process of learning and incorporating the core cultural values of another organisation.

Action research A participatory process of inquiry involving professional researchers and active participants of client organisation to generate practical solutions to pressing problems.

Ambidextrous strategic change The ability of change leaders to concurrently deploy different strategies across different business contexts or deploy different strategies in succession within a single or several business contexts.

Appreciative inquiry Focuses on the organisation as a positive force for change and on investigating ways to leverage what it does best to re-construct a better future.

Artefacts Concrete and highly visible elements such as company logos, symbols, dress codes and office layouts.

Assimilation The process of giving up one's own organisational culture to embrace that of another organisation.

Augmented reality The combination of software applications and hardware such as specially designed headsets, sensors and body wear to enable an interactive user experience blending computer-generated content and the real world.

Autocratic leadership Tends towards exploitive, controlling and dictatorial leadership styles based on the assumption that people dislike work and have to be closely supervised.

Background conversations Following Ford, Ford and McNamara, refers to different accounts or narratives of change which serve to create and sustain different types of resistance to change.

Balanced Scorecard (BSC) An evaluative tool developed by Kaplan and Norton in the early 1990s that integrates multiple perspectives and measures to enable a comprehensive and continuous assessment of change.

Basic underlying assumptions Mostly preconscious and hidden presuppositions or theories that can have a significant impact on decision-making and chosen courses of action.

Beliefs and values Conscious yet partially observable principles and standards of behaviour such as integrity, innovation, diversity, commitment, etc.

Bonini's paradox Named after Stanford professor Bonini and underlines the need for change models that are simple, clear and easy to understand and translate into practice.

Business Process Reengineering (BPR)   Generally involves a rapid and radical redesign of current business processes to achieve improvements in performance, productivity and quality.

Causal modelling   Diagnostic exercise through which change agents can generate thick causal explanations of organisational change and increase the likelihood of change success.

Causal models   Have a high *explanatory power* in that they allow for a grounded understanding of the complex web of causal relationships that underlie the change process and intended outcomes.

Change agency   The intentional action and causal power of agents in bringing about change geared towards certain desirable outcomes.

Change aversion   Refers to environments which nurture conservative beliefs and values that view change as something to be avoided or of last resort.

Change decay   Regression to old ways of working which can result in the loss of change gains.

Change evaluation   A process designed to determine the value of a change project against a set of indicators such as performance, intended outcomes and impact in order to improve its overall effectiveness.

Change management   A multidimensional process that aims to leverage the resources of an organisation to achieve its strategic goals and objectives and ensure its continuity and growth in the longer term.

Change readiness   Refers to environments that encourage progressive beliefs and values that promote a view of change as something to be embraced.

Change sustainability   The ability of an organisation to maintain certain new processes, activities or ways of working to achieve certain desired outcomes over a set period of time.

Collective leadership   Brings to the fore the notion of leadership as distributed across different levels and functional areas of the organisation.

Communication theory   One of the building blocks of change modelling that emphasises two-way communication and open dialogue as a key determinant of change success.

Communities of Practice   Informal groups of people brought together by a common interest in a particular domain of knowledge or area of organisational functioning to which they feel they can make a contribution while progressing their own learning and development.

Conceptual framework   Delimits the theoretical dimensions along which the contents of this textbook is developed.

Conceptual nugget   A valuable idea, concept or model arising from each of the key topics covered in this textbook representing its unique contribution to OCM.

Constructive mode of change   Van de Ven and Poole's conception of change as emergent, radical and revolutionary and progressing in an unstable and unexpected manner.

Contingency theory   Relates to the ability of change agents to effectively respond to the dynamic forces at play within their change situation.

Continuous change   Involves a form of planned change which is broken down into smaller stages over a period of time.

Continuums of leadership styles   Different ranges of leadership styles that vary between the two opposite poles of autocratic and democratic forms of leadership.

Control systems   Determine the way work processes and behaviours are monitored, evaluated, regulated and rewarded.

Coping cycle   Originates from Elizabeth Kübler-Ross' work charting the psychological responses an individual typically displays when going through a series of change transitions, including *Denial, Defence, Discarding, Adaptation* and *Internalisation*.

Cultural layers   Originates from the work of Edgar Schein which identifies three distinctive layers of culture with different degrees of visibility: *artefacts, beliefs and values,* and *basic underlying assumptions*.

Cultural paradigm   A complex set of ideas, values, beliefs and assumptions that define an organisation's cultural identity and shape its ways of thinking and doing things.

Cultural value system   Taken-for-granted assumptions, beliefs and values shaped over time through learning and adaptation and validated by experiences of past successes and failures.

Cultural web   Developed by Johnson and Scholes and consisting of six interrelated dimensions – *stories, symbols, power structures, organisational structures, control systems* and *rituals and routines* – the combined effects of which account for an organisation's dominant culture.

Culture   Based, according to Schein, on a set of assumptions that people hold and that find their expression in a shared system of beliefs, expectations and meanings.

Culture theory   Pays particular attention to the taken-for-granted assumptions, beliefs and values which can have a significant bearing on change outcomes.

Cuneiform   The first known writing system used in ancient Middle East around the 4th Century BCE.

Deep structures   Tushman and Romanelli's identification of the key domains of organisational activity, including strategy, culture, structure, power distribution and process.

Democratic leadership   Tends towards a collaborative and empowering work climate based on the assumption that people enjoy work and want to contribute to change success.

Determinism   Sees change agents as rather passive and locked in a reactive mode of thought and behaviour and with limited ability for intentional strategic action.

Dialogic approach to change   Carries the ideal of change initiatives brought under the binding principle of free dialogue to enable shared understanding and the coordination of action towards mutually beneficial goals.

Dialogic leadership   Places an emphasis on the constitutive role of open dialogue and its transformative impact on the leadership process.

Dialogic practice   Carries the ideal of a psychologically safe and socially empowering space for ongoing, free dialogue between change stakeholders.

Dichotomous conceptions   Types of organisational change viewed as binary opposites and split into two mutually exclusive categories.

Digital twin technology   Allows for the digital replication of real-world physical objects for practical purposes such as running simulations, monitoring and maintenance, and process integration.

Directed change implementation   Generally viewed as a hard approach to change, led from the top and driven by economic interests.

Discontinuous change   Involves a sharp and sudden break from current ways of working that occurs over a relatively short period of time.

Discourse theory   Sees dialogue as a cooperative conversation between equals and having a shaping influence on power relations, collective sense making, ideological commitments and chosen courses of action.

DMAIC   A five-step methodology used in Six Sigma interventions which stands for: *Define, Measure, Analyse, Improve* and *Control*.

Downward causation   A case where external causal factors impact the organisation.

Eco-leadership   A notion developed by Simon Western which promotes a systemic approach to change and reengages leadership with its ethical and environmental responsibilities.

Economic viability   When the financial returns and profits generated by a change initiative are high enough for an organisation to survive and prosper in the longer term.

Ecosystem   Locates the organisation as a living organism within its external environment with which it has a dynamic relationship.

Emergent strategic change   Represents an adaptive, ad hoc and reactive approach to strategic change in response to challenges and opportunities arising from the external environment.

Employee voice   Refers to the participation of employees and their right to have a say in organisational decision-making.

Enculturation   The process through which an individual or group learn and internalise the dominant culture of their own organisation.

Environmental protection   Demonstrating good stewardship of the natural environment whilst proactively contributing to its preservation, especially for the benefit of future generations.

Evolutionary change   Takes place incrementally or in small steps to ensure the organisation's survival and growth over time.

External causes   Macro-level and industry-level causal factors impacting organisational change.

Facilitated change implementation   Can be seen as a soft approach to change, entailing greater employee participation as a way of optimising change outcomes.

Feedback loop   A mechanism which allows the receiver to respond to the message sent by the sender.

Field theory   Warrants attention to the change situation as a whole and to the forces driving and constraining change.

Fordism   A system of mass production using assembly-line methods which was pioneered by the Ford Motor Company in the early 20th century to standardise production, maximise efficiency and minimise cost.

Gendered leadership   Pays attention to the gender-related factors impacting leadership roles and effectiveness.

Gestalt psychology   School of thought that focuses on how the human brain perceives and makes sense of things as a complete whole and not as isolated components.

Heijunka   A scheduling tool for levelling the production of multiple products in response to variations in customer demand.

Humanistic perspective   Supports the principles of humanism and exercises a duty of care to human beings, giving prime importance to their well-being, development and flourishing.

Identify and reply   When the change communication is focused on obtaining feedback from employees and addressing issues arising from the change initiative from their perspective.

Inbound logistics   The management of raw materials and other 'input resources' from external suppliers.

Incremental change   Typically low-intensity, localised change that entails a gradual process of step-by-step adjustments or modifications.

Infrastructure   The mode of governance, structures, relational networks, financial commitments, and quality standards that provide the foundation for all value chain work activities.

Integration   The process of adopting the cultural values of another organisation while maintaining one's own culture.

Internal causes   Causal factors within the organisation impacting change.

Internet of Things   A digital network of people, machines and electronic devices that can wirelessly communicate with each other over the Internet.

Jidoka   A visual quality control system that makes problems visible so that they can be addressed at source before the completion of the final product.

Just-in-Time   Describes a production and inventory management system that flows continuously and produces the right amount of goods only as and when needed.

Kaizen   Means *change for the better* and advocates the continuous improvement of the production process.

Leader–Member–Exchange (LMX) theory   Focuses on the quality of the dyadic (or two-way) relationship between a leader and their followers.

Leadership theory   Relates to characteristics, roles and responsibilities of change leaders in driving change success.

Lean   A set of tools and techniques designed to eliminate waste and maximise the efficiency of production processes.

Lean–Six Sigma (LSS)   A combination of Lean and Six Sigma.

Linear change models   Portray organisational change as a step-by-step process where one stage follows the other in a neat sequence.

Localised change   A type of change contained within a particular department or functional area or at a particular level of the organisation.

Logical incrementalism   Integrates elements of both planned and emergent approaches to change.

Marketing and sales   Includes activities such as advertising, brand-building, sales of goods and services.

Metaphor   A figure of speech that provides a range of relatable ideas, images and representations to facilitate understanding of a concept.

Motivation theory   A core element of change modelling that focuses on supporting mechanisms designed to optimise employee motivation, commitment and performance.

Muda   Refers to anything that can be considered wasteful and that does not add any value to the end product the customer is willing to pay for.

Mura   Refers to any form of irregularity or abnormality in the production process.

Muri   Occurs when someone or something is being overburdened and is operating beyond their power or capacity.

Noise   Any unwanted forms of distortion, disruption or barriers that can have a negative effect on the change message and 'corrupt' its intended meaning.

Operational change   Changes that are made to work structures, processes and activities in order to improve their effectiveness and efficiency.

Operations   Production processes that transform input resources into products and services that are valued by customers and that are designed to generate a profit.

Organisational development   Adopts a holistic and planned approach to maximise and sustain organisational well-being, effectiveness and performance.

Organisational silence   Arises from negative relational dynamics between change leaders and employees and entails the widespread withholding of information about change problems or issues from employees.

Organisational structures   Determine the way work is configured in order to achieve the strategic goals and objectives of an organisation.

Organisation-wide change   A type of change that encompasses the whole organisation and has a greater impact on business activities and organisational members.

Outbound logistics   The delivery of products and services to customers through various transportation methods.

Paradoxical tensions   Contradictory or opposing aspects of a role or activity that tend to co-exist and persist over time.

Path dependency   With regard to change evaluation, where an organisation persistently uses a particular evaluation system and refuses to change it even when better alternatives are available.

Pedagogical approach   The teaching philosophy and methodology used to impart knowledge in line with specific learning goals.

Performance management   Involves the application of particular processes, knowledge, skills and resources to achieve specific outcomes according to set standards within a set timescale and budget.

PESTLE analysis   Stands for *Political, Economic, Socio-cultural, Technological, Legal* and *Environmental* and is an effective diagnostic tool for scanning the external environment.

Planned strategic change (planned approach)   Represents a holistic, rational and proactive way of dealing with strategic change with a focus on long term effectiveness and performance.

Post-Fordism   A move away from the mass production of identical products to a more flexible and specialised mode of small batch production of differentiated products in response to customer demand.

Power structures   Determine the way power and authority are distributed and exercised across the organisation.

Pragmatics of human communication   The non-verbal, behavioural and relational dimensions of communication which account in a large measure for communication effectiveness.

Prescribed mode of change   Van de Ven and Poole's conception of change as planned, incremental, evolutionary and progressing in a fairly stable and predictable manner.

Process mapping   Creating a visual representation of a sequence of activities or tasks that are designed to transform an input into a desired output.

Process of becoming   A dynamic, emergent and continuously developing process or phenomenon.

Process theory   Promotes a view of organisational change as a continuous process and refers to the three-stage activity (*Input – Process – Output*) which underpins numerous change models.

Processual approach to change   Endorses a view of organisational change as an on-going, continuous and never-ending process of formation and development.

Psycho-social factors   A combination of psychological and social factors influencing individual dispositions and behaviours.

Punctuated equilibrium   A theory developed by Gould and Eldredge which views change as consisting of relatively longer periods of low-intensity, incremental change punctuated by shorter, compact periods of high-intensity, transformational change.

Quantum leadership   Emphasises the leader's ability to cope with uncertainty, ambiguity and complexity, and to adapt to fluctuations and chaotic disruptions in their change situation.

Quantum strategic change   The ability of organisations to harness innovations enabled by quantum technology as a catalyst for entrepreneurship and new business strategies and models.

Regenerative leadership   Founded on biophilic principles which warrant an ability of the leader to work towards the sustainability of both their organisation as a 'living system' and the 'wider living ecosystem' in which it operates.

Reify   Fix the meaning of something while downplaying its evolving nature and closing off the possibility of expanding understanding about it.

Resource-based   Places an emphasis on the necessary resources which have to be optimally configured to enable the successful implementation of a change strategy.

Revolutionary change   Entails a rapid and radical break from old and current ways of doing things.

Rituals   An ordered sequence of activities that are consciously carried out to achieve a specific purpose and generate certain desirable outcomes.

Routines   Repetitive processes or activities that need to be carried out regularly to ensure proper organisational functioning.

Scalable An intervention which can be transposed to other business domains once it has been successfully tried and tested in one part of the organisation.

Selective dissemination of information Where the content of a change message is filtered based on the assumption that its recipients do not need to know the full details.

Separation The maintenance of one's own culture with little interest in adopting the culture of another (partner) organisation.

Servant leadership Views an effective leader as primarily a servant who puts people first and empowers employees in taking ownership of change initiatives.

Simulation modelling A process of developing a digital prototype of an organisational system or activity to analyse the causal relationships which are necessary for its proper functioning and make predictions about its possible outputs.

Situated knowledge Knowledge that is located in a specific part of the organisation or embedded in a particular person or network of people.

Situational leadership Based on the assumption that there is no one best way to lead and the leader can switch between styles to fit different situations.

Six Sigma A statistically driven change tool for process improvement and quality management.

Social media A collective term for Internet communication platforms that enable the sharing of information and multimedia content across virtual networks and communities.

Social responsibility Creating social value and taking a leading role in making a contribution to the well-being and quality of life of key stakeholders and to society at large.

Socio-technical approach An approach to organisational change that integrates its social and technical aspects.

Spray and pray When all available information relating to a change initiative is given to employees in the hope that they will be able to make sense of its meaning.

Stories Oral or written narratives about specific people, courses of actions, strategic decisions or achievements that have contributed to the success of the organisation.

Strategic change The modification or major overhaul of an organisation's strategy and deployment of necessary resources to achieve competitive advantage and ensure long-term survival and growth.

Strategic change canvas Provides a visual and holistic framework for the groundwork that needs to be carried out prior to the implementation of the change strategy.

Strategic improvisation The ability of change leaders to reconfigure organisational resources to effectively address unanticipated opportunities and threats arising from their business environment.

Styles theory   Places an emphasis on leadership behaviours as opposed to the personality of the leader with a focus on what a leader *does* rather than what a leader *is*.

Subcultures   Develop when groups of employees cluster around a set of values, beliefs and ways of doing things that deviate from the dominant culture.

Sub-systems   The different parts that make up an organisation – e.g. technological, social, political, administrative, etc.

Sustaining change   Involves a series of proactive steps to both embed and stabilise new ways of working and maintain the momentum of change in pursuit of continuous improvement.

SWOT analysis   Stands for *Strengths, Weaknesses, Opportunities* and *Threats* and can complement the PESTLE analysis to match an organisation's resources to its operating environment.

Symbols   Highly visible objects created to promote an organisation's dominant cultural values and norms.

Synergistic effect   Where the combined effect of different things is greater than the sum of the separate effects.

Systemic approach to change   Views the organisation as a complex, adaptive ecosystem in a dynamic relationship with the forces of change within its external environment.

Systemic change models   Views the organisation as an open system with a focus on the dynamic relationships between its interconnected parts and their impact on organisational processes and outputs.

Systems theory   Places an emphasis on how the organisation evolves as a dynamic and organic entity within its wider environment and on the interaction between its different parts or sub-systems.

Taylorism   Principles of scientific management developed by Frederick Taylor in the late 19th century that aim to optimise efficiency by evaluating all the steps in a production process and breaking it down into specialised repetitive tasks.

Tell and sell   Where the change message aims to promote a change initiative in the hope that employees will commit to its pre-determined goals and objectives.

Theory of communicative action   Advocates the creation of a democratic space placed under the binding principle of free dialogue through which participants-in-communication can achieve shared understanding and coordinate their actions.

Traits theory   Posits that some people possess genetically determined, clearly identifiable and relatively stable characteristics and qualities that enable them to be effective as leaders.

Transactional leadership   Focused on short-term goals, close control, stability and order, and clear policies and procedures designed to provide a robust structure for day-to-day operations.

Transformational change   Typically high-intensity, organisation-wide change that can entail a major shift in an organisation's strategy, structures, product portfolio, production processes and cultural value system.

Transformational leadership   Views the leader as charismatic, inspirational and capable of transforming organisational reality and the people within it in pursuit of desired outcomes.

Tree infographic   A visual diagram in the form of a tree to highlight the key concepts, concerns or models which account for this textbook's unique contribution to OCM.

Triangulated evidence   Evidence gathered from different stakeholder perspectives to enable informed decisions and courses of action.

Typology of reactions to change   Refers to Kirkpatrick's three basic types of human reactions to change: positive, negative and mixed reactions.

Typology of resistance   Describes the different types of resistance to organisational change, including *Overt*, *Covert*, *Passive*, *Active* and *Adaptive* resistance.

Underscore and explore   Where the change message contains a broad outline of the change strategy while leaving the scope for employee feedback and input on how to best implement the change plan.

Upward causation   A case where an organisation has a causal impact on its wider operating context.

Value chain   Consists of multiple stages and a set of interrelated activities through which a company creates value in manufacturing a product or performing a service for its target customers.

Value Stream Mapping (VSM)   A visual tool usually used in Lean interventions to identify process inefficiencies and areas for improvement.

Voluntarism   Views change agents as having a degree of control over their environment and being able to exercise free will in making informed and intentional strategic choices.

VRIN   Stands for *Valuable, Rare, Inimitable* and *Non-substitutable* resources at the disposal of an organisation that are of strategic value.

VUCA business world   Stands for *Volatile, Uncertain, Complex* and *Ambiguous* and is used to describe the increasingly unstable and unpredictable global context facing modern-day business organisations.

Withhold and uphold   When the change message contains only a broad outline of the proposed change to get employees on board, leaving out strategic details to the care of the leadership team.

INDEX

3-step model of change, 90–2
4-D model, 319
5-Forces model, 40
9/11 terror attacks, 71

acculturation, 160, 170, 347
action, 203fig, 205, 343
action learning, 35
action research, 316tab, 318, 329, 347
active resistance, 128tab, 138
adaptation, 121fig, 123, 125fig, 126fig, 138
adaptive resistance, 128tab, 138
Aetna, 162–3
agile transformation, 171
Airbnb, 251
Airbus, 64
Alexander the Great, 177
Alibaba Group, 25–7
alignment, 97, 168, 170, 342
Amazon, 19, 20, 26, 53, 63, 187, 216
    Amazon QuickSight (AQS), 293–4
    Amazon SageMaker Canvas, 294
    Amazon Web Services, 293–4
ambidextrous strategic approach, 62–3, 65tab,
    75, 347
anger, 122–3
antiquity, 177
Apple, 62, 63, 187, 216, 307
appreciative inquiry, 316tab, 318–19, 329, 347
Argyris, C., 104
artefacts, 150tab, 170, 347
artificial intelligence, 20, 78, 267
assimilation, 160tab, 161, 170, 347
assumptions, 150tab, 151, 170
Atlassian, 225–6
audio, 228, 235
augmented reality, 315, 347
AutoCo, 236–40
autocratic leadership, 188–9, 220, 221, 223, 235,
    246, 252, 272, 347

background conversations, 132–4, 138, 347
Balanced Scorecard, 279, 286–91, 292,
    298–300, 347
beliefs and values, 85, 117, 150, 151, 170, 347
Bezos, Jeff, 53, 187
Biogen, 58
biophilia, 198
Blockbuster Entertainment Inc, 19–20

BMW, 64
Bonini's paradox, 88, 347
Booking.com, 295
Bosch Connected Industry, 266–7
Box, George E.P, 88
British Airways, 56, 57
Brundtland Report, 308
BuildCo, 330–4
Burke-Litwin model, 102–5, 107, 108–11
Burnes, B., 54–5, 59
Business Process Reengineering, 35,
    247–56, 257, 259, 264, 266, 272, 348
business strategy, 270, 273

Capricorn Investment Group, 207
Carnegie medal of philanthropy, 207
Case Western Reserve University, 318
causal complexes, 103
causal modelling, 2, 16, 29, 30–1, 40, 348
causal power, 30, 52, 53, 54, 75
cave paintings, 214–15
Champy, J., 248, 252
change
    case studies
        Henkel, 138–42
        Unite strike at Heathrow Airport,
            127–8
        Volkswagen scandal, 129–30
    communication of see change communication
    coping cycle, 121–6, 138, 349
    evaluation see change evaluation
    implementation see change implementation
    Kirkpatrick's types of reactions to,
        118–20, 137
    leadership see change leadership
    management see change management
    managing resistance as dialogic practice,
        135–7, 341–2
    models see change models
    reactions to, 116–21, 137, 357
    resistance to, 127–37, 138, 341–2, 357
    sustainability see change sustainability
    see also change implementation;
        organisational change
change agency, 52, 75, 348
change aversion, 116–17, 348
change communication
    case studies
        Atlassian, 225–6

AutoCo, 236–40
Nike, 222
choosing the right medium, 226–9
Clampitt's typology of communication
strategies, 222–6, 235
dialogic model, 230–4, 236, 247, 343–4
historical perspective, 214–17
Internet, 215–16
organisational silence, 6, 214, 221, 229–30,
236, 353
overview, 213–14, 216, 235
reasons for poor, 219–22, 235
remote forms of, 215, 216
Shannon and Weaver's model of
communication, 217–19, 230, 235
change decay, 326, 348
change evaluation
Balanced Scorecard, 279, 286–91, 292,
298–300, 347
case studies
Amazon Quicksight, 293–4
Ferienwohnung Thiele (FeWoT), 294–5
TATA Motor Group, 279
Tata Motor Group, 299–302
change leadership, 297
critical approach to, 295–8, 299, 344–5
operationalising a process model, 282–6
overview, 280, 298–9, 348
process model, 279, 280–2, 298
small and medium-sized enterprises (SMEs),
279, 292–5, 299
change implementation
Business Process Reengineering, 247–56, 257,
259, 264, 266, 272
case studies
Bosch Connected Industry, 266–7
T-Mobile, 254–5
Toyota Production System, 260, 273–6
directed change implementation, 246–8,
272, 350
facilitated change implementation, 247,
272, 351
filtering device for selecting methods, 270–2,
273, 344
Lean, 257–61, 264, 266, 267–70, 272–6, 352
Lean-Six Sigma (LSS), 268–70, 272–5, 352
overview, 245–6, 272–3
process mapping, 254–5, 272
Six Sigma, 263–70, 272–3, 355
Value Stream Mapping, 261–2, 272
change leadership
in antiquity, 177
case studies
Eric Schmidt, 190
Jeff Skoll, 207–9
Olivia Lum, 201–2
change evaluation, 297

change leaders, 182–4
collective leadership, 196–7, 206–7, 348
contemporary approaches, 179–80, 185tab,
196–202, 206–7
continuums of leadership styles, 188–9, 349
dialogic model of, 202–6, 209, 342–3, 350
eco-leadership, 196fig, 197–8, 206–7, 350
gendered leadership, 196fig, 200–2,
206–7, 351
Hersey and Blanchard's model of situational
leadership, 191–3
historical perspective, 177–81
key theories, 184–96
in late modern period, 178–9
leaders versus managers, 182–4, 206
leadership theories, 84–5, 352
leading change through conversational
practice, 208
and Lean, 260
meaning of, 176
in the Middle Ages, 177–8
overview, 175–6, 206–7
political versus organisational change,
180–1, 206
process model of change evaluation, 282, 285
quantum leadership, 196fig, 199, 206–7, 354
regenerative leadership, 196fig, 198,
206–7, 354
Renaissance, 178
servant leadership, 196fig, 199–200,
206–7, 355
situational leadership, 184tab, 190–3,
206, 355
styles approach, 86, 184tab, 188–90, 206
styles theory, 356
traits approach, 184tab, 185–8, 206, 356
transactional leadership, 194
transformational leadership, 184tab,
193–6, 206
change management
change managers, 85
conceptual framework, 1–2
dialogic approach, 2–3, 135
linear change models, 341, 352
models of, 88–108
versus organisational development and
project management, 34fig, 36–8
overview, 15, 33, 42, 348
processual approach, 2–3
systemic approach, 2, 38–41, 42–3, 44–5, 340
systemic change models, 5, 82, 83, 106,
107fig, 108, 342, 356
theories of, 82–7
change models
Burke-Litwin model of organisational
performance and change, 102–5,
107, 108–11

case studies
    Krakatau Steel, 93–4
    Sheraton Edinburgh, 108–11
    Unicorn, 99–100
characteristics of good, 88–9
Kirkpatrick's linear model, 92–4, 95
Kotter's eight-step checklist, 95–6
Kotter's integrative model of organisational
    dynamics, 100–2, 107
Lewin's 3-step model of change, 90–2
superior value of systemic change
    models, 106–8
Weisbord's six-box model, 96–100
change readiness, 116–17, 348
change sustainability
    action research, 316tab, 318, 329, 347
    appreciative inquiry, 316tab, 318–19, 329, 347
    case studies
        BuildCo, 330–4
        GSK Consumer Healthcare (GSKCH), 320–2
        IKEA, 314–15
        Tata Steel's Shikhar 25 programme, 327–8
    communities of practice, 316tab, 319–22,
        329, 348
    cultural values, 309fig, 310–11, 329
    economic viability, 309–10, 329, 331,
        332–4, 350
    embedding sustainability in the value chain,
        310–14, 329
    environmental sustainability, 309fig, 310,
        329, 331, 332–4
    historical roots, 308
    multidimensional approach, 308–9, 311–12,
        329, 330–1
    overview, 305–7, 329, 345–6, 348
    seven-step practical framework for, 322–8, 329
    simulation modelling, 40, 64, 317tab, 322–3,
        329, 330–4, 355
    social responsibility, 309fig, 310, 329, 331,
        332–4, 355
    strategies for sustaining change, 315–24, 329
Charlemagne, King of the Franks, 177–8
China
    Alibaba Group, 25–7
    protectionist trade wars, 29
choice management, 59
Cigna, 249–50
Cisco, 310
Clampitt, P.G, 214, 222–6, 235
Cleopatra, 177
cloud computing, 54
collective leadership, 196–7, 206–7, 348
communication theory, 83–4, 348
communicative action, theory of, 230–1,
    236, 343
communities of practice, 316tab, 319–22,
    329, 348

Community Health Partnerships, 44
Competing for the Future, 31
conceptual framework, 2, 348
conduit metaphor, 233–4
constructive mode of change, 24–5, 27fig, 28,
    42, 349
contingency theory, 86, 190, 349
continuous change, 23, 42, 349
continuous improvement, 313–14
continuums of leadership styles, 188–9, 349
control systems, 153fig, 155, 170, 349
conversational practice, 208
Cook, Tim, 187
coping cycle, 121–6, 138, 349
Coram, R., 54–5
covert resistance, 128tab, 138
COVID-19 pandemic, 18, 26, 29–30, 54–5,
    99, 108–11, 118, 127–8, 207, 214,
    236–40, 321–2
creation of meaning, 231–3, 236, 343
cultural change see culture change
cultural layers, 150–2, 349
cultural paradigm, 153fig, 156, 170, 349
cultural value system, 23–4, 40, 85–6, 349
cultural values, 309fig, 310–11, 329
cultural web, 145, 153–6, 157–9, 170, 349
culture
    case study: Mumbai Dabbawala, 152
    cultural change see culture change
    cultural web, 145, 153–6, 157–9, 349
    as iceberg, 148
    metaphors of, 146–50, 170
    in an organisational context, 148–9
    organisational subcultures, 156–9
    overview, 146, 170, 349
    as a river, 147
    Schein's layers of organisational culture,
        150–2, 170
    as software operating system, 147
    as traffic signs, 148
culture change
    acculturation, 160, 170, 347
    assimilation, 160tab, 161, 170, 347
    basic underlying assumptions, 347
    Business Process Reengineering, 252
    case studies
        Aetna, 162–3
        ING (Internationale Nederlanden
            Groep), 171–3
        Toyota Production System, 275
    dialogic model for managing, 167–70, 342
    enculturation, 160, 170, 350
    Hofstede's model of national cultures,
        164–7, 170
    integration, 160tab, 161, 170, 351
    and Lean, 260
    overview, 145–6

separation, 160tab, 161, 170, 355
strategies for managing, 160–3
culture mapping, 293
culture shock, 132
culture theory, 85–6, 349
cuneiform, 215, 349
customer dimension, 287fig, 288, 298
customer pull, 258fig, 259, 268

Darwin, Charles, 27
Davenport, T.H., 248
deep culture, 150tab, 151
deep structures, 28, 42, 44–5, 349
defence, 122–3, 125fig, 126fig, 138
delegating, 191fig, 192
democratic dialogue as conduit, 233–4
democratic governance, 313
democratic leadership, 74, 75–6, 188–9, 205–6,
247, 341, 349
denial, 121–2, 125fig, 126fig, 138
Denis, J-L., 197
depression, 123
determinism, 53, 54, 57–8, 75, 349
dialogic model
change communication, 230–4, 236,
247, 343–4
change leadership, 202–7, 209, 342–3, 350
culture change, 167–70, 342
dialogic leadership, 203–6
dialogic practice, 135–7, 138, 350
diesel dupe scandal, 129–30
digital twin technology, 350
directed change implementation, 246–8,
272, 350
discarding, 121fig, 123, 125fig, 126fig, 138
discontinuous change, 23, 42, 350
discourse theory, 231, 236, 343, 350
DMAIC process (Six Sigma), 264–5, 266–7, 269,
272, 350
dominant culture see cultural paradigm
Don't automate, obliterate, 250, 251
double-loop learning, 104
downward causation, 31, 350

eBay, 26, 207
eco-leadership, 196fig, 197–8, 206–7, 350
economic viability, 309–10, 329, 331,
332–4, 350
ecosystem, 38–9, 42, 340, 350
ecosystem approach, 63
eight-step checklist, 95–6
Eldredge, Niles, 27
emails, 228
embedding, 168fig, 171, 342
emergent approach, 55, 57–9, 60, 61, 73,
75, 341
emergent resistance, 325tab, 346

emergent strategic change, 60, 61, 247, 272, 350
emotional branding, 222
employee voice, 221, 350
enculturation, 160, 170, 350
environmental protection, 351
Environmental Protection Agency, 129
environmental scanning tool, 72, 75
environmental sustainability, 309fig, 310, 329,
331, 332–4
Eriksen, M., 205
Erin, Dr Timur, 138–42
evaluation see change evaluation
evidence-based change management, 282
evolutionary change, 23, 25, 42, 351
experimental learning, 74, 75–6
external causes, 29–30, 42, 351
external flows, 18
extraction of meaning, 231, 232fig, 233,
236, 343
Eyelliance, 208

Facebook, 216
face-to-face communication, 228, 235
facilitated change implementation, 247,
272, 351
Fairclough, N., 231, 236, 343
feedback loop, 217fig, 218, 235, 332, 351
Ferienwohnung Thiele (FeWoT), 294–5
Fiedler, Fred, 86, 190
field theory, 82–3, 90, 351
filtering device, 270–2, 273, 344
financial dimension, 287–8, 298
flat structures, 155
force-field analysis, 82, 342
Ford (company), 251
Ford, Henry, 252
Ford, J.D., 132, 135, 138
Fordism, 252, 257, 351
Forrester, Jay Wright, 322

Gandhi, Indira, 179–80
Gandhi, Mohandas Karamchand, 179
gendered leadership, 196fig, 200–2, 206–7, 351
General Motors, 29, 59
Gersick, C.J.G., 28
Gestalt psychology, 82, 351
GlasgowSmithKline, 320
Glaxo Pharmaceuticals, 201
Google, 64, 216
Gould, Stephen Jay, 27
Greenleaf, R.K., 199
Grossman survey, 219
Groupon, 207
GSK Consumer Healthcare (GSKCH)., 320–2

Habermas, J., 230–1, 233, 234, 236, 343
Hamel, G., 31, 32

Hammer, M., 248, 250, 251, 252
Harry, Mikel, 263
Harvard Business Review, 250, 251
Hayes, J., 28
Heathrow Airport, 127–8
Heijunka, 273fig, 274–5, 351
Hendry, C., 90
Henkel, 138–42
Heraclitus, 17
Hersey and Blanchard's model of situational
    leadership, 191–3
Hewlett-Packard, 31–2
hierarchical structures, 154–5
Hitler, Adolf, 178–9
Hofstede, Geert, 164–7, 170
Hosco, 43–6
human agency, 52–3, 54
Human Relations, 90
humanistic perspective, 313, 351
Hydrochem, 201
Hyflux, 201–2

IBM, 59
IBM Quantum Systems, 64
ideal speech situation, 230–1, 233, 236
identify and reply, 223fig, 224, 235, 351
IKEA, 314–15
iMac, 62
inbound logistics, 312, 351
incremental change, 23, 27fig, 28, 40, 42,
    43, 351
Individualism v. Collectivism – IDV, 164tab,
    167tab, 170
Indonesia, 93–4
Indulgence v. Restraint – IND, 165tab,
    167tab, 170
Industrial Internet of Things, 20
industry life-cycle model, 40
information and communication technologies
    (ICTs), 20
infrastructure, 83, 213, 311fig, 351
ING (*Internationale Nederlanden Groep*), 171–3
integration, 160tab, 161, 170, 351
integrative model of organisational dynamics,
    100–2, 107
intentional action, 52, 75
internal business dimension, 287fig, 288, 298
internal causes, 30, 42, 352
internal flows, 18
internalisation, 121fig, 124, 125fig,
    126fig, 138
Internet, 215–16
Internet of Things, 20, 49, 54, 216, 267, 352
internet-based messaging, 228, 235
intranet, 218, 221, 227fig, 228, 239
iPhone, 62
iPod, 62

Jefferson Award, 207
Jesus Christ, 177
Jidoka, 273fig, 352
Jobs, Steve, 62
John Lewis Partnership, 59
Johnson, Gerry, 145, 153–6, 170
Jones, D.T., 257–8, 259
Julius Caesar, 177
Just-in-Time, 259, 268, 269, 273fig, 274,
    275, 352

Kaizen, 260, 273fig, 275, 352
Kaplan, R.S., 286–7
King, Martin Luther, 179
Kirkpatrick, D.L., 92–4, 95, 118–20, 137
Knights, D., 127
Kotter, J.P., 95–6, 100–2, 107, 183
Krafcik, John, 257
Krakatau Steel, 93–4
Kramer, M.R., 310
Kübler-Ross, Elizabeth, 118
KUKA, 76–8

Lascaux, 214
LaserJet printer, 32
late modern period, 178–9
Leader-Member-Exchange (LMX) theory,
    194, 352
leadership *see* change leadership
Lean, 257–61, 264, 266, 267–70, 272–6, 352
Lean-Six Sigma (LSS), 35, 268–70, 272–5, 352
learning and growth dimension, 287fig,
    289–90, 298
Lee, A.S., 250
Lewin, K., 82, 89, 90–2, 318
life-cycle model, 40
linear change models, 341, 352
linear model, 92–4, 95
Local Destination Management
    Organisation, 295
localised change, 22, 42, 352
logical incrementalism, 59–60, 61, 75, 352
Long-term orientation v. Short term orientation –
    LTO–STO, 165tab, 167tab, 170
Lum, Olivia, 201–2

Ma, Jack, 25
Machiavelli, 178
managers *see* change management
Mandela, Nelson, 179
marketing and sales, 312, 352
Marx, Karl, 54
Marxist perspectives, 130–1
Masculinity v. Femininity – MAS, 165tab,
    167tab, 170
matrix structures, 155
McCalman, J., 129, 131

McGahan, A., 20
media
    level of interactivity, 227, 228, 235
    richness, 227–8, 235
medium (communication), 217fig, 218, 235
mergers and acquisitions, 66tab, 169, 246, 248
Merkel, Angela, 180
metaphors, 232, 352
microbusinesses, 292, 294–5
Microsoft, 32, 62
Middle Ages, 177–8
Mintzberg, H., 60–1, 73, 75, 341
modes of change, 25–7, 28, 42
More Sustainability Oriented State, 312
motivation theory, 84, 352
Motorola, 263
Muda, 273fig, 274, 275, 352
Mumbai Dabbawala, 152
Mura, 273fig, 274, 275, 352
Muri, 273fig, 274, 275, 352
Musk, Elon, 30, 53, 187
Myers, P., 219, 222, 247, 249–50, 266

nanotechnology, 54
Napoleon Bonaparte, 178
nature versus nurture debate, 117
negotiation of meaning, 231, 232fig, 233–4,
    236, 343
Netflix, 19, 216
network structures, 155
New Leadership Commitments
    (Henkel), 138–42
Nexeed Industrial Application System
    (NIAS), 267
NHS, 43–6
NHS England, 54–5
Nike, 29–30, 222
noise, 217fig, 218, 228, 235, 352
Norton, D.P., 286–7

Obama, Barack, 180, 185
Ohno, Taiichi, 273
open work, 225–6
operational change, 22, 42, 353
operations, 312, 353
Order of Canada, 207
order of discourse, 234
organisational change
    case study: Alibaba Group, 25–7
    causes of, 29–32
    definitions, 21
    dichotomous conceptions of, 22–4, 40,
        42, 350
    punctuated equilibrium, 27–9
    typology of, 22–7
    Van de Ven and Poole's modes of
        change, 24–7

Organisational Cynicism About Change, 195
organisational development, 25, 33, 34–5,
    36–8, 353
organisational silence, 6, 214, 221, 229–30,
    236, 353
organisational structures, 153fig, 154–5,
    170, 353
organisational subcultures, 170
organisation-wide change, 22, 42, 353
outbound logistics, 312, 353
overt resistance, 128tab, 138

paradoxical tensions, 183–4, 206, 353
Parmenides, 17
Participant Media, 207, 209
participating, 191fig, 192
participatory leadership, 195, 224, 272
passive resistance, 128tab, 138
path dependency, 285, 298, 353
Paton, R. A., 129, 131
PayPal, 207
pedagogical approaches, 1, 353
performance management, 56, 353
PESTLE analysis, 39, 65–7, 71–3, 75, 341, 353
Pfizer, 320
philosophy, 16–17, 21, 41
planned approach, 55–7, 59, 60, 61, 73,
    75, 341
planned strategic change, 353
political change, 180–1, 206
Poole, M.S., 24–7, 28, 42
Porter, M.E., 39, 310, 311fig, 312
Post-Fordism, 257, 258, 353
power distance index (PDI), 164tab, 166tab, 170
power structures, 153fig, 154, 170, 353
pragmatic competence, 234
The Pragmatics of Human Communication, 214
pragmatics of human communication, 214, 231,
    236, 343, 353
Prahalad, C. K, 31, 32
pre-historic artists, 214–15
prescribed mode of change, 24–5, 27fig, 28,
    42, 354
The Prince, 178
print, 227, 235
process mapping, 254–5, 272, 293, 299, 354
process model, 279, 280–6, 298
process of becoming, 176, 354
process theory, 83, 354
processual approach, 271, 273, 344, 354
product intimacy, 222
project management, 33, 34fig, 35–8
psychological contract, 131–2
psychological disposition, 117, 137
psycho-social factors, 117, 118, 354
punctuated equilibrium, 16, 27–9, 42, 43–6, 354
punctuation, 231, 234

Q, 293
quantum computers, 64
quantum information science, 64
quantum leadership, 196fig, 199, 206–7, 354
quantum revolutions, 63, 64
quantum strategic change, 63–5, 75, 354
Quinn, J.B., 59, 61, 73, 75, 341

Rapid Intervention Event, 259
receiver, 217fig, 218–19, 235
recording, 228, 235
Reddy, Michael, 233
reflection, 203fig, 205, 343
refreezing, 90fig, 91–2
regenerative leadership, 196fig, 198, 206–7, 354
reification, 176, 354
remote working, 55, 238–9
Renaissance, 178
resource-based approaches, 67, 354
revolutionary change, 23, 42, 354
rituals, 153fig, 155, 170, 354
robotics, 76–8
Romanelli, E., 28
routines, 153fig, 155, 170, 354

Samsung, 29
Sarker, S., 250
scalability, 249–50, 271fig, 272fig, 273, 344, 355
Schein, Edgar, 145, 146, 150–2, 170
Schmidt, Eric, 190
Scholes, Kevan, 145, 153–6, 170
Schön, D.A., 104
Sears Roebuck, 118–19
selective dissemination of information, 220,
    235, 355
self-organising, 63
selling, 191fig, 192
semantic noise, 233
sender, 217, 235
separation, 160tab, 161, 170, 355
September 11 terror attacks, 71
servant leadership, 196fig, 199–200, 206–7, 355
seven-step practical framework, 329
shallow culture, 150tab, 151
Shannon, C.L., 213–14, 217–19, 230, 235
shared meaning, 231, 232fig, 234, 236, 344
shared understanding, 167–8, 170, 342
Sheraton Edinburgh, 108–11
Short J.E., 248
Sigma, 263fig
simulation modelling, 40, 64, 317tab, 322–3,
    329, 330–4, 355
Single System Working, 43, 44fig, 45
single-loop learning, 104
situated knowledge, 129, 355
situational leadership, 184tab, 190–3, 206, 355
Six Sigma, 263–79, 355

Skoll, Jeff, 207–9
Skoll Centre for Social Entrepreneurship, 208
Skoll Foundation, 207, 208
Skype, 207
small and medium-sized enterprises (SMEs), 7,
    253, 261, 267, 272, 279, 292–5, 299
small enterprises, 292
Smith, Bill, 263
social entrepreneurs, 207, 208
social media, 228, 235, 355
social responsibility, 309fig, 310, 329, 331,
    332–4, 355
socio-cultural factors, 117, 137
socio-technical approach, 313, 355
solutions concept, 73
Space X, 53, 187
spray and pray, 223, 235, 355
stage-gate system, 328
steel, 327–8
Stogdill, R.M., 176
stories, 153–4, 170, 232, 355
strategic change
    ambidextrous strategic approach, 62–3, 65tab,
        75, 347
    case studies
        KUKA, 76–8
        NHS England, 54–5
    change agency, 52, 75, 348
    determinism, 53, 54, 57–8, 75, 349
    diagnostic tools, 65–71
    emergent approach, 55, 57–9, 60, 61, 73,
        75, 341
    environmental scanning tool, 75
    key features of, 50–1, 74–5
    logical incrementalism, 59–60, 61, 75, 352
    Mintzberg's pattern of strategy formation and
        development, 60–1, 75, 341
    overview, 22, 49–52, 54, 355
    PESTLE analysis, 65–7, 71–3, 75
    planned approach, 55–7, 59, 60, 61, 73,
        75, 341
    quantum strategic change, 63–5, 75, 354
    strategic change canvas, 69–71, 75, 355
    strategic improvisation, 61–2, 65tab, 75, 355
    SWOT analysis, 67–9, 71–3, 75
    voluntarism, 53–4, 57, 75
strategic change canvas, 69–71, 75, 355
strategic improvisation, 61–2, 65tab, 75, 355
styles approach, 86, 184tab, 188–90, 206
styles theory, 356
subcultures, 156–9, 170, 356
sub-systems, 2, 44, 45, 83, 340, 356
surface culture, 150tab, 151
sustainability see change sustainability
sustaining change, 305, 306, 307, 356
    see also change sustainability
switching, 63

SWOT analysis, 39, 67–9, 71–3, 75, 341, 356
symbols, 153fig, 154, 170, 356
synergistic effects, 268fig, 269–79, 356
systemic approach, 38–41, 42–3, 44–5, 271, 273, 340, 356
systemic change models, 5, 82, 83, 106–8, 341, 342, 356
systemic silence, 229, 230fig
systems practice, 73–4, 75–6
systems theory, 40, 43, 82–3, 356

talk, 203–4, 343
Taobao Tmall Commerce Group, 26
TATA Motors Group, 279, 299–302
TATA Steel's Shikhar 25 programme, 327–8
Taylor, Frederick, 252
Taylorism, 257, 356
Team of Experts model, 254
Tech-Meets-Talent initiative, 77–8
technology mapping, 293
TELECO, 250
tell and sell, 223–4, 235, 246, 356
telling, 191–2
Tesla, 30, 53, 187
Thatcher, Margaret, 180
theory of communicative action, 230–1, 236, 343, 356
thick causal explanations, 30, 42
T-Mobile, 254–5
Toyoda, Eiji, 273
Toyota Production System, 260, 273–6
traits approach, 184tab, 185–8, 206, 356
transactional leadership, 194, 356
transactional variables, 103fig, 104
transformational change, 23–4, 27fig, 28, 40, 42, 43, 44, 45, 357
transformational leadership, 184tab, 193–6, 205–6, 357
transformational variables, 103fig, 104
transmission, 168, 170, 342
tree infographic, 340, 357
triangulated evidence, 282, 285, 357
trust, 131
Tushman, M.L., 28

Uncertainty avoidance index – UAI, 165tab, 167tab, 170
uncertainty principle, 199
underscore and explore, 223fig, 224, 235, 247, 357
unfreezing, 90–1
Unicorn, 99–100
Unite, 127–8
upward causation, 29, 31–2, 40, 42, 357

value chain analysis, 40, 284tab
value flow, 258fig, 259
value specification, 258
value stream mapping, 258–9, 261–2, 272, 293, 299, 357
values, 85, 117, 150, 150tab, 151, 170, 347
Van de Ven, A.H., 24–7, 28, 42
video conferencing, 228, 235
Volkswagen scandal, 129–30
voluntarism, 53–4, 57, 75, 93, 357
VRIN, 69, 357
VUCA business world, 71–4, 75–8, 340–1, 357
Vurdubakis, T., 127

Waitrose, 59
Wal-Mart, 251–2
Walt Disney, 32
Waters, J.A., 61
Watzlawick, P., 214, 231, 234, 236, 343
Weaver, W., 213–14, 217–19, 230, 235
weighted direction, 103
Weisbord's six-box model, 96–100
Western, Simon, 197, 206
withhold and uphold, 223fig, 225, 235, 246, 357
Womack, J.P., 257–8, 259
World Tourism Organisation (WTO), 109–10
World Trade Centre, 71
Wu Zetian, 177, 178

Xerox, 59